STATUTORY PLANNING
IN VICTORIA

STATUTORY PLANNING IN VICTORIA

4TH EDITION

Des Eccles
BA (Melb), Dip Ed (Melb), Dip TRP (Melb)
Life Fellow, Planning Institute of Australia
Member, Planning and Environment List,
Victorian Civil and Administrative Tribunal

Tannetje L Bryant
LLB (Hons) (Melb), LLM (Mon), Dip Ed (Mon), Ph D (Mon)
Barrister and Solicitor of the Supreme Court of Victoria
Senior Lecturer in Law, Monash University
Former Member, Planning and Environment List,
Victorian Civil and Administrative Tribunal

THE FEDERATION PRESS
2011

Published in Sydney by
    The Federation Press
    PO Box 45, Annandale NSW, 2038.
    71 John St, Leichhardt, NSW, 2040.
    Ph (02) 9552 2200. Fax (02) 9552 1681.
    E-mail: info@federationpress.com.au
    Website: http://www.federationpress.com.au

First edition 1991
Second edition 1999
Third edition 2006
Reprinted 2010
Fourth edition 2011

National Library of Australia
Cataloguing-in-Publication entry

    Eccles, DJ (Desmond J)
    Bryant, Tannetje Lien

    Statutory planning in Victoria / Des Eccles and Tannetje Bryant

    4th ed.
    Includes index.
    ISBN 9781862878181 (pbk).

    City planning and redevelopment law – Victoria.
    Eminent domain – Victoria.

346.945045

©   The Federation Press
    This publication is copyright. Other than for the purposes of and subject to the conditions prescribed under the Copyright Act, no part of it may in any form or by any means (electronic, mechanical, microcopying, photocopying, recording or otherwise) be reproduced, stored in a retrieval system or transmitted without prior written permission. Enquiries should be addressed to the publisher.

Typeset by The Federation Press, Leichhardt, NSW.
Printed by Griffin Press, Salisbury, SA.

List of Chapters

1	Statutory Planning in Context	1
2	The Victorian Planning System	15
3	Planning Schemes	39
4	The Amendment of Schemes	74
5	Planning Permits	104
6	VCAT and Planning Reviews	147
7	Planning Enforcement	179
8	Heritage Conservation and Statutory Planning	194
9	Compensation	229
10	Where Are We Heading?	248

Contents

Preface	xv
Abbreviations	xvii
Table of Cases	xix
Table of Statutes	xxiii

1 STATUTORY PLANNING IN CONTEXT	1
Statutory planning and strategic planning	1
The limitations of statutory planning – some examples	2
Improving public transport	2
Improving residential streets	3
Heritage conservation	3
Planning as a process	4
Statutory planning and the planning process	4
The elements of the process	6
The process in practice – a hypothetical case study	8
The decision to plan and investigation of problems	8
The formulation of policies	9
The selection of mechanisms for implementing policies	10
Putting the mechanisms in place	13
2 THE VICTORIAN PLANNING SYSTEM	15
The system under the Town and Country Planning Act 1961	15
The State tier	16
The regional tier	17
The local government tier	19
Duplication and conflict between the tiers	19
The system under the Planning and Environment Act	21
The change from State, regional and local sections of schemes	21
State standard provisions, VPPs and local provisions	22
Planning authorities	24
Responsible authorities	25
Referral authorities	26
The powers of the Minister and the powers of municipalities	27
Subdivision and the planning system	29
Subdivision and planning permits	29

Referral authorities and planning permits for subdivision	30
Planning permit conditions for subdivision and the use of s 173 agreements	31
Time limits for decision and the matters the responsible authority must consider	33
Certification of a plan of subdivision	33
ResCode and subdivision	34
The Environment Effects Act and the planning system	36
When must an Environment Effects Statement be prepared?	36
Inquiries into the environmental effect of proposed developments	37

3 PLANNING SCHEMES — 39

The content of schemes – general powers	39
Objectives of planning in Victoria	39
The use, development, protection or conservation of land	40
The content of schemes – specific powers	41
Policies, specific objectives and strategy plans	41
Restrictions on the use and development of land	41
Requirements for the provision of public utility services	43
Creation or extinguishing of rights of way or other encumbrances	45
Specific information to be provided with an application for a permit	46
Underlying zoning	47
Incorporation of documents	47
Agreements	49
Classes of land, use or development exempted from s 96(1) or (2)	50
Classes of permit applications exempt from notification and review rights	50
Definition of the metropolitan Urban Growth Boundary	52
The format and structure of schemes	53
The VPPs and State standard provisions	53
The State Planning Policy Framework	54
The Local Planning Policy Framework (the MSS and local planning policies)	55
State standard zones and zone provisions	56
Overlays	60
Particular Provisions	62
General Provisions	62
Definitions	66
The ResCode provisions	68

CONTENTS

4 THE AMENDMENT OF SCHEMES — 74
- An overview of the scheme amendment process — 74
- Amendment of the VPPs — 76
- The normal scheme amendment process in detail — 78
  - Initiation of the proposed amendment — 78
  - Notification and exhibition of scheme amendments — 79
  - The lodging and consideration of submissions — 81
  - Panel hearing — 84
  - Adoption, approval and gazettal — 89
- The Growth Areas Authority and amendments which include precinct structure plans in the Urban Growth Zone — 92
- The lapsing of an amendment — 93
- The abnormal process — 94
  - Exemption from notification and other normal processes — 94
  - Fast-tracking of amendments — 96
- The combined amendment and permit process — 97
- Parliament and amendments — 98
  - Revocation of an amendment — 98
  - Amendment of the Urban Growth Boundary and Green Wedge subdivision controls — 98
  - Amendment of the Upper Yarra Valley and Dandenong Ranges Strategy Plan — 99
- Reviews and amendments — 99
  - Review of the merits of a proposed amendment — 99
  - Reviews in relation to amendment procedures — 100
- Agreements and amendments — 101

5 PLANNING PERMITS — 104
- The nature of planning permission — 104
  - A planning permit is not the same as a building permit — 104
  - What is permitted by a planning permit? — 105
  - A planning permit runs with the land — 105
  - The life of a permit — 106
- Making an application — 107
  - When is a permit required? — 107
  - The application form — 107
  - Time limits for making the decision — 108
- The duties of the responsible authority before it makes a decision — 109
  - Checking the details of the application — 109

CONTENTS

Checking that a permit is required and may be granted	110
Getting further information	111
Completing the register	112
Deciding if the application should be amended before notification	112
Sending the application to referral authorities	113
Notification of the application	114
Amending the permit after notification	117
Objections	118
Who may object?	118
Grounds of objection	119
The decision	120
Who makes the decision?	120
Permit conditions	132
Agreements and permits	133
Amending a permit	134
Some special cases	136
Licensed premises	136
Brothels	137
Gaming machines	140
Works approvals and licences	144
Permits required by responsible authorities and government departments	145

6 VCAT AND PLANNING REVIEWS 147

A brief overview of VCAT's functions	147
Jurisdiction of VCAT and its Planning and Environment List	147
Exclusion of courts from hearing or determining planning matters	150
Origins of the Planning and Environment List of VCAT	151
The Town Planning Appeals Tribunal	151
The Planning Appeals Board	153
The Planning Division of the Administrative Appeals Tribunal	154
Review by VCAT of the decisions of responsible authorities on planning permit applications	155
Review of decisions to refuse or grant a permit, of conditions in permits, and of failure to decide within the prescribed time	155
Lodging an Application for Review	156
Notice of the Application for Review and the lodging of grounds of review	158
Who are the parties?	158
The Major Cases List, the Short Cases List, and practice day hearings	159

CONTENTS

Preparing a submission for the review hearing	160
Order of appearance and representation at the hearing	163
Substitution of amended plans	164
Witnesses	164
Determination of questions of law	166
Compulsory conferences and mediation	166
Settlement	168
The decision of the Tribunal	168
Costs	169
Appeals to the Supreme Court on a question of law	174
Ministerial call-in of applications for review	175

7 PLANNING ENFORCEMENT — 179

The objectives of enforcement	179
Difficulties of collecting evidence	180
Enforcement mechanisms under the Planning and Environment Act 1987	181
Prosecution in the Magistrates' Court for breaches of a planning scheme, permit conditions or a s 173 agreement	181
Enforcement orders	182
Interim enforcement orders	184
Injunctions	186
Infringement notice	186
Cancellation of a permit and order to stop development	187
The conduct of enforcement proceedings before VCAT	188
The giving of evidence	188
Onus and standard of proof	189
Evidence and notes	190
Keeping everyone honest: the issue of costs in enforcement order proceedings	190
Enforcing enforcement orders	191
Prosecution in the Magistrates' Court for breach of an enforcement order or interim enforcement order	191
Contempt proceedings in VCAT	192
Injunction	192
Filing of VCAT order in the Supreme Court	192
Carrying out works required by the order	193
Special circumstances	193
Brothels and enforcement proceedings	193
Government and enforcement proceedings	193

CONTENTS

8 HERITAGE CONSERVATION AND STATUTORY PLANNING 194
World Heritage listing and the Environment Protection and Biodiversity Conservation Act 1999 (Cth) 194
   World Heritage listing 194
   Constitutional issues in the protection of World Heritage areas 195
   Protection of World Heritage properties under the Environment Protection and Biodiversity Conservation Act 1999 197
National Heritage protection 198
   The Australian Heritage Council 198
   The National and Commonwealth Heritage Lists 199
   Register of the National Estate 200
The Heritage Act 1995 (Vic) 203
   Background 203
   The Victorian Heritage Register 204
   The Heritage Council and the registration process 206
   Effect of registration 208
   The permit system 209
   Financial assistance 211
Heritage planning and Victorian planning legislation before the Planning and Environment Act 1987 212
   Heritage planning powers before 1972 212
   Heritage planning powers after 1972 213
   Heritage controls and the issue of compensation 214
   The example of St James Park 218
Heritage Conservation and the Planning and Environment Act 1987 219
   Heritage planning powers under the Act 219
   The Heritage Overlay provisions 220
   Land to which heritage controls may apply 224
Buildings on the Heritage Register and planning permits 225
Planning permits and Aboriginal heritage 226

9 COMPENSATION 229
Compensation issues and the impact of schemes 230
   Betterment 230
   Injurious affection 232
   Severance 233
   Planning blight 234
   Loss of development rights 235
   Heritage and environmental controls 235

CONTENTS

Compulsory acquisition and compensation	236
Voluntary acquisition and compulsory acquisition	236
The scope of compulsory acquisition powers	237
Land to be compulsorily acquired must first be reserved	238
The price paid	240
Other circumstances where compensation is payable under the Planning and Environment Act – planning compensation	243
Sale at a loss of reserved land	243
Refusal of planning consent for reserved land	245
Access restricted by closure of a road	245
Inaccurate planning certificate	246
Time limit on claims, who pays, and how disputes are resolved	246
Time limit on claims	246
Who pays?	247
Resolution of disputes	247
10 WHERE ARE WE HEADING?	**248**
Long-standing tensions in the Victorian planning system	248
The draft Planning and Environment Amendment (General) Bill	249
State significant developments	249
Planning scheme amendments	251
A "code assess" procedure for some permit applications	252
Conditions that can be included in permits	253
The need for bipartisan agreement and support	253
FURTHER READING	**255**
INDEX	**259**

Preface

This edition, like the previous editions, has been written primarily as a text and reference work for tertiary level students in the fields of planning, law and related areas. We hope it will also prove useful to non-specialist planners and lawyers, municipal councillors, and individuals and members of community groups on the receiving end of planning decisions who wish to know about how they can participate in the statutory processes relating to planning scheme amendments, planning permits, review proceedings before the Victorian Civil and Administrative Tribunal (VCAT), and the enforcement of scheme provisions and permit conditions.

We draw the attention of readers to the resources available on the website of the Department of Planning and Community Development at <www.dpcd.vic.gov.au> (including the VPPs on-line, planning schemes and planning scheme amendments on-line, and the publication *Using Victoria's Planning System*). We also draw attention to the VCAT website at <www.vcat.vic.gov.au>, which features information about the VCAT legislation, Practice Notes and Rules, a list of scheduled hearings, the daily law list and a selection of key decisions.

We have referred to a significant number of Court and Tribunal decisions, including decisions of the High Court, the Victorian Court of Appeal, the Supreme Court, and VCAT and its predecessors. Where discussion of these cases has been necessary we have attempted to avoid technical language without simplifying the complexity of the matters dealt with. The great majority of these decisions are available on the AustLII databases (<www.austlii.edu.au>).

Readers are encouraged to refer to the Butterworths publication *Planning and Environment Service Victoria* and to the newsletters of the Victoria Division of the Planning Institute of Australia (*Planning News*) and of the Victorian Planning and Environmental Law Association (*VPELA Newsletter*) to keep abreast of changes to legislation and the VPPs, and for discussion of recent Court and Tribunal decisions.

The Victorian planning system is constantly evolving and changing. We make no apology for including in this edition a good deal of historical material, as we did in the previous editions. Any student of the system should be concerned about the nature and the direction of change. If we don't know where we have been, how can we know where we are going?

In December 2009 the Draft Planning and Environment Amendment (General) Bill was released for comment. The Draft Bill followed a series of discussion and response papers which, along with the Draft Bill, are available on the Department of Planning and Community Development's website. The Draft Bill may yet be introduced into Parliament in its original or amended form following the change of government in the State election of November 2010. We have decided, with the

PREFACE

advice of our publisher, to prepare this fourth edition now. It may well be within a year or so that we will need to commence preparing a fifth edition which, at this stage, we think will be our swansong. We have both retired from full-time teaching and practice. By the time a sixth edition is due we hope to be enjoying full-time retirement.

Des Eccles
Tannetje Bryant
January 2011

Abbreviations

AAT	Administrative Appeals Tribunal
AATR	Administrative Appeals Tribunal Reports (Victoria)
ALJR	Australian Law Journal Reports
APA	Australian Planning Appeal Decisions
CC	City Council
CFA	Country Fire Authority
cl, cll	clause, clauses
CLR	Commonwealth Law Reports
EES	Environment Effects Statement
ESO	Environmental Significance Overlay
GDG/Good Design Guide	Good Design Guide for Medium Density Housing Revision 2, 1998
HO	Heritage Overlay
IDO	Interim Development Order
IPO	Interim Preservation Order
LGERA	Local Government and Environmental Reports of Australia (previously Local Government Reports of Australia)
LGRA	Local Government Reports of Australia
Melbourne 2030	Melbourne 2030: Planning for Sustainable Growth State of Victoria, October 2002
MMBW	Melbourne Metropolitan Board of Works
MMPS	Melbourne Metropolitan Planning Scheme
MSS(s)	Municipal Strategic Statement(s)
PAB	Planning Appeals Board
PABR	Planning Appeals Board Reports (Victoria)
r, rr	rule, rules
RDPs	Residential Development Provisions – Guidelines for Efficient New Residential Development November, 1988
reg/regs	Regulation(s)

ABBREVIATIONS

ResCode	A set of objectives and standards which apply to the construction of one or more dwellings on a lot and to the subdivision of land in residential zones, found at cll 54, 55 and 56 of planning schemes and Pt 4 of the Victorian Building Regulations
s, ss	section, sections
SC	Supreme Court
SC	Shire Council
SPC	State Planning Council
TPAT	Town Planning Appeals Tribunal
TCPB	Tow and Country Planning Board
UBR	Uniform Building Regulations
VCAT	Victorian Civil and Administrative Tribunal
VicCode 1	Victorian Code for Residential Development Subdivision and Single Dwellings 1992
VicCode 2	Victorian Code for Residential Development – Multi-Dwellings 1993
VPAD	Victorian Planning Appeal Decision
VPPs	Victoria Planning Provisions
VPR	Victorian Planning Reports, formerly Administrative Appeal Tribunal Reports (Victoria), and before that, Planning Appeals Board Reports (Victoria)
VR	Victorian Reports
VSC	Victorian Supreme Court

Table of Cases

ACT Nominees v Morrison (1984) 2 PABR 366: 88
Adams v Bayside CC [2000] VCAT 933: 172
Allen v Shire of Barrabool (1984) 16 APA 361: 93
Altona Petrochemical Co Ltd v City of Altona, Italian Soccer Club Altona Inc and Sixth P & C Nominees Pty Ltd (1985) 3 PABR 143: 177
Ampol Petroleum Ltd v Warringah Shire Council (1956) 1 LGRA 276: 127
Analed Pty Ltd v Roads Corporation [1998] VSC 174: 244
Analed v Shire of Melton (1994) 12 AATR 249: 93
Anastassiou v Port Phillip CC [2007] VCAT 248: 173
Antoniou v Roper (1990) 4 AATR 158: 96
Ashlyn Enterprises Pty Ltd v Yarra City Council [2003] VCAT 87; 13 VPR 132: 54, 126
Association of Franciscan Order of Friars v Boroondara CC [2002] VCAT 1085: 222
Attorney General ex rel Whitten v Shire of Gisbourne (1980) 45 LGRA 1: 101
Aussie Invest Corporation Pty Ltd v Hobsons Bay CC [2004] VCAT 2188: 174
Aust Defence Industries Ltd v City of Maribyrnong (1995) 15 AATR 78: 167
Australian Conservation Foundation v Minister for Planning [2004] VCAT 2029: 86, 88, 101
Avel Pty Ltd v City of Dandenong (1991) 7 AATR 271: 106
Azzure Investment Group Pty Ltd v Mornington Peninsula SC [2009] VCAT 1600: 227
B Marsh Nominees v City of Moonee Valley [2004] VSC 237: 32
B Smith v Shire of Flinders (1983) 1 PABR 183: 106
Bellan Constructions v City of Geelong (unreported, Planning Division of the AAT, P87/2252): 130
Bengold Pty Ltd v Kingston CC [2001] VCAT 1925; 9 VPR 9: 172
Bonus Pty Ltd v Leichhardt Municipal Council (1954) 19 LGR (NSW) 375: 64
Brandtmann v Shire of Lilydale and Barry (1989) 2 AATR 130: 190
Brichon Developments Pty Ltd v Glen Eira CC [2001] VCAT 497 (reported at 8 VPR 10): 126
Brown v Mornington Peninsula SC (No 1) [2003] VCAT 1796: 116
Cachia v Hanes (1994) 120 ALR 385: 173-174

Camberwell, City of v Nicholson (unreported, VSC, 2 December 1988): 175
Cardinia SC v De Haan [2004] VCAT 942: 189
Cardinia SC v Stoiljkovic (No 2) [2002] VCAT 918: 174
Cardwell SC v King Ranch Aust Pty Ltd (1984) 54 LGRA 110; 53 ALR 632: 44
Cascone v Shire of Whittlesea (1993) 11 AATR 175: 110
Castles v Bayside City Council [2004] VCAT 864: 131
Chambers v Maclean SC (2003) 126 LGERA 7: 110
Charnley Glen Pty Ltd v Boroondara City Council [2000] VSC 340; 6 VPR 93: 32
Child v City of Frankston (1983) 13 APA 474: 129
Christian Brothers Vic Property Ltd v Banyule City Council [2001] VCAT 2120; VPR 128: 44
Cohen Chalmers Pty Ltd v City of Stonnington (1994) 13 AATR 29: 172
Colin v Port Phillip CC [2000] VCAT 2073: 223
Commonwealth v Tasmania (1983) 158 CLR 1: 196
Convivial Company Pty Ltd v City of St Kilda (1991) 7 AATR 346: 111
Cope v Hobsons Bay City Council [2004] VCAT 2487: 31
Coptic Orthodox Patriarchate Archangel Mikhall and St Anthony Church Inc v Monash CC [2004] VCAT 948: 223
Coty (England) Pty Ltd v Sydney City Council (1957) 2 LGRA 117: 93
Craig v Port Phillip CC [2006] VCAT 2161: 223
Crampton v Frankston CC [2003] VCAT 1339; 15 VPR 49: 51
Crichton v City of Moorabbin (1991) 7 AATR 150: 106
Curry v Melton Shire Council [2000] VSC 352; 7 VPR 109: 43
Dahan v City of Richmond (1989) 3 AATR 80: 99
Dennis Family Corporation v Casey CC [2008] VCAT 691: 173
Dennis Marsden Subdivisional Services Pty Ltd v City of Heidelberg (1994) 13 AATR 7: 131
Doncaster Property Partnership v Manningham CC [2004] VCAT 2445: 124
Dooley v Port Phillip CC [2006] VCAT 2523: 223
Dowling v City of Malvern (1983) 1 PABR 86: 167

TABLE OF CASES

Dowling v Malvern and Aust Defence Industries Ltd v City of Maribyrnong: 168
Duffy v Alpine SC [2000] VCAT 1769; 5 VPR 340: 106
Eddie Barron v Constructions Pty Ltd v Shire of Cranbourne (1987) 28 APA 128; 6 AATR 10: 133
Equity Trustees Executors and Agency Co Ltd v MMBW [1994] 1 VR 534: 236
Fitzwood v City of Whittlesea (1994) 12 AATR 354: 93
Gala Homes and Sales Pty Ltd v MMBW [1970] VPA 259: 152
General Mutual Life Assurance Society Ltd [1976] VR 592: 61, 70, 123, 221
Glen Eira City Council v Gory [2001] VSC 306: 126
Glenwaye v Glen Eira CC [2006] VCAT 3000: 45
Golden Ridge v Whitehorse CC (Mitcham Towers) [2004] VCAT 1706: 54, 126
Graham v Stonnington CC [2010] VCAT 1224: 115
Grantham v Mornington Peninsula SC [2002] VCAT 424; 10 VPR 246: 106
Greater Geelong City Council v Geelong Markets Pty Ltd [2004] VCAT 781: 185
Green v Ballarat CC [2006] VCAT 2535: 173
Grollo Australia v Minister for Planning and Urban Growth (1993) 10 AATR 170: 96
Guinness Mahon Pty Ltd v Moonee Valley CC (1995) 15 AATR 176: 118
Halliday v Port Phillip CC [2000] VCAT 545: 222
Halwood Corporation Ltd v Roads Corporation (1995) 89 LGRA 280: 243-244
Halwood Corporation Ltd v Roads Corporation [1998] 2 VR 439: 245
Harding v Port Phillip CC [2002] VCAT 416: 222
Harmonious Blend Building Group v Shire of Yarra Ranges (unreported, 1996/48593): 131
Holt v South Gippsland SC [2003] VCAT 19: 182
Imperium Designs Pty Ltd v Glen Eira CC (2002) 12 VPR 182: 108
James W Sadler Pty Ltd v City of Keilor (1992) 11 AATR 176: 172
Johnson v Russell [2006] VSC 373: 174
Kentucky Fried Chicken Pty Ltd v Gantidis (1979) 140 CLR 675; 40 LGRA 132: 129
Kew, City of v MMBW (1983) 29 APA 341; 1 PABR 82: 172
King v Colac-Otway Shire Council (2002) 10 VPR 27: 63
King v Hepburn SC [2002] VCAT 928: 65
Kruska v Whittlesea City Council (2002) 11 VPR 66: 31
Lockett v Shire of Ballarat (unreported, Appeal No P89/0772): 100
Lowther Hall Anglican Grammar School v Moonee Valley CC (1999) 1 VPR 90: 172

Lyndale & Black Pty Ltd v MMBW (1983) 7 APA 470; 1 PABR 207: 93
McBride v Stonnington CC [2005] VCAT 2321: 115
McDonalds Properties (Aust) Pty Ltd v City of Stonnington (unreported, 1996/49075, 49104, 49091; editorial comment 22 AATR 2): 172
Macedon Ranges Conservation Society v Shire of Gisborne No 3 (1976) 7 VPA 232: 154
Macedon Ranges SC v Romsey Hotel Pty Ltd [2008] VSCA 45: 142
McNamara v Shire of Barrabool (1986) 26 APA 272: 106
Mainstay Australia Pty Ltd v Mornington Peninsula SC [2009] VCAT 145: 227-228
Marion v Shire of Orbost (1994) 12 AATR 268: 130
Marzorini v Mitchell SC [1999] VCAT 1826: 172
Mayor, Councillors and Citizens of the City of Traralgon v Sella Ira Pty Ltd and Paul Apostoleris Appeal P88/01616 (unreported): 189
Melbourne City Council v Starera Pty Ltd [2000] VCAT 569; 4 VPR 270: 64, 137
Micaleff v City of Keilor (1993) 11 AATR 139: 119
Mietta's Hotels Pty Ltd v Roper (1988) 1 AATR 354: 96
Minister for Planning and Environment v Braybridge (1988) 2 AATR 82: 177
Minnawood Pty Ltd v Bayside CC [2009] VCAT 440: 224
Mitchell v Port Phillip City Council [2002] VCAT 452 (11 VPR 127): 125
Moonee Valley CC v Quadry Industries Pty Ltd [1999] VSC 95; 6 VPR 196: 178
Morocco v City of Knox (unreported decision of the AAT, 88/0901, noted (1989) 2 AATR 25): 182
Murphyores Inc Ltd v Commonwealth (1976) 136 CLR 1: 196
Naprelac v Baw Baw SC [2005] VCAT 958: 45
Nascon Australia Pty Ltd v Maroondah (1997) 18 AATR 50: 130
National Trust of Australia (Victoria) v Australian Temperance and General Mutual Life Assurance Society Ltd [1976] VR 592: 61, 70, 123, 221
Nicholson v City of Camberwell (1988) 33 APA 151: 129
No 2 Pitt Street v Wodonga Rural City Council [1999] 3 VR 439: 150
Noonan v Boroondara CC [2001] VCAT 158: 174
Northcote Wholesalers v City of Northcote (1994) 13 AATR: 111
Nunawading, City of v Day [1992] VR 211; 6 AATR 346: 243
Nunawading, City of v Minister for Planning and Housing (unreported, VSC, Eames J, No 9888/92, 28 September 1992): 96

TABLE OF CASES

O'Connell Street Developments Pty Ltd v Yarra CC [2003] VCAT 448; 13 VPR 227: 55, 117, 127

Odyssey House v Benalal Rural CC [2003] VCAT 15; 13 VPR 69: 130

Oglesby v East Gippsland SC [2006] VCAT 2475: 172

Orientmix Australasia Pty Ltd v City of Melbourne (1982) 62 LGRA 152: 177-178

Perorad Care Pty Ltd v Frankston CC [2004] VCAT 2272: 51

Perth, Shire of v O'Keefe (1964) 10 LGRA 147: 64

Peterson v Rural City of Ararat [2003] VCAT 219; 14 VPR 202: 106

Pituri Pty Ltd v City of South Melbourne (1985) 3 PABR 200: 106

Polmac Pty Ltd v Whitehorse CC [1999] VCAT 209; 5 VPR 24: 111

Porchester Nominees Pty Ltd v William Renfrey (1987) 1 AATR 79: 87

Port Phillip v A and M Resi [2001] VCAT 489: 222

Port Phillip City Council v J & Evelyn Beckman (2003) 14 VPR 190: 64

Prahran, City of v Cameron [1972] VR 90: 190

Prizac Investments Pty Ltd v Maribyrnong CC [2009] VCAT 2616: 143

Queensland v Commonwealth (1988) 86 ALR 519: 197

R v King; Ex parte Westfield Corporation (Vic) Ltd (1981) 2 PABR 268: 88

Rajendran v Tonkin [2004] VSCA 43: 209

Rejfek v McElroy (1966) 39 ALJR 177; [1966] ALR 270: 190

Richards v City of Richmond (1984) 18 APA 323: 129

Richardson v Forestry Commission (Tas) (1988) 164 CLR 261; 77 ALR 237: 196

Ritchie's Stores Pty Ltd v Bass Coast SC [2003] VCAT 233; 14 VPR 82: 118

Romsey Hotel Pty Ltd v Victorian Commission for Gambling Regulation [2009] VCAT 2275: 142-143

Romsey Hotel v Victorian Commission for Gambling Regulation [2007] VCAT 1: 142

Rosanna Parklands Protection Association Inc v Banyule CC [2004] VCAT 2607: 184

Rosemeier v Greater Geelong City Council (No 1) (1997) 20 AATR 86: 133

Rowcliffe Pty Ltd v Stonnington CC [2004] VCAT 46 and [2004] VCAT 1370; 16 VPR 9: 54, 126-127

Rumpf v Mornington SC [2000] VSC 311; 2 VR 69; 6 VPR 314: 166

Salmal Constructions Pty Ltd v Richards (1998) 99 LGERA 423; 22 AATR 339: 221

Sammartino v Greater Geelong City Council (1997) 19 AATR 295: 130

Shalit v Jackson Clement Burrows Architects Pty Ltd [2002] VSC 528: 221

Sinclair v Boroondara CC [2001] VCAT 2203; 9 VPR 195: 111

Sinclair v Greater Geelong CC [2004] VCAT 588: 170

South Barwon, Shire of v Winstanley Bell & Co Pty Ltd (28 September 1970, unreported): 190

Springhaven Property Group Pty Ltd v Whittlesea City Council [2005] VCAT 816,: 44

Spurling v Development Underwriting (Vic) Pty Ltd [1973] VR 1: 128, 130

Staged Developments Aust v Minister for Planning, Heritage Victoria [2001] VCAT 1447; 8 VPR 131: 210

Stonnington City Council v Blue Emporium Pty Ltd [2003] VCAT 1954; 15 VPR 267: 184, 185

STY Building Supplies Pty Ltd v Greater Shepparton CC [2000] VCAT 1880: 111

Sunraysia Water Board v City of Mildura (AAT Appeal No 1994/013733): 116

Svanosio v Shire of Strathfieldsaye and Colwell (1989) 2 AATR 26: 189-190

Sweetvale Pty Ltd v Minister for Planning [2004] VCAT 2000: 171

Sweetvale Pty Ltd v VCAT [2001] VSC 426; 16 VPR 224: 51, 117

Taras Nominees Pty Ltd v Yarra CC [2003] VCAT 1952; 15 VPR 272: 112

Tasmanian Conservation Trust Inc v Minister for Resources (1995) 85 LGERA 296: 197

Tasmanian Conservation Trust Inc v Minister for Resources (1996) 30 LGERA 106: 197

Telford v Shire of Buln Buln (1990) 5 AATR 193: 172

Terence Casey Architects Pty Ltd v Colac Otway SC [2003] VCAT 1007; 14 VPR 70: 172

Thompson v VCAT [2001] VCAT 4: 192

Thorpe v Doug Wade Consultants Pty Ltd [1985] VR 433: 115

Tide Pty Ltd v Monash City Council [2000] VCAT 540: 108

TJ Love v Whittlesea Shire Council (2001) 7 VPR 268: 88, 101

Try Youth and Community Services Inc v Banyule CC [2000] VCAT 1123; 5 VPR 218: 130

Ungar v City of Malvern [1979] VR 259: 92, 152

Uniting Church v Moreland City Council (1996) 16 AATR 250: 129

Van der Meyden v MMBW [1980] VR 225: 217-218, 236

Varvanides v VCAT [2005] VSCA 231: 192

VBI Properties PL v Port Phillip City Council [2000] VCAT 885; 6 VPR 20, VCAT: 64

Vernia Pty Ltd v City of South Melbourne and J Licouski and C Simpas, noted at 1 AATR 2: 130

Victorian National Parks Association Inc v Iluka Resources [2004] VCAT 20: 61, 66, 123-124, 221

TABLE OF CASES

West Valentine Pty Ltd v Stonnington CC [2005] VCAT 224: 51
Westpoint Corporation v Moreland CC [2005] VCAT 2174: 135
White v Shire of Ballan (1986) 4 PABR 272: 63
Whittlesea City Council v Jala Pty Ltd [2000] VCAT 242: 31
Wilde v City of Moonee Valley (1997) 18 AATR 145: 131
Wilson v Port Phillip CC [2002] VCAT 811: 164
Zalcberg v City of Stonnington (1996) 18 AATR 122: 172, 174
Zuzek v Boroondara [2007] VCAT 2174: 135

Table of Statutes

Constitution
    s 51: 195-196
    s 52: 195
    s 109: 195-196

Commonwealth
Albury-Wodonga Development Act 1973: 18
Australian Heritage Commission Act 1975: 194, 198
    s 4(1): 200
    s 7: 200
Australian Heritage Council Act 2003: 194, 198, 200
    s 3(2): 201
    s 22(2): 200-201
    ss 22-23: 201
Conservation Legislation Amendment Act 1988: 196
Corporations Act 2001
    s 9: 140
Customs Act 1901: 196
Environmental and Heritage Amendment (No 1) 2003: 198
Environment Protection (Impact of Proposals) Act 1974: 197
Environment Protection and Biodiversity Conservation Act 1999: 197, 202
    s 12: 197-198, 200
    s 12(1): 198
    ss 316-320: 198
    ss 323-324: 198
    s 528: 201
    Part 3: 200
    Part 8: 197
Lemonthyme and Southern Forests (Commission of Inquiry) Act 1987: 197
    s 16: 197
World Heritage Properties Conservation Act 1983: 195-196

Victoria
Aboriginal Heritage Act 2006
    s 3(a): 226
    s 27: 202
    s 29: 202
    s 37: 202
    s 38: 202
    s 42: 226
    s 46: 226
    s 50: 226
    s 52: 226
    s 52(1): 227
    s 53: 226
    s 55: 226
    ss 61-67: 226
    s 116: 226
    s 130: 226
Aboriginal Heritage Regulations 2007
    reg 6: 226
    regs 7-19: 226
    regs 20-38: 226
    reg 40: 227
    regs 43-54: 227
    Part 4: 226
Administrative Appeals Tribunal Act 1984: 155
    s 25: 154
    s 52: 178
    s 52(1): 175
Administrative Law Act 1978: 174
Albury-Wodonga (Agreement) Act 1973: 18
Archaeological and Aboriginal Relics Preservation Act 1972: 202-203
Building Act 1993: 57, 68, 104
Building Control Act 1981: 35
Building (Single Dwelling) Regulations) 2001: 68
Building Regulations 1994: 68
Building Regulations 2006: 57, 68, 104
    Part 4: 69
Catchment and Land Protection Act 1994: 28, 80, 91, 148
Casino Control Act 1991
    Schedule 1: 25
Cluster Titles Act 1974: 30
Conservation, Forests and Lands Act 1987: 80, 91, 95
Development Areas Act 1973: 231-232
Docklands Authority 1991: 25
Environment Effects Act 1978: 21, 36, 38, 86, 114, 226
    s 2: 36
    s 3: 37
    s 8: 37
    s 9: 37
Environment Protection Act 1970: 26, 28, 136, 144, 148
    s 16: 123
    s 19B: 144
    s 19B(3): 144
    s 19B(4A): 144
    s 19B(4A)(b): 144
    s 19B(4A)(c): 144
    s 19B(4C)(b): 144
    s 19B(5)(c): 144
    s 19B(7A): 144
Environment Protection (Scheduled Premises & Exemptions) Regulations 2007: 144

TABLE OF STATUTES

Extractive Industries Development Act 1995
(Vic): 80, 148
Flora and Fauna Guarantee Act 1988: 31
Freedom of Information 1982: 154
    s 50: 154
Gambling Regulation Act 2003
    s 3.3.2(1): 141
    s 3.3.2(3): 141
    s 3.3.6: 141
    s 3.3.7: 141-143
    s 3.3.7(1): 141-142
    s 3.3.14: 141
    s 3.3.14(1): 142
Geelong Regional Commission Act 1977: 17, 19
Health Act 1958: 34
Heritage Act 1995: 1, 194, 202, 205, 219, 225
    s 3: 204, 208
    s 7: 206
    s 8: 206
    s 19: 203
    s 23: 206
    s 28: 206
    s 29(1): 206
    ss 30-31: 206
    s 31(9): 207
    s 32: 207
    ss 34-35: 207
    s 34A: 207
    s 41(6): 207
    ss 43-45: 207
    s 50: 207
    ss 55-62: 208
    s 64: 208
    s 65: 208
    s 66: 208, 225
    s 68: 209
    s 69: 209
    s 70: 210
    s 70(1)-(2): 209
    s 73: 209
    s 73(1)(b): 211
    s 74(2): 209
    s 75(3): 210
    s 76(2): 210
    ss 77-79: 210
    s 78(1)(b): 210
    ss 80-81: 211
    ss 85-86: 211
    s 120: 203
    s 135: 211
    ss 140-141: 211
    s 144: 211
    s 160: 208
    s 164: 208
    ss 166-168: 209
    s 182: 209
    Schedule 1, cl 2: 148
Heritage Overlay Provisions: 225
    cl 43.01: 220
    cl 43.01-1: 220
    cl 43.01-4: 221
    cl 43.01-5: 221, 223
    cl 43.01-6: 220
Historic Buildings Act 1974: 203, 205, 215
Historic Buildings Act 1981: 203-205, 225
Historic Buildings (Amendment) Act 1983: 204
Historic Buildings (Further Amendment) Act
1983: 204
Infringements Act 2006: 186
Interpretation of Legislation Act 1984: 49
    s 28: 63
Land Acquisition and Compensation Act 1986:
47, 211, 237
    s 5(1): 238-239
    s 5(2): 239
    s 5(3): 240
    s 5(4A): 240
    s 5(4B): 240
    s 37: 247
    s 40: 240-242
    s 41(1): 241
    s 41(2): 242
    s 44: 242
    s 45: 243
    s 45(1)(b): 243
    s 81: 247
    s 81(2): 247
    s 106(1): 247
Land Acquisition and Compensation Regulations
1998: 239
    reg 22: 243
Land Act 1958: 80, 95, 97
Latrobe Regional Commission Act 1983: 18
    s 6: 18
Liquor Control Reform Act 1998: 136
    s 16: 137
    s 87: 137
    s 87A: 137
    Part 5: 137
Local Government Act 1921: 15, 35, 62, 239
Local Government Act 1958: 34, 153
Local Government Act 1989: 46
    s 86: 120
    s 125: 23, 55
Local Planning Policy Framework (LPPF): 7, 22,
33, 222
    cl 55: 55
    cl 65: 123
Loddon Campaspe Regional Authority Act 1987:
17
Major Transport Projects Facilitation Act 2009:
146, 226, 249-250
Melbourne Planning Scheme
    cl 21.21: 124
    cl 61.01: 25
    cl 61.02: 27
Mineral Resources Development Act 1990: 27,
80, 91, 95
Monetary Units Act 2004: 182

TABLE OF STATUTES

Planning and Environment Act 1987: 1, 7, 13, 15, 21, 28-29, 37-38, 49, 53, 57, 74, 76, 96, 104, 137-139, 144-145, 147, 175-176, 194, 202, 206-207, 212, 229
    s 2: 252
    s 3: 21, 29, 40, 57-58, 104, 219-220, 237, 252
    s 4: 53, 82, 86, 130, 224
    s 4(1): 38, 81, 219
    s 4(1)(b): 220
    s 4(1)(d): 220
    s 4(1)(f): 40
    s 4(2): 26, 81
    s 4(2)(d): 155
    s 4B: 23, 49, 77
    s 4J: 77
    s 6: 82, 86, 219
    s 6(1): 39, 40, 219
    s 6 (1)(a): 29, 220
    s 6(1)(aa): 41
    s 6(1)(b): 40
    s 6(2): 41, 47, 219
    s 6(2)(a): 41
    s 6(2)(b): 41-42
    s 6(2)(c): 41-42
    s 6(2)(e): 42
    s 6(2)(f): 43
    s 6(2)(g): 45-46
    s 6(2)(ga): 46
    s 6(2)(gb): 46
    s 6(2)(h): 42
    s 6(2)(ha): 46
    s 6(2)(i): 241
    s 6(2)(j): 35, 47, 49
    s 6(2)(k): 49
    s 6(2)(ka): 50
    s 6(2)(kc): 50-51, 60-61, 114, 117
    s 6(2)(kd): 50-51, 60-61, 114, 117
    s 6(2)(1): 41
    s 6(3): 63, 150, 235
    s 6(4): 63
    s 7: 23, 53
    s 7(1): 22, 41
    s 7(2): 22-23, 54
    s 7(5): 53
    s 8: 24, 27, 51
    s 9: 24, 78
    s 9(2): 24
    s 10: 78
    s 10(1): 3
    s 11: 27, 78-79
    s 11(1): 90
    s 11(2): 90
    s 12(2): 81
    s 12(2)(b): 81
    s 12(2)(c): 81-82
    s 12A: 55
    s 12B: 8, 23
    s 12B(4): 23
    s 12B(5): 23
    s 13: 25, 27, 134
    s 13(a): 25
    s 13(b): 25
    s 13(c): 25, 27
    s 14: 179
    s 16: 145
    s 17: 94, 239, 246
    s 17(2): 101
    s 18: 94, 239, 246
    s 19: 80, 83, 90-91, 94, 97, 239, 243
    s 19(1): 80
    s 19(1)(c): 95
    s 19(1A): 81
    s 19(1B): 81
    s 19(2): 80
    s 19(3): 80
    s 19(4): 80
    s 19(7): 81
    s 20: 27, 49, 74, 77-78, 80, 93, 96, 99, 239
    s 20(2): 27
    s 20(3): 77, 95, 97, 239
    s 20(3)(b): 95
    s 20(3)(ba): 95
    s 20(3)(c): 95
    s 20(4): 27, 77, 94, 239, 250-251
    s 21: 81
    s 21(2): 83
    s 21(3): 77
    s 21A: 81
    s 22: 81
    s 22(1): 81-82
    s 22(2): 81
    s 23: 81
    s 23(c): 84
    s 24: 85
    s 24(a): 84
    s 25: 85
    s 26: 85, 90
    s 26(2): 90
    s 27: 90
    s 27(1): 89
    s 27(2): 89-90, 239
    s 27(3): 89-90, 95, 239
    s 29: 90
    s 30: 94
    s 30(1)(c): 94
    s 30(1)(d): 94
    s 30(2)-(3): 94
    s 31: 79, 85, 90
    s 32: 91
    s 33: 91
    s 34: 91
    s 34(1): 91
    s 34(2): 91
    s 35(1): 90
    s 35(4): 90-91
    s 35A(2): 90
    s 35A(3): 90
    s 35B: 79, 92
    s 36(1): 92
    s 36(2): 92
    s 37: 97

Planning and Environment Act 1987 (Vic) *(cont)*
  s 38: 92, 98
  s 39: 86, 86, 100-101, 149
  s 39(4): 100
  ss 46A-46G: 19
  s 46AA: 52, 98
  ss 46AG-46AJ: 99
  s 46AB: 52
  s 46AC: 52
  s 46AH: 99
  s 46AO: 92
  s 46AP: 92
  s 46AS: 92
  s 46AT: 93
  s 46D: 99
  s 46F: 99
  ss 46H-46QC: 43
  s 46N: 44
  s 47(b): 245
  s 47(1)(c): 109
  s 47(1)(d): 108, 110
  s 47(1)(e): 110
  s 48: 105, 108-109
  s 48(2): 108
  s 49: 109, 112
  s 50: 112, 117, 120
  s 50(1): 112
  s 50(4): 113
  s 50(5): 113
  s 50(6): 113
  s 50A: 112-113, 120
  s 51: 118
  s 52: 33, 50-51, 108, 114-118, 120, 135, 158, 187-188, 221
  s 52(1): 108, 116
  s 52(1)(a): 93, 187
  s 52(1)(ca): 116-117
  s 52(1)(cb): 116-117
  s 52(1)(d): 116, 187
  s 52(1A): 108, 114, 158
  s 52(1AA): 114, 116
  s 52(4): 117
  s 54: 47, 109, 111, 149
  s 54(1): 108, 120
  s 54(1A): 112
  s 54(1B): 112
  s 54(1C): 112
  s 54A: 112, 117, 120, 149
  s 54B: 112
  s 55: 26, 109, 113, 187
  s 56: 132, 144
  s 56(1)(a)-(c): 113
  s 56 (1A): 118
  s 57A: 117, 120, 149
  s 57A(4)-(5): 117
  s 57A(7)(a): 117
  s 57A(7)(b): 117
  s 57B: 5117
  s 57B(1): 117
  s 57B(2): 117
  s 57C:117-118
  s 57(1): 118
  s 57(2): 118
  s 57(2A): 118
  s 57(3): 118
  s 57(4): 118
  s 57(5): 118
  s 59: 108-109
  s 60: 33, 65, 120, 123, 127, 130, 138
  s 60(b)(ii): 55
  s 60(1): 123
  s 60(1): 127
  s 60(2)-(7): 46
  s 60(2): 131
  s 60(3): 51, 114, 117
  s 60(5): 131
  s 61: 27, 31, 132, 225
  s 61(1)(a)(aa): 132
  s 61(2): 26, 42, 113, 118, 187
  s 61(4): 132
  s 62: 31, 42, 120, 132
  s 62(1): 26-27, 42, 114, 118, 132, 187
  s 62(1)(a): 44
  s 62(2): 42, 44, 132
  s 62(5): 43-44
  s 62(6): 44-45
  ss 63-65: 120
  s 64: 132, 135, 221
  s 64(1)-(3): 50
  s 65: 132
  s 68(1)(b): 106
  s 69: 107
  s 71: 134
  s 72: 253
  s 72(1)(c): 135
  s 72(2): 136
  ss 72-76D: 134-136
  s 74: 135
  s 75: 149
  s 76: 149
  s 76C: 135, 149
  s 77: 148-149, 155
  s 78: 149
  s 79: 108, 148-149, 155
  s 80: 42, 149, 155
  s 81: 107, 149
  s 81(a)-(b): 149
  s 81(2): 112, 149
  s 82: 51, 117, 148
  s 82(1): 50, 93, 119, 149, 155
  s 82B: 119, 158
  s 82B(1): 149
  s 82B(4): 158
  s 82B(5): 158
  s 83A: 158
  s 84B: 92-93
  s 84B(1): 93, 116
  s 84B(1)(f): 90, 93
  s 85(1)(c)(ii): 119
  s 87: 116, 135, 253
  s 87(1): 116, 187
  s 87(3): 116, 149

TABLE OF STATUTES

s 87A: 224
ss 87-94: 179
s 88: 149
s 89: 116, 187
s 89(1): 149, 187
s 89(1)(b): 188
s 91(1): 116
s 91(2): 116
s 91(3): 116
s 91(3A): 116
s 92: 188
s 93: 116, 179, 188
s 94: 116, 188
s 95: 146, 178
s 95(2): 146
s 95(3)(c): 178
s 95(5): 146
s 95(6): 178
s 96: 50, 62, 145
s 96(1): 50
s 96(2): 50
s 96(6): 146
s 96(7): 146
s 96A: 97
s 96A(3): 97
s 96C: 97
s 96C(1): 97
s 96C(5): 97
s 96I: 97
s 96I(1): 97
s 96I(2): 97
s 96I(3): 97
s 96I(1A): 97
s 96J(4): 97
s 96M: 97
s 96N: 97
ss 97A-97M: 84, 121, 250
s 97B: 28
s 97E(2)-(3):121
s 97E(5): 121
s 97I: 135-136
s 97J: 135
s 97M: 28, 121
s 97MB: 121
s 97MD: 121
s 97MF: 121
s 97MH: 121
s 97MJ: 121
s 97MK: 122
s 97MW: 122
s 97MZT: 122
s 97P: 149
s 98: 243
s 98(1): 247
s 98(1)(d): 46
s 98(2): 245
s 99: 245
s 99(a)(i): 245
s 99(a)(ii): 245
s 99(c): 246
s 100: 242

s 102: 188
s 106: 244
s 106(1)(b): 244
s 106(2): 244, 246
s 107: 244
s 108: 245
s 109: 247
s 111: 244
s 111(3): 245
s 113: 234, 244, 247
s 114: 149, 180, 182, 184-185
s 114(3): 182
ss 114-119: 179
s 117(1): 188
s 118: 183
s 120: 149, 182, 184-185
s 120(2): 184
s 120(3): 184
s 120(3)(b): 185
s 120(6): 185
ss 120-121: 179, 185
s 123(1)(b): 193
s 123(2): 193
s 125: 179
s 126: 179
s 126(1)(2): 193
s 126(4): 193
s 127: 181, 188
s 130(3)-(5): 186
ss 130-132: 179
s 133: 180, 192
s 134(1)(c),(2): 180
s 134 (3): 180
ss 135-6: 180
ss 139-147: 189
ss 139-149: 190
s 148: 149
s 149: 149
s 149A: 121, 150
s 149B: 149-150
s 150: 99
s 150(1)-(3): 100
s 150(4): 101, 170
s 151: 84
s 153: 84, 238
s 159: 84
s 160: 87
s 161(1): 87
s 161(1)(b): 88-89
s 161(1)(d): 87
s 161(3): 88
s 161(5): 85
s 162: 84
s 163: 85
s 166: 89
s 167: 87
s 168: 87
s 169: 84
s 172: 193, 237
s 172(1)(a): 237
s 172(1)(b): 238

TABLE OF STATUTES

Planning and Environment Act 1987 (Vic) *(cont)*
    s 172(2): 238, 240
    s 172(3): 239
    s 173: 25, 31-32, 44, 49, 101, 123, 133,
        134, 149-150, 180-182, 184, 186, 191,
        249, 253
    s 173(1): 50
    s 173(3): 50
    s 174: 133
    s 175(2): 134
    s 177(1): 134
    ss 181-182: 134
    s 184(1): 150
    s 184(3): 150
    s 188: 120
    s 188(1)(a): 120
    s 188(2)(a): 90
    s 197: 109
    s 198: 241
    s 199(1): 246
    s 200(1), (2): 246
    s 201: 241
    s 201(1): 241
    s 201F: 240
    s 203: 78
    s 203(1): 78
    s 203(1)(c): 78
    Part 3A: 18
    Part 3B: 231
    Part 4: 99
    Div 2: 121
    Div 3: 121
    Div 5: 79
    Div 6: 136
    Part 4AA: 25, 121
    Part 6: 179
    Part 9: 99
    Part 9B: 45
Planning and Environment (Amendment) Act 1989: 78, 89, 95, 99-100
Planning and Environment (Amendment) Act 1993: 51
Planning and Environment Amendment (General) Bill 2009: 248-249
Planning and Environment Bill 1987: 4-5
Planning and Environment (Development Contributions) Act 2004: 43
Planning and Environment (General Amendment) Act 2004: 27, 80, 112, 117, 134
Planning and Environment (General Amendment) Bill 2004: 80
Planning and Environment (Growth Areas Infrastructure) Act 2010: 45
Planning and Environment (Metropolitan Green Wedge Protection) Act 2003: 52
Planning and Environment (Planning Schemes) Act 1996: 21-22, 35, 53
Planning and Environment Regulations 2005: 156
    reg 7: 80
    reg 8: 91
    reg 9: 80
    reg 10: 85, 90
    reg 13: 91
    reg 15: 107
    reg 19: 115
    reg 20: 109, 113
    reg 24: 108-109
    reg 25: 132
    reg 28: 132
    reg 57: 246
    Schedule 1 Form 3: 115
    Schedule 1 Form 4: 107
Planning Appeals Act 1980: 29, 166, 190
    s 40(2): 177
    s 41: 176-177
    s 41(1): 178
    s 41(2): 177
    s 41(3): 177
    s 41(5): 177
    Div 3: 166
Planning Appeals (Amendment) Act 1987: 154-155
Planning Appeals Board Act 1980: 29, 153, 155
    s 20: 154
    s 27-28: 153
    s 28(3): 154
    s 37: 153
    s 41: 154
    s 44: 153
    s 45: 153
    s 61-64: 154
Pipelines Act 1967: 80
ResCode: 36
[VicCode 1 was replaced in 2001 by the provisions of ResCode dealing with subdivision and set out at cl 56 of the VPPs (p 35)]
    cl 52: 58
    cl 54: 58, 62, 70-72
    cl 55: 58-59, 62, 66, 68, 70-73, 161
    cl 56: 62, 66, 68, 70, 72
Road Management Act 1983: 90
Sex Work Act 1994: 1
    s 22(1): 139
    s 23(1): 137, 139
    s 23(1)-(3): 138
    ss 33-70: 137
    s 33: 137
    s 36A: 140
    s 37: 140
    s 38: 140
    s 56: 140
    ss 71-79: 137
    s 71: 137
    s 72: 137
    s 72(a): 139
    s 72(b): 137
    s 73: 138-139
    s 73(a)-(k): 138
    s 73(b): 139
    s 73(e): 139
    s 74: 138
    s 74(1): 138-139

TABLE OF STATUTES

s 74(1)(a)-(d): 139
s 74(2): 138
s 75(1): 139
s 75(2): 140
s 75(3): 140
s 80: 193
s 82: 193
Part 3: 137
Part 4: 137, 193
Part 5: 193
State Planning Policy Framework (SPPF): 7, 14, 22, 23, 33, 54
    cl 11: 222
    cl 12: 55
    cl 14: 55
    cl 19.03-2: 223
Strata Titles Act 1967: 30
Subdivision Act 1988: 21, 28, 30-32, 148
    s 18: 31
    s 6: 34
    s 23: 45-46
    s 36: 46
Sustainable Resources (Timber) Act 2004: 80
Town and Country (Metropolitan Area) Act 1949: 16
Town and Country Planning Act 1944: 4, 15, 17, 19-21, 62, 95, 230
    s 13: 212
    s 204: 22
    Schedule, cl 5: 212-213
    Part 1: 22
Town and Country Planning Act 1958
    s 14(3): 151
    Second Schedule, cl 5: 213
Town and Country Planning Act 1961: 15, 19, 28, 40, 127, 130, 176-177, 180, 218-219, 225
    s 17: 212
    s 18B: 114
    s 21(1): 153
    s 42: 216-217
    s 42(1): 216
    s 42(2): 215
    s 42(6): 216
    s 49(2): 190
    Third Schedule: 40, 213, 219
    Third Schedule, cl 2: 468
    Third Schedule, cl 4: 29
    Third Schedule, cl 8: 213-216
    Third Schedule, cll 8A: 213-214, 216-217, 224
    Third Schedule, cll 8B: 213-216
Town and Country Planning (Amendment) Act 1968: 15-16, 151
    s 21(1)
Town and Country Planning (Amendment) Act 1972: 213
Town and Country Planning (Amendment) Act 1982: 218
    s 4: 216
Town and Country Planning (General Amendment) Act 1979: 20

Town and Country Planning (Transfer of Functions) Act 1985: 16
Transfer of Land Act 1958: 115
Upper Yarra Valley and Dandenong Ranges Authority Act 1976: 17
    s 12: 17
    s 17: 18
VicCode 1: 34-35
[Residential Development Provisions, renamed in 1992 The Victorian Code for Residential Development – Subdivision and Single Dwellings (and generally known as VicCode 1) p 34]
Victoria Planning Provisions (VPPs): 22-24, 29, 34, 229, 238, 252
    cl 52.01: 31
    cl 53: 18-19
    cl 56: 35-36
    cll 56.02-56.04: 36
    cll 56.02-56.10: 36
    cl 62.03: 30
    cl 65: 33
    cl 66.01: 30
    cl 66.02: 31
    cl 66: 26
Victorian Building Regulations 1983: 35
Victorian Civil and Administrative Tribunal Act 1998: 15, 29
    s 3: 148, 174, 183, 192
    s 13: 147
    s 14: 147
    s 16: 147
    s 21(4J)-(4K): 152
    s 25A: 147
    s 40: 148
    s 42(1): 148
    s 51(1): 148
    s 51(1)(d): 149
    s 51(2): 168
    s 52: 150, 175
    s 52(1): 150
    s 52(2): 150
    s 59: 174, 176
    s 60: 51, 158-159
    s 60(2): 159
    s 61(1)-(2): 159
    s 62(1): 163
    s 62(1)(c): 163
    s 62(7)(b): 164
    s 62(8): 163
    s 67: 182
    s 72: 158
    s 72(1): 182
    s 75(1)-(2): 169
    s 75(2): 174
    ss 77-94: 148
    s 78(a): 149
    s 78(2)(b)(ii): 166
    s 83: 167
    s 83(2), (4)-(5): 167
    s 85: 167

TABLE OF STATUTES

Victorian Civil and Administrative Tribunal Act 1998 (Vic) *(cont)*
  s 87: 170
  s 88: 167
  s 88 (6)-(7): 167
  s 89: 170
  s 92: 167
  s 93: 168
  s 94: 166
  s 95: 166
  ss 97-98: 166, 188
  s 98: 51
  s 98(1)(c): 159
  s 99: 163
  s 102(3): 164
  s 107: 166
  s 109: 169-171, 174, 190
  s 109(1)-(3): 169
  s 109(1): 170, 173
  s 109(3): 170-171
  s 109(3)(c): 173
  s 114: 182
  s 116: 183
  s 116(1): 168
  s 116(1)(b): 168
  s 117: 175
  s 117(1)-(2): 183
  s 117(1)-(4): 168
  s 117(6): 168
  s 118: 168
  s 119: 169, 183
  s 119(b): 183
  s 120: 182
  s 125: 186
  s 122: 192
  s 122(1): 192
  s 123: 186
  s 126: 157
  s 132: 157
  s 133: 183-184
  s 133(1): 183
  s 137(1)-(2): 192
  s 148: 150, 174-175, 178
  s 148(c): 175
  s 148(1): 174
  s 148(2): 175
  s 148(4): 175
  s 150(4): 174
  s 171(1): 182
  Part 3 Division 5: 166
  Schedule 1: 210
  Schedule 1, cl 2: 28, 176
  Schedule 1, cl 52: 166
  Schedule 1, cl 56: 158
  Schedule 1, cl 58: 28, 84, 121, 152, 175-177, 250
  Schedule 1, cl 59: 28, 84, 121, 152, 175-177, 250
  Schedule 1, cl 60: 175
  Schedule 1, cl 63: 170
  Schedule 1, cl 64: 164
  Schedule 1, cl 66: 166
  Schedule 3, cl 2: 148
Victorian Civil and Administrative Tribunal (Amendment) Act 2004: 176
Victorian Civil and Administrative Tribunal (Fees) Regulations 2001
  reg 4: 156
Victorian Civil and Administrative Tribunal Rules 1998: 182
  r 4.16: 168
  r 5.07: 158
Victoria Planning Provisions
  cl 11: 75
  cl 11.01: 40
  cl 12: 54
  cl 12.09: 54-55
  cl 19.03: 71
  cl 20: 125
  cl 31: 124
  cl 32.01-5: 58
  cl 32.01-2: 60
  cl 36.02-2: 58
  cl 36.02-7: 59
  cl 52.01: 31
  cl 52.05: 107
  cl 52.06: 107
  cl 52.29: 107
  cl 52.27: 136
  cl 52.28: 140
  cl 52.28-2: 140
  cl 52.28-3: 140
  cl 52.28-4: 140
  cl 52.28-6: 141
  cl 53: 18-19
  cl 54: 46, 61, 108-109
  cl 54.01: 70
  cl 54.01-4: 46
  cl 55: 46, 108-109
  cl 55.01-1: 46
  cl 56: 35-36
  cl 56.02-56.10: 36
  cl 56.04: 36
  cl 62.03: 30
  cl 63: 64
  cl 63.01: 63
  cl 63.02: 64
  cl 63.05: 64
  cl 63.08: 65
  cl 63.10: 65
  cl 65: 33, 66
  cl 65.01: 65
  cl 66: 26
  cl 66.01: 30
  cl 66.02: 31
  cl 66.02-1: 144
  cl 67: 50
  cl 67.01: 145
  cll 72-75: 110
  cl 74: 64
  cl 81: 47-48
Water Act 1989: 28

TABLE OF STATUTES

New South Wales
Albury-Wodonga Development Act 1974: 18

Tasmania
Gordon River Hydro-Electric Power Development Act 1982
    s 9: 196
    s 9(1)(h): 196

International
Convention for the Protection of the World Cultural and Natural Heritage (the World Heritage Convention): 194

Chapter 1

STATUTORY PLANNING IN CONTEXT

Statutory planning and strategic planning

Statutory planning is sometimes referred to as development control. It is the term normally used to refer to the formulation and administration of controls on the use and development of land. In Victoria these controls are contained for the most part in each municipality's planning scheme and operate primarily via a system of zoning. The matters that can be provided for in schemes, and the procedures for scheme amendment and scheme administration, are prescribed in the *Planning and Environment Act 1987*. However, not all controls on the use and development of land are necessarily included in schemes – as will be seen later, legislation other than the *Planning and Environment Act* can have a significant regulatory impact on specific land uses and developments, such as the *Heritage Act 1995* on buildings of heritage value and the *Sex Work Act 1994* on brothels, to name but two examples.

It has become something of a convention in Victoria, as in other States, to compartmentalise town planning or urban planning into statutory planning and strategic planning, with the latter term usually being used to refer to the research and policy development aspects of the planning process. Strategic planning is concerned with the formulation and evaluation of planning policies and the mechanisms (including planning schemes) put in place for implementing those policies. Land use and development policies come under the heading of planning policies and, like all policies, are statements of intent. They identify where it is intended that different land uses and development will locate and they may even establish priorities about the sequence in which it is intended that areas be developed. They may also identify those areas in which it is intended that redevelopment should occur and it is not uncommon for them to identify buildings and areas which are intended to be protected from development or redevelopment. The formulation of sound land use and development policies depends on systematic research into such matters as population and development trends; land and building characteristics; and the ways and means, including costs, of servicing land with physical and social infrastructure. Strategic planning involves more than this, though – it also involves researching the extent to which those statements of intent remain appropriate with the passage of time and, if they are still appropriate, whether the mechanisms put in place to implement them are having the desired effect. A crucial part of strategic planning is the monitoring and evaluation of the effects of controls on land use and development.

Unfortunately, the distinction between strategic and statutory planning has become institutionalised, for, in many municipalities, professional staff tend to work exclusively in either strategic planning or statutory planning. The corporate structures of these organisations reinforce that separation and as a result the functions of strategic and statutory planning become divorced from each other. But strategic and statutory planning are inter-related parts of a larger process which should involve research, policy formulation, the utilisation of various mechanisms (including planning schemes) to implement policy, and regular review of both policies and implementation mechanisms. As planning schemes impose different controls on different land uses and different areas of land, by their very nature they confer benefits and disbenefits in terms of land value, the uses for which land can be developed, and the level of access enjoyed by different sections of the community to shopping centres, employment nodes, schools, libraries, hospitals, entertainment areas and the rest of what we would generally call community facilities. The isolation of statutory planning from the larger process means that decisions which allocate benefits and disbenefits may be made on the basis of local political pressure and inventive legal argument rather than on the basis of considered policies which are a matter of public record. The end product may well be the closing-off of options for accommodating future development or for effective management of that development, rural and urban environments that are degraded in both environmental and social terms, and development patterns that cost the community dearly because they can be provided with physical and social infrastructure only at great expense.

The limitations of statutory planning – some examples

Planning schemes are not the only mechanism available for implementing land use and development policies. Other mechanisms may include the reorganisation and redirection of municipal activities and services and securing decisions and allocations of resources from other levels of government. The relevance of mechanisms other than planning schemes for implementing planning policies in general, and land use and development policies in particular, is shown by the following examples.

Improving public transport

Our public transport system seems to be a constant source of problems for the government and for the community. Encouraging the use of public transport and improving levels of access to public transport services are long-held and cherished planning principles. Management and control of land use and development via planning schemes may, over time, result in greater use of and access to public transport by promoting higher density development near current and planned train, bus and tram routes, and ensuring that future development is steered to appropriate locations. This is a core objective of *Melbourne 2030*, the metropolitan planning policy adopted by the State government in 2002. However, both increased use and improvement of access also depend on increasing the quality and frequency of services, the provision of new routes, fare prices and fare structures, improved security for passengers, and linkages between bus, tram and train systems. Improved access for particular groups, such as the elderly and the disabled, means removing the barriers of steps and steep slopes in and around railway stations, providing alternatives to steps for boarding trams and buses, and widening aisles in all modes of transport to accommodate wheelchairs. Planning schemes cannot achieve any of these things.

Improving residential streets

In reaction to the complaints of local communities, many municipalities in the inner urban areas of Melbourne have adopted the policy of improving the amenity of residential streets. Planning scheme provisions may have an impact in preventing development out of scale with existing buildings and uses not appropriate for a residential environment. But improvement of existing street amenity levels is likely to rely as much on a range of engineering and design initiatives as it does on planning scheme controls. Speed humps and textured road paving treatment at suitable intervals will have an impact on the volume and speed of traffic, as will roundabouts and narrowing and redesigning the alignment of carriageways to remove the long straight stretches that encourage higher speeds. Prohibiting entry from major roads into residential streets and even making some of them "one way" will reduce through traffic. The replacement of parallel parking by angle parking will increase on-street parking capacities, which is very important in areas with Victorian and Edwardian housing stock. Indented bays utilising nature strips will make safe parking available where none was possible because of narrow carriage ways. Sensitive replanting and landscaping of streets will have a significant impact on amenity, as will the resurfacing of footpaths, the repair and maintenance of street gutters and drains, and regular street cleaning.

Heritage conservation

In response to an increasing appreciation of our built heritage, often accompanied by pressure from interest groups such as the National Trust and residents associations, controls requiring planning consent for the alteration, removal or demolition of buildings of heritage value have been introduced in planning schemes. These statutory planning measures are certainly important for implementing heritage conservation policies, but in essence the effect of such controls is to prevent summary removal, alteration or demolition. Even in residential areas where pressures for redevelopment for commercial activity are not likely to be pronounced, these controls need to be supplemented if buildings are to be conserved (that is, kept in good repair and utilised). Education programmes on the care and maintenance of buildings, renovation advisory services, and even financial assistance in the form of grants and low-cost loans may be required for successful implementation of a heritage conservation policy. For commercial areas, incentives may be required to ensure that heritage value buildings are retained in part or whole, recycled for commercial use, or extended or modified in a sensitive manner. Development bonuses in the form of greater building scale and increased floor space than would normally apply could be granted for retaining all or part of the building on the same site. Alternatively, these bonuses could be transferred to another site. Perhaps rating concessions could be gained in return for retention. Even taxation concessions could be used as an incentive. Some of these measures are beyond the power of local government to deliver and would require the support of both the State and federal governments.

Many more examples could be used to demonstrate the limitations of statutory planning. The lesson is that statutory planning is a means to an end, but in many circumstances it may not be particularly relevant for the end sought. It is but one means of implementing (in part or in whole) land use and development policies which themselves may or may not be relevant for implementing other planning policies.

Planning as a process

Statutory planning and the planning process

Since 1944, with the passage of the Victorian *Town and Country Planning Act* of that year, planning schemes have been prepared, approved and administered in Victoria. Since that time a very large number of people have had direct contact with "planning". Perhaps they have found out that they cannot develop their land or use it for what they want without first securing planning permission. Perhaps they have discovered that their intended development or land use is prohibited by the local planning scheme. Many have been involved in lodging submissions either opposing or supporting a proposed scheme amendment and have subsequently appeared and presented their submissions to a panel appointed by the Minister for Planning. Many have lodged objections to a planning permit application for some proposed use or development in their local community and have subsequently become involved in what used to be called a planning appeal and is now called a review proceeding. For these people, planning is to do with zones and use definitions, notions such as amenity, legal argument and complicated procedures. However, as we have already seen, planning should not be equated with statutory planning, which is only one of a number of mechanisms used to implement land use and development policies.

This was recognised by the then Minister for Planning and Environment, the Hon J Kennan, who in his second reading speech to the Legislative Council on the Planning and Environment Bill in March, 1987, said (Victoria. Parliament. Legislative Council. Parliamentary Debates. 24 March 1987, pp 491–492):

> Honourable members will recall that the Bill is a total overhaul of the now outdated *Town and Country Planning Act.* I do not intend to waste the time of the House in repeating the many positive aspects of the proposed legislation, which I explained then. However, I must reiterate what the Government sees to be the purpose of the proposed legislation because the Government has received many submissions which have misunderstood the purpose of the Bill.
>
> The submissions have generated substantial debate about the scope generally of planning. "Planning" as envisaged by the Bill is about the use and development

of land. While this requires taking into account a wide variety of issues, they are to be taken into account insofar as they affect the use and development of land. Conversely, other kinds of planning may have an effect on the way land should be used and developed, and they could be implemented, where appropriate, through planning schemes.

> Planning schemes should not in themselves be seen as major statements of economic or social policy. Where it is desirable to influence the use and development of land to implement such policies, they should be stated or referred to in planning schemes.
>
> It was never intended to introduce a planning Act to precisely define the scope of planning, or tell planners, councils or anyone else how to plan. The Bill enables planning proposals to be implemented. Most planning, as such, does not need specific legislation.

Mr Kennan made some very important points about planning in this speech – not only is statutory planning a means of implementing land use and development policy but also it may be a means of implementing some aspects of broader social and economic policy. However, not all aspects of land use and development policy, and certainly very little of broad social and economic policy, can be implemented through statutory planning. In a letter published in the December, 1986, edition of *Planning News*, the newsletter of the Royal Australian Planning Institute (Victoria Division), the Minister explained that the Act established a framework for planning which emphasised process and reflected the theories of Andreas Faludi (see Further Reading).

The notion that planning may be viewed as a process capable of description and analysis is derived from cybernetics. Faludi views planning as a generic process that may be applied to not only urban and regional planning but also to community services planning, educational planning, corporate planning and so on. Applied to urban and regional planning, this process has become generally known as the systems or process approach to planning. While writers such as McLoughlin, Chadwick and Faludi (see Further Reading) have varied in their formulations of the process and of the relationships between the various stages and elements comprising it, nevertheless, all in one way or another distinguish between ends (that is, policy goals and objectives) and means (mechanisms selected and then implemented to achieve these policy goals and objectives). They also emphasise that in urban and regional planning, as in many other forms of planning, the policy goals and objectives are not static – they alter according to changes in economic, social, and political environments. Neither are the implementation mechanisms static – they alter in response to changes in policy goals and objectives and in response to evidence that the mechanisms are not achieving what they were intended to achieve or are having effects not foreseen at the time they were selected and implemented. The systems or process approach therefore views planning as a continuous activity rather than simply the production of a plan that gives a picture of some desired state to be achieved.

The elements of the process

While the systems or process approach is hardly new, it nevertheless does assist us in distinguishing between ends and means and allows us to view planning as something more than an arcane and mysterious activity understood only by the chosen few of town planners, engineers and architects who know something of zoning, and lawyers specialising in planning law. This is not to pretend it is a simple process – far from it. Apart from the technical skills involved, the activity itself is undertaken in a political environment, and often a highly charged one at that. However, the process is capable of description and analysis, at least in general terms, and this allows us to place in context the paraphernalia of legislation and schemes.

The following diagram is an oversimplification, but it illustrates the major components of the process.

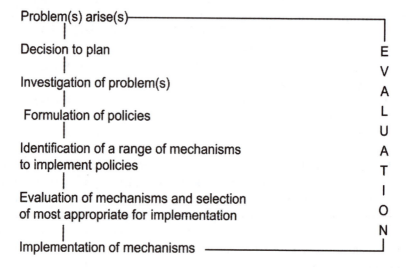

(After McLoughlin – see Further Reading.)

Most planning occurs in response to either existing or perceived future problems. Theoretically, having decided to tackle those problems (ie having decided to plan), the planning body needs to understand the nature of those problems and how they have arisen or are likely to arise, and on the basis of research and investigation formulate planning policies, including land use and development policies, to solve the problems, prevent them from occurring in the future or minimise their effects. There may be different ways of implementing policies, including the use of various statutory planning measures, and it is important for the planning body to identify these, evaluate their likely effects and then select those it considers to be appropriate. Putting the mechanisms into effect is the implementation phase.

Monitoring the impacts of the mechanisms put in place to implement policies is a crucial element in the planning process. It is essential if the planning body is to establish whether or not these measures are having the desired effects and whether or not they should be altered or abandoned in favour of other mechanisms. Monitoring is crucial in another sense, too, because changing economic, social and political conditions may give rise to new problems or alter the complexity of old problems. Therefore, policies may need to be altered or new policies may need to be developed. Without monitoring, the planning body will not become aware of the need to alter policies and implementation mechanisms until problems have become very pronounced, perhaps to the point where it is impossible to solve them, prevent them from occurring in the future or lessen their impacts. It is for this reason that the planning process is depicted as a continuous activity.

How does this theoretical view of the process of planning translate into reality? The systems or process approach is a model or construct of how planning in a general sense should operate, rather than a model derived from an examination of how it actually does operate, and reflects its origins in cybernetics. It is a model that could equally be applied at a general level to the planning of a holiday or to educational, community services, or business planning as it could to town planning. But, at a more detailed level, in town planning or urban and regional planning (as in most other types of planning) the process rarely conforms to a series of clear-cut stages. In town planning, more often than not, various stages in the process are characterised by heated contests between developers, State and local governments, individuals and community and special interest groups. The normal rules set out in legislation such as the *Planning and Environment Act* for dealing with these contests may not be followed because the Minister may decide to amend the planning scheme without the normal processes of public notification, the lodging of submissions, and the consideration of those submissions by an independent panel, or the Minister may call in and determine planning permit applications instead of the local council or call in and determine review proceedings instead of the Victorian Civil and Administrative Tribunal. At local and State government levels, decisions on planning scheme provisions and development proposals may be driven as much by political considerations as by policy considerations. The process is not antiseptic and machine-like. Perhaps because of this, there has been in the past very little monitoring and evaluation by local and State governments of their planning policies and the mechanisms put in place to implement them. This may explain why planning has been all too often a reactive process, occurring as a reaction to problems rather than as a means of preventing those problems from occurring in the first place.

Part of the difficulty of monitoring and evaluating the extent to which implementation mechanisms, including the administration of planning scheme controls, are achieving policy goals is the nature of the policies and the way in which they are expressed. Land use and development policies are now set out in the State Planning Policy Framework (SPPF) and Local Planning Policy Framework (LPPF) sections of planning schemes. In many instances, they are expressed in such broad terms that systematic monitoring and evaluation of them is well nigh impossible. The task is complicated by the fact that some policies inherently conflict with each other (for example, heritage conservation and urban containment policies). Therefore, determining whether or not planning controls and other mechanisms are having the desired outcomes is not a straightforward task. While this may be politically advantageous, it does mean that statutory controls on land use and development, and the administration of those controls via decisions on planning permit applications, tend to be viewed in isolation from the planning process as a whole. In the past, decisions on planning scheme amendments and planning permit applications have tended to get made in a knowledge vacuum as well as a policy vacuum, and strategic planning has become a form of crisis management rather than an integral and continuing part of the process. There is some evidence that this is changing, but a balanced judgement of the extent to which the situation has improved will only be possible after appropriate methodologies for reviewing schemes as required by s 12B of the Act have been developed.

The process in practice – a hypothetical case study

Let us take the hypothetical example of a municipality within commuting distance of the metropolitan area. This municipality is experiencing rapid population growth from people seeking variously a rural lifestyle and cheaper housing than can be found in the metropolitan area. The urban settlements in the municipality are expanding and there is an increasing demand for rural residential and hobby farm allotments. These pressures are throwing into relief a number of problems for the local council. Which areas should be used to accommodate rural residential and hobby farm developments? Where should these types of development be located in order to prevent the closing-off of options for the future expansion of the existing urban settlements? Should all the urban settlements be allowed to expand, given that it may be impossible to service all of them indefinitely with reticulated water and sewerage? As two of the urban settlements have a secondary school and a supermarket, would it be better to try to concentrate future shopping and community facilities in these centres, along with development which will result in local employment opportunities? How can sensitive rural environments be protected from urban development and how can the 19th-century buildings and precincts within the urban areas be retained in the face of pressures for redevelopment? These are just some of the familiar problems facing municipalities within commuting distance of Melbourne and the major provincial centres.

The decision to plan and investigation of problems

Clearly our hypothetical municipality has a series of problems that have to be tackled and one would hope that the council would quickly decide to develop policies (including land use and development policies) to deal with them. This would involve a good deal of research. Population and growth trends would need to be analysed, as would demand for suburban-style housing, rural residential allotments and larger hobby farms. The suitability of land to accommodate future development would need to be established. Servicing constraints and capacities would need to be determined, as would the current and future demand for community facilities and local employment. The sensitivity of rural environments to various forms of development would need to be documented, as would the heritage value of buildings and precincts in the urban settlements. The future plans of various government departments and agencies would need to be established and, if necessary, influenced by the council. How many schools are intended to be established and where? Is there any intention of expanding (or closing down) the local hospital? Will there be bypass roads built around the major towns? This is not intended to be an exhaustive list of issues, but it does serve to illustrate the magnitude of the task facing our council, which may find it necessary to appoint consultants to research some or all of these issues. Whether or not consultants are appointed, it is unlikely that investigations will have to start from scratch – the municipality has a planning scheme that has been in operation for many years and, while it is not adequate to allow council to effectively manage current and future development, it was probably based on some documented investigations, including at least a study of land characteristics and servicing capacities.

The formulation of policies

Armed with the results of research, and perhaps some recommendations from the researchers, our council is now in a position to formulate policies to guide the future development of the municipality. In many respects this is the most difficult part of the process for the council – some councillors wish to preserve the rural and small-town atmosphere of the municipality, some see development as a sign of progress, and others are concerned that expansion of the urban areas will alter the social composition of the municipality and lead to an erosion of community standards. Yet others are concerned about the implications of increased development for the conservation of both rural and urban environments and have recently been elected to council on a conservation platform. Some councillors believe that it is the duty of local government to govern and they wish to proceed with a minimum of community consultation about policies, fearful that consultation will create delays and result in weakening policies to a series of generalities which will provide minimum guidance for future decision-making. Others are strongly committed to community consultation, believing that the community should have a role in formulating policy and that the strength of any policy lies in the extent to which it is supported by the people to whom it applies. Clearly planning is a political activity and is subject to the pressures that can be brought to bear on both elected officials and professional officers.

After a trying period of debate (and hopefully not too long a period, otherwise the problems that initiated the exercise will have been exacerbated, perhaps to the point where they are no longer capable of solution), the council of our hypothetical municipality finally adopts a series of policy statements. These deal with future land use and development patterns, heritage conservation, local economic development and employment generation, and community services provision. The statement dealing with future land use and development patterns identifies the broad locations and directions of future urban expansion as well as areas for accommodating future rural residential and hobby farm development. It also identifies those areas that are to be retained for broad acre farming and the preferred urban centres for future major shopping and other major commercial and community facilities.

The conservation policy identifies in general terms rural and urban areas that are to be retained for their special qualities. For rural conservation areas, the statement goes on to express the principle that subdivision and development are to be restricted and that tree felling and the clearing of vegetation will be permitted only in exceptional circumstances. For urban conservation areas, it is stated that buildings should be retained, owners will be encouraged to keep these buildings in good repair and, where necessary, restore them, and new buildings should be constructed in a style that complements the old.

The policy dealing with economic development and local employment generation expresses the wish of council to encourage a range of businesses, including industry, to establish within the municipality in order to provide local employment opportunities and reduce the dependence of the community on commuting to work in the metropolitan area. Mention is made of the potential for tourism-related businesses to capitalise on the heritage qualities of precincts in the older settlements.

The community services policy contains the principle that the community should have access to local education, community health, recreation, and hospital facilities. Based on projected population increases, an assessment of the deficiencies of current facilities, and threshold ratios of population per facility, the policy identifies in general terms the extra services and facilities that council considers should be provided over the next 10 to 15 years.

The selection of mechanisms for implementing policies

Having taken at least a year to get from the decision to tackle the problems to the stage where it has developed its policies, our council now embarks on identifying how these policies can be implemented and then choosing and putting in place appropriate implementation mechanisms. In the meantime, other problems may have arisen, some problems that were originally thought to be potentially severe may not have eventuated, State government policies on the growth of metropolitan Melbourne and provincial centres may have changed, and the composition of council may have altered because of recent municipal. To complicate matters, the Chief Executive Officer, Town Clerk, Shire Engineer, and Town Planner may have all left and been replaced by people who hold different views on the role of local government, the importance of planning, and the role of community consultation in the planning process. You were warned that the diagram above of the planning process was an oversimplification!

The council will quickly become aware that translating its policies into implementation mechanisms is not easy. Most will need to be framed in the form of an amendment or series of amendments to the existing planning scheme. That may well mean amendments to the council's Municipal Strategic Statement and local

all the difficulties + hurdles

planning policies, the introduction of new zones and overlays and/or changes to the areas of land to which existing zones and overlays apply. In terms of future land use and development patterns, retaining land for broad acre farming can be achieved by amending the planning scheme so that for such areas subdivision into small allotments will be prohibited, as will a large range of non-farming uses. Where farm land has already been subdivided into small allotments but not yet developed, controls could be put in place requiring consolidation of titles into parcels of land of, say, 20 hectares in size before permission to establish a dwelling is granted. Both of these measures are likely to be resisted by land owners, including perhaps some councillors, who are aware of the vagaries of weather and wish to retain the option of subdividing off and selling a parcel of their land to tide them over a bad season. Some people will have purchased land on the perimeters of the existing urban settlements with the intention of either developing it themselves or selling it to developers as future building blocks. Either way, they expect to achieve a handsome profit. If the policy of restricting the expansion of some of these settlements is to be implemented and such land is to be subject to subdivision and minimum allotment size controls, there will be a great deal of pressure placed on councillors to alter the policy or make exceptions for particular areas and owners. Over time, freezing land for farming adjacent to expanding urban areas may impose severe financial burdens on owners, who are faced with ever-increasing rate bills as the value of their land inflates by virtue of the fact that it is close to an expanding urban area. Perhaps, in addition to statutory controls, implementation mechanisms should include a municipal rate concession for such owners. However, this is likely to be controversial too – if this is put in place for one farmer then why not for all farmers? And what about the townspeople? If some farmers are to effectively get a cut in rates, doesn't that mean the rest of the community will be required to pay higher rates?

The policy of confining future rural residential and hobby farm development to specific areas can be implemented by the mechanism of appropriate zoning with relatively small minimum allotment sizes and restrictions on the uses that can be established. However, this too will be controversial, for the same sorts of reasons as outlined for the broad acre farming areas. But the attraction of areas for rural residential and hobby farm development does not rely only on the characteristics of land and its zoning – the road pattern, access to town water supply, access to the sewerage network and even the garbage collection service in the case of rural residential land, and proximity to schools and other services are all important factors in the market attractiveness of these types of development. The council will quickly become aware that statutory measures are not only contentious; they are also not necessarily the only mechanisms that are relevant to implementing planning policy. Its own works programmes and the future locations of public facilities are also important and this is so regardless of whether the location is rural or urban.

Implementation of the policy of preferred urban centres for future major shopping and other community facilities depends on appropriate zonings and controls in both the preferred centres and the other urban settlements. But also locating the

... more things to consider in new growth

new municipal library, the new municipal recreation centre and the new municipal offices adjacent to one or other of the areas proposed for commercial expansion would be an important supporting measure. So would a willingness to promote the proposed commercial areas with private sector developers. This willingness may even extend to assistance with land acquisition and consolidation to secure a site for supermarkets or similar commercial developments. Upgrading of street networks and road widenings may also be relevant as supporting mechanisms. And, of course, all of these mechanisms or actions will have political consequences – residents and ratepayers who do not live in or close to the preferred centres will not be delighted at the prospect of having to travel to shop or use community facilities; more commercial development in the preferred centres will mean more traffic in nearby streets and most likely more difficulty in finding on-street parking, so local residents may be very vociferous in their opposition; and local shopkeepers may be opposed because of possible business competition.

To implement its heritage conservation policy, our council could include heritage overlay controls in its planning scheme, requiring planning permission to be granted for the demolition or alteration (even including painting) of buildings. The owners of buildings with heritage value in areas subject to redevelopment pressure, such as in the centres of the preferred urban areas where our council has a policy of encouraging future commercial development, face higher rate bills which reflect the redevelopment potential of their properties. This, plus controls preventing demolition to make way for such redevelopment, is likely to be seen as unreasonable, particularly if the buildings are incapable of being recycled for modern commercial uses or can be recycled only at significant expense. But, even if such controls are brought into effect, alone they may not achieve much aside from requiring permission to alter, remove or demolish buildings. Refusing a permit for alteration, removal or demolition of a building will not necessarily ensure that it is conserved, made use of and kept in good repair. As noted earlier in this chapter, implementation of heritage conservation policies may rely as much on education programmes and providing incentives for conservation as on statutory planning measures.

Our council's policies on economic development and local employment generation and on community services have less direct connection with statutory planning measures. Zoning appropriate land makes it possible for commercial and industrial activity to locate in the municipality, but that of itself will not ensure that such development occurs. Drawing the attention of prospective developers to the advantages of the municipality and the region, providing appropriate infrastructure, offering incentives in the form of rate concessions and premises (perhaps at subsidised rents for an initial period), and assisting with land assembly if land is zoned appropriately but fragmented in ownership may well be important policy implementation mechanisms. Some of these may be fraught with difficulty – some councillors are fearful of the bad press that can result from attempts to acquire property from ratepayers to facilitate development and others are ideologically opposed to such action; there is no guarantee that development will occur if council does acquire property and assemble sites and it may be left holding the bag if developers do not take up these sites; and rating concessions for commercial development will be difficult to justify to resident ratepayers, who are the majority of voters.

For its community services policy, our council can ensure that land is set aside at appropriate locations for future community services conducted by the public sector, including itself. The reservation of such land (by public acquisition overlays) is likely to be resisted, particularly by those who own the land, because the Public Acquisition Overlay indicates that the land will be acquired from them either by negotiation or by compulsory acquisition. While setting aside land for future public purposes is important, the implementation of the community services policy probably depends more on council's own decisions and funding allocations and on how it influences the decisions and funding allocations of other government departments and agencies, such as the Department of Education and the Department of Human Services.

Putting the mechanisms in place

From the discussion so far it should be clear that deciding on the policies and then selecting the appropriate implementation mechanisms are highly contentious activities. Both are essentially the results of trade-offs between what is desirable and what is politically sustainable, so the planning process is rarely as orderly as the diagram illustrating the systems approach to planning suggests. What also emerges is that implementation of planning policy does not necessarily rely on statutory planning measures.

Assisted perhaps by the reactions of land owners and residents at public meetings called to discuss its policies and how they should be implemented, our council has now selected the implementation mechanisms it sees as appropriate and politically sustainable. Obviously these implementation mechanisms may include a large number of amendments to the existing planning scheme and so the stage is set for the scheme amendment processes prescribed by the *Planning and Environment Act 1987* to be set in train. These (discussed in Chapter 4) will take some time – they normally involve public exhibition of the proposed amendments, the lodging of submissions, the consideration of those submissions by council, referral of submissions to a panel appointed by the Minister for Planning, a panel hearing, preparation by the panel of a report, consideration of that report by the council, and adoption by the council of the proposed amendments in part or in whole or in a modified form. The proposed amendments, accompanied by all relevant documents, including copies of all submissions, the panel's report, and copies of all submissions made to the panel, must then be forwarded to the Minister, who will then either approve and gazette them or not approve them, as the case may be. These formal statutory processes may take as long as two years to run their course. In the meantime, the environment in which the policies were formulated may alter, policies of other levels of government may change, and some of the assumptions made about growth rates may prove to be unjustified, all of which may result in a need to review these scheme amendments even before they have been approved. During that time the council must make decisions on planning permit applications for all sorts of uses and development, including subdivision. But these applications will be made and must be determined under the existing controls in the planning scheme, not the controls to be put in place pursuant to future planning scheme amendment(s), although, depending on how far the scheme amendments have advanced in the statutory amendment process, they may be given some weight as seriously entertained planning proposals. The ability of the council to administer its scheme as it exists to implement the policies it wants to see achieved for the future may be seriously hampered. Even deciding how to effectively monitor and evaluate in this environment, let alone actually undertake the task of monitoring and evaluation, poses real problems. But our council will be in a position to judge whether or not its policies and implementation mechanisms, including the scheme amendments, are appropriate only if it is committed to monitoring and evaluation, develops appropriate methodologies for doing so, and is prepared to commit resources to this crucially important part of the planning process.

The task of councils in the metropolitan area and the larger provincial centres to systematically develop policies and implementation mechanisms, put them in place and monitor and evaluate their performance is just as difficult as, and sometimes more difficult than, the task facing the council in our hypothetical case study. State planning policies on urban containment in the SPPF of schemes, derived from the State government's vision for the future of the metropolitan area set out initially in *Melbourne 2030* (2002), now part complemented by and part superseded by *Melbourne @ 5 Million* (2008), have resulted in very significant changes to the built environment in many suburbs. State policy is that medium density development within existing residential areas, and particularly within walking distance of activity centres, rail stations and tram and bus routes, should accommodate a major share of future population and household growth. Community reaction to the changes in local built environments which this has caused and continues to cause is more often than not negative, and has resulted in the formation of pressure groups and organisations committed to opposing what they see as inappropriate development. Save Our Suburbs is just one of these organisations. Permit applications for medium density developments, even just dual occupancy developments, are often bitterly contested. The result is often a very turbulent local political environment, with councillors seeking re-election experiencing a high rate of failure.

Chapter 2

THE VICTORIAN PLANNING SYSTEM

The system under the Town and Country Planning Act 1961

Statutory planning powers in Victoria date from 1921, when amendments to the *Local Government Act* gave councils the power to zone land for residential use. However, the first explicit planning legislation was the *Town and Country Planning Act 1944*, which established the Town and Country Planning Board (TCPB) and empowered it and municipal councils to prepare and administer planning schemes. Tracing in detail the development of the planning system since 1944 is beyond the scope of this book, but a brief description of the system before the *Planning and Environment Act 1987* was enacted has been included to assist the reader in understanding the current system.

A good deal of the basic structure of the planning system now in place in Victoria dates from 1968, when a number of significant amendments were made to the *Town and Country Planning Act 1961*. Since its creation in 1944, the TCPB had the function of advising the Minister whether or not schemes and scheme amendments prepared by municipalities should be approved and gazetted. It could also prepare schemes and scheme amendments at the request of the Minister and administer those schemes (that is, consider and determine planning permit applications). The 1968 amendments enhanced the power and status of the TCPB and it became responsible for promoting and co-ordinating planning throughout Victoria. Provision was also made for regional planning authorities, and a State policy formulation body – the State Planning Council – was established. Also established was an independent body to hear and determine appeals relating to planning permits – the Town Planning Appeals Tribunal (TPAT). In 1980 the TPAT became, with an expanded jurisdiction, the Planning Appeals Board (PAB), the functions of which were transferred to the Planning Division of the Administrative Appeals Tribunal of Victoria (AAT) in 1987. On 1 July 1988, the functions of the AAT were transferred to the Victorian Civil and Administrative Tribunal (VCAT) pursuant to the *Victorian Civil and Administrative Tribunal Act 1998*.

The 1968 amendments to the *Town and Country Planning Act* produced a three-tiered hierarchy of State, regional and local authorities, and an independent appeals body.

The State tier

The details of the system have been significantly modified over the years. At the State level, public sector restructuring resulted in the absorption in 1973 of the TCPB by a new Ministry for Planning, which in turn became the Department of Planning in 1981. The Department of Planning became the Ministry for Planning and Environment in September 1983, then the Department of Planning and Urban Growth in 1990. Restructuring of various parts of the State's bureaucracy and name changes have since resulted in the Department of Planning and Housing in 1991, the Department of Planning and Development in 1993, the Department of Infrastructure in 1996, the Department of Sustainability and Environment in 2002, and the Department of Planning and Community Development in 2007.

In 1985, under the *Town and Country Planning (Transfer of Functions) Act*, the planning powers of the Melbourne Metropolitan Board of Works (MMBW) were taken over by the then Ministry for Planning and Environment and the Minister became the regional planning authority for the metropolitan area. The MMBW was established late last century as the metropolitan water, sewerage and drainage authority for the metropolitan area, but it had been given the responsibility under the *Town and Country (Metropolitan Area) Act 1949* of preparing a metropolitan planning scheme. The development of the initial detailed scheme and its subsequent modifications to implement the metropolitan corridor strategy, and then later the metropolitan containment strategy, have been detailed by McLoughlin (see Further Reading).

The State Planning Council (SPC), established under the 1968 amendments to the *Town and Country Planning Act,* was empowered to prepare, with the advice and assistance of the then TCPB, Statements of Planning Policy which, when approved by the Minister and gazetted, became government policy and legally binding on both councils and regional authorities. The SPC was comprised of a relatively small number of representatives of government agencies and departments and both it and its successor, the State Co-Ordination Council (which was created in 1975 and ceased to exist in 1983), were responsible for developing a number of Statements of Planning Policy which were duly approved and gazetted. These statements were required to be taken into account and given effect by relevant regional authorities and councils in the preparation of scheme amendments and in consideration of planning permit applications. They were as follows:

Statement of Planning Policy 1 (Westernport) 1970. Varied 1976.
Statement of Planning Policy 2 (Mornington Peninsula) 1970.
Statement of Planning Policy 3 (Upper Yarra Valley and Dandenongs) 1971. Varied 1979.
Statement of Planning Policy 4 (Yarra River) 1971. Varied 1979.
Statement of Planning Policy 5 (Highway Areas) 1973.
Statement of Planning Policy 6 (Land Use and Aerodromes) 1973.
Statement of Planning Policy 7 (Geelong) 1973.
Statement of Planning Policy 8 (Macedon Ranges and Surrounds) 1975.
Statement of Planning Policy 9 (*Central Gippsland*) 1975.

After the State Coordination Council ceased to exist in 1982, the formulation of planning policy for the State as a whole and for key regions, such as the metropolitan area, became a function performed by the Minister and the departments which succeeded the TCPB, or the State Cabinet, depending on the significance of the policy and its relevance to and impact on the State economy and other government departments.

The regional tier

In 1968, when provisions were introduced into the Act to enable the creation of regional planning authorities, it was envisaged that authorities would be established for most, if not all, the regions of Victoria. It was also envisaged that Statements of Planning Policy would provide a "brief" or series of guidelines for the development by the new authorities of regional planning schemes. Regional schemes were conceived as incorporating detailed zoning and land use controls, much along the lines of the Melbourne Metropolitan Planning Scheme (MMPS) developed by the MMBW during the 1950s and finally gazetted in 1968. As in the metropolitan area, the role of municipal councils was envisaged as administering parts of the regional scheme under delegation from the regional authorities. This was certainly the model used for the establishment of the Westernport Regional Planning Authority in 1969 and the Geelong Regional Planning Authority in 1972, and for those regions detailed planning schemes were prepared and eventually brought into operation. However, government policy on regional planning altered. Due to a distinct lack of interest by municipalities in regional planning, and, in many instances, outright opposition (particularly to regional planning in the detailed regional planning scheme mould), very few regional planning authorities were established.

Generally speaking, those regional authorities that were established after Westernport and Geelong were given primarily a strategic planning rather than a statutory planning role. The Geelong Regional Planning Authority became the Geelong Regional Commission (GRC) under the *Geelong Regional Commission Act 1977*, which gave it the power to acquire and develop land for industrial and commercial purposes in addition to statutory planning functions. The GRC prepared a five-year strategy plan for its region and became actively involved in industrial estate development, the City By The Bay project in the City of Geelong, and a wide range of other economic and social development initiatives. The Loddon Campaspe Regional Planning Authority, established in 1973 under the *Town and Country Planning Act* and reconstituted under the *Loddon Campaspe Regional Authority Act 1987*, never embarked on the preparation of a regional planning scheme but was charged with the responsibilities of preparing a strategy plan for its region, carrying out land use planning for matters of regional significance, co-ordinating planning authorities in the region, and promoting the co-ordination of the works plans of public authorities in the region.

The Upper Yarra Valley and Dandenong Ranges Authority was established under the *Upper Yarra Valley and Dandenong Ranges Authority Act 1976*. Its primary role under s 12 of that Act was to carry out investigations and prepare regional strategy plans for its region. The Latrobe Regional Commission was established by the *Latrobe Regional Commission Act 1983*. Under s 6 of that Act, it was required to "co-ordinate the planning of the economic, physical, environmental and social development of the Latrobe region". It was also required to prepare and implement regional strategy plans, and to prepare infrastructure co-ordination plans and co-ordinated plans of works. Infrastructure co-ordination plans related to "prescribed development" (essentially the development of the brown coal resources of the Latrobe Valley), while co-ordinated plans of works related to major capital works programmes that the Minister directed to be included in the plan.

The Albury-Wodonga Development Corporation was unlike the other regional authorities in that it was established under Commonwealth, New South Wales and Victorian legislation and was partly modelled on the development corporations established for the post-war British New Towns programme. The Commonwealth *Albury-Wodonga Development Act 1973*, the New South Wales *Albury-Wodonga Development Act 1974*, and the *Victorian Albury-Wodonga (Agreement) Act 1973* provided the legislative base for the corporation. Its powers included acting as a development agency, including the construction of commercial and industrial buildings, and creating employment opportunities by encouraging the establishment of industries and investment in the growth centre of Albury-Wodonga.

There are now no regional planning authorities in Victoria. The Westernport Regional Planning Authority was abolished in 1981, the MMBW's functions as the metropolitan planning authority were transferred to the State's planning department (the then Ministry for Planning and Environment) in 1985, and the rest of the authorities were wound up during the period 1992–1995. But traces of Victoria's flirtation with regional planning remain. *Statement of Planning Policy 1* and *Statement of Planning Policy 2* are reference documents in the Mornington Peninsula Planning Scheme (see Chapter 3 for an explanation of the term "reference document"). *Statement of Planning Policy 8* is described in the Municipal Strategic Statement (MSS) of the Macedon Ranges Planning Scheme as a major State planning policy relevant to the strategic planning, land use and development within the Shire (see later in this chapter and also Chapter 3 for an explanation of the term "Municipal Strategic Statement"). The MSS states that implementation of the *Statement of Planning Policy 8* is one of the strategies for implementing the Shire's strategies for management of urban growth and development, protection for and encouragement of agricultural productivity, promotion of the Shire's cultural identity and community values, and the encouragement of economic development and tourism.

The *Upper Yarra Valley and Dandenong Ranges Strategy Plan* was prepared by the Upper Yarra Valley and Dandenong Ranges Authority and declared by the Minister pursuant to s 17 of the *Upper Yarra Valley and Dandenong Ranges Authority Act 1976* to be an approved regional strategy plan. Despite the repeal of that Act and the abolition of the authority, the regional strategy plan continues to have force and effect by virtue of Part 3A of the *Planning and Environment Act* and cl 53 of the Victoria Planning Provisions (VPPs), which has application only in the Shire of

Yarra Ranges. Sections 46A–46G of the *Planning and Environment Act* preserve the strategy plan. Many of the local policy provisions of the Yarra Ranges Planning Scheme are based on it. Clause 53 has as its purpose the facilitation of consistency between the Yarra Ranges Planning Scheme and the *Upper Yarra Ranges Valley and Dandenong Ranges Strategy Plan* and provides that, if there is any inconsistency between any provision in the schedule to this clause and any other clause or provision of the Yarra Ranges Planning Scheme, the requirements of the schedule prevail. The schedule contains controls based on key provisions of the strategy plan, such as controls on subdivision.

The local government tier

Under the *Town and Country Planning Act 1961* municipal councils could be responsible authorities. The term "responsible authority" as defined in this Act encompassed both "responsible authority" and "planning authority" as those terms are now defined under the *Planning and Environment Act*. That is, councils could prepare planning schemes, interim development orders (IDOs) and amendments to schemes and IDOs, and could administer and enforce the provisions of schemes and IDOs. The administration of planning controls means the consideration and determination of planning permit applications. Enforcement essentially means ensuring compliance with planning controls, including the conditions attached to planning permits (see Chapter 7).

An IDO was intended to be a temporary form of planning control imposed with the approval of the Minister, although some of them were in operation for years. The initial introduction of an IDO did not require any statutory public consultation, so it was essentially a device for quickly introducing the requirement to seek planning permission for the use and development of land where no scheme was in existence, or to control use and development while a scheme amendment was being prepared. Some IDOs were amended to introduce more and more detail as a scheme or scheme amendment was developed, so that the scheme or scheme amendment which finally replaced the IDO was indistinguishable from it, thus providing a smooth transition from one form of control to another. In instances where an IDO was taken out to protect a proposed scheme amendment, it was possible for a council to have two sets of planning controls in operation over an area.

Duplication and conflict between the tiers

Under the *Town and Country Planning Act*, not only councils but also the Minister and regional authorities constituted under the Act could be responsible authorities. The Minister could be a responsible authority for any part of Victoria. The Westernport Regional Planning Authority and the Geelong Regional Planning Authority were constituted under the Act and were responsible authorities, and when the Geelong Regional Planning Authority was reconstituted as the GRC in 1977 it retained its power as a responsible authority under the *Geelong Regional Commission Act*. The

Loddon Campaspe Regional Planning Authority, constituted originally under the *Town and Country Planning Act*, had the power to act as a responsible authority for its region but in fact confined its powers to being the responsible authority for the Whipstick Forest area in the then Shires of Marong and Huntly. Until 1985 the MMBW was specified in the Act as the responsible authority for the metropolitan area.

Theoretically a multitude of different and even conflicting scheme and IDO controls could apply to any parcel of land in the State under this system. It was relatively common for at least two sets of controls to apply – a situation usually referred to as "dual control". Permit applications were required under both sets of controls and had to be lodged with both responsible authorities, with the possibility that one would decide to grant and the other would decide to refuse. To establish the proposed use or development applied for, the permission of both bodies was required. The difficulties posed by dual control for applicants and the community at large were highlighted by the BADAC report of 1979 (see Further Reading), which advocated a "one stop shop" for permits and elimination of the requirement to seek more than one planning permit.

Most of the problems of the system revolved around its failure to establish the appropriate roles that should be performed by each tier. The legislation gave all tiers essentially the same role and this inevitably led to difficulties. For example, as the responsible authority for the metropolitan area the MMBW prepared a regional planning scheme (the MMPS), which was a detailed local scheme applied to a region. With its detailed zoning and land use controls it could be distinguished from schemes normally prepared by councils only by the fact that it applied to the whole metropolitan area. While local councils theoretically could prepare amendments to this scheme, in effect they had to get the permission of the MMBW to commence the amendment process. Therefore the regional authority controlled the scheme, which was also the case with the Westernport and Geelong Regional Planning Authorities. Like the scheme for the metropolitan area, the Geelong and Westernport regional schemes were detailed zoning plans.

There was a short-lived attempt to provide opportunities for councils in the metropolitan area to prepare local schemes under the local development scheme provisions of the *Town and Country Planning (General Amendment) Act 1979*. These schemes were to introduce even finer-grained zoning than that under the MMPS, provided they did not conflict with the MMPS. Only one such scheme was ever approved and gazetted (for the then municipality of Berwick) and the local development scheme provisions were repealed shortly thereafter.

Regional authorities and regional schemes also posed another problem. Who was to administer the scheme? In the metropolitan area the *Town and Country Planning Act* provided for the MMBW and, after 1985, the Minister to delegate to councils the power to consider and determine planning permit applications. Councils were the responsible authorities for the bulk of planning permit applications lodged under the MMPS. However, councils were not delegated the power to determine all applications

– certain classes of applications and all applications in some zones were made to and determined by the regional authority. These included applications in zones on the rural–urban fringe and in areas abutting main roads and watercourses. The rationale for this division of powers was that the regional authority should control land use and development on the rural–urban fringe in order to implement its policy on the shape and expansion of the metropolitan area. Regional authority control over land abutting main roads and watercourses was justified on the basis of ensuring consistency of decision-making across municipal boundaries. A similar system was put in place for other regional authorities constituted under their own legislation, so that the regional authority either determined or had the power of veto over applications for use and development that it was considered may have regional impact.

The system under the Planning and Environment Act

The *Planning and Environment Act 1987* did not change the basic structure of the system that developed under the *Town and Country Planning Act*. However, events since 1987, such as the restructuring of local government, the abolition of regional authorities and the requirements for new planning schemes prescribed by the *Planning and Environment (Planning Schemes) Act 1996* resulted in significant modifications to the system. To understand these modifications, and the duties, powers and responsibilities of the key bodies in the system now, it is essential to have an understanding of the main elements of planning schemes and their relationship to processes closely related to the planning process, such as the certification of plans of subdivision pursuant to the *Subdivision Act 1988* and environmental impact assessment under the *Environment Effects Act 1978*. It is also essential to come to grips with the terms "planning authority", "responsible authority" and "referral authority", each of which is defined in s 3 of the *Planning and Environment Act*.

The change from State, regional and local sections of schemes

Only one form of planning control is provided for by the *Planning and Environment Act* and that is a planning scheme based on the municipality to which the scheme applies. There is no provision for IDOs. Until the enactment of the *Planning and Environment (Planning Schemes) Act 1996*, the *Planning and Environment Act* provided for State, regional and local sections of planning schemes. For close to 10 years after the bringing into effect of the *Planning and Environment Act 1987*, all schemes had a State Section and a Local Section. Regional Sections were found only in schemes in the Metropolitan Region, the Geelong Region, the Latrobe Valley Region, the Westernport Region and the Upper Yarra Valley and Dandenong Ranges Region. There was no nexus between Regional Sections of schemes and regional planning authorities, as there was no Regional Section in schemes in the Loddon Campaspe region; schemes in the Westernport Region contained a Regional Section, but there had not been a Westernport Regional Planning Authority since 1981; schemes in the Victorian part of the Albury-Wodonga region did not contain a

Regional Section; and, while the Minister was not specified in the Act as the regional authority for the metropolitan area, there was a Regional Section in all metropolitan schemes and the Minister was the *de facto* metropolitan regional authority.

Matters of State significance were found in the State Section, and the Local Section contained the planning scheme maps and the great majority of detailed controls that applied to a particular municipality. However, on "Day One" of the new system, 16 February 1988, when all but Part 1 and s 204 of the Act commenced, institutional and administrative arrangements that had operated for many years resulted in some departure from this principle. For example, the Regional Section of Schemes in the Geelong region contained the great bulk of controls that applied in each municipality, reflecting not only the historical role of the Geelong Regional Planning Authority and the GRC in statutory planning in the region but also the detailed zoning and land use control provisions of the former regional planning scheme. In metropolitan schemes on "Day One", the Regional Section contained the provisions of the former MMPS and the Local Section contained little more than the relevant zoning maps. New plain English versions of these metropolitan schemes were brought into effect on 30 October 1989 and in these only the provisions of the former MMPS relevant to a particular municipality were included in the Local Section for that municipality.

Outside the metropolitan area only those schemes in the Geelong, Macedon Ranges, Latrobe Valley, Upper Yarra Valley and Dandenong Ranges, and Loddon Campaspe regions originally contained Regional Sections, reflecting the existence of former Statements of Planning Policy and/or the existence of regional planning authorities and commissions established between 1969 and 1983. These regional bodies no longer exist – most were wound up during 1994–1995. As a result of municipal restructuring, which also occurred during 1994–1995, the number of municipalities in Victoria was reduced from 210 to 78. Often what used be included in Regional Sections of schemes was transferred to the relevant Local Sections, reflecting the much larger geographical areas contained within the new municipalities. But the VPP-based schemes prepared pursuant to the *Planning and Environment (Planning Schemes) Act 1996* do not have Regional Sections. They must have a State Planning Policy Framework, and a Local Planning Policy Framework that contains the MSS for the relevant municipality and local planning policies. They also must contain State standard provisions selected from the VPPs.

State standard provisions, VPPs and local provisions

The *Planning and Environment (Planning Schemes) Act 1996* provided the legislative base for the format of the planning schemes now in place in Victoria. The first of these schemes was gazetted and brought into effect in late 1998. Section 7(1) of the *Planning and Environment Act 1987* requires planning schemes to include State standard provisions and local provisions. The State standard provisions must be selected from the VPPs, prepared by the Minister: s 7(2). The Ministerial Direction *The Form and Content of Planning Schemes* requires schemes to include the following from the VPPs: the State Planning Policy Framework, State standard zones,

THE VICTORIAN PLANNING SYSTEM

overlay controls, particular provisions that apply to specific categories of use and development, general provisions, definitions and incorporated documents. Some of these elements are introduced below, but all are discussed further in Chapter 3.

The State Planning Policy Framework sets out the State policies for land use and development in Victoria, including metropolitan Melbourne, and are in the form of broad general principles grouped under the headings of settlement, environment, housing, economic development, infrastructure, and particular uses and developments. The VPPs contain "stock standard" zones, overlay controls and provisions from which municipal councils must select when preparing schemes or scheme amendments. Zones primarily control the use of land but may also control the built form of a proposed development. Overlays provide another level of control over the built form of a proposal but may also control other matters such as vegetation removal. The discretion of councils in relation to the VPPs is limited to selecting the stock standard zones, overlays and other provisions which they see as appropriate for implementing their MSSs, and deciding to which land the zones and overlays are to apply: see s 12B. They cannot introduce new zones or overlays that are not contained in the VPPs; nor can the zones or overlays be varied: see s 10(1). Some zones and overlays may contain schedules dealing with local conditions, but these are limited to matters listed in the Ministerial Direction. The only way a new zone or overlay can be introduced is by an amendment to the VPPs, which only the Minister has the power to approve (although he or she can authorise another Minister, a public authority or a municipal council to prepare such an amendment: see s 4B).

Each planning scheme is required by s 7(2) of the *Planning and Environment Act* to contain an MSS, the content of which is prescribed: it must set out planning, land use and development objectives of the municipality and the strategies for achieving those objectives; it must provide a general explanation of the relationships between those objectives and strategies and the controls on the use and development of land; and it must include any other provision that the Minister directs to be included. Section 12B of the Act requires a council to review its planning scheme, including the MSS, no later than one year after each date by which it is required to approve a Council Plan under s 125 of the *Local Government Act 1989*, or within such longer period as determined by the Minister, or at any other time that the Minister directs. Pursuant to s 125 of the *Local Government Act*, a council must prepare and approve a Council Plan within the period of six months after each general election or by the next 30 June, whichever is later. The purpose of the review is to ensure that the planning scheme is consistent in form and content with the directions or guidelines issued by the Minister under s 7, sets out effectively the policy objectives for the use and development of land in the area to which it applies, and makes effective use of State provisions and local provisions to give effect to State and local planning objectives: s 12B(4). On completion of the review the council must without delay report the findings of the review to the Minister: s 12B(5).

Planning schemes are discussed in more detail in Chapter 3. In August 1993, Mr Maclellan, the Minister for Planning in the then newly-elected Kennett Government, launched the first of his Ministerial Statements *Planning a Better Future for all Victorians: New Directions for Development and Economic Growth*, in which he mapped out the government's plans for reform. A major part of that reform was to be the reform of planning schemes. The Minister made it clear that the new government viewed the current planning schemes as inhibitors of economic growth and job creation – they were cumbersome, too rigid, had far too many zones and were not consistent across the State in terms of zones and other controls, use tables, and definitions. He pointed to there being more than 140 different zones in place in the metropolitan area alone and stated his intention to reduce the number of residential zones in the state to about 10 (including rural residential zones), with similar reductions in the number of industrial commercial and rural zones to assist with the creation of opportunities for investment and jobs.

The VPPs originally contained 25 zones and 21 overlays. They now contain 33 zones and 22 overlays. In many respects planning schemes now are just as cumbersome and unwieldy, if not more so, as they were in pre-VPP days and, in the case of country areas where the old schemes were relatively slim and simply structured documents, they are even more so. The lengthy State Planning Framework section, often even lengthier MSSs, numerous local planning policies and a proliferation of schedules to zones and overlay have resulted in very big and complex documents. Those of us who have been in and around Victorian planning for a long time look back with nostalgia to the days when the ordinance of the most complex scheme in the State – the Melbourne Metropolitan Planning Scheme – could be carried around in one's pocket.

Planning authorities

A planning authority is defined by s 9 of the *Planning and Environment Act* as any person or body given power under s 8 to prepare a planning scheme or an amendment to a planning scheme. Note that preparation of a scheme or amendment is not the same as approval and gazettal – only the Minister has the power to do those things. Under s 8, the Minister may prepare a planning scheme or an amendment to a planning scheme applying to any land in any municipality. The Minister is also the planning authority for land not incorporated in any municipality, such as for French Island and Sandstone Island Planning Scheme, the Alpine Resorts Planning Scheme and the Port of Melbourne Planning Scheme.

A municipal council may prepare amendments to the State standard provisions and local provisions of its planning scheme (but must make application and be authorised to do so, pursuant to s 9(2)). But, if authorised to prepare an amendment to the State standard provisions, the power of the council is confined to rezonings using standard zones in the VPPs or altering the areas to which standard overlay controls in the VPPs apply. Any other Minister or public authority, with the authorisation of the Minister, may prepare an amendment to the State standard provisions or local provisions of a scheme. This allows the government department or authority concerned to prepare an amendment that applies to a number of schemes (such as reserving land for a public purpose to accommodate a freeway or highway by a Public Acquisition Overlay).

The Growth Areas Authority (GAA) is the planning authority for amendments which introduce Precinct Structure Plans (PSPs) for land in the Urban Growth Zone within the metropolitan urban growth boundary in metropolitan fringe planning schemes: see Chapter 4.

Responsible authorities

A responsible authority is defined by s 13 as the body responsible for the administration or enforcement of a scheme, or a provision of a scheme. A responsible authority is a body responsible for considering and determining planning permit applications (see Chapter 5) and for ensuring compliance with the scheme, permit conditions and agreements entered into pursuant to s 173 (see Chapter 7). In theory, the administration and enforcement of a scheme could be undertaken by different bodies under s 13, but in practice they are not.

The responsible authority is normally the local municipal council and it is with the relevant council that applications for planning permits are normally lodged. However, a responsible authority is a body that may be responsible for a provision or set of provisions of a scheme rather than the scheme as a whole. Moreover, while s 13(a) provides for a municipal council to be the responsible authority for a scheme that applies to land wholly or partly within its municipal district, it also qualifies this by "unless the planning scheme specifies any other person as the responsible authority". Under s 13(b) the Minister is the responsible authority if the scheme applies to any land outside a municipal district unless the scheme specifies any other person as the responsible authority, and s 13(c) authorises any person whom the planning scheme specifies to be a responsible authority.

While normally the local municipal council is the responsible authority, there are instances where it is not. In the Melbourne Planning Scheme (that is, the scheme which applies to the City of Melbourne) the Schedule to cl 61.01 provides that the Minister is the responsible authority for a large number of sites, precincts and types of development, including the Melbourne Casino Area, as delineated in Schedule 1 of the *Casino Control Act 1991*, the Docklands area, as defined in the *Docklands Authority Act 1991*, the Flemington Racecourse, the Melbourne Showgrounds, the Spencer Street redevelopment precinct, the Melbourne Convention Centre Development and the Melbourne Park Redevelopment Area, and for developments in the municipality with a gross floor area exceeding 25,000 square metres. The Minister is also the responsible authority for the French Island and Sandstone Island Planning Scheme, the Alpine Resorts Planning Scheme and the Port of Melbourne Planning Scheme.

Part 4AA of the Act, which became operational on 18 November 2009, provides for Development Assessment Committees (DACs), appointed by the Minister, to act a responsible authorities for permit applications for land in the Activity Centre Zone in metropolitan municipalities: see Chapter 5.

Referral authorities

The objectives of the planning framework (that is, the administrative system) established under the *Planning and Environment Act* are listed in s 4(2). They include the following:

(a) to ensure sound, strategic planning and co-ordinated action at State, regional and municipal levels;
(b) to establish a system of planning schemes based on municipal districts to be the principal way of setting out objectives, policies and controls for the use, development and protection of land;
(c) to provide for a single authority to issue permits for land use or developments or related matters, and to co-ordinate the issue of permits with related approvals.

The system is aimed at ensuring that one set of planning controls applies to any parcel of land anywhere in the State. The set of controls is included in the relevant planning scheme, the responsible authority for which is normally the local council, and it is with this body that planning permit applications are normally lodged. The system is aimed at preventing dual control and at the same time providing a mechanism whereby the requirements of agencies outside the system (such as servicing authorities) can be integrated into the development approval process. This is achieved via s 55 of the *Planning and Environment Act*, which requires that a copy of a planning permit application must be sent by the responsible authority to every person or body specified in the planning scheme as a referral authority for that type of application. Under s 61(2) the responsible authority must refuse to grant the permit if a referral authority objects to the permit being granted. If the referral authority does not object but requires conditions to be attached to the permit if the responsible authority decides to grant it, under s 62(1) the responsible authority must include these conditions and not include other conditions which would conflict with any condition required by a referral authority.

Referral authorities and the types of applications that must be referred to them are specified in the General Provisions of the VPPs at cl 66. This clause contains referral provisions for planning permits to subdivide land (see later in this chapter) and also in relation to use and development of land. For example, planning permit applications for subdivision must be referred to the relevant service agencies (the relevant water, sewerage or drainage authorities, the relevant telecommunications authority, the relevant electricity supply or distribution authority, and the relevant gas supply authority). Applications in areas to which the Wildfire Management Overlay applies must be referred to the Country Fire Authority (CFA). If the proposed use and/or development is to alter or provide access to a road in a Road Zone – Category 1, it must be referred to VicRoads. If the application is for a use or development requiring a works approval, a licence to discharge, or an amendment of a licence under the *Environment Protection Act 1970*, it must be referred to the Environment Protection Authority (EPA). Applications to use or develop land for mining must be referred to the Secretary to the Department administering the *Mineral Resources Development Act*. This is not an exhaustive list – referral is also required for applications to remove or destroy native vegetation, to use or develop land for a cattle feedlot, to use or develop land within extractive industry, to use or develop land within a Special Water Supply Catchment Area, to use or develop land for timber production by establishing a plantation, to use or develop land for extractive industry, and to use or develop land in some circumstances in industrial and some business zones.

The powers of the Minister and the powers of municipalities

Following is a brief outline of the main powers available to the Minister and to municipalities under the *Planning and Environment Act*. More comprehensive discussion of these powers is found in the following chapters, particularly Chapters 4, 5 and 6.

While municipal councils and other persons authorised by the Minister may prepare scheme amendments under s 8, it is the Minister who retains control over their approval and gazettal. Under s 11 of the Act, as amended by the *Planning and Environment (General Amendment) Act 2004*, if the Minister authorises a planning authority to prepare an amendment, the Minister may also authorise that planning authority to approve the amendment. If such authorisation is not given, it is the Minister who approves the amendment. There are some amendments for which authorisation for approval cannot be given and, for those where authorisation has been given, certification by the Secretary of the Department that the amendment is in an appropriate form must be secured before the planning authority can approve it. The Minister can therefore control the content of any scheme in the State.

The Minister may amend any part of any scheme in the State under s 8. Moreover, under s 20(4) the Minister may do so without any of the processes of notification and public consultation that normally apply to scheme amendments. Under s 20(2), provided that an amendment does not reserve land, close a road that provides access to land, or change provisions relating to land set aside or reserved as public open space, the Minister may exempt other planning authorities from the normal processes if he or she considers that such processes are not warranted, "or that the interests of Victoria or any part of Victoria make such an exemption appropriate". In other words, the Minister may amend a scheme simply by notice in the *Government Gazette*.

As has been noted above, the Minister is the responsible authority for areas not incorporated in a municipality and under s 13(c) may be specified as the responsible authority for all or part of a municipality's scheme (as in the Schedule to cl 61.02 of the Melbourne Planning Scheme). Pursuant to ss 13 and 20 the Minister may, in effect, take away the power of responsible authority from any council in the State merely by publishing a notice in the *Government Gazette*.

If specified as a referral authority in a scheme, the Minister has the power under s 61 to veto the decision of the relevant responsible authority to grant a permit. Alternatively, the Minister has the power under s 62(1) to impose conditions on the decision to grant. Theoretically, the Minister could be included in any or all schemes as a referral authority for particular types of applications and so have the power of veto, subject to review by VCAT, on all types of applications that may have bearing on a strategy or policy of the government of the day. However, that is unlikely given the Minister's powers to "call in" planning permit applications and also "call in" review proceedings from VCAT.

Section 97B, introduced into the Act in 1993, allows the Minister to call in a permit application and determine it with or without the advice of a panel if it appears to the Minister

> that the application raises a major issue of policy and that the determination of the application may have a substantial effect on the achievement or development of planning objectives, or the decision on the application has been unreasonably delayed to the disadvantage of the applicant, or that the use and development to which the application applies is also required to be considered by the Minister under another act or regulation and that consideration would be facilitated by the referral of the application to the Minister.

The Act is silent on the matter of what constitutes a major issue of policy or a substantial effect on the achievement or development of planning objectives, as it is on what constitutes unreasonable delay. Such determinations by the Minister are not subject to review by VCAT: see s 97M.

In situations where the Minister has not called in an application for a planning permit, applications for review of the decision of the responsible authority by applicants or objectors are normally considered and determined by VCAT. However, the Minister has the power to "call in" a review proceeding for Governor in Council determination if "it appears to the Minister administering the Planning and Environment Act that the proceeding raises a major issue of policy and that the determination of the proceeding may have a substantial effect on the achievement or development of planning objectives": *Victorian Civil and Administrative Tribunal Act 1989*, Schedule 1, cl 58. Again, the legislation is silent on what constitutes a major issue of policy or a substantial effect on the achievement or development of planning objectives. The Minister may direct the proceeding to be referred for Governor in Council decision or may invite VCAT to refer it. If invited, rather than directed, VCAT may refuse to refer it, in which case the Minister may direct VCAT to refer it. If the proceeding is referred to the Governor in Council it is the government of the day and not VCAT that makes the decision. The "call-in" power is not just restricted to review proceedings arising under the *Planning and Environment Act*, either. A review proceeding under another "planning enactment", such as the *Catchment and Land Protection Act 1994, Environment Protection Act 1970, Subdivision Act 1988* or *Water Act 1989* may also be called in: *Victorian Civil and Administrative Tribunal Act 1989*, Schedule 1, cll 2 and 59. Chapter 6 contains further discussion of the Minister's "call-in" power.

It should be noted that the power of the Minister to call in what were formerly called planning appeals and are now called planning reviews is not new. It was introduced into the *Town and Country Planning Act 1961* in 1978, following decisions of the then Town Planning Appeals Tribunal to allow planning permits, despite the Minister's opposition, for subdivision of land on the Boole Poole Peninsula and at Metung, both on the Gippsland Lakes, and for extension of the Tatra Hut restaurant in the Dandenong Ranges. The call-in power has been included in the planning appeals legislation ever since (it was included in the *Planning Appeals Board Act 1980*, and subsequently in the *Planning Appeals Act 1980*). Clearly the intention was to provide a mechanism for the government of the day to frustrate development in circumstances where it appeared likely that the decision at appeal would be for permission to be granted. However, since then it has been used more often to facilitate development proposals than to frustrate them.

Due to the formidable powers available to the Minister under the *Planning and Environment Act 1987* and the *Victorian Civil and Administrative Appeals Tribunal Act 1998*, the powers exercised by councils are those which the Minister allows them to exercise. The State standard provisions of schemes (that is, the VPPs), the fact that councils must get authorisation to prepare a scheme amendment, and the power of the Minister to amend a scheme without any notification or consultation processes limits the powers of councils as planning authorities. Their powers as responsible authorities depend on the extent to which the Minister is specified in their schemes as a responsible authority and also on whether or not the Minister decides to call in applications. Whether they will have a review proceeding brought by an applicant or objectors against their decisions on permit applications heard by the independent umpire, VCAT, depends on whether or not the Minister decides to call it in.

Subdivision and the planning system

Subdivision and planning permits

For many years planning schemes have contained controls relating to subdivision. For example, cl 4 of the Third Schedule to the *Town and Country Planning Act 1961* authorised the inclusion in schemes of controls "prescribing areas in which land or buildings are to be used for specified purposes, or prohibiting restricting or regulating the development and use of land within those areas (including the prescription of site requirements for specified purposes and the minimum size or dimensions of allotments into which land may be subdivided) …". Development was defined under that Act to include subdivision. Pursuant to s 6(1)(a) of the *Planning and Environment Act 1987*, a planning scheme "may make any provision which relates to the use, development, protection or conservation of land". Development is defined to include subdivision and consolidation of land.

Planning permission to subdivide land is normally required in all zones. Note that land is defined in s 3 of the *Planning and Environment Act* to include a building. Some zones specify the minimum allotment size permitted, should permission be granted. For example, in the rural zone not only is planning permission required for subdivision but also the minimum allotment size allowed, should that permission be granted, is 40 hectares in the absence of a local schedule (and if a schedule applies then it will specify for particular areas minimum allotment sizes smaller than 40 hectares). These provisions are buttressed by controls requiring consent for particular uses and developments and the land may also be subject to overlay controls dealing with areas of environmental significance, protection of landscape significance and protection of vegetation.

Certification of plans of subdivision, as distinct from granting planning permission to subdivide, is a power exercised in Victoria by municipal councils. Registration of a plan of subdivision by the Registrar of Titles, and therefore the issuing of separate titles to lots created by the subdivision, cannot occur without the plan first being certified. Before the coming into operation of the *Subdivision Act 1988*, certification was known as sealing a plan of subdivision and the processes for sealing were prescribed in the subdivision of land provisions of the *Local Government Act 1958*, the *Strata Titles Act 1967* and the *Cluster Titles Act 1974*. As planning consent was not necessarily required for conventional and strata subdivision, the processes of sealing a plan of subdivision were not integrated with the planning system. Where planning permission was required under scheme provisions for subdivision, both an application to seal and an application for a planning permit were necessary, each was processed under different legislation, both processes involved the exercise of discretion, and the processing of the two applications was not necessarily closely linked, particularly where the responsible authority for the planning permit application was not the council but a regional planning authority or the Minister. The *Subdivision Act 1988* repealed all previous subdivision legislation and integrated subdivision approvals into the planning system. The *Subdivision Act* does not distinguish between conventional subdivision, strata subdivision and cluster subdivision. Subdivision is treated simply as a process which leads to the creation of lots that are capable of being registered by the Titles Office and for which a Certificate of Title can be issued. Land is defined under the *Subdivision Act* to include buildings and airspace and a lot is defined as a part (consisting of one or more pieces) of any land (except a road, a reserve or common property) which can be disposed of separately.

The VPPs at cl 62.03 specify that planning permission is required for subdivision, except for the following: subdivision by an acquiring authority which does not create an additional lot; a subdivision by a public authority or utility service provider which does not create an additional lot other than for the purpose of a minor utility installation (provided that a permit is not required to subdivide pursuant to any overlay control); and, generally speaking, simple plans which involve the realignment of a common boundary between two lots.

Referral authorities and planning permits for subdivision

Planning schemes specify the referral authorities that must each be sent a copy of the planning permit application for subdivision. The powers of referral authorities have been outlined earlier in this chapter. For subdivision the referral authorities are set out in cl 66.01 of the VPPs and are, in the main, the relevant servicing agencies for water supply, sewerage, drainage, telecommunications, gas, and electricity. However, other authorities may also be referral authorities, such as the CFA, if the subdivision is outside the metropolitan area, the land is not serviced with reticulated water supply, and the subdivision creates a new road. If the application is for use and/or development of the land as well as for subdivision, a number of other referral authorities may be involved and these are set out in cl 66.02 of the VPPs. For example, if the subdivision involves clearance of native vegetation, the Secretary to the department administering the *Flora and Fauna Guarantee Act 1988* is a referral authority. For use or development requiring a works approval under the *Environment Protection Act* the EPA is a referral authority. The bodies specified in the planning scheme as referral authorities have the powers of referral authorities provided by s 61 and s 62 of the *Planning and Environment Act*.

Planning permit conditions for subdivision and the use of s 173 agreements

The imposition of conditions by a referral authority on a decision of the responsible authority to grant planning permission to subdivide does not exhaust the capacity of the responsible authority to impose additional conditions. Wide powers for responsible authorities to impose other conditions are afforded by s 62 of the *Planning and Environment Act*. The conditions imposed must be valid (see Chapter 5 for a discussion on the tests for validity of permits). Other legislation may also provide the power to impose conditions. For example, s 18 of the *Subdivision Act* provides a discretionary power for a council to require, in the absence of a planning scheme requirement for public open space, a public open space contribution of up to 5 per cent of the land or 5 per cent of the value of the land to be subdivided. But note that the Particular Provisions of the VPPs at cl 52.01 exempt certain cases of subdivision from public open space contributions, including subdivision of buildings used for commercial or industrial purposes and subdivision of buildings used for residential purposes and constructed before 30 October 1989.

Section 173 agreements (see Chapter 5) are often used, sometimes quite inappropriately, where land is to be subdivided. Once a Statement of Compliance has been issued under the *Subdivision Act* the permit holder may lodge the plan of subdivision at the Titles Office for registration, and following registration the lots created may be sold separately. At this point the permit for the subdivision may be "spent". It is arguable that at this point any ongoing conditions of the permit (such as limiting development on the lots to specific building envelopes) are no longer enforceable: see *Whittlesea City Council v Jala Pty Ltd* [2000] VCAT 242; *Kruska v Whittlesea City Council* (2002) 11 VPR 66; and *Cope v Hobsons Bay City Council* [2004] VCAT 2487. A condition requiring the owner of the land to enter into a s 173 agreement pursuant to which development may only occur within specified building envelopes, or a condition requiring the creation of a restriction on title (the restriction being that building can only occur within the envelope identified on the title), are alternatives to dealing with that situation.

Section 173 agreements are more appropriately used where a continuing obligation is imposed on the permit applicant, and subsequent owners of the land, such as a requirement to rehabilitate erosion, eradicate weed species and plant new vegetation over a relatively long period of time and then maintain the land in an erosion-free and weed-free condition and maintain planting and replace it as required. Do be aware that there are costs involved in drawing up and executing s 173 agreements and for that reason alone the question of whether they are necessary should always be asked. So should the question of whether such agreements should contain a sunset clause, specifying the date and under what circumstances they are to expire.

A planning permit for subdivision does not necessarily allow the lots created to be used or developed, say, with dwellings. In the case of single dwelling residential development, the zone controls or the overlay controls applying to the land may impose the requirement for a permit for the use (as in the Environmental Rural Zone, for example) and/or the construction or carrying out of buildings and works (as in land subject to an Environmental Significance or Significant Landscape Overlay). But there are instances where a single dwelling may be built on the lots created as a consequence of a permit being granted for subdivision, without the need for further planning permission, such as in the Residential 1 Zone in the absence of overlay controls. In the Residential 1 Zone the development of a single dwelling on a lot greater than 300 square metres in area normally does not require a planning permit. The exceptions are if there is a Schedule to the zone specifying that on lots between 300 and 500 square metres a permit is required to construct a single dwelling, or if an overlay imposes the requirement of a permit. But a permit is required to construct two or more dwellings on a lot. Therefore, instead of applying for a permit to develop two dwellings on a standard-sized lot of 700 square metres or so in an established residential area, in the absence of any overlay requiring a permit to construct a building the option is available of applying for a planning permit to subdivide the land into two lots of, say, 350 square metres each, thereby avoiding the need for a permit to develop a single dwelling on each of the lots. This "subdivision first" approach would seem to be a means of defeating the purpose of having controls on dual occupancy style development. But the Supreme Court held on appeal from VCAT in *Charnley Glen Pty Ltd v Boroondara City Council* [2000] VSC 340; 6 VPR 93 that this was a valid means of securing approval for a dual occupancy development. As discussed above, the responsible authority does have the power to impose a condition on a planning permit for subdivision requiring the owner to enter a s 173 agreement in relation to building envelopes, or a condition requiring the creation of restrictions on titles in the form of such envelopes. In *B Marsh Nominees v City of Moonee Valley* [2004] VSC 237 the Supreme Court, again on appeal from VCAT, followed *Charnley Glen* in holding that a planning permit application for subdivision of land into two lots did not have to be accompanied by an application for a dual occupancy development prior to or in conjunction with the application to subdivide, but it also held that a proposed building envelope alone or in conjunction with other mechanisms will not necessarily enable the issue of building bulk impact on a streetscape to be adequately resolved.

Time limits for decision and the matters the responsible authority must consider

Planning permit applications to subdivide are, in all respects, the same as any other planning permit application made under the *Planning and Environment Act* – they are subject to the same time limitations within which the responsible authority is required to make a decision; "stopping of the clock" provisions apply; the responsible authority is subject to the notification procedures specified under s 52; and applications for review may be lodged by applicants or objectors (for time limits and "stopping of the clock" see Chapter 5). Responsible authorities, when determining planning permit applications for subdivision, must take into account the matters listed in s 60 of the *Planning and Environment Act*. In addition to the matters contained in s 60, responsible authorities must also take into account, as appropriate, the matters listed in the decision guidelines set out in the General Provisions section of the VPPs at cl 65. These matters encompass the impacts of the proposed subdivision, the extent to which State and local policies have bearing on the subdivision and the details of the actual plan of subdivision proposed. The matters which the responsible authority must consider, as appropriate, include the following:

- the State Planning Policy Framework and the Local Planning Policy Framework, including the MSS and local planning policies;
- the purpose of the zone, overlay or other provision;
- the orderly planning of the area;
- the effect on the amenity of the area;
- factors likely to cause or contribute to land degradation, salinity or reduce water quality;
- the extent and character of native vegetation and the likelihood of its destruction;
- the degree of flood, erosion or fire hazard associated with the location of the land and the use, development or management of the land so as to minimise any such hazard;
- the suitability of the land for subdivision;
- the availability of subdivided land in the locality, and the need for creation of further lots;
- the density of the proposed development;
- the area and dimensions of each lot in the subdivision;
- the provision and location of reserves for public open space and other community facilities;
- the availability and provision of utility services, including water, sewerage, drainage, electricity and gas.

Certification of a plan of subdivision

Certification of a plan of subdivision under the *Subdivision Act* cannot occur until a planning permit has been issued, although the planning permit and certification procedures may occur in tandem if the applicant wishes to proceed with fully surveyed and detailed plans at the outset. Certification is required before the plan of subdivision can be registered with and certificates of title issued for the new lots by the Titles Office. Once a planning permit has been issued, under s 6 of the *Subdivision Act* and following receipt of an application for certification, council must certify if certain matters are complied with. Certification is an administrative procedure rather than an exercise of discretion, with matters relating to discretion and policy being dealt with at the planning permit stage. Applicants may seek review by VCAT of a failure or refusal of the council to certify.

It is beyond the scope of this book to discuss in detail the certification process. The purpose of this brief discussion has been to try to explain how the legislation enables the integration of what used be called sealing a plan of subdivision, and is now called certification of a plan of subdivision, into the planning system. Administrative efficiency has been a significant reason for the current approach to dealing with subdivision, but another reason is that subdivision is inherently a planning matter and that is so whether the subdivision is to create suburban residential allotments or to create rural residential allotments on the outskirts of a country town. If planning consent is granted and the appropriate conditions under which the subdivision may proceed are included as part of that consent, it is entirely appropriate that certification of the plan of subdivision be an administrative matter rather than a matter of discretion, as was the case under earlier legislation. For example, under the subdivision of land provisions of the *Local Government Act 1958* a referral system operated very much like that now in place under planning schemes. A council was required to refuse to seal a plan of subdivision if any of those referral authorities refused consent, or if the proposed subdivision did not comply with any provision of a planning scheme, had not been granted a planning permit under the relevant planning scheme, or did not comply with the *Health Act* or the provisions of any by-law. If none of these mandatory grounds of refusal applied, the council still had the discretion to refuse to seal on specified grounds. These grounds included a series of anachronistic matters, including "any ... new street road lane or passageway will not be connected at each end with another street road lane or passageway". Providing power for a council to refuse to seal because a proposed plan included courts is hardly in the best interests of administrative efficiency. Another discretionary ground of refusal was "not in the public interest", which was very broad indeed, and presumably encompassed a range of matters which were taken into account anyway when a planning permit was granted. The current system has the great advantage of requiring the issues of whether or not land should be subdivided, if so under what conditions, and whether the design and layout proposed is appropriate, to be examined and determined at the planning permit stage.

ResCode and subdivision

The *Residential Development Provisions*, renamed in 1992 *The Victorian Code for Residential Development – Subdivision and Single Dwellings* (and generally known as *VicCode 1*) were incorporated via the VPPs into every planning scheme in Victoria in 1989 pursuant to s 6(2)(j) of the *Planning and Environment Act*. The effect of this incorporation was that metropolitan municipalities were required to have regard to (and non-metropolitan municipalities could have regard to) *VicCode 1* when determining planning permit applications to subdivide land into residential allotments. *VicCode 1* applied to subdivisions containing residential allotments between 300 square metres and 4,000 square metres in size and was a set of design and engineering guidelines. It provided for not only small lots but also zero lot line building, swale drains, common trenching, footpaths down one side of the street only and other measures to reduce infrastructure costs and assist with urban consolidation. In the VPP-based planning schemes originally prepared pursuant to the *Planning and Environment (Planning Schemes) Act 1996,* all responsible authorities in the State were required to have regard to *VicCode 1* when determining planning permit applications for residential subdivision in urban and township areas. *VicCode 1* was replaced in 2001 by the provisions of *ResCode* dealing with subdivision and set out at cl 56 of the VPPs.

Before the incorporation of *VicCode 1*, residential subdivisions were subject to the allotment sizes, siting and setback standards contained in the *Victorian Building Regulations 1983* (VBRs) made under the *Building Control Act 1981*. The VBRs imposed a standard set of minimum siting controls (minimum allotment size and minimum setbacks from boundaries) for all buildings other than detached houses and buildings containing two or more dwellings (such as flats, villa units and townhouses). For detached houses and buildings containing two or more dwellings, a table in the VBRs provided five columns of minimum siting controls. Each municipal council was required to make a local law under the *Local Government Act* adopting the requirements of one of those columns for its municipality in part or whole, or prescribing requirements in excess of those specified in the table. In other words, a council could adopt different columns for different parts of the municipality. Many councils adopted for all or most of their municipalities minimum standards requiring a standard "quarter acre" allotment, with minimum frontage and side setbacks of, say, 9 metres and 1.5 metres respectively. Generally speaking, the VBR minimum standards for residential subdivisions included in municipal local laws exceeded by a considerable margin the standards provided by *VicCode 1*. VBR standards are responsible, for example, for the "30-foot" setback from the front boundary of much of the original housing in the middle to outer ring suburbs of metropolitan Melbourne. The impact of VBR standards on housing prices, their operation as devices which excluded the less well off from local housing markets, and their stultifying effects on dwelling design have been well documented (for example, see J Paterson et al in Further Reading). *VicCode 1* was aimed at reducing these effects and, particularly in the metropolitan area, assisting in the implementation of a consolidation policy and reducing the inevitably high servicing costs that result from low-density residential development.

VicCode 1 was superseded by cl 56 of the VPPs in August 2001. Clause 56 is part of the larger package of development objectives and standards relating to residential development known as *ResCode,* which is discussed further in Chapter 3. Clause 56 of the VPPs deals with residential subdivision and applies to subdivision in the Residential 1, Residential 2, Mixed Use and Township Zones. Clause 56 is structured under the headings of objectives and standards. An objective is defined as describing the desired outcome to be achieved in the completed subdivision. A standard is defined as containing the requirements to meet the objective. The clause states that a standard should normally be met, but, if the responsible authority is satisfied that an application for an alternative design solution meets the objective, the alternative design solution may be considered. There are 40 objectives and standards set out in cll 56.02 to 56.10. They deal with matters such as road layout, public open space networks, street design, intersection design, drainage, water supply, sewerage and utilities.

While responsible authorities must have regard to cl 56 when determining planning permits for residential subdivision in urban and township zones, that does not mean they have to impose or enforce its provisions in any mechanistic sense. As noted above, the objectives and standards contained in the clause are not mandatory requirements and in many instances are expressed in broad terms. For example, the residential diversity objective at cl 56.02-4 is "To provide residential areas that meet the diverse needs of the community with a wide choice in housing and associated public and commercial uses". The standard containing the requirements to meet that objective, Standard C4, states that the design of the neighbourhoods should provide for a variety of housing types and be arranged to encourage provision of local services, facilities and employment, in a manner that minimises land use conflicts. The standard also states that a mix of lot sizes should be provided within neighbourhoods that includes smaller residential lots and lots suitable for integrated medium-density housing in areas close to services, public transport and public open space. The extent to which a particular subdivision proposal meets the objectives and standards is a matter of judgement; it is not an exercise in measuring or comparing the proposal to a set of objectively expressed criteria or formulae.

The Environment Effects Act and the planning system

When must an Environment Effects Statement be prepared?

The Minister for Planning is responsible for administering the *Environment Effects Act 1978*. The mechanism contained in the Act for assessing the environmental effects of proposed development is an Environment Effects Statement (EES). An EES is an analysis of the existing environment, the proposed development, and the impact of the proposed development.

The Act applies to the following when they could have a significant effect on the environment: works declared to be public works for the purposes of the Act by Order of the Minister published in the *Government Gazette*. ("Public works" are defined in s 2 as "works undertaken or proposed to be undertaken ... by or on behalf of the Crown or for public statutory bodies, but does not include works undertaken by or on behalf of municipalities". It therefore applies to public, municipal and private sector proposals requiring a government or municipal decision. "Environment" is not defined in the Act, but the *Ministerial Guidelines for Assessment of Environmental Effects under the Environment Effects Act 1978*, which accompany the Act, define it to include "physical, biological, cultural, social, health, safety, and economic aspects of human surroundings, including the wider ecological and physical systems within which humans live".)

Under ss 3 and 8 the Minister is empowered to decide which proposals require an EES and to require the proponent of a development proposal to prepare an EES. The responsibility for preparing an EES lies with the proponent of the development, as is commonly the case with environmental impact legislation interstate and overseas. It has been suggested that the responsibility should lie with an independent agency, as it is not in the interest of the proponent to investigate thoroughly and report objectively. Certainly independent preparation would increase public faith in the process. The *Ministerial Guidelines* include a list of the types of environmental effects which form the criteria for deciding which projects should be referred to the Minister for determination as to whether a Preliminary Environment Report or Environment Effects Statement must be prepared.

Essentially the requirement to prepare an EES relies on the discretion of the Minister and the government of the day. If the Minister decides that an EES is required, the works or development proposed cannot proceed and no decision can be made on the relevant planning permit application or application for permit amendment, or adoption or approval of a planning scheme amendment, until the Minister and any person other than the proponent to whom the Minister requires be given a copy of the EES (such as another Minister or public authority, or planning authority, or responsible authority) have assessed it. If the development or works proposed requires planning permission or a planning scheme amendment, the Minister for Planning has formidable powers available under the *Planning and Environment Act* to ensure that recommendations are adopted – the Minister either approves or authorises other planning authorities to approve, and gazettes all planning scheme amendments, and may call in planning permit applications and review proceedings (see the discussion earlier in this chapter on the powers of the Minister).

Inquiries into the environmental effect of proposed developments

If an EES is prepared, the Minister may, with the approval of the Governor in Council, appoint one or more persons to hold an inquiry (whether in public or private, as he or she sees fit), into the environmental effects of the proposal: s 9. The *Ministerial Guidelines* state that an EES is normally exhibited for a period of 20 to 30 business days (but in exceptional circumstances the Minister may decide that a longer exhibition period is warranted), that public notice of exhibition will be required in at least one daily newspaper and in one or more local newspapers and on the department's website, and that submission to it may be made by members of the public. If the proposal involves a planning scheme amendment, a joint panel will be appointed to report under both the *Environment Effects Act* and the *Planning and Environment Act*. However, the very extensive discretionary powers of the Minister are matters for concern. The Act does not guarantee public exhibition and the opportunity to make submissions. Nor is a public inquiry guaranteed, and even if an inquiry is held, there is no guarantee that it will not be conducted in private. But, those things aside, it is the tendency of governments to announce that a project will proceed and then set in train EES preparation and enquiry processes that has caused a good deal of cynicism in the community. In the cases of the Bay Dredging (Port Phillip Bay Channel Deepening Proposal), the Desalination Plant (Wonthaggi Desalination Project), and the North–South Pipe (Sugarloaf Pipeline), the preparation of the ESSs followed the announcement that these projects would proceed. That does not inspire confidence that the process is transparent and *bona fide* – many in the community view the EES processes as a means of justifying what has already been decided.

Chapter 3

PLANNING SCHEMES

The content of schemes – general powers

Objectives of planning in Victoria

Under s 6(1) of the *Planning and Environment Act* a planning scheme "must seek to further the objectives of planning in Victoria within the area covered by the scheme" and "may make any provision which relates to the use, development, protection or conservation of any land in the area".

The objectives of planning in Victoria are contained in s 4(1) of the Act and are as follows:

(a) to provide for the fair, orderly, economic and sustainable development of land;

(b) to provide for the protection of natural and man-made resources and the maintenance of ecological processes and genetic diversity;

(c) to secure a pleasant, efficient and safe working, living, and recreational environment for all Victorians and visitors to Victoria;

(d) to conserve and enhance those buildings, areas or other places which are of scientific, aesthetic, architectural or historical interest, or otherwise of special cultural value;

(e) to protect public utilities and other assets and enable the orderly provision of public utilities and other facilities for the benefit of the community;

(f) to facilitate development in accordance with the objectives set out in paragraphs (a), (b), (c), (d) and (e);

(g) to balance the present and future interests of all Victorians.

This is a very ambitious list of objectives, all of which are not necessarily compatible with each other, and in practice they are not very useful as criteria for making decisions. For whom must the use and development of land be fair? Presumably the general community, particular sections of the general community who have to bear the immediate impact of both private and public sector development, and the proponents of that development. That is asking quite a lot, since the use and development of land confers benefits on some and disbenefits on others. Can the facilitation of development be compatible with conservation? Who determines the present and future interests of all Victorians and how might these interests be balanced when the future interests are unknown? Should equal weight be given to each of these objectives? These are just some of the more obvious questions that readily arise.

Section 4(1)(f) suggests that the over-arching objective is to facilitate development, albeit in accordance with the objectives set out above it, but the last of the objectives retreats from that position, with its emphasis on balancing the present and future needs of all Victorians. The question of balance is emphasised further in cl 11.01 of the Victorian Planning Provisions (VPPs), where it is stated:

> It is the State Government's expectation that planning authorities and responsible authorities will endeavor to integrate the range of policies relevant to the issues to be determined, and balance conflicting objectives in favour of net community benefit and sustainable development.

The objectives of planning in Victoria serve as a checklist of matters to be taken into account when schemes and scheme amendments are prepared. They do serve a purpose in drawing the attention of planning authorities to a range of environmental, social and economic considerations, and to notions of equity, efficiency and access. However, they do not provide a systematic methodology for making decisions.

The use, development, protection or conservation of land

Under the *Town and Country Planning Act 1961* the content of planning schemes was limited to the matters listed in the Third Schedule to that Act. Any matter included in a scheme but not listed in the Third Schedule could therefore be challenged in the Supreme Court on the grounds of *ultra vires* (meaning, in this instance, that there was no power conferred by the *Town and Country Planning Act* to include such a provision in a planning scheme). Parliament obviously took a restrictive approach to the powers that could be exercised by bodies authorised to prepare schemes and scheme amendments, even though the Third Schedule authorised a very wide range of scheme provisions. Under the *Planning and Environment Act* the approach is much more positive – s 6(1)(b) allows a scheme to make *any* provision which relates to the use, development, protection or conservation of any land in the area.

Scheme provisions must relate to land, which is defined by s 3 to include buildings and other structures permanently fixed to land, land covered with water, and any estate, interest, easement, servitude, privilege or right in or over land. Use, development, and conservation are also defined in s 3. Use "includes use or proposed use for the purpose for which the land has been or is being or may be developed". "Development" is defined to include the construction or exterior alteration or exterior decoration of a building, the demolition or removal of a building or works, the construction or the carrying out of works, the subdivision or consolidation of land, the placing or relocation of a building or works on land, and the construction, or putting up for display, of signs and hoardings. "Works" are also defined by s 3 to include any change in topography and the removal, destruction or lopping of trees and the removal of vegetation and topsoil. "Building" is defined by s 3 to include part of a building or structure, fences, walls, service installations, and a boat or pontoon that is permanently moored or fixed to land. "Conservation", as defined by s 3, includes preservation, maintenance, sustainable use, and restoration of the natural and cultural environment. The definitions of key terms such as "development", "works", "use", "buildings" and "conservation" are very wide and sometimes do not accord with normal everyday usage (such as demolition being included in development). The intention of the Act is to allow schemes to include the widest possible array of controls (that is, any provision which relates to the use, development, protection or conservation of land).

The content of schemes – specific powers

Section 6(2) sets out a list of specific matters that may be included in schemes. These do not limit in any way the broad power conferred by s (6)(1) but spell out how schemes may deal with the use, development, protection or conservation of land. In case any misunderstanding should arise, the last item on the list states that a planning scheme "may provide for any other matter which this Act refers to as being included in a planning scheme": s 6(2)(l).

Policies, specific objectives and strategy plans

Section 6(1)(aa) states that a planning scheme for an area must contain a Municipal Strategic Statement (MSS) if the scheme applies to all or part of a municipal district. Under s 6(2)(a) and (b) additional policies, specific objectives and strategy plans may be included in schemes. The State Planning Policy Framework (SPPF) section of all schemes, and local planning policies included as part of the Local Planning Policy Framework (LPPF) sections of schemes, are authorised by these sections and provided for by s 7(1).

Restrictions on the use and development of land

Section 6(2)(b) provides that a scheme may regulate or prohibit the use or development of land and s 6(2)(e) provides that a scheme may regulate or prohibit any use or development in hazardous areas or in areas which are likely to become hazardous areas. The means by which use or development is prohibited or regulated are zoning and overlay controls. Zoning is a feature of Victorian schemes and, generally speaking, in each zone some uses are prohibited, others require planning consent, and yet others may be established "as of right" (ie do not require planning consent). Zone provisions may also impose the requirement of a planning permit for development (such as, in a Residential 1 Zone, the requirement for a planning permit for the construction or extension of a dwelling on a lot of less than 300 square metres, the construction or extension of a dwelling on a lot between 300 and 500 square metres if a schedule to the zone specifies that a permit is required, the construction or extension of an additional dwelling on a lot, the construction of two or more dwellings on a lot, the construction or extension of a residential building, or for buildings and works associated with a use for which permission is required). Overlay provisions normally impose the requirement for a planning permit for development (including demolition or removal of a building in the case of a Heritage Overlay) and for the construction of a building and the construction or carrying out of works. When determining planning permit applications, the responsible authority is required to implement any mandatory conditions specified by the scheme, but it may also impose "any condition that it thinks fit" under s 62(2), subject, of course, to the requirements of referral authorities, and subject to meeting the tests for validity (see Chapter 5). Subject to review by the Victorian Civil and Administrative Tribunal (VCAT), referral authorities may veto a planning permit application or impose conditions on any decision by the responsible authority to grant the permit: ss 61(2) and 62(1).

Section 6(2)(e) appears to be redundant, because s 6(2)(b) is worded sufficiently broadly to apply to hazardous areas. It may be that the motivation for including s 6(2)(e) was to remove any doubt about the validity of schemes, including specific provisions relating to areas subject to bushfires, flooding, landslides and subsidence, and to areas in which dangerous goods are stored or dangerous products are manufactured.

Another form of regulation or prohibition is provided by the power in s 6(2)(c) for schemes to designate land as being reserved for public purposes. Scheme provisions specify the circumstances in which planning permission is required for the use or development designated as reserved. The Public Acquisition Overlay designates land as reserved for a public purpose. The purpose of this control includes "to identify land which is proposed to be acquired by a public authority" and "to reserve land for a public purpose and to ensure that changes to the use or development of land do not prejudice the purpose for which the land is to be acquired". Refusal of planning permission in relation to land that has been designated as reserved for a public purpose may result in a compensation claim for loss or damage under ss 98 and 99 (see Chapter 9). *weird*

Section 6(2)(h) provides for schemes to include provisions that require specified things be done to the satisfaction of the responsible authority or a referral authority. This is not to be confused with the power of a responsible authority to impose a condition on a planning permit under s 62 that certain things be done to the satisfaction of the responsible authority or to the satisfaction of a referral authority. These conditions are used when the responsible authority wishes to exercise a continuing supervisory role over some aspect of a development. It is quite common, for example, for planning permits to specify conditions that landscaping be maintained to the satisfaction of the responsible authority. The issue of maintenance is not one on which the responsible authority can decide to grant or refuse the permit, because it will not arise until the use or development has been established. Such conditions often lead to disputes because they do not contain any criteria for satisfying the responsible authority and may lead to review proceedings before VCAT under s 80. However, s 6(2)(h) applies to schemes, not to permits. For example, the Farming Zone Clause 32.03-2 provides that a lot may be used for one or two dwellings provided that certain conditions are met. Those conditions are that each dwelling must be connected to reticulated sewerage or that all wastewater must be treated and retained within the site to the satisfaction of the responsible authority; that each dwelling is connected to a potable water supply or have an alternative potable water supply, with appropriate storage capacity, to the satisfaction of the responsible authority; and that each dwelling must be connected to a reticulated electricity supply or have an alternative energy supply to the satisfaction of the responsible authority.

Requirements for the provision of public utility services

Section 6(2)(f) provides for schemes to set out requirements for the provision of public utility services to land, such as water, sewerage, drainage, electricity, telephone, and gas services. The section also allows schemes to specify levies or developer contributions to finance the provision of public utilities. Sections 46H–46QC deal with the preparation of approved development contributions plans as part of an approved planning scheme. Development contributions are payments or in-kind works or facilities provided by developers towards the cost of infrastructure, including roads, stormwater and drainage management systems, open space and community facilities. Development infrastructure is physical infrastructure required to be in place before a development commences, such as roads, drains, and land for community infrastructure. Community infrastructure is infrastructure which will be required as a community grows, such as pre-schools, community halls and maternal and child welfare centres.

A distinction must be drawn when using the term "development contributions" between a levy and an impact mitigation payment. Development contributions plans included as a part of a planning scheme are levies – that is, a fixed sum levied on owners, usually per lot or per dwelling. The amount represents the proportion of the cost of the infrastructure that will be shared by all development contributing to the need for that infrastructure. An impact mitigation payment is calculated by reference to the cost of the infrastructure in question, not by reference to a demand unit. It takes the form of provision of, or a direct payment of a specified sum for, particular works, services or facilities considered necessary as a result of a development.

Development contributions in the form of standard levies on development set out in the scheme are imposed via permit condition. They can only be imposed where a development contributions plan(s) has been approved as a part of the scheme: *Curry v Melton Shire Council* [2000] VSC 352; 7 VPR 109. Normally, the requirement to pay a development contributions levy is via the provisions of the Development Contributions Plan Overlay, which by a schedule or schedules identifies the land to which the levy applies, sets out the services or facilities for which the levy is imposed, and sets out the levy that is to be paid. Typically, the services and facilities include the costs of distributor roads, traffic management works, streetscape works, parks, active open space, community activity centres and drainage. The levy is applied per hectare of land or per new lot created and is typically $10,000–$12,000 per lot.

Before the enactment of the *Planning and Environment (Development Contributions) Act 2004*, s 62(5) provided that, in deciding to grant a permit, a responsible authority may include a condition that specified works which the responsible authority considers necessary as a result of the grant of a permit be provided on or to the land, or be paid for wholly or partly where the remaining cost is to be met by any Minister, public authority, referral authority or council providing the works. Section 62(6) provided that a responsible authority must not include in a permit a condition requiring a person to pay an amount for or provide services other than a condition required to implement an approved development contributions plan, or a condition requiring services or facilities be provided in accordance with an agreement under s 173. In *Christian Brothers Vic Property Ltd v Banyule City Council* [2001] VCAT 2120; VPR 128, the Tribunal held that, subject to the normal tests of validity, a responsible authority could include a condition in a permit requiring that works, such as roads, roundabouts and drains (as distinct from services or facilities) on or to the land or on nearby land, considered necessary by the responsible authority as a result of the grant of the permit, be paid for wholly or in part by the applicant, as such a condition was authorised by s 62(2). Section 62(2) provides that a responsible authority may include any condition on a permit it thinks fit, including specified conditions that are set out in that section. The Tribunal held that a condition imposed in the absence of an approved development contributions plan requiring the applicant to pay a share of the cost of constructing a roundabout necessitated by a subdivision, but at some distance from it, fell within the broad category of conditions held to be valid by the High Court in *Cardwell SC v King Ranch Aust Pty Ltd* (1984) 54 LGRA 110; 53 ALR 632.

But that no longer applies. Section 62(5) now provides that a permit may be granted which includes a condition required to implement an approved development contributions plan or a condition that specified works, services or facilities considered by the responsible authority to be necessary to be provided on or to the land or other land as a result of the grant of the permit, be provided by the applicant, or be paid for wholly by the applicant, or be provided or paid for partly by the applicant where the remaining cost is to be met by any Minister, public authority, or municipal council providing the works, services or facilities. Section 62(6) now provides that a responsible authority must not include in a permit a condition requiring a person to pay an amount for or provide works, services and facilities except in accordance with s 62(5) or s 46N, a condition that a planning scheme requires to be included as referred to in s 62(1)(a), or a condition that a referral authority requires to be included as referred to in s 62(1)(a).

In *Springhaven Property Group Pty Ltd v Whittlesea City Council* [2005] VCAT 816, which was an application for review of a failure to grant a permit within the prescribed time for a subdivision of land into 34 lots, the Tribunal held that a permit condition requiring the owner to contribute to the construction of a road, where the sum of that contribution was based on the area of land being subdivided on a per-hectare basis, was invalid. The Tribunal held that the approach taken in the *Christian Brothers* case was not available because of the inclusion in s 62(6) of "works", contributions to the cost of the roadworks from multiple owners were envisaged, and the condition sought to recoup moneys already spent on the road by the pioneer developer rather than the road works having been done or proposed to be done by any Minister, public authority or municipal council.

Before the *Planning and Environment (Development Contributions) Act 2004*, councils imposed by permit condition cash in lieu contributions towards the provision of car parking in and around busy shopping centres where parking is at a premium. Those cash in lieu contributions are no longer able to be validly imposed as permit conditions: see *Naprelac v Baw Baw SC* [2005] VCAT 958 and *Glenwaye v Glen Eira CC* [2006] VCAT 3000.

Section 62(6) provides that State agencies and public authorities may directly administer and collect development contribution levies provided for in a development contributions plan approved as part of a planning scheme, instead of having to rely on responsible authorities. Note that the requirements of these authorities other than those to do with the financing of service provision may be accommodated via the planning system if they are specified in schemes as referral authorities. For example, as was explained in Chapter 2, subdivision normally requires planning consent (the exception being subdivision of commercial and industrial buildings and the subdivision of residential buildings constructed before 30 October 1989). Planning permit applications for subdivision must be referred to the servicing agencies specified in the particular scheme (see Chapter 2). These referral authorities may object to an application, in which case the responsible authority must refuse to grant, or to impose conditions that the responsible authority must give effect to in any decision to grant.

Development contribution levies, imposed via an approved development contributions levy, must not be confused with the Growth Area Infrastructure Contribution (GAIC) provided for by Part 9B of the Act, inserted by the *Planning and Environment Amendment (Growth Areas Infrastructure) Act 2010*. The GAIC is intended to help pay for State infrastructure. It applies to land brought into the existing growth areas within the metropolitan Urban Growth Boundary since November 2005, and to all land within the new Urban Growth Boundary (ratified by Parliament in July 2010) that is zoned for urban development (ie the Urban Growth Zone in these new areas). For more discussion on the Urban Growth Boundary, see later in this chapter and also Chapter 4. Depending on whether the land is Type A, B or C (defined in s 201RC), the amount of contribution for the financial year 2010–11 varies between $80,000 and $95,000 per hectare: s 201SG.

Development contribution levies pursuant to an approved development contributions plan may be imposed in addition to the GAIC. The combined total of these may be between $20,000 and $30,000, which will almost inevitably be passed on to the consumer, thereby adding to the price of new housing in the our suburbs.

Creation or extinguishing of rights of way or other encumbrances

Planning schemes may regulate or provide for:
- the creation, variation or removal of easements or restrictions of land under s 23 of the *Subdivision Act 1988*: s 6(2)(g);

- the removal or variation of conditions in the nature of easements in Crown grants under s 23 of the *Subdivision Act 1988*: s 6(2)(ga);
- the creation or removal of easements or rights of way under s 36 of the *Subdivision Act 1988*: s 6(2)(gb).

These provisions are very similar to the power included in cl 2 of the Third Schedule to the *Town and Country Planning Act 1961*. Like under that Act, scheme provisions may not be effective without action also being taken under other legislation. Closure of a road over which a council has powers, for example, involves certain procedures under the *Local Government Act 1989*.

Scheme provisions creating or extinguishing rights of way or encumbrances on land may result in compensation claims against the planning authority. Section 98(1)(d) provides for the owner or occupier of any land to claim compensation for financial loss suffered as the natural, direct and reasonable consequence of access to land being restricted by the closure of a road by a planning scheme (see Chapter 9). This would apply, for example, in the creation of pedestrian malls in existing shopping centres. However, it is not enough to allege financial loss, and in the case of malls that may be very difficult to prove – the experience with most malls is that they have resulted in financial benefits in the form of increased levels of trading.

"Restriction" in s 6(2)(g) has the same meaning as in the *Subdivision Act* – that is, a restrictive covenant. Note that a responsible authority may, subject to appeal, grant a planning permit which allows the variation or removal of a restrictive covenant: s 60(2)–(7). These provisions, when originally introduced in 1991, allowed for the variation or removal of a covenant by means of either a planning scheme amendment or by a planning permit. Subsequent amendments to s 60(2)–(7) have for the most part made the permit method ineffective for removing covenants registered, lodged for registration or created on or before 25 June 1991 in all except consent cases where no one objects to the removal. See Chapter 5 for a more detailed discussion on permits for the variation or removal of restrictive covenants.

Specific information to be provided with an application for a permit

Section 6(2)(ha) provides that a scheme may require specified information to be provided with an application for a planning permit. For example, where a permit is required for a dwelling on a lot pursuant to cl 54 of the VPPs (see "The format and structure of schemes" and "The ResCode provisions" below), or where, pursuant to cl 55, a permit is required to construct an additional dwelling on a lot, construct two or more dwellings on a lot, extend a dwelling if there are two or more dwellings on a lot, or construct or extend a residential building, the permit application must be accompanied by a neighbourhood and site description, the contents of which are set out at cll 54.01-4 and 55.01-1, respectively. Further, the responsible authority must inform the applicant in writing, before notice of the application is given or, if notice is not required to be given, before it makes a decision on the application, that the neighbourhood and site description is either satisfactory or not satisfactory. If it is not considered satisfactory, the responsible authority may require further information from the applicant under s 54 of the Act.

Underlying zoning

The notion of underlying zoning is largely redundant because all land to which a planning scheme applies is included in a zone and, if it is to be acquired for public use, that intention will be indicated by the Public Acquisition Overlay. Before the VPP-based planning schemes, land was included in either a zone or a reservation. A Future Public Purposes Reservation applied to land that was intended to be acquired for public sector use. The underlying zoning was the zoning that would have applied if there had been no Future Public Purposes Reservation in place.

Section 6(2) provides for schemes to state the provisions that would have applied to land reserved for public purposes if the land were not so reserved. Reserved land is land "earmarked" or identified as land to be acquired by the public sector at some point in the future and used for a public purpose, such as a government school, public hospital, park et cetera. In other words, a scheme may specify the zoning that would have applied had the land not been reserved. Underlying zoning is linked to the notion of market value in the *Land Acquisition and Compensation Act 1986* (see Chapter 9). Land reserved for a future public purpose (by the Public Acquisition Overlay as provided for in the State standard provisions of schemes) is land intended to be acquired by the public sector. When the land is acquired, the base price paid will be the market value or the value that would apply had the land not been reserved (that is, if the Public Acquisition Overlay had not been in place).

Incorporation of documents

Section 6(2)(j) provides for schemes to apply, adopt or incorporate any document which relates to the use, development or protection of land. This allows documents to be incorporated in planning schemes by reference – they do not have to be physically included in the scheme. A list of incorporated documents is a statutory part of the planning schemes via the VPPs. Councils can choose whether additional documents, such as development plans, strategies, guidelines or outline development plans, or reports on matters such as the conservation value of certain areas, are to be incorporated documents or reference documents and then seek to include them in their planning schemes via a planning scheme amendment. A document is only incorporated if it is included in the list of incorporated documents in cl 81 of the planning scheme, or in the schedule to that clause. It is then part of the planning scheme and can only be amended as an incorporated document by a planning scheme amendment.

Generally speaking, incorporated documents contain guidelines or policies or plans that are required to be taken into account when decisions are made on planning permit applications. Incorporated documents must not be confused with reference documents, which are the background or database documents for the MSS and local policies in the LPPF sections of the planning scheme. For example, a local planning policy dealing with heritage matters may refer to heritage studies undertaken by or on behalf of the relevant council. A local planning policy dealing with neighbourhood character may refer to a neighbourhood character study undertaken by or on behalf of the council. A reference document *per se* carries little or no weight in determining applications for planning permits. However, an incorporated document is part of the planning scheme and must be taken into account if relevant to the proposed use and development which is the subject of a permit application.

The distinction between incorporated documents and reference documents becomes a little blurred where a council has included the recommendations of a heritage study or neighbourhood character study as a local planning policy and included the relevant study as an incorporated document, as has been done in the City of Port Phillip, where the *Port Phillip Heritage Review* Version 2, 2000, and the *City of Port Phillip Heritage Policy Map* are incorporated documents in the Port Phillip Planning Scheme.

Documents incorporated in the new schemes have local application as detailed by the scheme itself. As at mid July 2010, 30 documents were incorporated in all planning schemes, including the following:

- *Code of Forest Practices for Timber Production*, 2007;
- *Victorian Code for Cattle Feedlots*, August 1995;
- *Guidelines for Environmental Management – Code of Practice – Septic Tanks*, Publication 891, Environment Protection Authority, March 1999;
- *Private Tennis Court Development Code of Practice*, Revision 1, March 1999;
- *Code of Practice, Piggeries*, Department of Planning and Housing and Department of Food and Agriculture, 1992;
- *Building in bushfire-prone areas*, CSIRO and Standards Australia (SAAHB36-1993), May 1993;
- *Apiary Code of Practice*, May 1997;
- *Victorian Code for Broiler Farms*, 2009;
- *Policy and Planning Guidelines for Development of Wind Energy Facilities in Victoria*, 2009;
- *Victoria's Native Vegetation Management – A Framework for Action*, August 2002;
- *Growth Area Framework Plans*, Department of Sustainability and Environment September 2006.

A schedule to cl 81 may include documents of relevance to the particular municipality in the scheme as incorporated documents. For example, in the Moonee Valley Planning Scheme in mid July 2010 the schedule to cl 81 listed 11 documents, including the following:

- *Lower Maribyrnong River Concept Plan* 1986;
- *Moonee Ponds Creek Concept Plan*;
- *Development Concept Plan – Former Essendon & District Memorial Hospital*;

- *Penleigh and Essendon Grammar School – Essendon Campus Master Plan* August 2004;
- *Penleigh and Essendon Grammar School – Moonee Ponds Master Plan* August 2000;
- *2-12 Hood Street, Airport West – The Good Guys Head Office Redevelopment* August 2007.

Section 6(2)(j) poses a number of problems. As it is not necessary for incorporated documents to be physically appended to schemes, it is often difficult to establish what the controls are without obtaining copies of a large number of additional documents which, taken together, may be larger than the scheme which incorporates them. Not all these documents are readily available to members of the public, so it is no easy task finding out the guidelines that may apply to particular types of development or to aspects of those developments. Even if copies of the relevant incorporated documents are obtained, some were prepared for purposes other than incorporation in schemes and they may not fit readily within the context of other controls and so be difficult to interpret or apply to a particular case.

If a document is incorporated in a scheme and then is subsequently amended, does this mean the scheme is also amended? The question has a good deal more point when it is considered that these documents may be prepared and amended by bodies outside the planning system, such as the Environment Protection Authority. And what of documents drawn up by a particular municipality and incorporated only in its scheme? Can they be amended by council vote? Can the scheme amendment processes prescribed by the *Planning and Environment Act* be by-passed? Analysis of the *Interpretation of Legislation Act 1984* indicates that the document incorporated in a scheme is the document as it stood at a particular date. Any amendment of the document has no force as part of the scheme unless it is also amended under the procedures for amendment laid down in the *Planning and Environment Act*. However, having said that, it is also important to note that s 4B of the Act allows the Minister to prepare an amendment to the VPPs and s 20 of the Act allows the Minister to exempt planning authorities, including himself or herself, from the processes of notification, submission and panel hearing and essentially amend a scheme, including by amending the VPPs, by the stroke of a pen (see Chapter 4).

Agreements

Section 6(2)(k) explicitly authorises a scheme to provide that any use or development of land is conditional on an agreement being entered into with a referral authority or the responsible authority. In the Farming Zone, for instance, a permit is required to subdivide land, and each lot created by the subdivision must have an area of 40 hectares unless a schedule to the zone specifies otherwise. A permit may be granted to create smaller lots if the subdivision is to create a lot for an existing dwelling, or if the subdivision is the re-subdivision of existing lots and the number of lots is not increased. However, in both instances an agreement under s 173 of the Act must be entered into between the owner of each lot created and the responsible authority, which ensures that the land must not be further subdivided. The agreement must be entered on title and is therefore binding on future owners.

However, agreements may be used in the absence of scheme provisions that the use or development of land is conditional on an agreement being entered into. Section 173(1) states that "a responsible authority may enter into an agreement with the owner of land in the area covered by a planning scheme for which it is the responsible authority". Section 173(3) provides for agreements to be made with prospective owners – a recognition that planning permit applicants and proponents of scheme amendments are not necessarily the owners of the land in question but may hold, for example, a purchase option on the property. The use of agreements in relation to permits for subdivision has been discussed in Chapter 2. The use of agreements is discussed further in Chapters 4 and 5.

Classes of land, use or development exempted from s 96(1) or (2)

Section 96 states that, where a responsible authority itself requires a planning permit or where a person requires a permit for the use or development of land owned or managed or occupied by a responsible authority, application must be made to the Minister. However, s 6(2)(ka) states that a planning scheme may provide that specified classes of land, use or development are exempted from this requirement. In October 1990 the Minister approved an amendment to the then State section of planning schemes which removed this requirement, so that applications were made to the relevant responsible authority. The VPP-based planning schemes continue these arrangements via cl 67 of the VPPs. Essentially, if a responsible authority requires planning permission, it applies to itself (see Chapter 5).

Classes of permit applications exempt from notification and review rights

Section 6(2)(kc) states that a planning scheme may set out classes of permit applications exempt from the notice requirements under s 52 of the *Planning and Environment Act*. Section 6(2)(kd) provides that a planning scheme may exempt classes of applications the decisions on which are exempt from the requirements of ss 64(1), (2) and (3) and 82(1).

Section 52 requires that applications for planning permits must be notified to owners and occupiers of adjoining land (unless the responsible authority is satisfied that the grant of the permit would not cause material detriment to any person) and to others if the responsible authority considers that the grant of the permit may cause material detriment to them.

Section 64(1), (2) and (3) provide that a responsible authority must give a copy of its decision on a permit application to each objector and must not issue a permit until the expiration of the period in which an objector may lodge an application for review. In the case of a decision to grant where there have been objectors, that would be 21 days after the objectors receive the Notice of Decision to Grant (see Chapter 5). Section 8 provides that an objector to a permit application may apply to VCAT for review of a decision to grant a permit.

Section 60(3) makes it clear that a responsible authority is not *required* to consider any objection lodged to a planning permit application if the application was not required to be notified under s 52. However, an exemption from giving notice of an application and the lodging of objections does not prevent the responsible authority from giving notice, and from considering any objections it receives. If a scheme creates exemptions from the normal notification requirements, it does not operate to preclude objections being made by persons with a relevant interest but simply renders it more difficult for such persons to ascertain the existence of the permit application; the provisions of the Act concerning exemptions, if implemented in a scheme, will tend to limit the opportunities for objectors to learn of an application and to bring an application for review before a permit has in fact been issued: *Sweetvale Pty Ltd v VCAT* [2001] VSC 426; 16 VPR 224. The exemption in relation to review rights applies only to decisions to grant a permit. Where the application comes before VCAT (as in an application for review of a refusal or for review of a failure of the responsible authority to decide within the prescribed time), the Tribunal is not bound to consider objectors' submissions but, pursuant to s 98 of the *Victorian Civil and Administrative Tribunal Act 1988*, it may grant leave to objectors to make submissions and leave may be given where it thinks fit: *Crampton v Frankston CC* [2003] VCAT 1339; 15 VPR 49. It is also possible for the Tribunal to join a person or persons as a party to a proceeding pursuant to s 60 of the *VCAT Act*. However, it was held in *West Valentine Pty Ltd v Stonnington CC* [2005] VCAT 224 that, even if it is open to the Tribunal to join an objector as a party to a proceeding where they are otherwise exempt from review rights, there would need to be very unusual circumstances to justify doing so contrary to the explicit scheme of exemption from reviews in certain classes of permit application. Section 82 states that an objector cannot seek review of a decision on a permit application if the application is exempt. However, a subsequent amendment of a permit application cannot operate to exclude persons who have legitimately become parties before that amendment: *Perorad Care Pty Ltd v Frankston CC* [2004] VCAT 2272. If the permit sought requires multiple consents under the provisions of the scheme and an application for review of a decision to grant is lodged by objectors then VCAT is obliged to disaggregate the submissions in relation to those consents which are exempt from third party review rights and those which are not: *Sweetvale Pty Ltd v VCAT* [2001] VSC 426; 16 VPR 224.

Section 6(2)(kc) and (kd) were inserted by the *Planning and Environment (Amendment) Act 1993*. Planning schemes now contain a very significant number of exemptions, found particularly in the provisions relating to Residential 2, Commercial, Industrial, Public Land and Special Purpose Zones and to overlay controls. For example, in the Residential 2 Zone medium density housing and residential buildings are exempt from the normal notification and third party application for review processes. In Industrial 1 and Business 1 Zones, applications for subdivision are also exempt, subject to some exceptions (such as the land to be subdivided is not within 30 metres of land in a Residential Zone or Business 5 Zone, or land used for a hospital or school), and permit applications for buildings and works are similarly exempt. For land subject to the Heritage Overlay, development exempted from the normal notification and review processes includes demolition or removal of an outbuilding (including a carport, garage, pergola, shed or similar structure) unless it is identified in a schedule to the overlay; demolition or removal of a fence, unless it is identified in a schedule to the overlay; external painting of a building; and construction of a fence, swimming pool, or tennis court. For land subject to the Incorporated Plan Overlay, a permit application that is generally in accordance with the incorporated plan is also exempt from the normal notification and third party review processes.

Definition of the metropolitan Urban Growth Boundary

Provision for the inclusion in specified metropolitan planning schemes of an Urban Growth Boundary were inserted into the Act by the *Planning and Environment (Metropolitan Green Wedge Protection) Act 2003*. Section 46AB provides that an Urban Growth Boundary is a boundary that is specified or is to be specified as an Urban Growth Boundary in a metropolitan fringe planning scheme. Section 46AA provides that a metropolitan fringe planning scheme is one applying to all or part of the municipal districts listed in that section alphabetically, from Brimbank City Council to Yarra Ranges Shire Council. The metropolitan growth boundary is shown on the planning scheme maps for those municipalities. Land outside the metropolitan growth boundary is shown as Green Wedge land (see s 46AC) and is generally included in a Green Wedge Zone. Land within the boundary which has been identified as land that is to accommodate subdivision and urban growth has generally been rezoned from Farming Zone to Urban Growth Zone.

The metropolitan Urban Growth Boundary was introduced as one of the mechanisms for implementing *Melbourne 2030* (2002), the Government's metropolitan planning strategy. That strategy was based on the assumptions that metropolitan Melbourne's population would increase by a million people by 2030, generating demand for an additional 620,000 dwellings, and that approximately 30 per cent of these additional dwellings would be required in green field locations (within the Urban Growth Boundary), while approximately 70 per cent would be accommodated within the existing built up metropolitan area. However, *Melbourne @ 5 Million* (2008), the Government's revised metropolitan strategy, updated the population and household formation forecasts contained in *Melbourne 2030* and identified that by 2030 an additional 600,000 dwellings over and above the existing 2008 number will be required by 2030. The revised strategy recognised that the targets in *Melbourne 2030* were not being achieved and reflected the political reality of widespread community opposition to the "densification" of the built-up area by the growth in medium density housing developments, in turn placing at risk the slim majorities held by Labor in some key inner suburban seats. It forecast that only 53 per cent of the required dwellings will be built within the existing built-up area and approximately

47 per cent will be in growth areas on the rural urban fringe. In accordance with these revisions, the Urban Growth Boundary was amended by Amendment VC68. The amendment was approved by the Minister in June 2010 and ratified by Parliament at the end of July 2010 (for amendment of the Urban Growth Boundary and Green Wedge subdivision controls, see Chapter 4).

Under Amendment VC68 approximately 46,000 hectares were added to the area within the Urban Growth Boundary, with approximately 24,500 hectares rezoned to Urban Growth Zone. The amendment also introduced the Public Acquisition Overlay over some 15,000 hectares of native grasslands (thereby reserving these grasslands for public acquisition), and Environmental Significance Overlays over approximately another 5,000 hectares. In addition, the amendment introduced the Public Acquisition Overlay for the alignments for future transport links such as the Outer Metropolitan / E6 Transport Corridor Link and the Regional Rail Link, included in the *Victorian Transport Plan*.

Planning is very much a political process, whether it be at the metropolitan or the local level, but we do question whether the expansion of the Urban Growth Boundary was necessary. Woodcock et al (2010) (see Further Reading) conclude that modest height limits in activity centres and of four to five storeys along transport corridors would easily be enough to accommodate the population growth projections in *Melbourne 2030* and *Melbourne @ 5 Million* and would directly affect only approximately 7 per cent of the current built-up area and therefore protect the character of most urban areas. They suggest that this could be implemented without the fear of a resident backlash which has become a brake on urban containment policy.

The format and structure of schemes

The VPPs and State standard provisions

All the planning schemes in place in the State were prepared pursuant to the *Planning and Environment (Planning Schemes) Act 1996*, which amended the *Planning and Environment Act 1987*, and have a standard format and structure. The 1996 amending Act provided for the Minister to prepare a set of State standard provisions – the VPPs. The VPPs are not a planning scheme – they are the source document from which new schemes are to be constructed and they include the SPPF and the State standard zones, overlays, Particular Provisions, General Provisions and definitions.

Section 7 of the *Planning and Environment Act* requires schemes to include State standard provisions and local provisions. The State standard provisions must consist of provisions selected from the VPPs. The Ministerial Direction *The Form and Content of Planning Schemes*, issued under s 7(5) of the *Planning and Environment Act*, requires the following parts of the VPPs to be included in schemes:

- Objectives of Planning in Victoria (reproduced from s 4 of the *Planning and Environment Act*).
- Purposes of the planning scheme (to provide a clear and consistent framework within which decisions about the use and development of land can be made; to

express State, regional, local and community expectations for areas and land use; and to provide for the implementation of State, regional and local policies affecting land use and development).
- Contents (modified to include only those zones and overlays selected from the VPPs and included in the planning scheme).
- User Guide.
- SPPF.
- Standard zones and zone provisions included in the scheme.
- Standard overlay controls and provisions included in the scheme.
- Particular Provisions.
- General Provisions.
- Definitions.
- Incorporated documents.

The Ministerial Direction states that a planning scheme must not include any zone or overlay clause not included in the VPPs and that if a provision is selected from the VPPs for inclusion in a scheme (such as a zone or overlay provision) then the entire provision, including any subclauses, must be selected without any modification.

The local provisions must include an MSS and any other provision the Minister directs to be included: s 7(2).

The State Planning Policy Framework

The purpose of the SPPF included in all schemes is to inform planning authorities and responsible authorities of those aspects of State level planning policy which they are to take into account and give effect to in planning and administering their respective areas.

Principles of land use and development planning are set out in SPPF under the headings of Settlement, Environment, Housing, Economic Development, Infrastructure and Particular uses and development. Under each of these headings are stated broad objectives, some guidelines for implementation, and a set of strategies (essentially a list of matters and documents that planning and/or responsible authorities are to have regard to as are relevant when preparing amendments to schemes, or their own MSS, or when determining planning permit applications).

Melbourne 2030, although released in 2002, was not even referred to in the SPPF until September 2005, when cl 12 was introduced via an amendment to the VPPs (VC34). It is now one of the documents listed in cl 12.09 as an incorporated document to which planning and responsible authorities must have regard (as relevant).

Before *Melbourne 2030* being included in cl 12.09 as an incorporated document to which planning authorities and responsible authorities must have regard, it was given significant weight by VCAT in a series of controversial decisions, including *Ashlyn Enterprises Pty Ltd v Yarra City Council* [2003] VCAT 87; 13 VPR 132, *Rowcliffe Pty Ltd v Stonnington CC* [2004] VCAT 46 and [2004] VCAT 1370; 16 VPR 9, and *Golden Ridge v Whitehorse CC (Mitcham Towers)* [2004] VCAT 1706 (see the discussion in Chapter 5 on the role of policy in deciding on permit applications). In *O'Connell Street Developments Pty Ltd v Yarra CC* [2003] VCAT 448; 13 VPR 227 the Tribunal held that the strategy, as distinct from its accompanying implementation plans and advisory note, was a final strategy adopted by the Minister which may be considered by the Tribunal and must be considered pursuant to s 60(b)(ii) of the Act if the circumstances appear to so require. Now, of course, by virtue of cl 12.09 and its status as an incorporated document, it is clear that it must be considered by planning authorities and responsible authorities, and by VCAT standing in the shoes of a responsible authority, in application for review proceedings.

At the time of writing, cl 12 of the SPPF had not been amended to reflect the policy changes flowing from *Melbourne @ 5 Million*. Presumably this will occur at some point in the future. However, cll 12 and 14 have been amended by Amendment VC66 to reflect the Government's policy on regional development and settlement *Ready for Tomorrow – A Blueprint for Regional and Rural Victoria* dated June 2010.

The Local Planning Policy Framework (the MSS and local planning policies)

The content of the MSS is prescribed by s 12A of the Act. The MSS must set out the strategic planning, land use and development objectives of the planning authority, the strategies for achieving the objectives, the land use or development opportunities, and constraints that are relevant to the municipality. It must provide a framework for local planning decisions, a general explanation between those objectives and strategies and the controls on the use and development of the land in the planning scheme, and any other matter that the Minister directs to be included. The MSS must also be consistent with the council's current Council Plan prepared under s 125 of the *Local Government Act 1989*. The detail provided in MSSs varies a good deal from scheme to scheme. For metropolitan municipalities the MSS may be a lengthy document of 40 or 50 pages. In many rural schemes the MSS may run to only half a dozen pages. Having examined a large number of MSSs over the years, our conclusion is that the typical MSS is devoted mainly to describing the characteristics of the municipality and contains a much shorter section attempting to set out a strategic direction for the future.

In addition to the MSS, the LPPF may also include local policies. The extent to which schemes contain local policies varies a great deal. Very often local policies amount to nothing more than a restatement of policies in the SPPF. In the metropolitan area, local planning polices dealing with housing and residential areas tend to be "loaded up" in an attempt to cushion or reduce the impact of elements of the SPPF, such as the urban consolidation policy set out in cl 12, or attempt to set out broad "standards" or "requirements" that are more stringent or onerous than those set out in cl 55 (the *ResCode* provisions dealing with medium density development, discussed later in this chapter). For example, a policy that is aimed at discouraging medium density development in residential areas except those close to shopping centres and public transport routes is an attempt to narrow the application of cl 12 and the purpose *interesting + important*

of the Residential 1 Zone that applies to most metropolitan residential areas. In many instances, policies are not buttressed by zone or overlay controls which would allow the policy to be implemented. For example, in the vast majority of areas zoned Residential 1, a policy to retain the existing housing stock in the area in the absence of any control on the demolition of buildings cannot be implemented. In the absence of overlay controls, an existing house may be demolished and a new house built in its place without any planning permission being required for either the demolition of the existing building or the construction of the new building. A policy to retain existing trees cannot be implemented without an appropriate overlay that imposes the requirement for a permit to lop, remove or destroy trees. In the absence of such an overlay, trees can be lopped, removed or destroyed with impunity so far as the planning system is concerned.

In some instances, a policy may be at odds with the provisions of the controls that apply to the land. For example, a policy would be at odds with the provisions of the Heritage Overlay if it held that proposals which would result in the removal of heritage fabric will not be supported in areas subject to a Heritage Overlay. The provisions of the Heritage Overlay clearly contemplate that a permit may be granted for the alteration, removal or demolition of a building and require that each case be considered on its merits. The weight policies must be given in determining planning permit applications is discussed in Chapter 5.

State standard zones and zone provisions

The zones and zone provisions in each scheme are those selected from the VPPs and approved as implementing the SPPF and the LPPF, including the MSS and local planning policies. The VPPs provide for the following zones.

Residential	**Industrial**	**Business**
Residential 1	Industrial 1	Business 1
Residential 2	Industrial 2	Business 2
Low Density Residential	Industrial 3	Business 3
Mixed Use		Business 4
Township		Business 5
Residential 3		

Rural	**Public Land**	**Special Purpose**
Environmental Rural	Public Use	Special Use
Rural Living	Public Park and Recreation	Comprehensive Development
Green Wedge	Public Conservation and Resource	Urban Floodway

PLANNING SCHEMES

Rural	**Public Land**	**Special Purpose**
Green Wedge A	Road	Capital City
Rural Conservation		Docklands
Farming		Priority Development
Rural Activity		Urban Growth
		Activity Centre

There is no ability for planning authorities to vary the zones or to introduce local zones. However, some degree of local variation may be achieved by the use of schedules, as set out in the Ministerial Direction *The Form and Content of Planning Schemes*.

Each zone has a Use Table which is divided into three sections – Section 1 (as of right uses), Section 2 (discretionary uses) and Section 3 (prohibited uses). For example, in the Residential 1 Zone, the zone normally selected to apply to most urban residential areas, planning permission is not required for the uses listed in Section 1 of the Use Table (agriculture, bed and breakfast, carnival, dwelling etc.), provided that any condition specified is met – these are the "as of right" uses. Planning permission is required if the relevant conditions specified for a Section 1 use are not met. Planning permission is required for the uses listed in Section 2 of the Use Table (known as discretionary uses) and any condition specified in Section 2 must be met or planning permission cannot be granted. Uses listed in Section 3 are prohibited (that is, planning permission cannot be granted). Note that at the end of the uses listed in Section 2 for the Residential 1 Zone is "any use not in Section 1 or 3", which is known as the "innominate" use category. Normally, an innominate use is included in the Section 2 discretionary use section of the Use Table for the relevant zone. Chapter 5 deals with planning permits. However, it might be wise at this stage to distinguish between a building permit and a planning permit, and between a planning permit for the use of land and a planning permit for the development of land.

Pursuant to the *Building Act 1993*, a building permit may be issued by either the local council or a private sector licensed building surveyor who may or may not reside or work in or anywhere near the municipality in which the building is to be constructed. The primary purpose of the building permit/approval system is that of ensuring that the building to be constructed will meet the minimum standards of construction specified in the *Building Regulations 2006*. A building permit is required for any construction. Planning permits are issued pursuant to the *Planning and Environment Act 1987*. They are not always required – as, for example, for Section 1 uses as discussed above. The primary purpose of planning permits is to ensure that uses and development are located appropriately in relation to State and local policies and also in relation to other uses and development and do not interfere with the amenity of adjoining and nearby land. But there is a distinction between *use* and *development*. "Development" is defined in s 3 of the *Planning and Environment Act 1987* and includes construction of a building or works, the demolition or removal of a building or works, and the subdivision or consolidation of land.

If we return to Section 1 uses in the Residential 1 Zone, no planning permission is required to use land for a dwelling (other than bed and breakfast), but the clauses accompanying the Use Table (specifically cl 32.01-4) state that a planning permit is required to construct or extend a dwelling on a lot of less than 300 square metres (or on a lot of less than 500 square metres if a schedule to the zone so specifies); construct a dwelling if there is at least one dwelling on the lot; construct two or more dwellings on a lot; extend a dwelling if there are two or more dwellings on a lot; and construct or extend a residential dwelling. Application requirements and decision guidelines are specified for these developments, including the requirement that the responsible authority must consider, when deciding on an application, the *ResCode* provisions at cl 54 or cl 55, depending on the nature of the development proposed. However, to establish the use "home occupation" (a home business) in an existing dwelling, a planning permit is not required (but Particular Provisions included in cl 52 impose a set of conditions which must be met by the home occupation, otherwise a permit is required). Section 2 uses require planning permission for both use and development (that is, for buildings and works as well as use) pursuant to cl 32.01-5. So use of an existing building for a medical centre requires planning permission, as does the construction of a building to be used as a medical centre (and in both instances car parking provisions are specified in the Particular Provisions of the scheme). Note that "construct" is defined in s 3 of the Act, so construction includes reconstruction or the making of structural changes.

The Public Use, Public Park and Recreation, Public Conservation and Resource, and Road Zones show land used for public purposes. The Public Acquisition Overlay shows land which has been reserved for future public acquisition and future public use (see Chapter 9). The provisions of some of these zones give rise to some concerns. In the Public Park and Recreation Zone, the majority of Section 1 uses must meet specified conditions, otherwise planning permission is required. It is of some concern that the uses "store" and "retail premises", and the innominate "any other use not in Section 3" do not require planning permission, provided they are conducted by or on behalf of the relevant public land manager. This may well lead to increasing commercialisation of our public parks. Clause 36.02-2 specifies that planning permission is required to construct a building or construct or carry out works on land subject to the Public Park and Recreation Zone, but not for buildings or works carried out by or on behalf of a public land manager or by or on behalf of Melbourne Parks and Waterways. So a large range of commercial premises may be established in public parks without even having to get planning permission for the use or for any buildings or works associated with the use. For any use listed in Section 2, planning permission is required. Section 2 uses such as "retail premises" and "store" must be "associated with public land use" but are not required to be conducted by or on behalf of a public land manager. Restaurants, take-away food outlets and even hotels and taverns are included within the definition of "retail premises" and may well be "associated with public land use", so therefore could establish in public parks with planning permission for use. They could even establish without a permit for the buildings to accommodate them, pursuant to a schedule accompanying the zone. Planning permission is required to subdivide land or to construct a building or construct or carry out works, except those building and works specified in cl 36.02-2. However, cl 36.02-7 provides for the provisions of the zone to be overridden in that a schedule may exempt the requirement for planning permission for the use of land, or for construction of a building, or for the construction or carrying out of works.

The lesson is that the zone provisions, any schedules accompanying the zone, and the Particular Provisions of the scheme need to be checked in order to establish the circumstances in which planning permission is not required, is required, or cannot be granted. And on top of all this, the land may be subject to overlay controls which may impose requirements additional to those contained in the zone provisions and the particular use provisions. Generally speaking, overlays deal with development, as distinct from use, and impose the requirement for a permit for building and works either where none is required by the zone which applies to the land or additional to any permit requirement for building and works required by the zoning of the land. However, an overlay may also impose a requirement for a planning permit to remove, destroy or lop vegetation (see, for example, the Vegetation Protection, Significant Landscape, and Environmental Significance Overlays). The VPP-based schemes are not easy for the lay person to use, but then neither were the old ones they have replaced. But the VPP-based schemes provide significantly more flexibility (and therefore less certainty) than the old schemes, and in many instances they have removed third party objection and review rights (see earlier in this chapter for a discussion of exemption provisions in schemes).

In the metropolitan area the Residential 1 Zone, generally speaking, applies to land which was subject to the Residential C Zone in the pre-VPP planning schemes. In the Residential C Zone, planning permission was required for the use and development of land for flats (a term defined to include flats, villa units and townhouses). In the Residential 1 Zone, the use of land for a dwelling is "as of right", with the construction of two or more dwellings requiring planning permission. A responsible authority cannot refuse planning permission for flats and other forms of medium density development because the use is not appropriate for the site or location (perhaps because of the adjoining land uses, or the distance of the site from community and commercial facilities), as they could under the Residential C Zone. Neither can objectors, either in objections or before VCAT in review proceedings, validly mount such an argument. Now the use does not require planning permission – the assessment of a medium density proposal revolves around the details of the development, the number of dwellings, their design and layout on the site, the number of car spaces to be provided, the extent to which it respects the character of the neighbourhood and so on, taking into account the relevant parts of the SPPF, the *ResCode* provisions at cl 55, and any relevant local policies in the LPPF. "Bed and breakfast" and "place of worship" appeared as Section 2 uses in the Residential C Zone but are now in Section 1. In the old Residential C Zone, a total of 69 uses were listed in Section 3, but only 16 uses are listed in Section 3 in Residential 1 Zone. It is appreciated that the definitions in the new schemes account for some of the difference in these numbers in Section 3, but clearly there has been a significant change towards making formerly prohibited uses discretionary uses. The level of certainty about the uses and development which cannot establish in residential areas has been diminished and the barriers to establishing medium density development have been reduced.

The opportunities for local residents and others who may be affected by a proposed development to lodge objections to a planning permit application and then either initiate or be parties to review proceedings before VCAT have also been significantly reduced. As was explained earlier in this chapter, s 6(2)(kc) and (kd) of *the Planning and Environment Act 1987*, introduced by amendment in 1993, provide for a planning scheme to exempt applications from the normal third party notification, objection and review rights under the Act. These provisions have been utilised mainly in the Residential 2, Commercial, Industrial, Public Land and Special Purpose Zones and in some overlay controls. They are also included even in the Residential 1 Zone – see cl 32.01-2 dealing with subdivision.

In 1993 Mr Maclellan, the Minister for Planning in the then new Kennett Government, launched the first of his Ministerial Statements, *Planning a Better Future for all Victorians: New Directions for Planning and Economic Growth*, in which he made it clear that the new Government intended to make the planning system the servant of economic growth and job creation and that planning schemes in the future would facilitate investment and development, not inhibit it. The increased flexibility of the zones in the VPP-based schemes and their exemption provisions are consistent with this aim.

Overlays

As with zones, standard overlays are included in the VPPs, and planning authorities must select from these overlays to implement State and local policies. Generally, overlays apply to a single issue or a related set of issues, such as heritage, environmental concerns, flooding and so on. Where more than one issue applies to land, multiple overlays can be used. Many of the overlays may have schedules to specify local objectives and controls. The format of these schedules is prescribed in the Ministerial Direction *The Form and Content of Planning Schemes*. Generally, overlays may only specify requirements about development, not use, and they do not change the intent of the zone that applies to the land concerned.

The overlays provided for in the VPPs are as follows.

Environment and Landscape
Environmental Significance
Vegetation Protection
Significant Landscape

Heritage and Built Form
Heritage
Design and Development
Incorporated Plan
Development Plan
Neighbourhood Character

PLANNING SCHEMES

Land Management	Other
Erosion Management	Public Acquisition
Salinity Management	Airport Environs
Floodway	Environmental Audit
Land Subject to Inundation	Road Closure
Special Building	Restructure
Wildfire Management	Development Contributions Plan
State Resources	City Link Project

As noted above, generally speaking overlays impose the requirement for a permit for building and works over and above any permit requirement imposed by the zoning that applies to land and in some instances may impose the requirement to remove, lop or destroy vegetation (for example, the Vegetation Protection, Significant Landscape, and Environmental Significance Overlays). The requirements imposed by the Heritage Overlay include to construct, demolish or remove a building, subdivide or consolidate land, externally alter a building, construct or display a sign, (unless a schedule identifies that no paint controls apply to the heritage place) externally paint an unpainted surface, and remove, destroy or lop a tree if a schedule identifies the heritage place as one where tree controls apply (see Chapter 8).

As explained in Chapters 5 and 8, it is an established principle of planning law that, in determining a planning permit application, the responsible authority's discretion is limited to the matters included in the clause which triggered the application: see *National Trust of Australia (Victoria) v Australian Temperance and General Mutual Life Assurance Society Ltd* [1976] VR 592 and *Victorian National Parks Association Inc v Iluka Resources* [2004] VCAT 20. In other words, if the zoning of the land is such that a permit is not required for a use or development, but a permit is required under the Environmental Significance Overlay, the responsible authority is confined to considering matters authorised by the provisions of the overlay. In the case of the Heritage Overlay, in the Residential 1, Residential 2, Mixed Use and Township Zones, if the requirement for a permit for the development or extension of a dwelling is triggered not by the zoning but by the Heritage Overlay, this principle does not apply. This is because, for such applications, cl 54 must be considered. This clause deals with the amenity and neighbourhood character impacts of the proposed development. Therefore the responsible authority must consider these issues as well as heritage issues in making its decision.

Many of the planning permit applications made pursuant to the Heritage Overlay are exempt from the normal third party notification, objection and review provisions of the *Planning and Environment Act*. The exemptions are authorised by s 6(2)(kc) and (kd), as was explained earlier in this chapter, and include demolition or removal of an outbuilding (including a carport, garage, pergola, shed or similar structure) unless it is identified in a schedule to the overlay; demolition or removal of a fence (unless it is identified in a schedule to the overlay); external painting of a building;

construction of a fence, swimming pool or tennis court; and construction or display of a sign. Any or all of these may be of significant interest to nearby owners and occupiers. But, in the absence of schedules requiring planning permission, the first that nearby owners and occupiers may know of such actions is that they are occurring or have occurred – and they have no right to initiate or be a party to review proceedings before VCAT.

Particular Provisions

Planning schemes include a set of standard Statewide Particular Provisions specified in the VPPs for a range of uses and developments. Particular Provisions not included in the VPPs cannot be included in schemes, but planning authorities may use local policies to address additional matters if they wish. The matters which the VPP Particular Provisions deal with include subdivision, easements and restrictions; specific sites and exclusions; advertising signs; car parking, loading and unloading of vehicles; mineral exploration and mining; extractive industry and the search for stone; uses with a potential for offence or risk; home occupation; service stations; car washes; motor vehicle, boat and caravan sales; heliports; post boxes; native vegetation; timber production; convenience restaurants and take-away food premises; private tennis courts; crisis accommodation; shared housing; community care units; crematoriums; cattle feedlots; licensed premises; gaming; and paintball games facilities. The Particular Provisions section also includes the *ResCode* provisions at cll 54, 55 and 56. For the sake of convenience, these provisions are discussed separately below.

General Provisions

General Provisions are a set of standard Statewide provisions from the VPPs included in all schemes. They standardise the operational requirements of schemes and deal with existing use rights, referral of planning permit applications to referral authorities, applications under s 96 of the Act (that is, applications relating to land owned or occupied by responsible authorities, including applications made by responsible authorities) and broad decision guidelines. Referral authorities are discussed in Chapter 2. Section 96 applications are discussed briefly earlier in this chapter and also in Chapter 5. Some specific discussion of existing uses and decision guidelines is warranted.

Existing uses

An existing use is sometimes referred to as a non-conforming use. A non-conforming use in the days before the VPP-based schemes was a use prohibited by a planning scheme but established before the controls which prohibited it came into effect. Because the first planning schemes in Victoria date back to the years subsequent to the enactment of the *Town and Country Planning Act 1944* (although zoning by-laws were authorised under the *Local Government Act* in 1921), much of the development of the inner parts of the metropolitan area and provincial centres occurred in the absence of planning schemes. In many areas this resulted in a mixture of land uses, so when a scheme was brought into effect it was not unusual for some of the uses found in a particular area to be prohibited by the zoning. For example, if an area containing a mixture of residential and industrial uses was zoned residential, the industrial uses would be prohibited by the scheme. Both the original scheme and subsequent scheme amendments may have produced non-conforming uses. Such uses, provided they were lawfully in existence before the scheme or scheme amendment which made them non-conforming was approved, were allowed to continue. They had existing use rights.

In the current VPP-based schemes, existing use rights extend to more than just non-conforming uses. Clause 63.01 provides that an existing use right is established if any of the following apply:

- The use was lawfully carried out immediately before the approval date of the scheme or amendment that prohibited it.
- A permit for the use had been granted immediately before the approval date and the use commences before the permit expires.
- A permit has been granted for an alternative use pursuant to cl 63.08 and the use commences before the permit expires.
- Proof of continuous use for 15 years is established.
- The use is a lawful continuation by a utility service provider or other private body of a use previously carried on by a Minister, government department or public authority, even where the continuation of the use is no longer for a public purpose.

Existing use rights apply to land, not to owners or others with an interest in land, such as lessees. The rights are not affected if the land is sold or if a new lease is taken out on the property. The principle of existing use rights is protected by s 28 of the *Interpretation of Legislation Act 1984*, which provides that legislation shall not operate retrospectively. However, the *Planning and Environment Act* also contains provisions relating to existing uses. Section 6(3) provides that nothing in a planning scheme shall prevent the lawful existing use of land, building and works. These provisions do not apply under s 6(4) to a use which has stopped for a continuous period of two years, a use which has stopped for two or more periods which together total two years in any period of three years or, in the case of a use which is seasonal in nature, if the use does not take place for two years in succession.

It has long been established that "lawful" means lawful in terms of planning law: see, for example, *White v Shire of Ballan* (1986) 4 PABR 272 and *King v Colac-Otway Shire Council* (2002) 10 VPR 27. But cl 63.11 provides a mechanism for extending existing use rights to a use which did not lawfully establish (either because it was prohibited by the scheme at the time the use was established or at that time the scheme imposed the requirement of a planning permit for that use and no permit was granted) if it can be established that the use has been conducted continuously for 15 years. The time limit of 15 years has relevance in a number of circumstances, including enforcement proceedings. For example, a defence in enforcement proceedings where it is alleged that land is being used contrary to the provisions of the scheme may be that the use is protected by existing use rights. The person claiming this defence would need to prove that the use has been carried out continuously for 15 years. There are some qualifications on making a claim under the 15-year rule – it cannot be used if during that time the use has been declared illegal by a court or tribunal or during that period the responsible authority has clearly and unambiguously given a written direction for the use to cease by reason of non-compliance with the scheme. It was held by VCAT in *Port Phillip City Council v J & Evelyn Beckman* (2003) 14 VPR 190 that the 15-year period was satisfied if the use had continued for any 15-year period and had not ceased during that period, and could not then be destroyed by the giving of a clear and unambiguous direction.

In the context of existing use rights, the word "use" has a narrow meaning and the courts have consistently drawn a distinction between "use" and "purpose" to clarify that meaning. For premises used for the purposes of a butcher's shop, the existing use rights are confined to "butcher's shop" and do not extend to the general use of the premises as a shop: *Bonus Pty Ltd v Leichhardt Municipal Council* (1954) 19 LGR (NSW) 375; *Shire of Perth v O'Keefe* (1964) 10 LGRA 147. Similarly, if the use was a bakery, the rights apply to a bakery, not a general category of industry: *City of Nunawading v Harrington* [1985] VR 641. Clause 63.02 of schemes provides, via the VPPs, that if a use is being characterised to assess the extent of any existing use right, it is to be characterised by the purpose of the actual use at the relevant date, subject to any conditions or restrictions applying at that date, and not to the classification in the table to cl 74 (the land use definitions section of the VPPs) or in Section 1, 2 or 3 of any zone. In other words, cl 63 provides that the distinction between use and purpose must be applied and the actual use as distinct from the broad category of use at the relevant date must be determined. VCAT (and its predecessors) have generally followed the principles set out in the *Bonus, City of Nunawading* and *Shire of Perth* cases. For example, in *VBI Properties PL v Port Phillip City Council* [2000] VCAT 885; 6 VPR 20, VCAT held that the purpose of the use should not be characterised by a definition or expression used in a planning scheme but by asking what is the purpose being served by the use. It held that the current use of premises as a backpackers' hostel was a different use from the former use as a boarding house and was not protected by existing use rights. See also *Melbourne City Council v Starera Pty Ltd* [2000] VCAT 569; 4 VPR 270, where it was held that the appropriate use served by the use of land as a hotel was that of a nightclub or late-night function centre.

Clause 63.05 provides that a use in Section 2 or Section 3 of the Use Table for the zone in which the land is now located may continue provided:

- No building or works are constructed or carried out without a permit. A permit must not be granted unless the buildings or works complies with any other building or works requirement in the scheme.
- Any condition or restriction to which the use was subject and which applies to the use in Section 2 of the zone continues to be met. This includes any implied

restriction on the extent of the land subject to the existing use right or the extent of activities within the use.
- The amenity of the area is not damaged or further damaged by a change in the activities beyond the limited purpose of the use preserved by the existing use right.

The field of existing use rights is a complex one and it is beyond the scope of this book to explore it in detail. What constitutes stopping of a use? How is the land to which existing use rights apply to be identified? For discussion of these and other issues, see Byard, Code, Porritt and Testro in Further Reading.

Can a building housing a use for which an existing use right has been established be reconstructed if it is destroyed in a fire? Clause 63.10 provides that, if at least 50 per cent of the floor area of such a building or 50 per cent of the floor area of any works is damaged or destroyed (whether by fire or some other cause) so that the use cannot continue without the building or works being reconstructed, the land must be used in conformity with the scheme unless a permit is granted to continue the use and to construct or carry out building or works.

Clause 63.08 provides that, if land is used for a Section 3 use for which an existing use right has been established, a permit may be granted to use the land for an alternative use that does not comply with the scheme. However, the responsible authority must be satisfied that the new alternative use will be less detrimental to the amenity of the locality. Of course, there may be other considerations to take into account as well as the amenity impacts of the alternative use. For example, local policies as well as basic planning principles may militate against the granting of a permit for the alternative use of land as a shop in a residential area remote from the commercial centre of a country town: see *King v Hepburn SC* [2002] VCAT 928.

Decision guidelines

The General Provisions include a list of matters that must be taken into account within the context provided by s 60 of the Act when the responsible authority considers applications. These matters are guidelines for the exercise of the discretionary powers by the responsible authorities to grant permission, refuse permission, or grant permission subject to conditions. They operate in addition to any controls that the application must satisfy and in addition to any decision guidelines included in the specific zone and overlay provisions that apply to the land in question. Clause 65.01 of the General Provisions requires the responsible authority to consider, as appropriate, before deciding on an application or approval of a plan:

- the matters set out in s 60 of the Act;
- the SPPF and the LPPF, including the MSS and local planning policies;
- the purpose of the zone, overlay or other provision;
- any matter required to be considered in the zone, overlay or other provision;
- the orderly planning of the area;
- the effect on amenity of the area;

- the proximity of the land to any public land;
- factors likely to cause or contribute to land degradation, salinity or reduce water quality;
- whether the proposed development is designed to maintain or improve the quality of stormwater within and exiting the site;
- the extent and nature of native vegetation and the likelihood of its destruction;
- whether native vegetation is to be or can be protected, planted or allowed to regenerate;
- the degree of flood, erosion or fire hazard associated with the location of the land and the use, development or management of the land so as to minimise any such hazard.

The responsible authority must also consider another list of matters specified in cl 65 when deciding on applications to subdivide land. Note that each zone and overlay control also includes decision guidelines for particular uses and developments. In the Residential 1 Zone, for example, the responsible authority must consider, before deciding on a permit application to subdivide land, the *ResCode* provisions at cl 56 (see Chapter 2). When considering applications for medium density housing and residential buildings in this zone, the responsible authority must consider the *ResCode* provisions at cl 55 (see later in this chapter).

Morris J observed in *Victorian National Parks Association Inc v Iluka Resources* [2004] VCAT 20 that in practice most decisions revolve around one or two key considerations (see Chapter 5).

Definitions

The definitions section contains standard Statewide definitions from the VPPs. It sets out the meaning of terms used in the scheme. The section contains definitions of General Terms (such as building height, frontage, gross floor area, ground level), Outdoor Advertising Terms (such as animated sign, floodlit sign, panel sign, sky sign), and Land Use Terms. Land Use Terms are arranged in the form of a nested hierarchy in that a term listed in the first column of the table includes the terms listed in the third column, which in turn are included in any term listed in the fourth column. For example, a dwelling is a building used as a self-contained residence which must include a kitchen sink, food preparation facilities, a bath or shower, and a closet pan and wash basin. The use "dwelling" includes the uses "bed and breakfast" and "caretaker's house" and in turn is included in the broad category of use "accommodation". "Accommodation" is defined to include camping and caravan park, corrective institution, dependent person's unit, dwelling, group accommodation, host farm, residential building, and residential village, all of which are also defined.

In the Residential 1 Zone "dwelling (other than bed and breakfast)" is a Section 1 use and therefore this use does not require planning permission in this zone. As "caretaker's house" is included in "dwelling", it is also a Section 1 use. However, "dwelling" does not include "dependent person's unit," so it is listed separately in Section 1. In Section 2 "accommodation (other than a dependent person's unit and dwelling)" is listed. Therefore, all the other uses included in the definition of "accommodation" are Section 2 uses – that is, camping and caravan park, corrective institution, group accommodation, host farm, residential building and residential village. However, the broad category of use "industry (other than car wash)" is a Section 3 or prohibited use in the Residential 1 Zone. "Industry" is defined in the Table of Land Use Terms and includes materials recycling, refuse disposal, refuse transfer station, research and development centre, rural industry and service industry, all of which are also defined in the Table of Land Use Terms.

Note that the way in which terms are used in the general community may not be the way they are used in planning schemes. Where does a video hire outlet, such as a Movieland store, fit into the Use Table for the Residential 1 Zone? There is no definition provided for this specific use, so does that mean it falls into the innominate use category in Section 2 and so can establish in the zone with planning permission? No, it cannot, because the use "retail premises" is defined as "land used to sell goods by retail, or by retail and wholesale, sell services, or hire goods". The video hire outlet is therefore included in "retail premises" and is included in the Section 3 or prohibited uses section of the Land Use Table for the zone. What is prohibited is "retail premises (other than community market, convenience shop, food and drink premises, and plant nursery)". The video store is clearly not a convenience shop, which is defined as "a building with a leasable floor area of no more than 240 square metres, used to sell food, drinks, and other convenience goods. It may also be used to hire convenience goods". There is no definition provided for "convenience goods", but the hire of convenience goods would include the hire of videos. So a milk bar (provided it has a leasable floor area of less than 240 square metres) could hire out videos and still fall within the definition of convenience shop and so establish in the Residential 1 Zone with planning permission. But the Movieland store could not establish in this zone, because such stores do not sell food, drinks and other convenience goods. They also usually have a leasable floor area in excess of 240 square metres.

The definitions are a crucially important part of planning schemes. As the examples above demonstrate, the definitions must be examined to determine if a use does not require planning permission, does require planning permission, or is prohibited by the zoning of the land. That may not always be a simple, straightforward task. Is a proposed PubTAB agency in a hotel a separate use from the hotel, or is it a use ancillary to the hotel use? Are retail, entertainment and leisure uses associated with a cinema complex separate uses from the cinema, or uses ancillary to the cinema use? Is a manual car wash an industry? Is a Bunnings hardware superstore a shop? It is beyond the scope of this book to deal in detail with the principles of how uses are to be characterised and how dominant and ancillary uses are to be ascertained, but there is some discussion of these questions in Chapter 5.

The ResCode provisions

Broadly speaking, *ResCode* is a set of development standards and policies applying to residential subdivisions, the development of a dwelling on a lot where planning permission is not required, the development of a dwelling on a lot where planning permission is required, and the development of two or more dwellings on a lot. *ResCode* was brought into effect in August 2001. That part of *ResCode* dealing with the subdivision of land has been discussed in Chapter 2. The *ResCode* provisions are at cll 54 and 55 in the Particular Provisions section of planning schemes. They are discussed separately below.

ResCode where no planning permission is required for a single dwelling

In many instances the development of a single dwelling on a lot does not require planning permission. For example, in the Residential 1 Zone, the standard suburban zone which applies to most of the suburban areas of metropolitan Melbourne and urban areas elsewhere in the State, "dwelling" is a Section 1 or as of right use. In the Residential 1 Zone a permit is required to construct or extend a dwelling on a lot with an area of less than 300 square metres, or on a lot between 300 and 500 square metres if specified in a schedule to the zone, but otherwise no permit is required pursuant to the zoning. In the absence of an overlay control (such as a Heritage Overlay, a Significant Landscape Overlay, or an Environmental Significance Overlay) requiring permission to construct a building or to construct or carry out works, no planning permission is required to construct or extend a single dwelling on a lot (provided the lot has an area greater than 300 square metres and provided that there is no schedule to the zone imposing the requirement for a permit on lots between 300 and 500 square metres in area).

Before the VPP-based schemes came into effect there were no overlay controls, although in some respects Urban Conservation Zones operated in similar fashion to a Heritage Overlay. Generally speaking, a planning permit was not required for a detached dwelling on residentially zoned land in the suburban areas of metropolitan Melbourne and other provincial centres. This resulted in many houses being constructed, particularly two-storey houses, which have had severe amenity impacts on abutting land through overlooking and overshadowing. A possible solution would be to require a planning permit for the development of all single dwellings as well as two or more dwellings on a lot, but this would result in councils having to deal with a huge number of permit applications. Even if the requirement for a permit for a single dwelling on a lot were limited to two-storey dwellings, the volume of applications would still be overwhelming, and in any event single-storey dwellings may have severe amenity impacts on abutting land, particularly if the area is steeply sloping and the house is built on a site that is higher than abutting land.

As part of *Rescode* package the amenity impacts resulting from the construction and extension of a single dwelling on a lot where no planning permission is required are dealt with outside the planning system via the *Building Regulations* made pursuant to the *Building Act 1993*. The *Building Regulations 1994* were amended by the

Building (Single Dwelling) Regulations 2001, now contained in Part 4 of the *Building Regulations 2006*. The amendment introduced 14 standards dealing with such matters as street setback, building height, site coverage, car parking, side and rear setbacks, overlooking, overshadowing, walls on boundaries, daylighting of habitable room windows, private open space and front fence height. Note that these are essentially amenity aspects of the proposed development. The standards do not deal, except in a very indirect way, with the impact of the proposal on the character of the neighbourhood. The *Building Act* provides that a building surveyor must not issue a building permit unless he or she is satisfied that the building work and building permit will comply with the Act and the *Building Regulations*. If a proposed building would not meet the *ResCode* standards in the *Building Regulations* (or the other requirements of the *Building Regulations*), a building surveyor may prepare a Report and Consent Notice to the relevant council (the reporting authority) to obtain its approval to vary the relevant standard or standards.

A Ministerial Guideline titled *Siting and Design of Single Dwellings*, issued 24 August 2001, deals with variations of the standards. It lays down decision guidelines for each standard which set out the circumstances that must apply before the council may give its consent to a variation. The Ministerial Guideline *Involvement of Adjoining Owners in Siting Appeals*, issued 16 June 1994, directs that adjoining owners be notified where a request is made to allow a reduction in setback requirements. This Ministerial Direction states that, if an adjoining owner objects to the proposal and the objection is not considered frivolous, the council, in deciding the issues, should bear in mind that refusal would create a situation where the applicant may lodge an appeal to the Building Appeals Board and this gives the affected adjoining owner the opportunity to appear as a witness of the council at the appeal. But a request to vary a standard may be made in relation to standards dealing with matters other than setbacks, and therefore adjoining owners are not required to be notified in accordance with the Minister's Direction. If they are not notified, they cannot lodge an objection because they would not know that a Report and Consent Notice had been lodged. But even if they are notified and lodge an objection, they do not have any third party right of appeal to the Building Appeals Board against a decision of the council to reduce the requirements of a standard. And if council refuses to reduce the requirements of a standard, adjoining owners may only appear as witnesses before the Building Appeals Board if called by the Council – they may not appear as parties in their own right. The lack of third party rights under the *Building Act* is a cause for concern. So is the fact that the Building Appeals Board is not required to give reasons for its decisions.

ResCode where planning permission is required for a single dwelling on a lot

Clause 54 of the VPPs applies to a planning permit application to construct or extend a single dwelling on a lot under the provisions of a Residential 1 Zone, a Residential 2 Zone, a Mixed Use Zone, or Township Zone, or Neighbourhood Character Overlay if the land is in one of those zones. Until 1 September 2005, when Amendment VC33 was gazetted, cl 54 also applied where the requirement for a permit was triggered only by a Heritage Overlay and the land was included in these zones. The circumstances in which the Residential 1, Mixed Use, and Township Zone provisions give rise to a requirement for a permit for a single dwelling on a lot are limited to where the lot is less than 300 square metres in area or, in addition, where a schedule to the zone specifies that a permit is required for lots between 300 and 500 square metres in area. On land subject to a Neighbourhood Character Overlay, a permit is required to construct a building or carry out works (but a permit is not required to construct a swimming pool or to construct or extend an outbuilding normal to a dwelling, unless a schedule to the overlay specifies a permit is required). On land subject to a Heritage Overlay, a permit is required, *inter alia*, to construct or extend a building. Note that, in relation to land subject to a Neighbourhood Character Overlay or a Heritage Overlay, for cl 54 to be triggered, the land must be also in a Residential 1, Residential 2, Mixed Use, or Township Zone and, if it is in one of those zones, the clause applies to all lots, regardless of their size. The triggering of cl 54 by a Heritage Overlay is a departure from the principle established in *National Trust of Australia (Vic) v Australian Temperance and General Mutual Life Assurance Society Ltd* [1976] VR 592 that the ambit of discretion is bounded by the purpose for which the discretion is conferred and therefore the amenity considerations are irrelevant when the requirement for a permit is triggered by heritage controls (see the discussions on the ambit of discretion earlier in this chapter and in Chapters 5 and 8). The decision guidelines in the provisions of the relevant zones and overlays for the construction and extension of one dwelling on a lot require the responsible authority to *consider* (not *apply* or *implement*) the objectives, standards and decision guidelines of cl 54.

The purpose of cl 54 includes to encourage residential development that is responsive to the site and neighbourhood. As with cll 55 and 56, Clause 54 sets out objectives (the desired outcomes to be achieved) and standards (the requirements to meet the objective), but, while a standard should be met, the clause states that, if a responsible authority is satisfied that an alternative design solution meets the objective, the alternative design solution may be considered. The requirements set out in cl 54 are that a development *must* meet all the objectives of the clause and *should* meet all the standards of the clause. Clause 54.01 imposes the requirement that a permit application must be accompanied by a neighbourhood and site description and a design response, and specifies what should be included in each. Twenty objectives and accompanying standards are set out in cl 54, dealing with such matters as impacts on neighbourhood character, overlooking, overshadowing, setbacks, site coverage, walls on boundaries, solar access to north-facing habitable room windows, and daylighting into the habitable room windows on abutting land. The standards for each of the objectives may be varied by a schedule to the zone in which the land is located or, if the land is subject to a Neighbourhood Character Overlay, by a schedule to that overlay. There is no logical reason why standards should vary across municipal boundaries – variations in standards via a schedule appear very much to be a response to local political pressure.

While the objectives must be met and the standards should be met by a proposed development, they cannot be applied in a mechanistic fashion. The objectives are statements of principle expressed in general open-ended terms. The neighbourhood character objective includes "To ensure that the design respects the existing neighbourhood character or contributes to preferred neighbourhood character". Note that the word used is *respects*, not *copy* or *replicate*. The objective for integration with the street includes "Dwellings should be designed to promote the observation of abutting streets and any abutting open space". The extent to which a proposed dwelling meets these objectives is a matter of judgement and involves a good deal of subjectivity. Similarly, the extent to which a particular standard is met may involve a subjective assessment. Standard A1, to meet the neighbourhood character objective, is "The design response must be appropriate to the neighbourhood and site. The proposed design must respect the existing or preferred neighbourhood character and respond to the features of the site". There is no objective test for "appropriate" or "respect". While each of the objectives and some of the standards of cl 54 are expressed in terms of a principle or a goal to be achieved, many of the standards are expressed in numerical terms or in such a way that they can be applied objectively, such as the standards for site coverage, street setbacks, permeability, walls on boundaries, and overlooking. For example, Standard A6 states that at least 20 per cent of the site should not be covered by impervious surfaces. But the word "should" is used here and in the other standards too, not "must". Clause 54 should not and cannot be applied in a mechanistic and formulaic manner.

ResCode, medium density development and residential buildings

Clause 55 of the VPPs superseded the *Good Design Guide for Medium Density Housing* and applies to a planning permit application to construct a dwelling if there is at least one dwelling on the lot, to construct two or more dwellings on a lot, to extend a dwelling if there are two or more dwellings on a lot, and to construct or extend a residential building in a Residential 1 Zone, a Residential 2 Zone, a Mixed Use Zone or a Township Zone. (A residential building is a backpackers' lodge, boarding house, hostel, nurses' home, nursing home, residential college or residential hotel.) In all of these zones a permit is required for such permit applications, but cl 55 is not triggered by applications to construct or extend a development of four or more storeys, excluding a basement. As with cl 54, the decision guidelines in the relevant zones require the responsible authority to *consider* cl 55 in assessing an application. For proposed residential development of four or more storeys, a November 2004 amendment to cl 19.03 of the VPPs requires that an urban context report and a design response accompany the permit application and that responsible authorities should have regard to the *Design Guidelines for Higher Density Housing* (Department of Sustainability and Environment, 2004) in assessing the design and built form aspects of the proposal.

The *Good Design Guide for Medium Density Housing* Revision No 1 1997 was incorporated into all of the VPP-based planning schemes, as was Revision 2 of April 1998. Revision 2 introduced the requirements of a site analysis and design response to accompany permit applications. The *Good Design Guide* applied, essentially, to the same sorts of applications that now trigger cl 55. Decision guidelines in the zone provisions required the responsible authority, before deciding on such applications (except applications for a development of five or more storeys, excluding a basement) to *consider* (not *apply* or *implement*) the *Good Design Guide*.

An earlier version of the *Good Design Guide* – the *Victorian Code for Residential Development – Multi Dwellings* (known as *VicCode 2*) – was incorporated into the then State section of planning schemes in 1993. *VicCode 2* was subsequently replaced by the *Good Design Guide* 1995 as an incorporated document. In determining planning permit applications for medium density development in the metropolitan area, responsible authorities were required to have regard to *VicCode 2* from 1993 and then the *Good Design Guide* from 1995. Outside the metropolitan area, responsible authorities could have regard to *VicCode 2 / Good Design Guide* but were not required to. Like the *Good Design Guide* and the *ResCode* provisions in cl 55, *VicCode 2* was aimed at not only improving the design and layout of medium density development and ensuring that the amenity impacts of medium density housing were not unreasonable but also assisting the implementation of urban consolidation policy. The introduction of the VPP-based schemes represented a significant change in that all responsible authorities were required to consider the *Good Design Guide* when determining permit application for medium density housing and residential buildings, whether or not they were in the metropolitan area.

The *ResCode* provisions in cll 54, 55 and 56 (and in the *Building Regulations*, as discussed in Chapter 2) follow the structure used in the *Good Design Guide*, which was a performance-based code dealing with elements such as privacy, overlooking and overshadowing, on-site car parking, on-site open space, building envelope, site density, site layout landscaping, dwelling entry, and neighbourhood character. For each of these elements, objectives were specified, as were criteria for achieving those objectives. The objectives specified the desired outcomes for each element to be achieved. The criteria were designed to provide a basis for judging whether the objectives had been met. A proposed development was required to be assessed against all of the criteria for each element, but it was not required to satisfy them all. The objectives and the criteria were capable of very different interpretations and did not provide any objective benchmarks for each element. However, for the elements of site density, visual and acoustic privacy, car parking and vehicle access, and private and communal open space, techniques were also specified. These techniques were benchmarks, mainly expressed in the traditional form of regulations, such as the number of car parking spaces per dwelling that should be provided, the amount of open space per dwelling to be provided, and so on. Compliance with the techniques was assumed to satisfy the relevant element objectives and criteria, so in a sense the techniques were "fall-back" standards if it could not be demonstrated by an applicant that the development would satisfy the element objectives and criteria by other means. However, the *Good Design Guide* also provided that a responsible authority could diverge from a prescribed technique (that is, impose a more stringent standard than provided for by a technique) if it believed that compliance with the technique would not satisfy the objectives and criteria of a design element.

The *ResCode* provisions at cl 55 of the VPPs set out 34 objectives and accompanying standards. The requirements set out in the clause include that a development *must* meet all the objectives of the clause and *should* meet all the standards of the clause. But, at the risk of being repetitive, we point out that these requirements sit within the context established by the decision guidelines in the relevant zones and those decision guidelines only require the responsible authority to *consider* the provisions of cl 55 before deciding on a permit application. The objectives are each expressed in terms of a principle or a goal to be achieved. Many but not all of the standards are expressed in numerical terms in such a way that they can be applied objectively, such as the standards for site coverage, street setbacks, permeability, walls on boundaries and so on. However, deciding whether an objective is achieved, or whether some standards are achieved, of necessity involves subjective assessment. This is not generally understood in the community.

Chapter 4

THE AMENDMENT OF SCHEMES

An overview of the scheme amendment process

The Minister approves and brings into effect amendments to planning schemes in Victoria. The normal process of scheme amendment prescribed by the *Planning and Environment Act 1987* is, in summary, as follows:

- initiation of the amendment;
- notification of owners and occupiers who may be affected;
- lodging of submissions by those affected;
- consideration by the planning authority of the submissions lodged;
- referral to a panel appointed by the Minister of submissions unable to be accommodated by the planning authority;
- hearing of submissions by the panel;
- consideration of the panel's report by the planning authority and adoption or abandonment of the amendment;
- if the amendment is adopted by the planning authority, consideration by the Minister, who may approve or not approve it;
- if the Minister approves the amendment, gazettal and bringing the amendment into effect.

The process is complex and is discussed in detail below. Not all these stages may occur, because the Minister has the power under s 20 to exempt a planning authority (including himself or herself) from the normal exhibition and notification requirements and approve an amendment by a notice in the *Government Gazette*.

Because the process is complex, it is all too easy to get lost in the detail and lose sight of the issue of the criteria on which decisions to adopt and approve are based. Most planners, and indeed most lawyers, would claim that the test which should be used by planning authorities in deciding whether or not to adopt, by panels in recommending whether or not planning authorities should adopt, and by the Minister in deciding whether or not to approve, is whether or not the amendment is in the public interest. The notion of the public interest could mean at least four things in this context. The first is that, ideally, the amendment is consistent with a coherent and explicit planning policy adopted by State or local governments after a process of public consultation; the second is that, ideally, it must benefit the whole community, and not just a particular individual or group of individuals; the third is that, ideally, the amendment does not cause disbenefits to either individuals or the community at large; and the fourth is that, ideally, while it may cause disbenefits to individuals, these are outweighed by the benefits that will flow to the wider community. We have used the word "ideally" because the fact of the matter is that State policies are not always coherent and are not always adopted after a consultation process and most amendments, by and large, deliver benefits to some (such as the owners of land where that land is rezoned to allow a wider range of uses and more intensive development) without delivering any immediate benefits to anyone else.

State and local planning policies are, inevitably, broad-brushed statements of intent, and, as we have seen in Chapter 3, are sometimes internally inconsistent and even contradictory (the State policy of urban consolidation is at odds with other State and local policies on heritage conservation, for example). Therefore, assessment of scheme amendments may involve integrating the range of policies relevant to the issues to be determined, and balancing conflicting objectives in favour of net community benefit and sustainable development as provided for by cl 11 of the Victoria Planning Provisions (VPPs). The extent to which consideration of State and local policies are relevant in assessing an amendment will depend on the type and scale of the amendment proposed. For an amendment involving the rezoning of a relatively small area of land, State policy, and even local policies, may not be particularly relevant.

For many amendments there is more than one public or one community to be considered, depending on the scale at which we are talking. In that sense there may be a number of public interests involved, not just one. An amendment to allow a jail or a freeway to be developed may be opposed vehemently, and with good reason, by those whose land will be acquired to accommodate the facility and by those who have to live near it. However, the wider community may be very much in favour of it, because the facility proposed will confer a perceived benefit or address a deficiency or problem. A jail, for example, may have very significant spin-offs in terms of generating local employment either directly or through contracts for providing goods and services such as food, maintenance and cleaning. A freeway may mean greater ease in commuting to work and elsewhere and may even cause property values to rise in areas that experience this benefit. In both cases, the disbenefits borne by a few may be justified in terms of the benefits conferred on a wider community.

In some instances the disbenefits may not necessarily revolve around externalities such as noise, traffic generation, smells and the like. Nor may they necessarily involve a decline in property values due to these factors. An amendment which would allow the development of suburban style housing in an area currently devoted to rural residential development may be opposed by those who currently live in the area, despite the fact that property values may rise, because it was precisely the rural residential ambience which attracted them in the first place. The fact that there may be a desperate need to provide land in the area for suburban style housing may not be a particularly compelling argument to those who are fighting to protect their lifestyle.

At the extremes we can identify what is not in the public interest, such as toxic waste dumps close to housing or the pollution of land and streams to the point where they are incapable of restoration for any sustainable use. However, many amendments (and indeed many planning permits) will not necessarily have extreme environmental, social or economic effects, and some will have a mixture of both positive and negative effects. Obviously the public interest cannot be determined on the basis of a referendum of those immediately affected by a proposed amendment (or, indeed, by a planning permit application). The mere fact that some, or even a majority, of people oppose an amendment is not sufficient reason why it should not be approved. If that were so then few scheme amendments would ever be approved and the community would be locked into the status quo of current land use and development patterns. What is in the public interest (and what will damage or diminish the public interest) must be determined on a case-by-case basis. There is no scientific method of arriving at an answer – in each case it is a matter of considered judgement. Individual beliefs, attitudes and opinions will colour that judgement. What is important is that, in the context of the process laid down by the legislation, that judgement is based on a disinterested analysis of the evidence submitted by the various parties, including the planning authority, the proponent of the amendment (if it has been initiated by someone other than the planning authority), members of the community in favour, and members of the community against.

The legislation cannot dictate the quality of submissions, nor can it ensure that decisions will always be based on the notion of the public interest, however much we may believe they should be. The decisions to place on exhibition and adopt amendments are made by the Minister or local councillors and it is the Minister who decides whether or not to approve amendments. Local councillors and the Minister are, first and foremost, politicians and are subject to the normal political imperatives. So how can legislation limit the power of whim and political expediency in the amendment process? First, it can ensure that the ambit of evidence contained in submissions and required to be taken into account by the decision-makers is not so narrowly drawn that only a limited range of issues is canvassed. Secondly, it can ensure that there is ample and equal opportunity for each party involved to make submissions. Thirdly, it can ensure that there is ample and equal opportunity for parties to challenge each other's submissions. Fourthly, it can ensure that independent advice based on dispassionate analysis of the amendment and on the evidence for and against it is available when the decisions to adopt and approve are taken. Finally, it can ensure that decision-makers bear the political consequences of decisions that are not based on that independent advice. The extent to which the *Planning and Environment Act* does these five things is a major concern of this chapter.

Amendment of the VPPs

In preparing an amendment to its scheme, a council is essentially restricted to:
- rezoning land by substituting a different State standard zone from the VPPs to the one which currently applies to the land;

- substituting a different State standard overlay from the VPPs to the one which currently applies to the land;
- introducing or amending a schedule to a State standard zone or overlay from the VPPs;
- amending its Municipal Strategic Statement (MSS) or local policies.

The question then arises as to how the VPPs may be amended. An amendment to the VPPs may be prepared at any time by the Minister or, with the authorisation of the Minister, by any other Minister, public authority, or municipal council: s 4B. Note that the authorisation of the Minister is required for the preparation of an amendment to the VPPs by anyone other than the Minister. The provisions of the Act dealing with notification, submissions, consideration of submissions, panel hearings and so on apply to an amendment to the VPPs as if such amendments were amendments to planning schemes: s 4B. However, when approving an amendment to the VPPs that the Minister has prepared, the Minister may exempt himself or herself under s 20(4) from any or all of the normal processes of notification and subsequent submission and panel hearing processes. If the amendment has been prepared by any other Minister, or by a public authority or municipal council, the Minister may exempt the amendment from the notification, submission and panel hearing processes, subject to the constraints imposed by s 20(3). The power of the Minister in relation to s 20 is discussed in more detail later in this chapter. Note that power of exemption under s 20 can be applied to all amendments, not just an amendment to the VPPs.

If the Minister does not exempt himself or herself, or any other Minister, public authority or council, from the normal notification, submission and panel hearing processes, submissions may be lodged (and must be considered) which request a change to the terms of a State standard provision: s 4B. In other words, submissions may be made about the content of the VPPs. But submissions in relation to a planning scheme amendment, as distinct from an amendment to the VPPs, are not entitled to include requests to change the terms of a State standard provision: s 21(3). Submissions to a planning scheme amendment about State standard provisions are essentially confined to whether a standard zone should be replaced by some other standard zone, whether a standard overlay should be introduced, replaced by another standard overlay or deleted, or whether a schedule to a zone or overlay should be introduced, deleted or modified.

An amendment to the VPPs may also provide for an amendment to one or more schemes: s 4J. Approval of such an amendment is deemed to be an amendment of these scheme(s). Notice of approval of such a deemed amendment is also deemed to be an amendment of the planning scheme(s). An amendment to the VPPs is a "V" amendment and is identified by the letter "V" and given an amendment number allocated by the department (for example, V1, V2 et cetera). An amendment to both the VPPs and one or more schemes is identified by the letters "VC" (VC1, VC 2 et cetera). An amendment to a planning scheme only is identified by the letter "C" (C1, C2 et cetera), with the number allocated by the municipality, whether or not it is the planning authority.

The normal scheme amendment process in detail

Initiation of the proposed amendment

As was explained in Chapter 2, s 8 of the Act empowers the Minister to prepare an amendment to any part of any planning scheme anywhere in Victoria. With the authorisation of the Minister, municipal councils may prepare amendments to the local provisions of their schemes, but such amendments are confined to the Local Planning Policy Framework (LPPF) and to replacing for areas of land zones set out in the VPPs with other zones set out in the VPPs, replacing overlays set out in the VPPs with other overlays set out in the VPPs, or including, deleting or amending schedules to these zones and overlays. Under ss 9 and 11 the Minister may authorise any other Minister or public authority to prepare an amendment to a planning scheme, but for State standard provisions this power also extends only to inclusion or deletion of a State standard provision, not to the terms of a State standard provision: s 10.

There is no procedure specified in the Act for the private sector to apply for scheme amendments. The Act implies that amendments will be policy driven – that they will be initiated by planning authorities on the basis of their own strategic planning. In fact, many amendments are initiated by the private sector, by developers large and small who seek amendments, such as rezonings, and convince the relevant council or the Minister to place an amendment on exhibition. This involves lobbying the local council and may also involve lobbying the Minister. The effect of the amendment sought may be to allow a permit to be applied for and considered for use and development prohibited under the current scheme provisions, or for a use and development to proceed as of right, or as of right provided specified conditions are met. Where the amendment sought is to allow use and development to proceed as of right (that is, without a planning permit), or as of right provided certain specified conditions are met, the effect of the amendment, if approved, is the same as granting planning permission.

While the Act does not contain formal procedures for developers or any other private person to apply for a scheme amendment, s 203 recognises that in fact the initiation of the amendment process may be the result of representations to the relevant planning authority or to the Minister. Section 203(1)(c), introduced via the *Planning and Environment (Amendment) Act 1989*, provides for the Governor in Council to make regulations prescribing fees for consideration of amendments to planning schemes. These fees may be charged for, but are not limited to, considering a proposal for an amendment, any stage in the amendment process, and considering whether or not to approve an amendment. The process of scheme amendment imposes a cost on planning authorities and the Department of Sustainability and Environment. Apart from amendments where exemption from the normal process is granted under s 20, the requirements of notification and panel hearing are two significant sources of cost. Where an amendment has been placed on public exhibition as a result of representations from the private sector, there is nothing intrinsically wrong with recouping those costs by fees, just as there is nothing wrong with levying fees under s 203(1) for considering applications for permits. However, unlike the permit process, where applicants and third parties have the right to seek review by the Victorian Civil and Administrative Tribunal (VCAT) of decisions of the responsible authority (provided, of course, that the scheme provisions do not exempt the proposed use and/or development from the normal notification, objection and review processes, or that the Minister does not "call in" the permit application, or that the Minister does not "call in" the application for review), there is no opportunity for review by VCAT of the merits of a proposed amendment. Reviews in relation to amendments are confined essentially to matters of procedure rather than substance. In other words, the merits or otherwise of proposed amendments cannot be the subject of a review proceeding (see later in this chapter).

Before the advent of the VPP-based schemes, the introduction of fees for scheme amendments may well have encouraged planning authorities to exhibit site-specific amendments, particularly where schemes did not contain a strategic basis in the form of land use and development policies and zone objectives. There was a danger that such amendments would be exercises in *ad hockery*, for, in the absence of a policy base, panels and the Minister tended to consider each amendment in isolation and in a policy vacuum, potentially leading to a situation where the provisions of schemes could become littered with exceptions, perhaps to the point where they made a nonsense of providing any certainty to developers and the community about what may and may not be developed in any area. The VPP-based planning schemes require a much more developed policy base than was formerly the case, particularly via MSSs and local policies in the LPPF. The system of State standard provisions does not necessarily prevent site-specific rezonings occurring, but it does make them much more difficult to justify and much less likely to occur. That is not to say that site-specific amendments are always inappropriate, because they may be necessary deal with drafting errors, rectify anomalies, or alleviate inequitable situations. At the time the VPP-based planning schemes were put in place they were not seen or used as an alternative means of securing planning consent for use and development prohibited under scheme provisions that would otherwise apply. That appears to have changed – site-specific amendments are now not uncommon.

Notification and exhibition of scheme amendments

Authorisation must be given in writing by the Minister for another Minister, public authority or council to prepare a planning scheme amendment: s 11. The Minister's authorisation must state whether the planning authority is also authorised to approve the amendment under s 35B or whether the amendment must be submitted to the Minister for approval under s 31. The Minister cannot authorise a planning authority to approve an amendment under s 35B if it is an amendment to a metropolitan fringe planning scheme that inserts or amends an urban growth boundary, has the effect of altering or removing controls on the subdivision of any Green Wedge land to allow the land to be subdivided into more lots or lots smaller than allowed for in the planning scheme, or if the amendment is to be considered concurrently with an application for permit under Division 5 of Part 4 (see later in this chapter).

The authorisation provisions were introduced into the Act by the *Planning and Environment (General Amendment) Act 2004*.

The second reading speech on the Planning and Environment (General Amendment) Bill 2004 stated that these provisions would ensure that a proposed amendment is assessed against State policy before it can be prepared and that, where an amendment is of local significance only, a simplified approval process will occur. It was stated that the ability for a planning authority to approve an amendment if authorised by the Minister would remove an unnecessary stage in the amendment process and would allow quicker approvals for about two-thirds of planning scheme amendments every year. Well, it all depends on what "quick" and "quicker" mean. It is not uncommon for relatively small and uncomplicated amendments to take up to two years from initiation to approval and gazettal.

Unless an exemption is granted by the Minister under s 20, it is mandatory under s 19(1) for the planning authority to give notice of its preparation of an amendment. Those who must be notified by the planning authority are:

- every Minister, public authority and municipal council it believes may be materially affected;
- the owners and occupiers of land it believes may be materially affected;
- any Minister, public authority, municipal council or person prescribed (under reg 7 of the *Planning and Environment Regulations 2005*, those prescribed are any municipal council where it is not the planning authority and the amendment affects land within its municipal district for which it is responsible, the Minister administering the *Conservation, Forests and Lands Act 1987*, the Minister administering the *Catchment Land Protection Act 1994*, the Minister administering the *Sustainable Resources (Timber) Act 2004*, the Minister administering the *Mineral Resources Development Act 1990*, the Minister administering the *Extractive Industries Development Act 1995*, and the Minister administering the *Pipelines Act 1967*;
- the Minister administering the *Land Act 1958*, if the amendment provides for the closure of a road wholly or partly on Crown land.

In addition, the planning authority must publish notice of a proposed amendment in a newspaper generally circulating in the area and in the *Government Gazette*: s 19(2) and (3). Regulation 9 of the *Planning and Environment Regulations 2005* requires the notice given under s 19 to give the title of the amendment, give a brief description of the effect of the amendment, give a general description of the land affected, state where the amendment may be inspected and give the name and address of the planning authority for the receipt of submissions. Under s 19(4) the closing date for submissions is at least one month from the date on which the notice appeared in the *Government Gazette*. This notice must be published on the same day as the last of the notices given under s 19, or after all other notices have been given, to ensure that those who have been notified have at least one month in which to lodge a submission.

The purpose of notification is to inform people of what the proposed amendment is about and their right to make a submission if they see fit. How well does it do that?

Sometimes it does it well and sometimes not at all well. Owners and occupiers the planning authority believes may be materially affected include at least the owners and occupiers of land that is the subject of the proposed amendment and may also include the owners and occupiers of adjacent and nearby land. If the amendment may affect a large number of owners and occupiers, the planning authority is not required to give notice individually to them if it considers the number affected makes it impractical to do so, in which case the newspaper notice is crucially important, as are other actions the planning authority may take to ensure that people are informed that an amendment has been prepared: s 19(1A) and (B). The newspaper notice has its limitations, but it can have the effect of informing a wider community. What is crucial is the wording of the statement included in the notice explaining the effect of the amendment and in the documents available for inspection at the places specified in the notice. Planning authorities often lose sight of the fact that the proposed amendment itself will be all but incomprehensible to most people. On the whole planning authorities, particularly councils, do a good job in ensuring that documents are displayed for inspection and are not just available on request, and in notifying as widely as possible. Section 19(7) specifically provides for a planning authority to "take any other steps it thinks necessary to tell anyone who may be affected by the amendment about its preparation". However, much more could be done in providing explanatory statements that express the effect of proposed amendments in terms understood by the lay person.

The lodging and consideration of submissions

Any person may make a submission under s 21. In other words, people other than those who were notified under s 21 have the right to make a submission, which may oppose or support the amendment. Joint submissions are provided for by s 21A so that a number of people may make one submission. It is common for petition-style submissions signed by a large number of people to be lodged either in favour or in opposition to an amendment. Note that no-one is entitled to make a submission which requests a change to the terms of any State standard provision to be included in the planning scheme, but anyone is entitled to make a submission which requests that a State standard provision be included in or deleted from the scheme: s 21. Aside from that, the Act is silent on the grounds of support or objection that may be included in a submission and which therefore must be considered by the planning authority and any subsequent panel. However, the objectives of planning in Victoria contained in s 4(1) and the objectives of the planning framework established by the Act contained in s 4(2) imply that the grounds may be very broad. This is supported by s 12(2), which deals with the matters to which a planning authority is to have regard to in preparing a scheme or scheme amendment. Under s 12(2)(b) a planning authority must take into account any significant effects the scheme or amendment might have on the environment, or which it considers the environment may have on any use or development envisaged by the scheme or amendment. Under s 12(2)(c) the planning authority may also take into account the social and economic effects of a scheme or amendment. While the Act says a planning authority "may" take into account social and economic effects, planning authorities may not simply decide that they will not take such matters into account. The inclusion of s 12(2)(c) in the Act is to ensure that the consideration of economic and social effects of an amendment is valid if the use or development envisaged by the scheme or amendment is likely to have such effects. An amendment to allow the establishment of a regional shopping centre, for example, would clearly have social and economic effects and these must be taken into account. How significant those effects are likely to be and therefore how much weight should be placed on these effects in assessing submissions is a matter that the planning authority and any subsequent panel would need to establish.

The relevance of the social and economic effects of a proposal that is the subject of a planning permit application is discussed in Chapter 5. Rarely will the economic or social effects of a proposal be relevant to the consideration of a planning permit. Responsible authorities, in exercising their powers of discretion in relation to planning permit applications, are not concerned with regulating economic competition. Responsible authorities administer planning scheme provisions that have been approved by the Minister and gazetted. Planning authorities, in a sense, are advising the Minister as to what those planning provisions should be. In coming to a conclusion about what planning policies and controls on shopping centres should be included in a planning scheme, it is appropriate for the planning authority to consider the strategic implications, for example, of the development of out-of-town shopping centres on the central business district of a regional centre. In doing so the planning authority is not considering the economic competition between individual businesses but whether the impact of proposed new centres would lead to unacceptable vacancy rates, underutilisation of land and underutilisation of existing infrastructure, and would have undesirable impacts in terms of lengthening journeys to shop. These are essentially community impacts, as distinct from the impact of one business on another. They are valid considerations for a planning authority to take into account in deciding whether a planning scheme amendment should be supported or not. But taking into account the economic impact on an existing business of a proposed new business which is the subject of a planning permit application is a different matter – economic impacts of that sort are normally not able to be validly considered by responsible authorities. (See "The social and economic effects of a proposal" in Chapter 5.)

A submission to an amendment will only be relevant if it raises planning issues and is related to the amendment. It must be about the amendment if it is to be considered: s 21(1). Having said that, the potential scope of submissions set by ss 4 and 6 are broad. Depending on the specific amendment, submissions dealing with air quality; noise; flora and fauna; water quality; drainage; soil contamination; soil erosion and land degradation; landscaping; visual environment and aesthetics; buildings and sites of historical, architectural or archaeological interest; compatibility with urban conservation zones; traffic generation and management; and parking may be relevant. Again, depending on the specific amendment, submissions dealing with the need for and access to community facilities and services, providing greater or lesser choice in housing, shopping, recreational and leisure services, may be relevant, as may submissions dealing with the generation or reduction of employment opportunities; the supply and demand in the local area for whatever is being proposed; the multiplier effects on the local economy; access to facilities, services and employment opportunities; choice and affordability of goods and services; and the use of existing urban infrastructure.

Submissions should be as explicit and as detailed as possible. If a number of people are affected by an amendment they should consider as a group engaging a lawyer or town planner to prepare and lodge a joint submission on their behalf. There is no set format for a submission, but it should:

- identify the amendment it refers to by specifying the amendment number;
- explain how the amendment will affect the submittor and why the submittor supports or opposes it;
- state whether the submittor would like the planning authority to abandon, adopt or modify the amendment (modification may include excluding certain land from the amendment, for example);
- provide the submittor's name, address and contact telephone number(s);
- if the submission is made jointly on behalf of a number of people, specify a representative or spokesperson for the group to whom notices (such as notice of a subsequent panel hearing) may be sent.

The planning authority must make a copy of each submission lodged with it available for any member of the public to inspect: s 21(2).

Submissions lodged on or before the date set out in the notice given under s 19 must be considered by the planning authority: s 22(1). However, the planning authority must not consider a submission which requests a change in the terms of any State standard provision to be included in the planning scheme: s 22. Late submissions may be considered, and must be considered if the Minister so directs: s 22(2). But there is no guarantee that a late submission will be considered – so get your submission in on time! After considering submissions, the planning authority must accommodate them by changing the amendment, or it must abandon the amendment, or it must refer the submissions to a panel: s 23. As in most instances, some submissions will support the amendment and others will oppose it – the planning authority has little choice but to refer them to a panel if it wishes to proceed to the next stage of the process.

Some planning authorities arrange public meetings either before or during the exhibition stage. This enables the amendment to be explained and for the planning authority and the proponent, if there is one, to respond to any concerns that people have. This at least ensures that there will be fewer submissions based on a misunderstanding of what the effect of the amendment is likely to be. Some planning authorities also give a hearing to submittors as part of the consideration stage, although they are under no obligation to do so. This often has the effect of reassuring submittors that their concerns have been listened to, provides the planning authority with an opportunity to correct misunderstandings about the amendment, and may result in the withdrawal of objecting submissions. However, this type of community consultation is the exception rather than the norm.

Panel hearing

If a planning authority cannot accommodate all submissions by changing the amendment and it does not wish to abandon the amendment, it must refer the submissions to a panel of one or three persons appointed by the Minister. Planning Panels Victoria is the management body for panels appointed under s 153 to hear submissions in relation to planning scheme amendments and report to the planning authority. Panellists are drawn from a pool of full-time and sessional members with expertise in planning and related disciplines. The functions of a panel are to provide submittors with an opportunity to appear in person and have their submissions heard and considered by a body independent of the planning authority, and to provide independent advice to the planning authority and the Minister about the amendment and the submissions referred to it. The panel provides advice – it may recommend that an amendment be abandoned, modified or adopted, but it is a recommendation only. Mind you, the panel's advice must be made public, so its recommendations carry a good deal of weight, even if only in the political sense.

It should be noted that Planning Panels Victoria is also the management body for advisory committees and other panels appointed or established by the Minister, such as those appointed under the *Environment Effects Act*, and advisory committees established by the Minister under s 151 of the *Planning and Environment Act*, such as the Central City Standing Advisory Committee (to advise the Minister on planning permit applications for which the Minister is the responsible authority in the City of Melbourne), panels appointed by the Minister on permit applications which have been "called in" by the Minister pursuant to ss 97A–97M (see Chapter 2), and committees appointed by the Minster to advise on applications for review "called in" by the Minister pursuant to cll 58 and 59 of Schedule 1 to the *Victorian Civil and Administrative Tribunal Act 1998* (see Chapters 2 and 6).

Section 23(c) provides that a planning authority may refer to a panel submissions that do not require a change to the amendment, which would include those submissions in favour. It is usual for all submissions to be referred, including those which do not oppose and those which support the proposed amendment. The panel must consider all submissions referred to it and give a reasonable opportunity to be heard to any person who has made a submission which has been referred to it: s 24(a). Submittors may appear in person and be heard, or may engage lawyers, town planners or other persons to represent them: s 162. If a large number of submittors wishes to be heard, on the first day of the hearing the panel will arrange a timetable. Section 159 provides that a panel may give directions about the times and places of hearings, matters preliminary to hearings and the conduct of hearings. A panel may refuse to hear any person who does not comply with a direction given under s 159.

Panels have the power to enforce their own directions. Under s 169 any person who, without lawful excuse, disobeys a direction of a panel is guilty of an offence and is liable to a penalty of up to 60 penalty units (currently, approximately $7,200). Other offences attracting a fine of up to this amount are also created by this section. A person who insults, assaults or obstructs either a panel member while that member is performing functions or exercising powers as such, or any other person attending a hearing, is guilty of an offence. A person who "misbehaves at a hearing before a panel or without lawful excuse repeatedly interrupts a hearing before a panel" is also guilty of an offence. What constitutes misbehaviour is not specified.

Under s 161(5), submissions and evidence may be given to the panel orally, in writing, or partly orally and partly in writing. One of the matters that panels are frequently required to give directions on is the exchange of documents before the commencement of the hearing. It is relatively common for representatives of parties, particularly proponents, to make very detailed written submissions and to call expert witnesses who table and speak to highly technical reports. As a requirement of natural justice, all parties must be given reasonable opportunity to digest witness reports and other reports and prepare questions and counter-submissions. If it is discovered that expert witness submissions and supporting documents have not been exchanged between parties, this may lead to adjournments, delay and a great deal of inconvenience, not only for proponents who may be carrying high holding charges and costs but also for submittors, who have often made arrangements at their place of work or with child minding so that they can attend the hearing. A panel may report and make recommendations on a submission without hearing the person who made the submission if the person is not present or not represented at the time and place appointed for the hearing of the submission: s 163.

As noted above, a primary function of a panel is, having heard submissions, to provide disinterested or dispassionate advice in the form of a report to the planning authority and to the Minister as to whether or not an amendment should be adopted in part or whole, or abandoned. Under s 25, the Act only requires that a report be prepared – there is no mandatory requirement for the report to contain recommendations, although it is difficult to see how a panel could discharge its responsibilities without giving advice in the form of recommendations. Therefore in practice reports do contain recommendations. It is up to the planning authority whether or not it accepts this advice, but a copy of the panel's report must be forwarded to the Minister at a later stage in the process (see s 31 of the Act and reg 10 of the *Planning and Environment Regulations 2005*) and it is the Minister who decides whether or not an amendment should be approved. Section 26 also requires the panel's report to be made available for public inspection no later than 28 days after it has been received by the planning authority, so the planning authority must bear the political consequences of not taking advice if it decides to adopt an amendment contrary to the recommendation of the panel. So must the Minister, if he or she approves and gazettes an amendment contrary to the panel's advice.

A panel is required under s 24 to give a reasonable opportunity to be heard to any person who has made a submission referred to it, the planning authority, any responsible authority or municipal council concerned, any regional planning authority concerned, and any person whom the Minister or the planning authority directs it to hear. A panel can refuse to consider a submission referred to it (or part of a submission) if the submission (or the part of it) is irrelevant to the amendment and it can refuse to give a submittor an opportunity to be heard if the submittor seeks to advance a submission which is irrelevant to the amendment: *Australian Conservation Foundation v Minister for Planning* [2004] VCAT 2029. However, as was noted above, the terms of ss 4 and 6 of the Act are such that the scope of matters with which a submission may deal and remain relevant is broad. In the *Australian Conservation Foundation* case, which arose as a result of a referral to VCAT pursuant to s 39 of the Act, a panel had been appointed pursuant to both the *Planning and Environment Act* and *Environment Effects Act* to hear submissions to a scheme amendment to facilitate the continued operation of the Hazelwood Power Station in the Latrobe Valley. The Minister's terms of reference for the panel directed that it not consider matters relating to greenhouse gas emissions from the power station. Morris J held that the amendment, if approved, would make it more probable that the power station will continue to operate beyond 2009, which in turn may make it more likely that the atmosphere will continue to receive more greenhouse gas emissions than would otherwise be the case, which may be an environmental effect of significance; that the panel failed to consider submissions to that effect; and that the Minister had no power to issue terms of reference to a panel in relation to its duty to consider submissions about an amendment to a planning scheme.

The normal procedure is for the planning authority to be heard first. The representative of the planning authority outlines the background to the amendment, details the notification that was undertaken, summarises the submissions that were lodged, and indicates why the planning authority either accepted or rejected the submissions. If there is a proponent of the amendment (that is, the amendment was placed on exhibition at the request of someone other than the planning authority) then the proponent is heard next. It is normal for proponents to be represented by lawyers or consulting town planners, and, depending on the complexity of the amendment, for expert witnesses to be called. While in theory there is ample and equal opportunity for all parties to test each other's evidence to the panel through cross-examination of expert witnesses, unrepresented submittors are usually unfamiliar with the technique of questioning and may be intimidated by the often large array of professionals assembled by proponents. Submittors are heard next and may themselves call expert witnesses. Finally, the proponent and/or the planning authority sums up the points raised and attempts to address the issues raised by submittors, particularly objecting submittors. It should be noted that, depending on the nature of the amendment, the complexity of the issues raised and the number of submittors involved, panel hearings may go on for weeks.

Submittors do not always appreciate that all of the submissions referred to it by the planning authority have been read by the panel before the hearing commences. If the amendment applies to a specific site or specific area, in many instances the panel will also have conducted a field inspection. If it has not conducted a field inspection, it will certainly do so during the hearing, or after the hearing has finished. While the panel will normally explain that it has examined all submissions referred to it, this does not always prevent people from trying to read out what has already been read by the panel. Emotions do sometimes run high and submittors often feel that they should have their day in court (as it were), even if what they wish to say is identical to what they have already said in their original written submissions, or identical to what a large number of other people have said or wish to say. The advice contained in a panel's report will depend on the merits of the case, not on the number of people who oppose or support the amendment.

Using Victoria's Planning System (available at <www.dpcd.vic.gov.au>) contains some useful hints for the presentation of a submission to a panel, including avoiding repeating points made by others, ensuring that the submission relates to planning matters, and providing the panel member(s), the planning authority, and the proponent of the amendment, if there is one, with copies of both the submission itself and any documents referred to in it. If the oral submission is essentially the same as the written submission considered by the planning authority, the oral submission should be in the form of a summary.

Under s 161(1), panels are required to act according to equity and good conscience without regard to technicalities or legal forms, are bound by the rules of natural justice, are not required to conduct hearings in a formal manner, and are not bound by the rules of evidence. They may regulate their own proceedings: s 167. Panel proceedings are essentially adversarial in nature and it is common for planning authorities and proponents to be represented by lawyers or town planners. It is also becoming common for other submittors, particularly objecting submittors, to be represented, but many objecting submittors are not represented, doubtless because of cost. If submittors (particularly objecting submittors) are not highly organised, or are not represented, they are often at a disadvantage at a panel hearing. As noted above, they usually lack the skills to effectively cross-examine expert witnesses called on behalf of proponents, and they also usually lack the finances to call their own expert witnesses. Where a hearing lasts for a long time, it may not be possible for many submittors to attend for any more than one or two days, simply because of work and other commitments. In these circumstances, rebutting the evidence submitted on behalf of proponents becomes very difficult. However, panels are not passive in the sense that they must rely only on the submissions put to them. Under s 161(1)(d) a panel is not bound by the rules of evidence but may inform itself on any matter in any way it thinks fit and without notice to any person who has made a submission. Under s 168 a panel may take into account any matter it thinks relevant in making its report and recommendations. These two sections provide a solid foundation for a panel to question the planning authority, the proponent, submittors and expert witnesses and so establish the nature of the amendment and its effects. A panel has a duty to satisfy itself of the nature of the amendment and the effects it will have if it is approved: *Porchester Nominees Pty Ltd v William Renfrey* (1987) 1 AATR 79.

Under s 160, hearings must be conducted in public unless a submittor objects on the ground of confidentiality and the panel is satisfied that the submission is of a confidential nature. The authors are not aware of the public ever being excluded from a panel hearing on the basis of the confidentiality of a submission. As hearings are

[Margin note: natural justice?]

bound by the rules of natural justice under s 161(1)(b), it is doubtful if other parties to a hearing could be excluded on the grounds of confidentiality, and, where there may be literally hundreds of submittors as parties, to all and intents and purposes they are the general public.

While panel hearings are not required to be conducted in a formal manner, it is sometimes very difficult to avoid formalities and at the same time conform to the rules of natural justice. Submittors must be given reasonable opportunity to be heard and the testing of evidence by cross-examination of expert witnesses called by the various parties is normally an essential component of natural justice. However, under s 161(3) a panel may prohibit or regulate cross-examination in any hearing. It may not decide before the hearing commences that no witnesses will be cross-examined: *R v King; Ex parte Westfield Corporation (Vic) Ltd* (1981) 2 PABR 268. However, cross-examination is regulated in the sense that lawyers and other professionals may be directed to modify their style of questioning of expert witnesses. The vigorous and even abrasive questioning of witnesses that can occur in a court of law is not appropriate in a panel hearing.

A panel may consist of one or more persons. As panels are subject to the rules of natural justice, great care must be exercised to ensure that not only are panel members not biased but also that a reasonable person could not conclude that they are biased. Where an amendment is to allow the development of a commercial enterprise, such as a shopping centre, it may well be in the financial interests of competitors to delay the process of amendment for as long as possible. One way of achieving a delay is to have a Supreme Court challenge to the panel hearing upheld on the grounds that one or more of the panel members is biased. "In assessing the likelihood of compromise or bias, the test is that of what a reasonable man would perceive to be the fairness or otherwise of the procedures in question", said Nathan J in delivering judgement in *ACT Nominees v Morrison* (1984) 2 PABR 366. In this case it was held that a panel member was biased because she had retained on another matter counsel who appeared before her representing one of the parties to the panel hearing. In the same case, one of the other panel members was alleged to be biased in that he winked and made facial expressions of a familiar kind to one of the contending counsel. But Nathan J was satisfied, having read the transcript of the hearing and the panel member's response to the question that was put to him at the time, that the allegation was not sustained.

Obviously, if a panel member or one of his or her immediate family owned or had an interest in property affected by an amendment, a reasonable person would conclude that there was a likelihood of bias. But there are other instances where the issue of bias may occur, such as panel members speaking to one party to a hearing in the absence of other parties, and conducting site inspections in the company of only one party. Panel members must be meticulous in their conduct to ensure the issue does not arise.

In *TJ Love v Whittlesea Shire Council* (2001) 7 VPR 268, which, like the *Australian Conservation Foundation* case, resulted from a referral to VCAT pursuant to s 39 of the Act, the issues of bias and denial of natural justice were considered in relation to a panel member's decision to refuse an adjournment requested by a submittor. Mr Love owned land adjacent to a former tip site that was to be rezoned from Public Park and Recreation to Industrial 1. His submission to the council as the planning authority for the amendment was that the former tip site land was unsuitable for industrial use due to drainage and leachate impacts on his land and nearby land, including the Merri Creek. At the directions hearing before the commencement of the panel hearing, he requested an adjournment because he was awaiting a decision on a freedom of information request on the Environment Protection Authority (EPA) to provide reports on investigations it had conducted on the former tip site. He submitted to the panel member that the information requested of the EPA was necessary for him to brief an expert environmental witness on whose evidence he could rely at the panel hearing. The panel member declined to grant an adjournment, ruling that the EPA information was not relevant to the rezoning of the land. The Tribunal held that, because the amendment would provide automatic use rights and limit third party rights, and because the planning authority was the proponent of the amendment, the desire of Mr Love to place environmental evidence before the panel was entirely reasonable. The Tribunal declared that Mr Love was not afforded natural justice under s 161(1)(b) of the Act and that the decision of the panel regarding the relevance of the evidence which he intended to call would give rise to an apprehension of bias in the mind of a reasonable and fair-minded observer. The Tribunal ordered that the panel be reconstituted and that the panel hearing not commence until after the EPA provided Mr Love with the relevant documents.

It sometimes becomes clear during the course of a panel hearing that the planning authority has not complied with the procedures specified in the Act in relation to the preparation and notification of the amendment. Section 166 provides that in these circumstances a panel may continue to hear submissions and make its report, or, if it thinks that the non-compliance has been substantial, adjourn the hearing and make an interim report. Such a report may recommend that the planning authority give notice to a specified person or body.

Adoption, approval and gazettal

Section 27(1) requires the planning authority to consider the panel's report before deciding whether or not to adopt the amendment. However, this requirement is modified by s 27(2) and (3), both of which were introduced into the Act by the *Planning and Environment (Amendment) Act 1989*. Under s 27(2) the Minister may exempt a planning authority from considering the report if it has not been received within six months of the panel's appointment or within three months of the completion of the hearing, whichever is earlier. One would hope that planning authorities would never be able to claim exemption on this basis. Section 27(3) provides that the Minister may exempt a planning authority from considering a panel's report if the Minister considers that delay in considering whether or not to adopt the amendment would adversely affect the planning of the area. The Minister may impose conditions to which the exemption is subject.

Assuming that an exemption has not been granted under s 27, the planning authority is required to consider the panel's report and then may decide to adopt the amendment in part or whole, modify it, or abandon it: s 29. If the planning authority decides to abandon the proposed amendment, it must, under s 28, inform the Minister in writing. For a municipal council, adoption would require a formal resolution to that effect: s 188(2)(a). Note that an adopted amendment has legal status in that under s 84B(1)(f) of the *Planning and Environment Act 1987*, VCAT is required, in determining an application for review, to have regard to any scheme or amendment adopted by the relevant planning authority but not yet approved by the Minister. Following adoption, the proposed amendment must be submitted to the Minister with the prescribed information: s 31. Regulation 10 of the *Planning and Environment Regulations 2005* details this prescribed information, which includes the reasons for the amendment, copies of submissions on the amendment received by the planning authority, the panel's report (if a panel was appointed), and a description of, and reasons for, changes made to the amendment before adoption.

Panel reports are required to be made public under s 26. The report must be made available for inspection free of charge during office hours within 28 days of the planning authority receiving it, but, if the planning authority decides whether or not to adopt the amendment within a shorter period of time, it must be made available forthwith. Once made available for inspection, it must be kept available for two months after the amendment comes into operation or lapses: s 26(2). The requirement to make the report public applies even if an exemption is granted under s 27(2) or (3). This is potentially embarrassing for the planning authority and the Minister if the decision to adopt or not adopt in the absence of the report is at variance with, or even in contradiction to, the recommendations contained in the report. So they should be embarrassed, and even more so than if the report had been considered and the decision to adopt or not adopt ran counter to its recommendations.

If a planning authority has been authorised pursuant to s 11 to approve an amendment, it must not do so until the amendment has been certified by the Secretary to the Department as being in an appropriate form: s 35A(2). Before certifying, the Secretary may require any changes that are necessary to ensure that it is in an appropriate form: s 35A(3). An amendment for which authorisation to approve has not been given pursuant to s 11(1), or for which authorisation was given and then subsequently withdrawn pursuant to s 11(2), must be forwarded to the Minister for approval. The Minister may, under s 35(1), approve the amendment in whole or part, or subject to such conditions as the Minister wishes to impose. The Minister may also refuse to approve. The power of the Minister is limited by s 35(4), which requires that approval must not occur without the consent of "a Minister prescribed under s 19, if that Minister so requires for a prescribed reason; or the Minister administering the *Road Management Act 1983*, if the amendment or part provides for the closure of a freeway or an arterial road declared road within the meaning of that Act". Prescribed

Ministers are those who are required to be notified of the preparation of a proposed amendment at the beginning of the formal scheme amendment process, and are listed in reg 8 of the *Planning and Environment Regulations 2005*. Prescribed reasons are listed in reg 13 of the Regulations and include that the amendment:

- may unreasonably prejudice the use or development of land owned, controlled or managed by the Minister administering the *Conservation, Forests and Land Act 1987*;
- may unreasonably prejudice the most suitable use of land in the public interest, for which there is a special area plan under the *Catchment and Land Protection Act 1994*;
- may unreasonably prejudice the use or development of land for timber production; and
- may unreasonably prejudice the exploration or the use and development of land for mining purposes under the *Mineral Resources Development Act 1990*.

The test of what may constitute "unreasonably prejudice" seems to be at the discretion of the Minister concerned and, in the event of a conflict with the Minister for Planning and Community Development, the matter is presumably resolved at cabinet level.

Before making a decision to approve or not approve an amendment, the Minister may, under s 32, direct the planning authority to give more notice of it if the Minister thinks the notice given was inadequate, even if the planning authority complied with all the notification requirements of s 19. This would set in train a rerun of the process, involving consideration of submissions, panel hearing, adoption and resubmission to the Minister: ss 33–34.

A proposed amendment may be altered by the planning authority after considering submissions and the panel's report. The Minister may, after it has been forwarded for approval, also wish to alter it, perhaps as part of the process of securing the consent of other Ministers under s 35(4). The issue arises of providing opportunity for persons affected (including proponents as well as objectors) to make submissions to a proposed amendment which has been modified substantially from what was placed on public exhibition at the start of the process. Section 33 allows the Minister to direct the planning authority to give notice of any changes and s 34(1) provides that the Minister *may* allow any person to make a submission, but this time to the Minister, not the planning authority. Section 34(2) provides that the Minister *may* refer such submissions to a panel, which is required to hear any person who made a submission. The panel reports to the Minister and must set out in its report recommendations on the changes. Note that there is no guarantee that modifications, even substantial modifications, will result in a second round of submissions and modifications. It is up to the Minister to allow submissions under s 34(1) and, even if submissions are allowed, it is again a matter of Ministerial discretion as to whether or not submissions are referred to a panel.

There are potential problems that may arise in relation to the powers of the Minister to make last-minute changes to a proposed amendment. It may well be that attempts are made to influence the Minister through lobbying, using arguments such as the potential employment that may flow if the amendment is approved, or pointing to the potential revenue that may be generated for the State Government. The Minister may place much more weight on these arguments than may be placed by a planning authority or a panel. There is also the issue of equal access to the Minister – it is unlikely, for example, that objecting submittors who are ordinary members of a community could secure the same level of access as a proponent company which also happens to be a significant contributor to the State economy.

For amendments which have been approved by the Minister, or approved by a planning authority authorised to do so, the Minister must publish notice of approval in the *Government Gazette*, specifying the place or places at which persons may inspect the amendment: s 36(1). The planning authority must give notice of approval in a manner satisfactory to the Minister: s 36(2). Usually this means a notice in one or more newspapers circulating in the area; there is no requirement that those who made submissions must be notified. An amendment comes into force on the date on which the notice of approval was published in the *Government Gazette*, or on any other later date specified in that notice: s 37. The date is important for establishing existing use rights (see Chapter 3). It is also important in another context too – the scheme provisions VCAT is required to take into account under s 84B when determining review proceedings are the provisions in force at the time of the determination, not the provisions that applied at the time the application was made, nor at the time the application was determined by the responsible authority: *Ungar v City of Malvern* [1979] VR 259.

Section 38 requires the Minister to lay a notice of approval of an amendment, including an amendment approved by a planning authority pursuant to s 35B, before each House of the Victorian Parliament within 10 sitting days of it being approved. The amendment may be revoked in whole or part by either House within 10 sitting days after the notice has been laid. Revocation automatically restores those provisions of the scheme that the amendment replaced.

The Growth Areas Authority and amendments which include precinct structure plans in the Urban Growth Zone

The Growth Areas Authority (GAA) was established in 2006 and is the planning authority for the preparation of precinct structure plans for land in the Urban Growth Zone, which applies to land within the metropolitan growth boundary identified as growth areas in the municipalities of Cardinia, Casey, Hume, Melton, Mitchell, Whittlesea and Wyndham: see ss 46AO and 46AP.

The GAA's members are appointed by the Governor in Council on the recommendation of the Minister. Its functions are set out at s 46AS of the Act, and include the co-ordination of development, infrastructure and services provision in growth areas. The GAA may do all of the things that are necessary or convenient to enable it to perform its functions and achieve its objectives: s 46AT.

The principal mechanism now for identifying urban growth areas is the Urban Growth Zone, included in the VPPs by Amendment VC60 in 2009. The purpose of the zone includes to manage the transition of non-urban land into urban land in accordance with a precinct structure plan; to provide for a range of uses and the development of land in accordance with a precinct structure plan; to contain urban use and development to areas identified for urban development in a precinct structure plan; and to provide for the continued non-urban use of the land until urban development in accordance with a precinct structure plan occurs. Approved precinct structure plans are included as incorporated documents in the relevant planning schemes. They are prepared as amendments to the relevant schemes and are normally subject to the processes for scheme amendment discussed in Chapter 4 (notification, exhibition, lodging of submissions, panel hearing et cetera.). However, by virtue of s 20 the Minister has the power to exempt himself or herself, or other planning authorities, for these normal processes.

The GAA is the planning authority for the preparation of precinct structure plans. Their preparation, of necessity, involves consultation with and participation by the relevant municipal councils and government agencies. Once a precinct structure plan has been approved and included as an incorporated document in a planning scheme, a permit application for a use and/or development which is generally in accordance with it is exempt from the normal notice requirements pursuant to s 52(1)(a), and any person who becomes aware of the application being lodged, even though it has not been given notice, has no right to seek review of a decision to grant the permit pursuant to s 82(1).

The lapsing of an amendment

Section 84B of the *Planning and Environment Act* lists the matters to which VCAT is required to have regard when determining an application for review. The list includes s 84B(1)(f), which requires VCAT to have regard to any planning scheme or amendment adopted by a planning authority but not, as on the date on which the review proceeding is determined, approved by the Minister. In addition, s 84B(2) states that the matters listed in s 84B(1) are in addition to any other matters which the person or body in respect of whose decision gave rise to the appeal could properly take account of or have regard to in making its decision. One of those matters is a proposed amendment, even if it has not yet been adopted by the planning authority. For many years the courts have held that the existence of a "seriously entertained planning proposal" is an important circumstance to be taken into account in the exercise of planning discretion: *Coty (England) Pty Ltd v Sydney City Council* (1957) 2 LGRA 117. There are numerous instances where VCAT and its predecessors have followed this principle: see, for example *Lyndale & Black Pty Ltd v MMBW* (1983) 7 APA 470; 1 PABR 207; *Allen v Shire of Barrabool* (1984) 16 APA 361; *Analed v Shire of Melton* (1994) 12 AATR 249; and *Fitzwood v City of Whittlesea* (1994) 12

AATR 354. However, the weight given to a proposed amendment will vary according to the stage it is at in the amendment process – one which has been exhibited will be given more weight than one which is still in its drafting stage.

Because VCAT is required to have regard to proposed amendments, it is important that there are "sunset" provisions included in the *Planning and Environment Act* for amendments that have uncertain status, otherwise quite conflicting amendments at various stages in the process may apply to the same parcel of land. Alternatively, an amendment that has been proposed but not proceeded with beyond the stage of consideration of submissions may become an important factor in a review decision. If a proposed amendment is not adopted within two years of the date on which notice of its preparation appears in the *Government Gazette* under s 19 at the beginning of the process, or if the Minister does not allow a longer period for adoption, it lapses: s 30. It also lapses if the Minister is notified in writing that the planning authority has abandoned it, or if the Minister refuses to approve it: s 30(1)(c) and (d). In all three situations where an amendment lapses, the Minister must publish a notice in the *Government Gazette* setting out the date on which it lapsed and that is conclusive proof of the date on which it lapsed: s 30(2) and (3).

The abnormal process

Exemption from notification and other normal processes

Section 20(4) allows the Minister to exempt himself or herself from any of the requirements of ss 17, 18 and 19 of the Act and any of the *Planning and Environment Regulations* in respect of an amendment the Minister prepares. It should be remembered that the Minister may prepare an amendment to any section of any scheme in Victoria. The effect of s 20(4) is to allow the Minister to exempt himself or herself from any or all of the normal notification requirements. If the exemption applies to all of ss 17, 18 and 19, the Minister may amend a scheme by simply publishing a notice in the *Government Gazette*, without the stages of lodging of submissions, consideration of those submissions, panel hearing, and consideration of the panel's report.

Exemption may occur "if the Minister considers that compliance with any of these requirements is not warranted or that the interests of Victoria or any part of Victoria make such an exemption appropriate". In addition to exempting himself or herself from the normal requirements, the Minister may exempt any other planning authority from any of the requirements of s 19. Under s 17 a copy of an amendment must be given by the planning authority to the relevant municipal council (if the planning authority is not that council), the Minister, and any other person whom the Minister specifies. Therefore, as the exemption can only be given in relation to the requirements under s 19, these provisions still apply. However, if the amendment is prepared by a municipality then in effect no notification need be given under s 17.

Unlike exemptions granted by the Minister to himself or herself under s 20(4), there are some limitations on exemptions granted to other planning authorities and these are specified in s 20(3). The Minister may not grant an exemption from the requirement to notify owners and occupiers of the land affected if the amendment provides for the reservation of land for public purposes or proposes to close a road. Therefore, owners and occupiers of land affected by such an amendment must be notified, giving them the opportunity to make submissions and then have access to a panel hearing, should the planning authority not accommodate those submissions by changing or abandoning the amendment. This is in accord with the recommendation of the Morris Report (see Chapter 9) that persons whose land is to be acquired should have the opportunity to contest the decision to acquire. However, there is nothing in the Act to compel a planning authority to accept any recommendation contained in a panel report and, as a result of the *Planning and Environment (Amendment) Act 1989*, s 27(3) now allows the Minister to exempt a planning authority (presumably including himself or herself) from considering a panel report if the Minister considers that delay in considering whether or not to adopt would adversely affect the planning of an area. The end result is that the Act guarantees that only non-Ministerial amendments providing for the reservation of land or for the closure of roads will be notified, but even for these there is no guarantee that a panel report will be even considered, let alone acted upon.

Other limitations on the Minister's power to grant exemption to another planning authority from the normal notification requirements are found in s 20(3). Under s 20(3)(b) and (c), the requirement to notify any Minister required under s 19(1)(c) still applies – these are the Minister administering the *Conservation, Forests and Lands Act 1978*, the Minister administering the *Mineral Resources Development Act 1990*, and, if the amendment provides for the closure of a road on Crown land, the Minister administering the *Land Act 1958*. Under s 20(3)(ba), exemption cannot be granted from the requirement to place a notice in a newspaper and the *Government Gazette* if an amendment "proposes a change to provisions relating to land set aside or reserved as public open space". But these instances of notification have nothing to do with notification of members of the community or people whose land may be directly affected, nor do they set in train the normal submission and panel hearing processes.

It may be argued that the Minister should have the power to grant exemption from the normal process and approve an amendment at "the stroke of a pen" to deal with minor amendments, such as inconsistencies and mistakes in scheme provisions, which would otherwise lead to the expenditure of a great deal of time and money by requiring notification, submission and panel hearing procedures. Where the State government wishes to amend its Statewide planning policies and controls (the VPPs), it may be appropriate that the Minister is able to exempt himself or herself from the normal requirements. There is even a case to be made for using the exemption power to introduce the requirement on an interim basis for all uses and development to seek planning permission in order to protect scheme amendments that are being processed according to the normal procedures. It should be remembered that there is no equivalent under the Act to an interim development order as provided for under the *Town and Country Planning Act*. And it should also be noted that there have been residents' groups that have benefited from the exemption power, because they have successfully persuaded the Minister to approve amendments without notification where applications for review have been lodged in relation to permit applications for use and development which they have vehemently opposed and it has appeared that under existing scheme provisions the Tribunal would have had little option but to determine the reviews in favour of the permit applicants. But the power is a double-edged sword – it can be used to facilitate development as well as stop it, without any chance of independent evaluation of that development and its impact via the normal submission and panel hearing procedures. It is for this reason that the exercise of the Ministerial exemption power under s 20 is a matter of concern. Without that scrutiny the suspicion inevitably arises that amendments may be approved for short-term political gain at the expense of proper planning considerations, or to assist political friends or supporters.

Before 1993, s 20 of the Act provided for the Minister to exempt himself or herself, or other planning authorities, from the normal processes if, after consultation with the relevant planning authority, "the Minister considers that compliance with any of these requirements is not warranted or that the over-riding interests of Victoria necessitate exemption". Four Supreme Court challenges to the Minister's exemption power were determined between 1988 and 1992, all involving Mr Tom Roper, Labor Minister for Planning: *Mietta's Hotels Pty Ltd v Roper* (1988) 1 AATR 354; *Antoniou v Roper* (1990) 4 AATR 158; *City of Nunawading v Minister for Planning and Housing* (unreported, VSC, Eames J, No 9888/92, 28 September 1992); and *Grollo Australia v Minister for Planning and Urban Growth* (1993) 10 AATR 170. The judgements in these cases were not all consistent, leaving in some doubt the circumstances in which the Minister could validly exercise the exemption power under s 20. Those doubts were removed by the Kennett Government in 1993, when s 20 was amended to remove the requirement to consult with the relevant planning authority and to change the wording of the section to "that the interests of Victoria or any part of Victoria make such an exemption appropriate". That has made it well nigh impossible to challenge the exercise of the power of the Minister to amend a planning scheme at the stroke of a pen.

Fast-tracking of amendments

There is no specific fast-track legislation in Victoria under which the normal development control processes are avoided or speeded up. However, there is no need for separate legislation when the current provisions of the *Planning and Environment Act* are considered. The power of the Minister to amend any provision of any scheme in the State and his or her power to do so without the normal procedures of notification, submissions and panel report is a very powerful method of fast-tracking, as are Ministerial "call-ins" of permit applications and applications for review (see Chapters 5 and 6).

The combined amendment and permit process

Readers are advised to consult *Using Victoria's Planning System*, available at <www.dpcd.vic.gov.au>, for more detail on this process.

Section 96A provides that a person who requests a planning authority to prepare an amendment may also apply to the planning authority for a combined amendment and permit process. This allows the planning authority to simultaneously prepare and give notice of an amendment and give notice of an application for a permit, even if the permit could not be granted under the existing scheme provisions: s 96A(3). There is no right of review of a decision of the planning authority to refuse to combine the preparation of an amendment with consideration of a permit application.

Notice of a combined amendment and permit application must be given pursuant to s 96C, not s 19. Pursuant to s 96C(1), notice must be given to every Minister, public authority and council the planning authority believes may be materially affected by the amendment; the owners and occupiers of land who the planning authority believes may be materially affected; any Minister, public authority, council and person prescribed by the regulations; the Minister administering the *Land Act* if the amendment provides for closure of a road wholly or partly on Crown land; the relevant responsible authority, if it is not the planning authority; the owners and occupiers of land adjoining the land to which the permit application applies; and the owners and occupiers of land benefitting from any registered restrictive covenant which applies to the land if the permit would allow the variation, removal or breach of the covenant. A notice must also be placed in a newspaper circulating in the area, and, if the amendment would allow the variation or removal of any registered restrictive covenant applying to the land, on the land. There must also be a notice published in the *Government Gazette*. The notice must set a date for submissions to the planning authority and that date must be not less than one month after the date on which the notice appears in the *Government Gazette*.

As with scheme amendments prepared by a planning authority other than the Minister, the Minister may grant an exemption from the notice requirements pursuant to s 20(3). The Minister may not grant an exemption from the requirement to notify owners and occupiers of the land affected if the amendment provides for the reservation of land for public purposes or proposes to close a road. Section 96C(5) provides that a failure to give notice under s 96C(1) does not prevent the adoption of the amendment by the planning authority or its submission to the Minister for approval, or the grant of a permit. Unlike a normal planning permit application, the permit application in the combined process is not required to be referred to any relevant referral authority specified in the scheme. Also unlike a normal planning permit application, it is the Minister who determines it: s 96I. The decision of the Minister is not subject to review by VCAT: s 96M. The Minister may grant the permit, grant it subject to conditions the Minister thinks fit, or refuse to grant it on any grounds the Minister thinks fit: s 96I(1). The permit may be granted at the same time as the approval of the amendment to which the permit applies: s 96I(3). If the grant of a permit would breach a registered restrictive covenant applying to the land, the

Minister must refuse to grant the permit unless the approved amendment provides for the variation or removal of the covenant or a permit has already been issued or decision has been made to grant a permit to allow such removal or variation: s 96I(1A).

Even if no permit has been applied for, or even if a panel has not recommended the grant of a permit (assuming that exemption from the normal lodging of submissions, consideration of submissions and panel hearing processes has not been granted by the Minister), the Minister may grant a permit if the Minister considers it appropriate as a result of changes to the amendment during the amendment process: s 96I(2). Any permit granted by the Minister must be issued by the responsible authority at the direction of the Minister: s 96J(4). Once the permit is issued it becomes the responsibility of the responsible authority: s 96N. That includes responsibility for enforcing the conditions of the permit.

We have grave concerns about the combined process. It provides almost unlimited potential to by-pass what most would consider to be an acceptable level of community consultation and participation in both scheme amendment and permit granting processes. There is no guarantee that those who would be affected by either or both the amendment being approved and the permit being granted have the right to make submissions and have their submissions considered by the planning authority or by a panel. On top of that, they have no avenue to VCAT to seek review of the Minister's decision to grant a permit. The overriding concern from a public policy point of view is that, in the absence of any real brake or fetter on the powers available to the Minister in the combined process, decisions may be made on the basis of political expediency and/or to assist powerful friends of the government, whatever its party political hue, rather than on planning merits.

Parliament and amendments

Revocation of an amendment

Parliament may revoke an amendment. Pursuant to s 38 of the Act, the Minister must cause notice of the approval of every amendment to be laid before each House of the Parliament within 10 sitting days after approval. Either House may revoke the amendment, provided that it does so within 10 sitting days of the notice being laid.

Amendment of the Urban Growth Boundary and Green Wedge subdivision controls

The provisions of the Act dealing with the Urban Growth Boundary and Green Wedge land have been outlined in Chapter 3. The Urban Growth Boundary is shown on the planning scheme maps of metropolitan fringe municipalities listed in s 46AA. Green Wedge land is land in a metropolitan fringe municipality but outside the Urban Growth Boundary. An amendment to a metropolitan fringe planning scheme which amends or inserts an Urban Growth Boundary, or which has the effect of altering or removing controls over the subdivision of Green Wedge land to allow for more lots or smaller lots, is subject to the same procedures that apply to other amendments, including exemptions from the normal process granted by the Minister pursuant to s 20 (see above). But ss 46AG–46AJ impose an additional requirement in that such an amendment must be ratified by each House of Parliament. Section 46AH provides that the Minister must lay before each House a copy of the amendment within seven sitting days after the amendment has been approved. The amendment does not take effect unless it has been ratified by a resolution passed by each House within a further 10 sitting days.

Amendment of the Upper Yarra Valley and Dandenong Ranges Strategy Plan

The *Upper Yarra Valley and Dandenong Ranges Strategy Plan* and its linkage to the Yarra Ranges Planning Scheme were discussed briefly in Chapter 2. Section 46F provides that, despite anything to the contrary in the Act, an amendment to a planning scheme which is inconsistent with an approved regional strategy plan must not be approved. The Minister may at any time prepare an amendment to the *Upper Yarra Valley and Dandenong Ranges Strategy Plan*, and, subject to s 46D, the procedures specified in the Act for the amendment of schemes (including the granting of exemptions pursuant to s 20) apply. Section 46D provides that the Minister must lay before each House a copy of the amendment within seven sitting days after the amendment has been approved. The amendment does not take effect unless it has been ratified by a resolution passed by each House within a further 10 sitting days.

Reviews and amendments

Review of the merits of a proposed amendment

Before the *Planning and Environment (Amendment) Act 1989*, s 150 of the *Planning and Environment Act* provided as follows:

(1) Any person who is affected by the decision or failure to decide by a planning authority or responsible authority under this Act may refer that decision or failure to the Administrative Appeals Tribunal for review.
(2) The Tribunal may review a decision or failure referred to under Sub-section (1) and direct the planning authority or responsible authority to take any action the Tribunal considers appropriate.
(3) Sub-section (1) does not apply to any decision under Part 4 or Part 9 or a decision for which a specific right of appeal is given under this Act.

Parts 4 and 9 of the Act deal with, respectively, planning permits and general administrative powers. Section 150 was never intended to allow appeals in relation to the merits of scheme amendments. However, the Administrative Appeals Tribunal (AAT) held in *Milner v Minister for Planning and Environment* (1998) 1 AATR 217 that s 150 provided power for it to review the decision of a planning authority to prepare and/or adopt an amendment to a scheme, but that this power did not extend to reviewing the decision of the Minister to approve an amendment. In *Dahan v City of Richmond* (1989) 3 AATR 80 this power was reaffirmed and the AAT directed the City of Richmond to prepare and place on exhibition an amendment to the Richmond planning scheme which it had twice previously refused to do. In *Lockett v Shire of Ballarat* (unreported, Appeal No P89/0772) the AAT directed the planning authority to set aside a decision not to proceed with a site-specific rezoning and to refer to a panel the submissions it had received to the proposed rezoning. The *Planning and Environment (Amendment) Act 1989* repealed s 150 (1), (2) and (3) and so removed from the system the ability of the AAT (now VCAT) to review the merits of the decisions of planning authorities in relation to the exhibition and adoption of amendments.

There is a school of thought that says the repeal of s 150(1), (2) and (3) was a retrograde step, because it removed the avenue of reviewing the decisions of planning authorities to not exhibit amendments proposed by the private sector. It may be argued by proponents that all amendments should be exhibited and that the submission and panel hearing stages of the process will establish their merits or otherwise. For the argument to be consistent, it must recognise that, if proponents were to be given the right to seek review where the decision of the planning authority was to not exhibit, equity considerations dictate that third parties must be given that right where the decision was to exhibit. Whatever the decision of the planning authority was, it would mean a round of review on the merits during the amendment process, and, if the amendment were subsequently approved by the Minister, this would almost certainly encourage objecting submittors to lodge objections and applications for review in relation to permits required under the amendment. The time and cost involved would be very considerable. There is also the important question of whether or not it would be appropriate for the same body to determine both types of review. The question of impartiality arises if the Tribunal were to hear and determine an application for review of a permit application if it had already determined that the amendment under which the permit application was made should be exhibited.

Apart from enforcement proceedings, the primary function of the Planning and Environment List of VCAT is to review on the merits the exercise of discretionary power by responsible authorities in relation to planning permit applications. It is not appropriate for it to have the power to review the substantive merits of land use and development policy and the scheme amendments devised to implement such policy. That is a matter for State and local governments to determine.

Reviews in relation to amendment procedures

Section 39(1) of the Act provides that "a person who is substantially or materially affected by a failure of the Minister, a planning authority or a panel to comply with Division 1 or 2 of this Division or Part 8 in relation to an amendment which has not been approved may, not later than one month after becoming aware of the failure, refer the matter to the Tribunal for its determination". Section 39(4) authorises VCAT to make any declaration it thinks appropriate, or direct that the planning authority must not adopt the amendment or a specified part of the amendment, or direct the

Minister not approve an amendment or a specified part of it, unless action which the Tribunal specifies is undertaken.

Section 39 is designed to allow breaches of the procedures specified in the Act for the notification of amendments, the consideration of submissions, referral of submissions to a panel, and the conduct of panel hearings, to be reviewed by VCAT as an alternative to mounting a challenge and securing an injunction in the Supreme Court: see, for example, *Australian Conservation Foundation v Minister for Planning* [2004] VCAT 2029 and *TJ Love v Whittlesea Shire Council* (2001) 7 VPR 268, discussed earlier in this chapter.

It is important to appreciate that s 39 does not allow the substantive merits of an amendment to be reviewed. However, the lesson is to mount a challenge before the amendment is approved – once it has been approved, the decisions of the planning authority, the Minister or the panel cannot be challenged before VCAT, although they may be challenged before the Supreme Court, provided the person or persons seeking review can establish sufficient standing under common law or under the *Administrative Law Act 1978*.

Persons seeking VCAT review under s 39 must be substantially or materially affected. It is not enough to feel outraged that the procedures were not adhered to – there must be detriment of a real, rather than of a trivial or imaginary, nature: *Attorney General ex rel Whitten v Shire of Gisbourne* (1980) 45 LGRA 1. If review is sought for some ulterior motive, such as delaying the processing of the amendment, it could prove costly for the person or persons seeking the review. Section 150(4) provides that the Tribunal may order compensation and costs to be paid by the person who brought proceedings before it if it is satisfied that the proceedings have been brought vexatiously or frivolously and any other person has suffered loss or damage as a result.

Agreements and amendments

Agreements were discussed briefly in Chapter 3. While the provisions of an amendment, if approved, may require that an agreement be entered into between the applicant and the responsible authority as a precondition for planning consent for use and/or development, the opportunities for using agreements in association with, but not part of, an amendment are limited. Note that s 17(2) provides that the documents which must be exhibited with a planning scheme amendment include a copy of any s 173 agreement if the agreement or part of it will not come into operation fully unless the amendment comes into operation.

Let us assume a site-specific amendment has been proposed by a developer to allow a particular use or development to establish, subject to planning consent. While the amendment may allow for a wide range of developments and uses, subject to the granting of a permit, in fact a particular development is envisaged, and the proponent has convinced the planning authority to exhibit the amendment on the understanding that only that particular development will be the subject of a planning permit application if the amendment is approved. In these circumstances the planning authority may wish to ensure that the proponent will develop what he or she has proposed and not apply for a permit, if the amendment is approved, for some entirely different development. After all, even if the planning authority, subsequently acting as a responsible authority, refuses permission for an entirely different type of development, the applicant has the right to seek review of the decision and VCAT may rule in his or her favour.

However, there are some difficulties in implementing an agreement under these circumstances. Not least of all is the difficulty posed by the fact that the Act provides only for agreements between responsible authorities and owners of land, or with the anticipated owners of land (such as when someone holds a purchase option or agreement to purchase). But in scheme amendment mode the relevant authority is a planning authority, not a responsible authority. The intention seems to be that the planning authority will set the parameters of the proposed amendment, and the responsible authority can then enter into the agreement after notice of the amendment has been given. But why should the proponent enter into any such agreement? The responsible authority cannot agree, in advance of the amendment being approved and in advance of a planning permit application being lodged, that it will grant planning permission. To do so would be to abrogate its responsibility to consider on their merits objections lodged to the permit application. Even if it did agree to grant planning permission, objectors to a permit application have the right to seek review of that decision before VCAT, provided the scheme provisions do not exempt the permit application from the normal notification, objection and review provisions of the Act, so the planning authority has little to offer the applicant as an inducement to enter into the agreement. Whether or not the proponent is already the owner of land which is the subject of the amendment, he or she is unlikely to want to be tied down to a detailed proposal, because, even if the amendment is approved, it may well take some considerable time for the stages of notification, submissions and panel hearing to occur – perhaps as much as two years or more. Changing circumstances, particularly the impact of changing interest rates, may make the specific proposal uneconomic. The establishment of competitors in the area in the intervening period may also make it uneconomic.

More often than not, where a particular development is envisaged as establishing on a site subject to planning consent and subsequent to the approval of an amendment, the amendment arrives at the panel hearing with no agreement being entered into. Nevertheless the planning authority, the proponent, and often the objectors and the supporters of the amendment make submissions as though a particular development will be established on the site. In fact, detailed plans of the proposed development may have been exhibited with the amendment and other documents under s 18. In the absence of an agreement the panel has no option but to consider these plans and the proposed development as only indicative of the development that may establish subject to planning consent, should the amendment be approved. After all, there is no reason why the proponent may not apply for a planning permit for an entirely different development. Nor is there any reason to prevent the proponent selling the property to another person who may also see fit to make application for an entirely different development. In these circumstances, it is not helpful to the panel if the proponent or the planning authority make submissions as if the panel hearing were a hearing on a specific planning permit application.

Chapter 5

PLANNING PERMITS

The nature of planning permission

Under the *Planning and Environment Act 1987* numerous discretionary powers are bestowed on responsible authorities and planning authorities. The exercise of broad discretionary power is an integral feature of all town planning schemes and the most frequently exercised discretion is the power to grant or refuse planning permits. The importance of this discretion cannot be underestimated, as the sheer volume of permit applications considered each year indicates that it is the most frequent type of contact the public has with the exercise of planning power. Decisions to grant planning permission can directly or indirectly affect the whole nature of an area by influencing such matters as the pattern of land use, the scale and intensity of building, traffic congestion, and population density. These decisions can therefore affect the wellbeing of communities.

A planning permit is not the same as a building permit

The difference between a planning permit and a building permit was discussed in Chapter 3. A planning permit will be required when the planning scheme says it is. In most instances the requirement for a permit will be triggered by the provisions of the zone that applies to the land or of any applicable overlays, or both (see Chapter 3). But there are things other than the use or development of land that also trigger the requirement for a permit – for example, illumination of domestic tennis courts. "Use" and "development" are defined in s 3 of the Act. "Development" includes both works and subdivision of land (for a further discussion on the relationship between planning permission and the certification of plans of subdivision, see Chapter 2). Planning permission must be sought for discretionary uses (that is, those uses which are permitted under the scheme but not permitted as of right). These are sometimes referred to as consent uses.

A planning permit is not a building permit under the *Building Act 1993*. A building permit is, primarily, a certification that the building or alteration to the building meets minimum standards of construction as specified in the *Building Regulations 2006*, made pursuant to that Act. The planning permit system is aimed at ensuring, among other things, that land uses are appropriately located, that buildings and uses do not interfere with each other, that some degree of harmony of scale and character between structures is achieved, that development will not harm the environment unduly, and that buildings and neighbourhoods of conservation or other significance are not summarily altered or destroyed.

What is permitted by a planning permit?

A planning permit gives permission for a particular use and/or development proposal on a particular area of land and is normally subject to particular conditions. The permit therefore specifies the consent(s) granted, identifies the land to which the permit applies, if the proposal involves development or works, ties the permission(s) granted to a particular set of plans, and sets out the conditions which apply. The consents granted will depend on the nature of the proposal and the planning controls in place. In a Residential 1 Zone, for example, the development of two or more dwellings on a lot requires permission for development but not for the use. If the land is also subject to a Heritage Overlay and the proposal involves the demolition of an existing building, permission is required for the demolition of the existing building as well as the construction of the new development on the land. In such circumstances the permit will state that it grants permission, for example, for the demolition of the existing building(s) on the land and the development of three dwellings. The land will normally be identified in the permit by the street name and number and the name of the suburb or township. In some circumstances, such as in rural areas, it may be necessary to identify the land by specifying its title particulars. It is difficult to imagine the circumstance in which a permit, particularly a permit for development as well as use, is not subject to conditions. Whether it contains conditions or not, the consent(s) are tied to a particular proposal by words such as "in accordance with the plans submitted with the application". If the permit contains conditions requiring some modifications to the proposal, the first condition will normally require the submission, approval and endorsement by the responsible authority of amended plans "generally in accordance with the plans submitted with the application, but modified to show ...", with the modifications then specified. If the permit is granted pursuant to an order of VCAT following its determination of an application for review, and VCAT has allowed the substitution of amended plans for the plans accompanying the permit application, the condition will normally include a reference to the plans allowed to be substituted, with these plans identified by a date or reference number or both. Even for a small proposal such as the development of three dwellings on a lot, a permit may contain 20 or more conditions dealing with amended plans, the provision and maintenance of landscaping, drainage of the land, construction of crossovers, the location and concealment from general view of plant and equipment such as heating and airconditioning units, and the period of time within which the development must be commenced and completed.

A planning permit runs with the land

The applicant for a permit does not have to be the owner of the land, but the owner must be informed that an application has been made: *Planning and Environment Act*, s 48. A planning permit normally "runs with the land". While the permit is granted to a particular applicant, the permit applies to a particular piece of land and normally continues to apply even after a change of ownership. Therefore, in considering whether or not to grant a permit, a responsible authority must carefully assess whether the proposal is an appropriate one for the land in question, both now and in the future.

Town planning is concerned with the use and development of land and not the identity of the particular applicant who puts it to that use. Although a permit "runs with the land" and cannot be transferred to another allotment of land, there are circumstances where, in effect, they are made "personal" to the applicant in order to protect amenity. VCAT and its predecessors have consistently held that only on very rare occasions should a planning permit be made personal to the applicant. In the case of brothels and electronic gaming machines, the licences required (see later in this chapter) restrict the operation of those uses to individuals or companies rather than permit conditions. But, unless there are exceptional grounds which indicate that only a particular applicant can be trusted to properly develop and use the land in accordance with the law, permits should not be made personal: see, for example, *Pituri Pty Ltd v City of South Melbourne* (1985) 3 PABR 200 at 227; *McNamara v Shire of Barrabool* (1986) 26 APA 272 at 278; *Crichton v City of Moorabbin* (1991) 7 AATR 150; *Avel Pty Ltd v City of Dandenong* (1991) 7 AATR 271; *Peterson v Rural City of Ararat* [2003] VCAT 219; 14 VPR 202; *Duffy v Alpine SC* [2000] VCAT 1769; 5 VPR 340 at 346. Even where made personal to the applicant, a permit still applies to a particular piece of land.

The Tribunal has upheld permit conditions and inserted conditions which have made the permit personal to the applicant on the basis that how the use or development is managed is crucial to protecting amenity. For example, in *B Smith v Shire of Flinders* (1983) 1 PABR 183, a permit for a broiler chicken farm was made personal to the applicant because:

> the degree of nuisance caused by poultry farming depends to a large extent upon the quality of management and that the characteristics of the proposed user ... will be relevant if the characteristics or qualities are distinctive, or peculiar and will be significant in the case of the land from a town planning point of view.

It is also common for permits for animal boarding establishments (dog kennels and catteries) to be made personal to applicants: see, for example, *Grantham v Mornington Peninsula SC* [2002] VCAT 424; 10 VPR 246.

The life of a permit

A permit for "development" expires if the development (or any agreed stage of it) does not commence within the time specified in the permit, or is not completed or commenced within two years. If no time is specified in the permit, it then expires if the development or any stage of it is not completed within two years: see s 68(1)(b). A permit for "use", as distinct from "development" (for example, to establish a use in an existing building), expires if the use is not established within the time period specified in the permit, or, if no time is specified, within two years. A permit for a use also expires if the use is discontinued for a period of two years. Thus, a permit not "actioned" within two years expires, and may expire within a shorter time than two years depending on the conditions inserted in permit.

If a permit has been acted on (for example, the development and use is completed and established within the two-year time limit, or such shorter time as required by a condition attached to it) and the life of the permit is not limited by a time condition then it has an unlimited life, provided that the use to which the permit applies is not discontinued for more than two years, and provided that the permit is not cancelled. (The cancellation of permits under the *Planning and Environment Act* is discussed in Chapter 7.)

Responsible authorities normally include standard time conditions on permits, such as "the development must commence within two years of the date of the permit and be completed within four years of the date of the permit but these times may be extended if a request is made in writing before the permit expires or within three months afterwards". Extensions of time are authorised by s 69 of the Act. The responsible authority may grant or refuse such extensions, depending on the merits of the application, and refusals are subject to an application for review by the applicant to VCAT: s 81 (see Chapter 6).

Making an application

When is a permit required?

One must go to the particular scheme in question to determine whether or not a permit is required for any particular use or development. The zoning of the land and any overlays that apply to it must be established. The zoning, Use Table and other provisions for the zone must be examined. If an overlay applies to the land, it may trigger the requirement of a permit for the construction or carrying-out of buildings and works, or for removal of vegetation. However, there are controls in schemes other than zones and overlays which may trigger the requirement for a permit, such as cl 52.05, dealing with advertising signs; cl 52.06, dealing with reduction or waiving of car parking requirements; and cl 52.29, dealing with creation or alteration of access arrangements for land adjacent to a Road Zone – Category 1, or in a Public Acquisition Overlay, if the purpose of the acquisition is for a Category 1 Road (see Chapter 3 as to how planning schemes are structured). It is not uncommon for a development proposal to trigger the requirement for as many as four or five planning consents.

The application form

An application for a planning permit is made to the relevant responsible authority (normally the local council – see Chapter 2) on the standard form prescribed by the *Planning and Environment Regulations 2005*, Part 4, reg 15, Form 4 (Schedule 1). The application must also be accompanied by the prescribed fee (see reg 7 of the *Planning and Environment (Fees) Regulations* 2000). There is a sliding scale of fees based on the value of the use and development. Fees are levied to defray administrative costs. They are not refunded if the application is refused.

An application for a permit may be made by any person, such as a natural person or a company, but not an unincorporated association, group, or committee. An application may be made by an agent acting on behalf of a person and it is commonplace for applications to be made by architects, town planners or lawyers acting as agents. The applicant does not have to be the owner of the land. If the applicant is not the owner, the applicant must, under s 48 of the Act, get the application signed by the owner or include a declaration that the owner has been notified of the application. Section 48(2) of the Act provides for penalties for false declarations.

The application form for permits requires a good deal of information to be provided, such as the location of the property, and details about the use or development for which permission is sought. These details normally require that detailed plans of the proposed development are submitted with the application. Enough detail must be supplied to enable the responsible authority and potential objectors to establish what the likely impact of the proposed use or development will be. The planning scheme may specify additional information that must accompany the permit application, such as a neighbourhood and site description pursuant to cll 54 and 55 (see Chapter 3). If the land is burdened by a registered restrictive covenant, the application must be accompanied by a copy of the covenant, and, if the application is to allow the variation or removal of a registered restrictive covenant, information clearly identifying each allotment or lot benefited by the covenant and any other information required by the regulations: s 47(1)(d) and (e). Under s 54(1) of the Act, the responsible authority may refuse to consider an application until all relevant information is provided. Failure of the applicant to respond to repeated requests for further information may result in the applicant having to start the process again: *Tide Pty Ltd v Monash City Council* [2000] VCAT 540.

Time limits for making the decision

The times for making a decision on a permit application are governed by s 59 of the Act and reg 24 of the *Planning and Environment Regulations 2005*. Generally speaking, the responsible authority has 60 days from the lodging of the permit application in which to make a decision, otherwise the applicant may seek review of the failure to decide pursuant to s 79. The responsible authority may decide on an application without delay if:

- the responsible authority is not required to give notice of it pursuant to s 52 (either because it decides to refuse the application without notification or because the application is exempt by provisions in the scheme from the requirement to notify) and no objections have been lodged; and
- the application in its original or amended form is not required to be referred to the relevant referral authority or authorities specified in the scheme.

If notice of the permit application is given pursuant to s 52(1) or (1AA), the responsible authority must not make a decision before the 14-day period specified in the notice for the lodging of objections has expired, otherwise its decision would be contrary to law and be invalid: *Imperium Designs Pty Ltd v Glen Eira CC* (2002) 12 VPR 182. If a copy of the application is required to be sent to a referral authority, the responsible authority may make its decision 28 days from the day on which the referral authority is given a copy of the application. However, if the referral authority requires further information, the responsible authority may make its decision 28 days from when the responsible authority gives that information. If a copy of the application is required to be sent to a referral authority, is sent within 28 days of the application being lodged, and the referral authority then requires further information and says so within 21 days of receiving the copy of the application, the 60-day "clock" stops until the information is received by the referral authority: s 59 and *Planning and Environment Regulations 2005*, reg 24. The responsible authority may itself require further information from the applicant, and if that requirement is made within 28 days of the permit application being lodged, the 60-day "clock" stops until that information is supplied: s 54 and *Planning and Environment Regulations 2005*, reg 20. The philosophy of responsible authorities dealing with matters expeditiously is expressed in general terms in s 197 of the *Planning and Environment Act*.

The duties of the responsible authority before it makes a decision

Checking the details of the application

On receiving a planning permit application, a responsible authority should check that it is the responsible authority for the use or development proposed. If it is not then the application must be forwarded to the relevant responsible authority. It is possible that the scheme specifies the Minister as the responsible authority for some types of applications. A responsible authority should also check to see that the applicant is a person. The applicant must have a legal personality (for example, an unincorporated association, such as a local progress association, is not a legal person). Legal persons include a corporation, an individual and a partnership. All responsible authorities should then check the following details:

- all the consents required pursuant to the zones, overlays and other provisions of the planning scheme;
- if the application is required to be sent to referral authorities under s 55;
- whether the application is:
  - allowed as of right without a permit;
  - permitted subject to conditions; or
  - prohibited under the relevant planning controls;
- that the application contains sufficient detail for the responsible authority to determine the exact location of the subject land and the nature of the proposal (s 47(1)(c));
- the application is accompanied by the appropriate plans and any additional information required by the planning scheme (for example, see cll 54 and 55 of the VPPs);
- the application has been made with the knowledge of the landowner (s 48);
- whether or not expert advice is required;
- that the register is filled in for the application (see s 49);
- that the prescribed fee accompanies the application.

If the land is burdened by a registered restrictive covenant, an application must be accompanied by a copy of the covenant: s 47(1)(d). In addition, if the application is for a permit to allow the removal or variation of the covenant, the applicant must submit information which clearly identifies the land benefited by the covenant and any other information required: s 47(1)(e).

Checking that a permit is required and may be granted

Due to misunderstanding or misinterpretation of the planning scheme provisions, sometimes permit applications are lodged for uses or developments that are prohibited, or that do not require planning permission. An application for a use or development that is prohibited by the planning scheme is a nullity in that the responsible authority has no power to consent to it: *Chambers v Maclean SC* (2003) 126 LGERA 7. And, of course, a responsible authority cannot issue a valid permit for a use or development that does not require planning permission. Ascertaining whether a proposed development, as distinct from use, requires planning permission is normally a relatively straightforward task. Ascertaining whether a proposed use requires planning permission, or is subject to specific requirements, normally requires the application of the definitions and nesting diagrams included in cll 72–75 of the planning scheme. These clauses are included in the VPPs and are therefore the same in all schemes. Even then, the task of establishing if a use does or does not require planning permission, or is prohibited, may not be simple. In *Cascone v Shire of Whittlesea* (1993) 11 AATR 175 at p 190, the Supreme Court set out six principles for characterising a proposed use:

(1) In characterising the proposed use, it is always necessary to ascertain the purpose of the use.

(2) It is wrong to determine the relevant purpose simply by identifying activities, processes or transactions and then fit them to some one or more uses defined by the scheme.

(3) It is wrong to approach the ascertainment of purpose of a proposed use on the footing that it must be within one or more of the uses defined in a scheme; at least that is so where there is provision for innominate uses in the scheme.

(4) The ascertainment of purpose of a proposed use may yield the result that the purpose revealed very largely falls within a defined use. The extent to which it does not may be so trifling that it may be ignored and in that instance the purpose should be taken as to fall within the defined use.

(5) The ascertainment of purpose may yield the result that more than one separate and distinct purpose is revealed. If one is dominant and the other is ancillary to the dominant use, and the dominant use is as of right, then the ancillary use is legitimised – in planning terms there is but one use. But if there are no dominant and ancillary uses, but two separate uses, each must

be as of right otherwise they will require permission, provided that they are not prohibited by the scheme. The mere fact that one use may be either as of right or discretionary does not prevent the other from being prohibited.

(6) In resolving the problem of the characterisation, the purpose of the use is the real and substantial purpose of the use.

The Supreme Court in *Northcote Wholesalers v City of Northcote* (1994) 13 AATR concluded that there is no single test to determine what are dominant and ancillary uses. There have been various methods used to determine whether a use is ancillary, including comparing the actual or expected sales receipts from each use, the number of customers of the uses and the likely duration of their stay, the floor area to be given over to each use, whether the customers of the purported ancillary use are likely to be also customers of the purported dominant use, and whether there is to be physical separation of the uses. In *Convivial Company Pty Ltd v City of St Kilda* (1991) 7 AATR 346 the Tribunal held that a PubTAB sub-agency in a hotel was a separate use. It found that the income from the PubTAB would be between 1.5 per cent and 3.5 per cent of the hotel's income, the number of customers would be small, the space it occupied would be approximately 4 per cent of the area of the hotel, the customers of the hotel would be principally hotel patrons, the length of stay of patrons would be short, and the entry to the PubTAB would be separate from the entry to the hotel. The Tribunal placed significant weight on the fact that the entrances would be separate.

In *Polmac Pty Ltd v Whitehorse CC* [1999] VCAT 209; 5 VPR 24 the Tribunal found, applying the principles set out in the *Cascone* case, that a proposed 14-screen cinema complex, retail area, food outlets and redesigned car park in Box Hill District Centre was a "cinema based entertainment facility" as defined in the VPPs and that the retail and other uses to be physically and functionally associated with the cinemas were ancillary uses. In *Sinclair v Boroondara CC* [2001] VCAT 2203; 9 VPR 195 the Tribunal held that the use of Camberwell Civic Centre for a regular "computer swap meet" was ancillary to the primary purpose of the use of the civic centre. In *STY Building Supplies Pty Ltd v Greater Shepparton CC* [2000] VCAT 1880 it was held that a Bunnings hardware superstore proposed for land in a Business 4 Zone was not a shop ("shop" was prohibited in the zone) but fell within the planning scheme definitions for a number of as of right uses and one discretionary use for the zone. See Part 5.5 of the *Planning Appeal Casenotes* volume, Butterworths' *Planning and Environment Service Victoria,* for more examples of decisions on dominant and ancillary uses.

Getting further information

Further information may be required by the responsible authority from the applicant or by the referral authority from the responsible authority (s 54). Where such a requirement is made, time does not start to run until the date on which that information is received by the party who requested it. This applies only if the requirement for more information is made within 28 days of receipt of the application, or if the requirement is made by a referral authority within 21 days of receiving a copy of the application, provided that it received the copy of the application from the responsible authority within 28 days of lodgement (see "Time limits for making the decision", above). Otherwise the clock continues to run. An applicant may apply to VCAT for review of a requirement for further information. In *Taras Nominees Pty Ltd v Yarra CC* [2003] VCAT 1952; 15 VPR 272 the Tribunal stated that it is an impermissible use of s 54 for a responsible authority to require further information when it is really seeking to have the application changed.

Sections 54(1A), (1B) and (1C), 54A and 54B were inserted into the Act by the *Planning and Environment (General Amendment) Act 2004*. Section 54(1A), (1B) and (1C) enables a responsible authority to set a time by which further information is to be provided and any notice requiring further information must state that the application will lapse on the date specified (which must not be less than 30 days after the date of the notice) unless the information is provided. Section 54A provides that an applicant may seek an extension of the time by which the information is to be provided, provided that a request for extension is made within the lapse date specified, and the setting of a new lapse date. If the responsible authority refuses to extend the time as requested it must provide the applicant with a written notice of its decision. If the decision is made after the lapse date has passed or will occur within 14 days of the decision to refuse, the notice must set out a new lapse date which is 14 days from the date of the decision. An applicant may apply to VCAT for review of a refusal to extend time: s 81(2). Section 54B deals with determining a final lapse date of an application.

Completing the register

The responsible authority must keep a register as prescribed in the regulations. This register must be available for public inspection free of charge: s 49. A further means of record keeping is some form of computer database in which all details of application outcomes are entered. Most councils have in place computer systems to track the progress of permit applications and the stages they have proceeded through in the process of decision making. In some municipalities members of the public can access the tracking systems online.

Deciding if the application should be amended before notification

Sections 50 and 50A were inserted into the Act by the *Planning and Environment (General Amendment) Act 2004*. Section 50 enables an applicant to request the responsible authority to amend an application before notification of it is given. Section 50(1) provides that an amendment may include an amendment to the use or development proposed, to the description of the land to which the application applies, and to any plans and documents accompanying the application. The request must be accompanied by the prescribed fee and, if the applicant is not the owner of the land, it must be signed by the owner or include a declaration that the owner has been notified about the request. The responsible authority may refuse to amend the application if it considers that the amendment is so substantial that a new application should be made, otherwise it must amend the application as requested: s 50(4) and (5). The responsible authority must make a note in the register if an amendment is made to the application: s 50(6). This is to ensure that anyone looking for information about the application is made aware that it has been amended. An amended application is to be taken as the application for the purposes of the Act and to have been received on the day the request for amendment was received. This is important in determining the date for calculating the 60-day period within which a decision on the application must be made.

Section 50(A) enables the responsible authority to initiate an amendment to the application before notification is given. The responsible authority may amend the application with the agreement of the applicant. The amendment may include the same things that an amendment requested by the applicant may include. The responsible authority may require the applicant to notify the owner of the land or make a declaration that the owner has been notified, if the applicant is not the owner. As with an amendment requested by the applicant, there must be a note made on the register and the amended application is taken to be the application for the purposes of the Act and to have been received on the day the applicant agreed to the amendment.

Sending the application to referral authorities

Referral of some permit applications to referral authorities will be mandatory under the provisions of the relevant scheme. Even where a mandatory requirement for referral does not exist, it may be appropriate to refer certain applications to expert bodies for technical advice. However, if they are not authorities to which a mandatory referral is required, any objections or suggestions as to permit conditions they may make are advice only.

A responsible authority must give a copy of an application for a permit to every person or body that the planning scheme specifies as a referral authority for that type of application: *Planning and Environment Act 1987*, s 55. Section 55 is designed to cover a range of situations and includes the power to fetter the decision of the responsible authority. A referral authority must consider every application referred to it within the time specified (28 days under reg 20 of the *Planning and Environment Regulations 2005*). The referral authority may tell the responsible authority that it does not object to the granting of the permit, or does not object if the permit is subject to the conditions it specifies. Alternatively, it may object to the granting of the permit, in which case the responsible authority must refuse to grant the permit: *Planning and Environment Act*, s 56(1)(a), (b), (c). A referral authority's silence is construed as it having no objection to the application.

The responsible authority, before coming to a determination on an application, must consider the decision of the referral authority and must refuse to grant the permit if the relevant referral authority objects to granting it: *Planning and Environment Act*, s 61(2). If the responsible authority decides to grant a permit, it must include any condition the referral authority requires and not include any other conditions which would conflict with any condition required by the referral authority: s 62(1). For newly developing areas on the rural urban fringe, servicing agencies are specified in the scheme as referral authorities. For areas subject to the Wildfire Management Overlay, the Country Fire Authority is specified as a referral authority (See Chapter 2).

Comments from expert bodies such as the local drainage authority, the Department of Sustainability and the Environment and the local water supply authority may be particularly useful in environmentally sensitive areas. Expert views from bodies such as local historical societies, the regional tourist organisation and the council of an adjoining municipality et cetera can also be useful in certain circumstances. These bodies may be able to recommend permit conditions which will result in a better quality of development. But such recommendations have the status of recommendations only. They do not have to be included in any permit granted, as would be the case pursuant to s 61(2) if such bodies were referral authorities.

If a responsible authority believes that a proposal might have a significant effect on the environment it may, under the *Environment Effects Act 1978*, seek the advice and assistance of the Minister before making its determination. The Minister may in fact request that a responsible authority seek such advice. If an Environment Effects Statement (EES) is required then no decision on the permit application can be made by the responsible authority until the EES procedures are completed (for a discussion of the *Environment Effects Act*, see Chapter 2).

Notification of the application

A responsible authority may refuse to grant a permit without notice being given of the permit application: s 52(1A). But in all other circumstances (save for those applications which are exempt from notification pursuant to ss 6(2)(kc), (kd) and 60(3) – see Chapter 3) notification must occur pursuant to s 52(1) and (1AA). Notice of application (ie advertising) may be given by the applicant or the responsible authority. If the latter, the applicant pays the costs of such advertising.

Section 52 must be read against some historical background. Under the *Town and Country Planning Act 1961*, advertising occurred under s 18B, which stated that "where the responsible authority is of the opinion that the grant of the permit may cause substantial detriment to a person other than the applicant" then advertising was to occur to provide opportunities for objection. If at least one objection was lodged then the objector and others could appeal against the decision of the responsible authority to grant the permit.

However, there were no criteria in the *Town and Country Planning Act* as to when or in what circumstances the responsible authority was required to form an opinion that substantial detriment would be caused. In effect, advertising was at the discretion of the responsible authority. If no advertising occurred and no objections were lodged then no person other than the applicant could appeal. If the applicant was granted the permit then the first thing a nearby resident might know about the use or development was when it was being built, and then there was no avenue of appeal open at all. The infamous Brockhoff silos in Waverley and the saga of the extensions to Doug Wade's house in Parkville came about essentially because there was no advertising and therefore no opportunity for objections to be lodged.

In the *Wade* case (*Thorpe v Doug Wade Consultants Pty Ltd* [1985] VR 433) a permit was granted without notification of the application being given to those who may have been detrimentally affected. Because the applicant's architect had secured the initials of adjoining owners on proposed plans for extension, the responsible authority, the City of Melbourne, determined not to advertise the application. Having received no objections to the proposal, the Melbourne City Council decided to grant the permit. Neighbours first became aware of the development when work commenced. Residents were not able to appeal under the *Town and Country Planning Act* and were therefore put to the expense of seeking an injunction in the Supreme Court. They failed to secure an injunction and the costs of the proceedings were awarded against them. They then appealed to the Full Bench, were unsuccessful, and again had costs awarded against them.

Pursuant to s 52 of the *Planning and Environment Act*, if the responsible authority does not require the applicant to give notice then it must itself give notice of the application in the prescribed form (see *Planning and Environment Regulations 2005*, reg 19 and Form 3, Schedule 1) to the following:

(a) to the owners (except persons entitled to be registered under the *Transfer of Land Act* 1958 as proprietor of an estate in fee simple) and occupiers of allotments or lots adjoining the land to which the application applies unless the planning scheme exempts it or the responsible authority is satisfied that the grant of the permit would not cause material detriment to any person; and

(b) to a municipal council, if the application applies to or may materially affect land within its municipal district; and

(c) to any person to whom the planning scheme requires it to give notice; and

(ca) to the owners (except persons entitled to be registered under the *Transfer of Land* 1958 as proprietor of an estate in fee simple) and occupiers of land benefited by a registered covenant, if anything authorised by the permit would result in a breach of the covenant; and

(cb) to the owners (except persons entitled to be registered under the *Transfer of Land* 1958 as proprietor of an estate in fee simple) and occupiers of land benefited by a registered covenant, if the application is to remove or vary the covenant; and

(d) to any other persons, if the responsible authority considers that the grant of the permit may cause material detriment to them.

"Adjoining land" is land contiguous with (ie touching) the land to which the planning permit application applies: *Graham v Stonnington CC* [2010] VCAT 1224. Land across the street is not adjoining land. Nor is land separated from the land to which the permit application applies by a laneway. "Material detriment" need not be substantial detriment. It may be minor, but real, as distinct from imagined or perceived detriment: *McBride v Stonnington CC* [2005] VCAT 2321.

"Persons entitled to be registered under the *Transfer of Land Act* 1958 as proprietor of an estate in fee simple" are persons who have purchased land but the sale has not been completed and the fee simple ownership of the land has not yet been transferred to them and is not shown on title. In these situations the responsible authority cannot be expected to be aware that the land has been sold. The new owners, if they become aware later in the process that a permit application is the subject of an Application for Review by VCAT, may lodge a Statement of Grounds and seek leave to be joined with other objectors as a party to the review proceedings.

Under s 52(1) all these persons, except those included in (d), must be given notice by mail or by direct delivery. Furthermore, in addition to the requirements under s 52(1)(ca) and (cb), notice of an application to remove or vary a registered covenant must also be given by placing a sign on the land which is the subject of the application and by publishing a notice in a newspaper generally circulating in the area in which that land is situated: s 52(1AA). For persons included in (d), notice may be given by displaying a notice of the proposed application on the site of the proposed development, or placing an advertisement in a newspaper circulating in the area, or both.

VCAT may cancel or amend a permit if it considers any of the circumstances set out in s 87(1) of the Act apply. Those circumstances include any failure to give notice in accordance with s 52. A request for cancellation or amendment of a permit may be made by the responsible authority, a person under s 89, a referral authority, or the owner or occupier of the land concerned: s 87(3). Section 89 states that a person who objected or would have been entitled to object to the issue of a permit may ask the Tribunal to cancel or amend a permit if any of the circumstances set out in that section apply. Those circumstances include that the person believes that the person should have been given notice and was not given notice. At the hearing of a request to the responsible authority, VCAT must give reasonable opportunity to be heard to the owner and occupier of the land concerned, to any person who made the request under s 87, the Minister, and to any relevant referral authority. In determining a request for cancellation or amendment of a permit, VCAT must take into account the matter set out in s 84B(1) as if the request were an application for review, plus any other matters it may properly take into account or have regard to: s 89. After hearing a request, VCAT may direct the responsible authority to cancel or amend a permit and to take any action required in relation to the permit, and the responsible authority must comply with those directions without delay: s 91(1) and (2). However, VCAT must not direct the responsible authority to cancel or amend a permit unless it is satisfied that certain circumstances apply: s 91(3) and (3A). In the case of a person who objected or would have been entitled to object to the issue of a permit and who believes that he or she should have been given notice and was not given notice, those circumstances are that the person could not reasonably have been expected to be aware of the permit application in time to lodge an objection, and was substantially disadvantaged by the matter set out in the request, and it would be fair and just in the circumstances to cancel or amend the permit. In *Brown v Mornington Peninsula SC (No 1)* [2003] VCAT 1796 the Tribunal followed *Sunraysia Water Board v City of Mildura* (AAT Appeal No 1994/013733) in holding that exclusion from the planning process is not of itself sufficient to amount to substantial disadvantage and that the requestor needs to demonstrate substantial disadvantage arising from the grant of a permit.

The determination of a request to cancel or amend a permit may give rise to a liability for costs: ss 93, 94. Cancellation and amendment of a permit in the context of planning enforcement is discussed in Chapter 7.

This discussion of notification and the following discussion on objection assumes that the relevant planning scheme does not exempt the particular use or development from the normal notification requirements. However, as was explained in Chapter 3, ss 6(2)(kc), (kd), 52(4), 60(3) and 82 of the *Planning and Environment Act* provide that a scheme may set out classes of applications which are exempt from the normal notification, objection and review processes. But, pursuant to s 52(4), a planning scheme may not exempt applications from the notice requirements under s 52(1)(ca) and (cb) – that is, the owners and occupiers of land benefiting from a restrictive covenant must be notified if the permit would authorise anything that would result in a breach of the covenant or if the application is to remove or vary the covenant. Schemes may contain numerous instances where such exemptions apply (see Chapter 3). However, an exemption from giving notice of an application and the lodging of objections does not prevent the responsible authority from giving notice, and from considering any objections it receives: *Sweetvale Pty Ltd v VCAT* [2001] VSC 426; 16 VPR 224.

Amending the permit after notification

Sections 57A–57C were inserted into the Act by the *Planning and Environment (General Amendment Act) 2004*. Section 54A provides for the amendment of applications at the request of the applicant after notice has been given pursuant to s 52. Aside from sub-s (1), s 57A is generally expressed in the same terms as s 50 (see above). The responsible authority may refuse to amend the application if it considers that the amendment is so substantial that a new application should be made, otherwise it must amend the application as requested: s 57A(4)–(5). If the applicant is not the owner of the land, the request must be signed by the owner or the applicant must submit a declaration that the owner has been informed of the request. On the amendment of the application the amended application is taken to be the application for the purposes of the Act and to have been received on the day the request was received by the responsible authority: s 57A(7)(a). All objections made in relation to the original application are to be taken to be objections to the amended application pursuant to s 57A(7)(b), which preserves the review rights of objectors in the event that they are not notified of the amended application.

If an application is amended under s 57A the responsible authority must determine whether and to whom notification of the amendment must be given and, if notice is to be given, the nature and extent of that notice: 57B(1). In determining whether or not and to whom notice should be given, the responsible authority is required to consider whether, as a result of the amendment, the grant of the permit would cause material detriment to any person: s 57B(2). The responsible authority may give notice or require the applicant to give notice of the amended application. The responsible authority must give a copy of the amended application to the relevant referral authority or authorities unless the responsible authority considers the amendment to the application would not adversely affect the interests of such authority or authorities: s 57C. There does not appear to be any explicit provision enabling referral authorities to exercise their powers under ss 61(2) and 62(1) in relation to amended applications.

These sections provide a formal opportunity for applications to be amended in response to objections lodged as a result of notification undertaken pursuant to s 52. They also recognise that negotiations may be initiated by responsible authorities between applicants and objectors and may result in compromise and therefore alterations to the application. Such alterations may satisfy objectors so that at least some withdraw their objections, a better development may result, and the likelihood of an application for review being lodged by objectors may be reduced if the responsible authority decides to grant the permit.

Objections

Who may object?

Any person who may be affected by the grant of the permit may lodge an objection to a planning permit application, whether or not the permit application has been notified. Section 57(1) of the Act states that "any person who may be affected" may object. An owner or occupier of any land benefited by a registered restrictive covenant is deemed to be a person affected by a permit which would remove or vary the covenant, or authorise a use that would breach the covenant: s 56(1A). However, s 57(2A) provides that the responsible authority may reject an objection "which it considers has been made primarily to secure or maintain a direct or indirect commercial advantage for the objector".

You do not have to be an owner or occupier in the near vicinity of the site to be affected. Objections have to be in writing: s 57(2). There is no prescribed form that must be used, although responsible authorities provide a standard form that may be used. If a group of people all put in separate objections all specifying the same grounds (for example, a community group, each member separately signing and submitting a duplicated letter or standard objection form) then one person may be informed by the responsible authority of its decision on the application: s 57(3) and (4). Section 57(2) provides that an objection must state how the objector would be affected by the grant of the permit. However, the absence of such a statement may not make the objection invalid: *Ritchie's Stores Pty Ltd v Bass Coast SC* [2003] VCAT 233; 14 VPR 82 and *Guinness Mahon Pty Ltd v Moonee Valley CC* (1995) 15 AATR 176. Note that the application itself and all copies of objections must be available for inspection under ss 51 and 57(5) at the office of the responsible authority.

Grounds of objection

The grounds of objection to the grant of the permit should relate to planning considerations as to why that use or development should not be permitted. Common grounds that are often used in objections are an increase in noise and traffic, overlooking, detrimental effect on the amenity of the neighbourhood, increase in density et cetera. But planning considerations, in some limited circumstances, can include the social and economic impact of a proposed development; in particular, where the use or development will have an impact on the community in that area (see below).

The permit application and the plans for the proposal should be inspected before deciding whether or not to lodge an objection. There is no point objecting on the grounds that the proposed development will unreasonably overshadow and result in unreasonable overlooking of your property if the plans show that there will be no overshadowing beyond the boundaries of the subject site and there are no windows facing your property or, if there are windows, they will be screened to prevent overlooking. Objectors often claim that if the permit is granted the values of their properties will fall. A decline in property values *per se* is not a valid town planning consideration: see, for example, *Micaleff v City of Keilor* (1993) 11 AATR 139. A decline in property values may reflect the amenity impact of a proposal, but it is almost impossible to prove that values will fall. For example, it is possible that a permit for a medium density development will inflate the value of surrounding properties by creating an anticipation on the part of developers and buyers that similar developments will be permitted on those properties.

If the responsible authority makes a decision to grant the permit, persons who have objected have a right to apply to VCAT for review of that decision: *Planning and Environment Act 1987*, s 82(1). Any other person who is affected may lodge a Statement of Grounds and apply to be joined as a party to the review proceedings. But note that other persons may lodge a Statement of Grounds and seek to be joined only where at least one written objection to the grant of the permit was received by the responsible authority: *Planning and Environment Act*, s 82B. If the responsible authority fails to make a decision on the permit application within the prescribed time, the applicant has the right to make an application to VCAT for review of that failure. If that occurs, VCAT notifies the objectors and if they lodge a statement of grounds they are parties to the review. If there has been at least one objection lodged, others may also lodge statements of grounds and apply to be joined as parties. If no objections were received by the responsible authority, only the applicant has the right of review under the Act. If the applicant does seek a review, VCAT has the power to require the advertisement of the application: *Planning and Environment Act*, s 85(1)(c)(ii). But the crucial point is that, if no objections are lodged, no-one other than the applicant may have the right to seek a review. Applicants are likely to seek a review against a decision to grant only if they consider that any condition imposed is too onerous.

The decision

Who makes the decision?

Normally it is the relevant local council, acting as the responsible authority, which makes the decision. Responsible authorities may delegate certain decision-making powers to a committee or officer "by instrument": s 188. In this context, "instrument" means a resolution of council. The wording of s 188 of the Act enables the responsible authority to delegate "any of its powers" in relation to making decisions on permit applications. This enables the responsible authority to decide which powers it delegates.

In relation to planning permits, the following may be delegated:
- requiring more information under s 54(1) before dealing with the application;
- granting an extension of time within which further information must be provided, under s 54A;
- amending the application before giving notice, under ss 50 and 50A;
- deciding to give notice under s 52;
- amending an application after the giving of notice, under s 57A;
- considering objections under s 60;
- determining permit applications under ss 60, 63–65;
- framing permit conditions under s 62.

In other words, essentially all permit decisions may be delegated to an officer or committee. Surf Coast Shire Council has appointed, pursuant to s 86 of the *Local Government Act 1989*, a Planning Committee which has as its members five persons from the community who are neither councillors nor officers of the council, and one council officer. The community members have full voting rights. The officer has the right to debate but not vote on matters before the committee. The committee has been delegated, pursuant to s 188(1)(a) of the *Planning and Environment Act*, the power to decide on planning permit applications where objections have been received to an application, or a council officer is recommending refusal of the application, or an application of major significance or sensitivity has been referred to the committee by the responsible authority. An application may be referred to the council for determination by the Senior Planning Officer or the Planning Committee, or may be called in by the council with the agreement of at least five councillors. This system has been in operation in one form or another since 1994. Under it, each year approximately 80 per cent of permit applications are determined by delegated officer, approximately 20 per cent are determined by the Planning Committee, and less than 2 per cent are determined by the council. A major advantage of this system claimed by Surfcoast Shire is that it takes local politics out of decision making on permit applications. However, it does give rise to concerns about the accountability of the decision makers. It seems likely that there will be a continuing debate about whether it is appropriate for decisions on planning permit applications to be made by persons who are neither councillors nor council officers, and whether the Surfcoast model is one which other councils should emulate.

Generally speaking, responsible authorities are reluctant to delegate all their powers. The types of matters usually delegated by councils to officers, or to a committee of councillors, or to a committee of councillors and officers, include the power to advertise, consider objections, frame permit conditions, and make a final decision on applications only where no objections have been lodged.

The Minister may "call in" a permit application and make the decision under ss 97A–97M of the *Planning and Environment Act* (see Chapter 2). When an application is "called in" then, subject to some exceptions in s 97E(5), the application must be referred for report and recommendations to a panel appointed under Part 8 of the Act. Such a panel must give objectors reasonable opportunity to be heard (s 97E(2)–(3)) and must consider objections and submissions made to it (see Chapter 8).

Where the Minister has made a decision, there are special mandatory provisions that apply and also special provisions as to the amendment of a permit issued by the Minister under these provisions. The normal rights and remedies (that is, a right to seek review to VCAT under Part 4, Division 2, including amendment or cancellation of the permit under Division 3 and referral under s 149A) are excluded by s 97M.

The calling-in of applications is a major incursion into third party rights in the planning process. When the power is exercised by the Minister, responsible authorities have no input into the decision. Third party rights are given some recognition by providing a panel to which they can make submissions. However, the panel can only make recommendations to the Minister. The final determination will be made by the Minister (a politician with no requirement to be impartial and who may lack expertise) and not by an independent quasi-judicial tribunal (VCAT is presided over by a Supreme Court judge and the Planning and Environment List consists of a body of experts).

As noted in Chapter 2, Part 4AA of the *Planning and Environment Act*, inserted into the Act in 2009, provides for Development Assessment Committees (DACs), which may act as responsible authorities for planning permit applications for land in the Activity Centre Zone in metropolitan suburbs specified in s 97M. Section 97MB provides that the Governor in Council, on the recommendation of the Minister, may establish DACs by order published in the *Government Gazette*. The order establishing a DAC must specify the class or classes of application to be determined by the order and the area or areas in the relevant Activity Centre Zone or Zones for which the DAC has been established. Sections 97MD, 97MF and 97MJ provide that, in deciding applications for permits and for amendment of permits, a DAC has all the powers that the responsible authority would have had to decide on the application if it were not a DAC application. Section 97MH provides that the decision, or failure to make a decision, of a DAC is taken to be a decision, or failure to make a decision, of the responsible authority. Therefore an Application for Review of a decision or a failure to make a decision may be made to VCAT, and VCAT will determine such applications, provided the Minister does not exercise the call-in power pursuant to cll 58 and 59 of Schedule 1 of the *VCAT Act* (see Chapter 6).

The membership of a DAC comprises a chairperson nominated by the Minister, two other members nominated by the Minister, and two other members nominated by the relevant council, who must be drawn from a list of five persons who are councillors or council staff who have been nominated by the council: s 97MK. Sections 97MW to 97MZT deal with probity requirements for and conflicts of interest of DAC members. Alternative members are required for each position.

Applications for appointment to the first DAC (for the Doncaster Hill Activity Centre) were called for in mid-August 2010. The role statement prepared by the Department of Planning and Community Development for these positions states that DACs are "to provide for partnership between State and Local Government in the consideration and determination of planning permit applications for projects of Metropolitan significance within Melbourne's 26 Principal Activity Centres". It goes on to state that DACs are to meet and determine permit applications on an as-needed basis and will be supported through the department, that permit applications are to be lodged with the relevant municipal council, including giving third party notice where required and the preparation of an Officer's report in respect of each application, and that DAC decisions, including failure to decide, can be reviewed by VCAT.

The rationale for establishing DACs is not clear. It is difficult to see how they will necessarily result in councils becoming more amenable to making decisions faster or more consistently with the metropolitan policy of encouraging significantly more intense development in and around activity centres. And there remain at this stage a large number of unknowns. Will a responsible authority be able to lodge an objection or otherwise make a submission to a DAC? If so, how is the issue of bias to be avoided for those members who are councillors or officers of the responsible authority? Why should a responsible authority defend before VCAT a decision that it does not agree with? How can it be expected to defend a decision it did not make? Is a responsible authority itself able to seek review of a DAC decision? If a council is required to defend a DAC decision before VCAT, who is to provide the resources for it to do that? Is the relevant DAC a party to review proceedings?

The ambit of discretion

In making its decision on whether or not to grant a permit application, the responsible authority is exercising a discretionary power. The discretion of the decision maker must be exercised in accordance with the purpose for which the discretion is conferred. In exercising its discretion to grant or refuse a permit application and impose conditions on an application, the responsible authority (and VCAT on review of that decision) is confined to considerations that are relevant to the subject matter of the provision. In most instances those considerations are broadly based, particularly where the permit application may be for multiple consents under the zoning and overlays which apply to the land and perhaps also under other provisions of the planning scheme. But, as also explained in Chapters 3 and 8, it is an established principle of planning law that, in determining a planning permit application, the responsible authority's discretion is limited to the matters included in the clause that triggered the application: see *National Trust of Australia (Victoria) v Australian Temperance and General Mutual Life Assurance Society Ltd* [1976] VR 592; *Victorian National Parks Association Inc v Iluka Resources* [2004] VCAT 20. If, for example, the requirement for a permit is triggered only by the provisions of an Environmental Significance Overlay which applies to the land, the responsible authority is confined to considering matters authorised by the provisions of the overlay. If the requirement for a permit is triggered only by the provisions of a Heritage Overlay, the responsible authority must consider heritage issues only in making its decision.

Matters the responsible authority must consider

The matters the responsible authority or the delegate acting on behalf of the responsible authority must consider in making the decision are specified in s 60. They include the relevant planning scheme, the objectives of planning in Victoria, all objections and other submissions which it has received and which have not been withdrawn, all decisions and comments of referral authorities and any significant effects on the environment of the proposed use or development, or vice versa: see s 60(1). The requirement to consider any significant effects the environment may have on the use or development may arise, for example, where the proposal is for a medium density development in a Residential 1 Zone and where industrial uses on abutting land operating under existing use rights may have a detrimental impact on the development.

Note that planning schemes contain State policies set out in the State Planning Policy Framework (SPPF), Municipal Strategic Statements (MSSs) and local planning policies set out in the Local Planning Policy Framework (LPPF), over-arching decision guidelines at cl 65 and then specific decision guidelines which accompany each zone and overlay.

In addition to these mandatory considerations, s 60 provides that the responsible authority may consider, *if the circumstances appear to so require*, a number of other matters. They include any significant social and economic effects of the use or development, any approved regional strategy plan and any amendment to it not adopted but not yet approved by the Minister, any relevant State environment protection policy declared in any Order made by the Governor in Council under s 16 of the *Environment Protection Act 1970*, any other strategic plan, policy statement, code or guideline which has been adopted by a Minister, government department, public authority or municipal council, any amendment to the planning scheme adopted by the responsible authority but not approved by the Minister or a planning authority, any agreement made pursuant to s 173, and any other relevant matter.

As Morris J observed in another context:

> [T]he *apparent* scope of relevant considerations is extremely broad. This is typically the case with planning permit decisions. Yet if all apparently relevant factors need to be considered in a particular case, with reasons being articulated as to how the matter was taken into account, the making of decisions on planning permit applications would be quite impossible. In the real world, most decisions revolve around just one or two

key considerations ... (*Victorian National Parks Association Inc v Iluka Resources* [2004] VCAT 20)

The role of policy in decision-making

A policy must not be applied as if it were a mandatory requirement of the planning scheme. In the great majority of cases, to do so would inevitably involve a selective application, given the multitude of policies contained in the SPPF and LPPF. What is required is a balancing of conflicting policies in favour of net community benefit and sustainable development, as required by VPP provision at cl 11 of planning schemes.

In *Doncaster Property Partnership v Manningham CC* [2004] VCAT 2445, the Tribunal affirmed a decision of the responsible authority to refuse a permit for a new two-storey building to house a car dealership and service centre opposite Westfield Shoppingtown in Doncaster on the grounds that the proposal would be an underdevelopment of the site, given the policies and strategic vision for the area set out in the Manningham Planning Scheme. Westfield Shoppingtown is identified in *Melbourne 2030* as a principal activity centre. The strategic vision for the centre is set out in cl 21.21 of the scheme and was introduced into the scheme by Amendment C33. That vision is based on the Doncaster Hill Strategy adopted by Manningham City Council in October 2002 and described by the Tribunal as the culmination of planning for the Doncaster Hill area since the 1980s. The vision for the precinct within which the subject land was located is the development of a high-density, mixed-use area including cafes, restaurants and outdoor seating at ground floor level.

In the *Doncaster Property Partnership* decision at paras [50]-[61], the Tribunal discussed the role of policies in determining permit applications and we have taken the liberty of reproducing most of that discussion:

> 50. It is sometimes argued that if a use or development is permitted by the planning scheme, then it ought to be approved and an applicant should not be forced to do something more with his land than suits his purpose or his means. In this respect, it is said that planning policy may encourage a use or development but cannot compel it.
>
> 51. However, the limitations of this argument are that it ignores the role of policy in planning schemes. Planning schemes based on the Victoria Planning Provisions are based on policy and decisions must be Predicated on the degree to which they will implement policy. For example, clause 31 of the Victoria Planning Provisions states:
>> Because a use is in Section 2 does not imply that a permit should or will be granted. The responsible authority must decide whether the proposal will produce acceptable outcomes in terms of the State Planning Policy Framework, the Local Planning Policy Framework, the purpose and decision guidelines of the zone and any of the other decision guidelines in Clause 65.
>
> 52. The purpose of all zones, overlays and various other provisions expressed throughout the planning scheme includes
>> To implement the State Planning Policy Framework and the Local Planning Policy Framework, including the Municipal Strategic Statement and local planning policies.
>
> 53. A council wears two hats in the planning process – as planning authority and responsible authority. It is the role of the planning authority to set policy and

include that policy in the planning scheme. It is the role of the responsible authority to administer the planning scheme and to make decisions that will seek to implement the policy it contains. It is not open to the responsible authority to ignore policy in the process of decision-making because it may no longer agree with it or does not like the outcome it produces in a particular set of circumstances. To change policy requires an amendment to the planning scheme by the planning authority. The same constraints apply to the Tribunal on review where it stands in the shoes of the responsible Authority.

54. When policy is adopted into the planning scheme it goes through a process set out in the *Planning and Environment Act 1987*, which will normally involve public participation through exhibition of an amendment, the opportunity to make submissions and to be heard by an independent panel. A planning authority has an obligation to prepare a municipal strategic statement (MSS) for its municipal district which must contain the Strategic planning, land use and development objectives of the planning authority. The planning authority also has an obligation to review its MSS every three years or as directed by the Minister and to regularly review all the provisions of the planning scheme for which it is a planning authority. The Victoria Planning Provisions envisage that an MSS will change and evolve over time to reflect the strategic planning for an area. Clause 20 states:

> The MSS is dynamic and enables community involvement in its ongoing review. The MSS will be built upon as responsible authorities develop and refine their strategic directions in response to the changing needs of the community.
>
> When preparing amendments to this scheme and before making decisions about permit applications, planning and responsible authorities must take the MSS into account.

55. If a policy is included in a planning scheme, the Tribunal should be cautious before finding that the Policy is not capable of implementation or is not a pragmatic policy and therefore should be disregarded. The Tribunal must seek to implement the planning scheme objectives and apply policy where relevant even if this leads to outcomes that the Tribunal, applicants, objectors or even the council do not like or agree with. The consequences of a proper application of policy rest with the planning authority. It is always open to the planning authority to change a policy that is not working, that is producing unwanted or undesirable outcomes or where the needs of the community change. Indeed, these are matters that each council should consider when it undertakes its three-yearly review of the planning scheme.

56. As Member Keaney said in the case of *Mitchell v Port Phillip City Council* [2002] VCAT 452 (11 VPR 127) with respect to a particular policy favouring a *"preference for somewhat larger dwellings with larger areas of open space which might be attractive to households other than single persons or couples"*:

> The Tribunal believes that Council is entitled to have that strategic view. It is a view which has been publicly tested. It is a view which has been considered by a Planning Panel. It is a view now sanctioned by the State Government. Under new format planning schemes therefore it is a policy position of some importance which should only be overturned for very good reason. The Tribunal is not in a position of reviewing the merits of that policy; it is simply trying to implement it.

57. Of course there are instances where it will not be appropriate to implement a policy. Situations will arise where there are competing policies, in which case the responsible authority and the Tribunal must be guided by the principles set out in clause 11 of the Victoria Planning Provisions:

It is the State Government's expectation that planning and responsible authorities will endeavour to integrate the range of policies relevant to the issues to be determined and balance conflicting objectives in favour of net community benefit and sustainable development.

Planning, under the *Planning and Environment Act 1987*, is to encompass and integrate relevant environmental, social and economic factors. It is directed towards the interests of sustainable development for the benefit of present and future generations, on the basis of relevant policy and legislation. Planning authorities and responsible authorities are responsible for the effective planning and management of land use and development in their districts for the broad interests of the community, through the preparation of strategic plans, statutory plans, development and conservation plans, development contribution plans, and other relevant plans to achieve the objectives of the Act.

58. In other cases, the policy may be ambiguous, unintelligible or produce an absurd outcome. In situations such as this the Tribunal may well reach the conclusion that a particular policy should not or cannot be applied, as the Tribunal observed in the case of *Brichon Developments Pty Ltd v Glen Eira CC* [2001] VCAT 497 (reported at 8 VPR 10), where Member Read said:

[29] ... However, the application of any policy still has to be 'tempered' by considering whether the policy is meaningful in the particular (or any) situation. If this is not the case, it is appropriate to set the policy aside or vary its interpretation. I do not accept the attitude that, merely because a policy is incorporated into the planning scheme it will necessarily always (or ever) make sense. There have been plenty of examples, or situations, where approved policies can be found to be inapplicable, or not open to sensible or useful interpretation.

59. There will also be cases where the Tribunal finds that a policy is not relevant or applicable to the facts before it. A decision about whether a policy is applicable or relevant will always turn on the facts and circumstances of the case. Equally, as Justice Balmford said in the Supreme Court case of *Glen Eira City Council v Gory* [2001] VSC 306 with respect to the obligation to consider policy 'as appropriate': *"To consider is not necessarily to adopt or to follow."*

60. However, presuming that a policy is relevant, it makes sense and there are no competing policies or any overriding community interest to the contrary, we consider the Tribunal should seek to implement that policy. This may mean refusing a permit on the grounds that it constitutes an underdevelopment of a site, which would undermine or prejudice the long-term achievement of the policy objectives. It is important though to bear in mind that it is the role of the Tribunal in each case to consider and determine if in fact the policy is relevant, if it makes sense, whether there are competing policies (and if so how they should be balanced) and ultimately if there is any overriding community interest to the contrary.

Before cl 12 of the SPPF was inserted into the VPPs in September 2005, *Melbourne 2030* was given significant weight by VCAT in decisions such as *Ashlyn Enterprises Pty Ltd v Yarra City Council* [2003] VCAT 87; 13 VPR 132, *Rowcliffe Pty Ltd v Stonnington CC* [2004] VCAT 46 and [2004] VCAT 1370; 16 VPR 9, and *Golden Ridge v Whitehorse CC (Mitcham Towers)* [2004] VCAT 1706. In *Ashlyn,* sometimes referred to as the "cheesegrater" case because of the appearance of part of the proposed development, the proposal was for 152 dwellings, two cafes and associated car parking in Mixed Use Zone in Fitzroy. A Heritage Overlay applied to some of the parcels of land comprising the site. The Tribunal granted a permit holding that the contemporary architecture was not inappropriate in the location, and that the proposal was an appropriate design response to the heritage significance of the area and its neighbourhood character. In *Rowcliffe,* where the proposal was for seven buildings containing between two and six levels in a Residential 1 Zone, the Tribunal took the view that it was obliged to consider *Melbourne 2030.* In *Golden Ridge* the proposal was for residential towers of eight and 14 storeys above a three-level podium devoted mainly to car parking, located about 20 metres from one of the entrances to Mitcham Railway Station and in a Mixed Use Zone. The Tribunal held that *Melbourne 2030* was an important consideration in this case.

In *O'Connell Street Developments Pty Ltd v Yarra CC* [2003] VCAT 448; 13 VPR 227, a guideline decision dealing with the status of *Melbourne 2030,* the Tribunal held that, as distinct from its associated Draft Implementation Plans, *Melbourne 2030* was an adopted policy of the State government which the Tribunal may consider and, if the circumstances so require, must consider pursuant to s 60(1)(b), because it is a strategy in its final form, it has been adopted after an extensive consultation process, and the Minister and the State government are pursuing its implementation on a serious basis. The Tribunal stated that it was entitled to give weight to *Melbourne 2030* in balancing competing policies and other provisions of the planning scheme, but it also sounded a note of caution by stating:

> The primary obligation of a responsible authority and the Tribunal when deciding on a permit application is to apply the existing law, being the appropriate legislation and the planning scheme currently in force, and whilst it is desirable that discretion be exercised in a way that does not compromise the Metropolitan Strategy, until it is incorporated into the planning scheme, it should not be the basis for the approval of a proposal that is inconsistent with or contrary to the controls or policies of the existing planning scheme.

The social and economic effects of a proposal

The extent to which economic and social considerations may be used as grounds of review merits close analysis, because s 60 of the *Planning and Environment Act* provides that responsible authorities may consider, if the circumstances appear to so require, any significant social and economic effects of the use or development for which application is made. The *Town and Country Planning Act* made no reference to social and economic effects in relation to decisions on planning permit applications, but nevertheless such effects had been established for many years by the courts and tribunals as legitimate and proper planning considerations in certain circumstances. The decisions indicated that planning consents are not concerned with private economic and social impacts. However, the courts distinguished between different economic and social considerations in an attempt to determine when these matters will or will not be a relevant consideration.

In *Ampol Petroleum Ltd v Warringah Shire Council* (1956) 1 LGRA 276, Sugerman J stated at 279:

> It is difficult to express the precise distinction between what considerations may fall within the scope and object of the subject legislation and what considerations fall outside it ... probably the true distinction under clause 27, is that between what has been referred to in some of the decisions as "town planning considerations" and, on the other hand, social or economic considerations of a general character, not specifically related to town planning; between, that is to say, on the one hand, the responsible authority, which is the local municipal or shire council, directing its mind to considerations of town planning and, on the other hand, its directing its mind to considerations which go beyond town planning and are of a general social or economic nature, more appropriate to be dealt with by the central government ...

The Court held in this case that it was beyond the scope of a responsible authority's town planning powers to attempt to rationalise a product market. The authority had refused a permit for a service station on the ground that there was already an adequate number of service stations to serve the community. The case is an illustration of an authority improperly taking into consideration a particular and not a general economic consideration, the former being irrelevant and the latter relevant in the consideration of a permit application. The refusal of a permit for a service station may have a general economic effect in stifling competition and thereby, say, increasing the cost of petrol, unlike, for example, the effect of the proposed development on the cost of living, on transportation, in travelling time of commuters generally et cetera.

The issue has been discussed in a number of cases concerning regional shopping centres. In *Spurling v Development Underwriting (Vic) Pty Ltd* [1973] VR 1, it was argued and accepted by the Supreme Court of Victoria that it was irrelevant that shopkeepers in neighbouring centres would lose customers if a proposed regional shopping centre was permitted. However, the Court went on to say that, where a neighbouring shopping centre would suffer an unjustifiable economic impact as a result of the proposed development, this would have an adverse effect on the amenity of the residents who use the shops and would thus be relevant. Stephen J said at 12–13:

> In my view, it is a proper planning consideration to inquire whether or not the establishment of some competing regional shopping centre will adversely affect existing shopping facilities or will render unlikely of execution some existing plan to improve existing shopping facilities for local residents of the area, to that extent possibly prejudicing amenity.

Thus, where a neighbouring shopping centre will suffer an unjustifiable economic impact as a result of permitting a new shopping complex, a responsible authority may refuse the permit on these grounds. What is unjustifiable must be determined on a case-by-case basis.

It is clear from the cases that *private* economic considerations are clearly not proper planning considerations (for example, whether the applicant will lose money on the development or whether the development will cause devaluation of individual property values in the area). However, if the proposed development has an economic effect on the community generally, that may be a relevant and proper consideration;

the courts and tribunals have in certain instances been able to justify the consideration of social or economic matters on the basis that the effect goes further than, for example, merely affecting competition and so becomes a matter of public economics.

The principles expounded in *Spurling's* case were further clarified by the High Court in *Kentucky Fried Chicken Pty Ltd v Gantidis* (1979) 140 CLR 675; 40 LGRA 132. A council took into account economic competition feared or expected from a proposed use. The Court held that the council had not properly considered the permit application, as this was not a planning consideration within the terms of the scheme ordinance. Barwick CJ stated at p 681:

> [I]t is in my opinion that economic competition feared or expected from a proposed use is not a planning consideration within the terms of the Planning Scheme Ordinance governing the matter. Nothing said by my brother Stephen in *Spurling* ought to be taken as deciding otherwise.

However, if the proposal would jeopardise the amenity of the area, permission may properly be refused; that is, in certain circumstances the competition may have an effect on the amenity of the area. Stephen J, agreeing with the Chief Justice, stated at p 687:

> If the shopping facilities presently enjoyed by a community or planned for it in the future are put in jeopardy by some proposed development, whether that jeopardy be due to physical or financial causes, and if the resultant community detriment will not be made good by the proposed development itself, that appears to me to be a consideration proper to be taken into account as a matter of town planning. It does not cease to be so because the profitability of individual existing businesses are at one and the same time also threatened by the new competition afforded by that new development ... However, the mere threat of competition to existing businesses if not accompanied by a prospect of a resultant overall adverse effect upon the extent and adequacy of facilities available to the local community if the development be proceeded with, will not be a relevant town planning consideration.

If the proposed use would have the effect of putting the existing facilities at risk then the effect of the proposed development on the amenity of the area is a proper town planning consideration. There must be, however, a threat of loss of that facility to the community, otherwise the economic effect is not a relevant consideration.

As with economic considerations, social considerations are not of themselves necessarily regarded as proper planning matters that may be taken into account by a responsible authority or the Tribunal in the consideration of a planning application. For example, the cases clearly establish that planning is not concerned with the social and moral effects of a proposed brothel: *Child v City of Frankston* (1983) 13 APA 474; *Nicholson v City of Camberwell* (1988) 33 APA 151. The Planning Appeals Board stated in *Richards v City of Richmond* (1984) 18 APA 323 that it is not the function of the Board to impose on the community its own views of morality. The Tribunal has also held that it was in no doubt that gaming raises important social and economic questions but it did not believe it could decide a case on the basis of the effects of gambling generally in Victoria, since gambling is legal: *Uniting Church v Moreland City Council* (1996) 16 AATR 250. Similarly, the Tribunal has stated that, whilst there was a widely held perception that the social effects of tabletop dancing were significant, it is a use which is discretionary under the relevant planning scheme: *Sammartino v Greater Geelong City Council* (1997) 19 AATR 295. In *Odyssey House v Benalal Rural CC* [2003] VCAT 15; 13 VPR 69, the Tribunal overturned the decision of the responsible authority to refuse a permit for a drug rehabilitation centre on the outskirts of a small rural settlement approximately 18 kilometres west of Benalla, holding that the proposal was not inconsistent with the purposes of the Rural Zone, unlikely to undermine the social cohesion of the local community, there was a demonstrated need for the facility, and it would result in a net community benefit.

In *Nascon Australia Pty Ltd v Maroondah* (1997) 18 AATR 50 at 71, the Tribunal held that:

> It is now firmly established in law ... that planning can and should have regard to the economic effect of a proposal and that proposals may be rejected on such grounds as adverse economic effects for the community at large.

The Tribunal held in *Marion v Shire of Orbost* (1994) 12 AATR 268 that, in the particular circumstances which applied in the case, the effect of the proposal on the economic viability of another establishment was a relevant consideration. It disallowed an appeal against a refusal to grant a permit for a proposed convenience store and petrol sales outlet and found that the well-established and recognised activity and social role of an existing general store in an isolated community should not be put at risk by the economic impact of the proposal: the community as a whole would suffer if that occurred.

It is clear that sectional and individual economic considerations do not come within the ambit of the provisions (see, for example, *Bellan Constructions v City of Geelong* (unreported, Planning Division of the AAT, P87/2252); *Vernia Pty Ltd v City of South Melbourne and J Licouski and C Simpas*, noted at 1 AATR 2). The principles enunciated by Stephen J in *Spurling* continue to apply.

In the light of the precise wording of s 4 and s 60, and on the basis of decisions made by the Tribunal, it would appear that the law has not radically changed in this area since the days of the *Town and Country Planning Act*. The fact is that individual competition or individual dislike of a particular use will not of itself be relevant unless it can be tied to broader community effects consisting of a social problem or a social benefit, or an economic advantage or disadvantage. The matter will be a relevant consideration when it affects "the community" rather than the individual in an advantageous or detrimental way but normally only where the community in question has particular characteristics such that a use or development may have an impact much greater than on other communities. Planning controls must not be used to stifle economic competition, and even charitable organisations are not exempt from that principle: *Try Youth and Community Services Inc v Banyule CC* [2000] VCAT 1123; 5 VPR 218.

The tests to be applied for variation or removal of covenants

A registered restrictive covenant is a restriction on a property title which continues despite changes in ownership. Before the advent of planning legislation and planning schemes, registered restrictive covenants were often used as a private form of land use and development control, prohibiting land uses such as industry and quarrying, or restricting to one only the number of dwellings which could be built, or requiring dwellings to be constructed of brick or stone.

The responsible authority must not grant a permit which allows the removal or variation of a restrictive covenant unless it is satisfied that the owner of any land benefited by the covenant (other than an owner who has in writing consented to the grant of the permit) will be unlikely to suffer financial loss, loss of amenity, loss arising from change to the character of the neighbourhood or any other detriment: s 60(2). In the case of a restrictive covenant registered on or before 25 June 1991, the responsible authority must not grant a permit which removes or varies it unless the responsible authority is satisfied that the owner of any land benefiting from the restriction (other than an owner who has in writing consented to the grant of the permit) will be unlikely to suffer any detriment of any kind, including any perceived detriment, and if that owner has objected to the grant of the permit, that objection is vexatious and not made in good faith: s 60(5).

Where a restrictive covenant benefits only the lot or parcel of land that is the subject of the permit application and owned by the applicant, or where such owner has consented to the permit being granted, s 60(2) or (5) do not provide any significant bar to a permit being granted. However, a registered restrictive covenant commonly applies to more than one lot or parcel and so more than one owner benefits from it. For covenants registered after 25 June 1991 the tests that must be satisfied before the responsible authority may grant a permit to remove or vary are onerous. They are significantly more onerous for covenants registered on or before 25 June 1991, because the responsible authority must be satisfied that the owner of any land benefiting from the restriction will be unlikely to suffer any detriment of any kind, including perceived detriment. This means that in the great majority of instances such restrictions may only be removed or varied by consent. But the test of "perceived detriment" may not be an insuperable barrier in all situations. The Tribunal concluded in *Dennis Marsden Subdivisional Services Pty Ltd v City of Heidelberg* (1994) 13 AATR 7 that the test of perceived detriment in s 60(5) must be an objective one; that there must be, at the least, a reasonable basis for believing that the perception of detriment has some foundation. In *Wilde v City of Moonee Valley* (1997) 18 AATR 145, the Tribunal followed *Dennis Marsden* and found that perceived detriment does not mean a perception of detriment, but there must be an actual detriment that someone perceives. In *Harmonious Blend Building Group v Shire of Yarra Ranges* (unreported, 1996/48593; editorial comment (1997) 18 AATR 242) the Tribunal held that perceived detriment must be a real detriment capable of objective analysis, and that it must be probable in that it must not be unlikely. In *Castles v Bayside City Council* [2004] VCAT 864, it was held that the test is unlikelihood rather than absolute certainty, although the detriment is a bar if it is likely and minor, even if it would be outweighed by other considerations.

Communicating the decision to those concerned

The decision of the responsible authority can be to grant, to grant subject to conditions, or to refuse. If a referral authority objects under s 56 of the Act then the responsible authority must refuse under s 61. In addition, pursuant to s 61(4), if the grant of a permit would authorise anything that would result in a breach of a registered restrictive covenant, the responsible authority must refuse to grant the permit unless a permit has been issued or a decision made to grant a permit to allow the removal or variation of the covenant. The decision must be communicated to the applicant, to objectors, if there have been any, and to referral authorities. A Notice of Decision to Grant must be sent to the applicant and objectors if there have been objections lodged and the responsible authority has decided to grant a permit (it cannot issue the permit because objectors and others have the right of review): *Planning and Environment Act*, s 64; *Planning and Environment Regulations 2005*, reg 25, Form 5, Schedule 1. A Notice of Refusal is sent to objectors and the applicant if the decision was to refuse: *Planning and Environment Act*, s 65; *Planning and Environment Regulations 2005*, reg 28, Form 6, Schedule 1.

It is not unknown for responsible authorities to play local politics and refuse the application if there has been a flood of objections. Rather than examine the merits of an application and, where appropriate, frame conditions to address the concerns of the objections, they refuse the application or fail to make a decision within the prescribed time and so effectively force the applicant to seek a review, thereby leaving it to VCAT to make the decision.

Permit conditions

Section 62(1) provides that certain types of conditions must be included on planning permits, namely:

- any condition which the planning scheme or a relevant referral authority requires to be included;
- if the grant of the permit would authorise anything which would result in a breach of a registered restrictive covenant, a condition that the permit is not to come into effect until the covenant is removed or varied. (s 61(1)(a), (aa))

Section 62(2) of the *Planning and Environment Act* lays down the ambit of conditions that may be included in a permit. Section 62(2) is not an exhaustive list but is prefaced by the words "any other condition that it thinks fit, including ...". For example, a condition may specify things which are to be done to the satisfaction of the responsible authority, the requirement of car parking, landscaping of the site and so on.

In addition to s 62 of the Act, the courts and tribunals have established certain criteria for determining whether a responsible authority has properly exercised its right to impose conditions. These are whether the condition is fair and reasonably related to the permitted development, whether it is reasonable, whether the condition is reasonably certain and whether the condition involves excessive delegation.

A condition will be fairly and reasonably related to the permitted development if there is a connection between the permission granted and the limitation imposed. However, the condition must also be reasonably capable of being related to the implementation of planning policy as set out in the Act or the planning scheme. Even where a condition relates to the permission granted, it can be struck down for being unreasonable in that it is so unreasonable that no reasonable responsible authority would have imposed it. A condition should also clearly set out the obligations imposed. That is, it should not be vague or uncertain. See *Rosemeier v Greater Geelong City Council (No 1)* (1997) 20 AATR 86, where the Tribunal provides an in-depth analysis of the relevant case law and tests applied on the validity of planning conditions.

In *Eddie Barron v Constructions Pty Ltd v Shire of Cranbourne* (1987) 28 APA 128; 6 AATR 10, the Tribunal identified four criteria which must be satisfied before, in that instance, a condition imposing a monetary contribution to be paid by the permit applicant is valid. These include need, equity, and nexus. There must be a need for the condition in the sense that the consequence of the use or development must give rise to the condition being proposed. There must be a nexus between the use and/or development for which consent is being granted and the condition being imposed. For example, a condition being imposed to rectify an existing problem (such as a drainage problem) not caused nor exacerbated by the use and/or development would be invalid. A condition must not be inequitable. A condition requiring the applicant to surface, or pay for the entire cost of surfacing, the entire length of a road or laneway to which the subject land and other properties have frontages would be invalid. It would be inequitable because other properties which also have frontage to the laneway would also benefit but would not be contributing to the cost.

Conditions must be framed so that they are capable of enforcement. That is, the requirements set out in the condition must be clear, certain and unambiguous. For example, "the proprietor shall cease trading at 11 pm" could mean that he or she could close at 11 pm and open again at 11.01 pm.

The issue of conditions dealing with the imposition of development levies was discussed in Chapter 3. The issue of "spent" conditions in relation to permits for subdivision was discussed in Chapter 2. For examples of valid and invalid conditions, see Parts 5.40 to 5.45, *Planning Appeal Case Notes* volume in Byard, Code, Porritt and Testro, *Planning and Environment Service Victoria* in Further Reading.

Agreements and permits

Under s 173 of the *Planning and Environment Act* a responsible authority may enter into an agreement with the owner of the land. The form and content of the agreement are set out in s 174. The agreement can restrict the use or development of land and can subject the land to special conditions. The responsible authority can also impose a condition in the permit that an agreement be entered into between it and the owner of land. The types of agreements that have been entered into include an agreement that there be no further subdivision of the allotment created by a subdivision (see, for example, cl 37.07-3 of the Farming Zone provisions), an agreement which outlined the steps required to be taken to ameliorate the detrimental effects of television reception, and an agreement to create a buffer zone (for other examples, see Part 7, *Planning Appeal Case Notes* volume in Byard, Code, Porritt and Testro, *Planning and Environment Service Victoria* in Further Reading). In general, agreements are used where it is intended to impose a continuing obligation on the land owner, such as to eradicate pest animals and weeds and maintain the land pest-free, and/or revegetate the land over a period of time and then maintain that vegetation.

The advantage of imposing a condition that a particular agreement be entered into between the applicant and the responsible authority is that it may be a means of imposing restraints which may not be regarded as within the scope of the power to impose conditions. Another advantage of using a s 173 agreement is that one can provide within the terms of the contract the mechanism for costs and a default clause. If the provisions are not complied with, contractual remedies are available to enforce the agreement.

Where possible, s 173 agreements should contain sunset clauses. But care should be taken in deciding if an agreement is the most appropriate mechanism to use in the first place, such as by a restriction on title, imposed as a condition which must be complied with before the use or development for which permission is sought commences. Such restrictions are negative in nature and cannot be used to require an owner to undertake actions, and so may not be appropriate in particular circumstances. Agreements may be ended by a sunset clause in the agreement itself, specifying that it ends partly or wholly on the happening of a specified event, or at a specified time, or on the cessation of the use or development of the land for a specified purpose: s 177(1). In the absence of a sunset clause, an agreement can only be ended in whole or part with the approval of the Minister, or by agreement between the responsible authority and all persons who are bound by any covenant in the agreement: s 175(2).

Sections 181 and 182 deal with the registration of agreements and entering of their registration on title. In the absence of s 13 agreements being executed in this way, the agreement may not be able to be enforced against future owners of the land.

Amending a permit

Section 71 provides the power for a responsible authority to correct mistakes in a permit, whether or not the permit was issued at the direction of VCAT. The power is confined to correcting clerical errors, or an error arising from an accidental slip or omission, or an evident miscalculation of figures or mistake in the description of any person, thing or property referred to in the permit.

Pursuant to ss 72–76D, introduced into the Act via the *Planning and Environment (General Amendment) Act 2004*, a person who is entitled to use or develop land in accordance with a permit may apply to the responsible authority for an amendment to the permit. An amendment includes an amendment to any plans, drawings or other documents approved under a permit: s 72(1)(c). Leaving aside for the moment secondary consents, which are discussed below, if the permit was issued at the direction of the Tribunal, any application for its amendment must be made to the Tribunal pursuant to s 87, which sets out the circumstances in which an amendment may be made, including any material misstatement or concealment of fact in relation to the application, and any material change of circumstances which has occurred since the grant of the permit. If the permit was issued after being called in and determined by the Minister, an application for its amendment must be made to the Minister, who may appoint a panel to consider the application and provide advice as to whether the permit should be amended: ss 97I, 97J. An application to amend a permit must be treated by a responsible authority as if it were an application for a permit (and therefore must be notified in accordance with s 52). If no-one has objected to the application to amend the permit, or if notice of the amendment is not required to be given to objectors under s 64 because it is exempt from the normal notification requirements, the responsible authority must issue an amended permit: s 74. If the application to amend is not exempt, a decision to grant is subject to review by VCAT: ss 75 and 76C. If the application to amend is refused, that decision is subject to review by VCAT: s 76C.

Permits may also be amended by the responsible authority by a secondary consent or by the permit amendment provisions set out at ss 72–76D, or by VCAT. "Permit" includes any plans, drawings or documents approved under a permit: see *Zuzek v Boroondara* [2007] VCAT 2174. Secondary consent amendments may be granted whether or not the permit was issued at the direction of VCAT following its decision on an Application for Review. But, for a secondary consent to be granted, the terms of the permit must allow such a consent. If a permit contains a condition to the effect that the development shown on the endorsed plans must not be altered without the consent of the responsible authority then a secondary consent to changes to the plans is authorised and may be granted. Similarly, conditions which specify operating hours or maximum numbers of persons on premises, but also contain words to the effect that these hours or number must not be altered without the consent of the responsible authority, authorise secondary consents, which may then be granted. In essence, relatively minor amendments may be made by secondary consent provisions in the permit, such as changes to the internal layout of buildings, or minor changes to the footprint or height of a building, or minor changes to the operating hours of a business, or the time limits within which a development must commence or be completed. However, if the changes proposed are likely to have any significant amenity or other impacts on other land, such as may happen with a change in the footprint or height of a building, then the secondary consent mechanism must not be used. If the change would require an additional consent, such as a change in the footprint or setbacks of a building, which would then trigger a permit requirement under a Vegetation Protection Overlay, for example, then the secondary consent mechanism must not be used. *Westpoint Corporation v Moreland CC* [2005] VCAT 2174 sets out parameters

for the use of secondary consents. A secondary consent may be used (provided that the permit authorises the use of a secondary consent) if:
- it does not result in the transformation of the proposal;
- it does not authorise something for which primary consent is required;
- it is of no consequence, having regard to the purpose of the planning control under which the permit was granted;
- it is not contrary to a specific requirement, as distinct from an authorisation within the permit, which itself cannot be altered by consent.

The amendment of permit provisions set out at ss 72–76D do not apply to permits issued by the Minister under Division 6 of the Act. Division 6 sets out the powers of the Minister to call in a permit application from a responsible authority and decide the permit application himself/herself (see Chapter 2 below). Applications for amendment for such permits must be made to the Minister: see s 97I. Nor do they apply to permits issued at the direction of VCAT (s 72(2)): aside from amendments by secondary consents, such permits may be amended only by VCAT.

The amendment of permit procedures set out in ss 72–76D are essentially the same as for a new permit application, involving notification, consideration of objections and so on.

Some special cases

In a number of situations, special provisions apply to the granting and refusal of permits. These include permits for licensed premises and brothels and permits requiring works approval or discharge licences under the *Environment Protection Act*.

Licensed premises

The provisions set out in cl 52.27 of schemes via the VPPs apply to premises licensed, or to be licensed, under the *Liquor Control Reform Act 1998*. Pursuant to cl 52.27 a planning permit is required to use land to sell or consume liquor if a licence is required under the *Liquor Control Reform Act*, a different licence or class of licence is required from that which is in force, the hours of trading allowed under any licence are to be extended, or the number of patrons allowed under any licence is to be increased. The purpose of cl 52.27 is:

> To ensure that licensed premises are in appropriate locations.
>
> To ensure that the impact of licensed premises on the amenity of the surrounding area is considered.

For practical reasons, a planning permit is normally a prerequisite to a licence being granted by the Director of Liquor Licensing. The intention is that planning issues relating to planning permit applications will be considered and determined before application is made to the Director of Liquor Licensing for a licence or variation of an existing licence. The decision guidelines in cl 52.27 require the responsible authority to consider, *inter alia*:

The impact of the sale or consumption of liquor permitted by the liquor licence on the amenity of the surrounding area.

The impact of the hours of operation on the amenity of the surrounding area.

The impact of the number of patrons on the amenity of the surrounding area.

The cumulative impact on any existing and the proposed liquor licence, the hours of operation and the number of patrons, on the amenity of the area.

Section 16 of the *Liquor Control Reform Act 1998* makes it a condition of every licence and BYO permit, save for a limited licence or a pre-retail licence, that the use of the licensed premises does not contravene the planning scheme that applies to the licensed premises under the *Planning and Environment Act 1987*. Compliance must therefore be continuous and, in the event that licensed premises are used for a purpose substantially different from a previous use, existing use rights may be taken to be abandoned and a planning permit required. See *Melbourne City Council v Starera Pty Ltd* [2000] VCAT 569.

Decisions by responsible authorities on planning permit applications for licensed premises are subject to review proceedings before VCAT. Such reviews should not be confused with reviews of the decisions of the Director of Liquor Licensing on licence applications pursuant to Part 5 of the *Liquor Control Reform Act 1998*. Section 87 of that Act provides that specified persons, including the applicant for a licence and a person who lodged an objection to the grant of a licence, may apply to VCAT for review of a decision by the Director in respect of an application for the grant, variation, transfer, or relocation of a licence or BYO permit, including a decision to impose a condition on the grant, variation, transfer or relocation. It also provides that the licensee or permittee may apply to the Tribunal for review of a decision of the Director to vary the licence or BYO permit. Section 87A provides that a licensee of licensed premises to which a late-hour entry declaration applies may apply to the Tribunal for review of the Director's decision to make or vary the declaration.

Brothels

Before applying for a planning permit for a brothel, the applicant must obtain a licence under s 33 of the *Sex Work Act 1994*. A licence is also required for escort agencies. Applications for licences are determined by the Business Licensing Authority. Licensing of brothels is dealt with in Part 3 of the *Sex Work Act* (ss 33–70).

Part 4 of the *Sex Work Act* (ss 71–79) deals with planning controls on brothels. Words and expressions used in this part of the *Sex Work Act* have the same meaning they have in the *Planning and Environment Act 1987*: see *Sex Work Act 1994*, s 71.

An application for a planning permit to use or develop land for a brothel can only be made by a person who holds a licence under the *Sex Work Act* as a prostitution service provider: see s 72. Apart from an exception in s 72(b), the holding of such a licence is a mandatory requirement. The exception is in favour of small owner-operated brothels, exempted by s 23(1) of the *Sex Work Act* from the requirement to hold a licence. This exception applies to a brothel conducted in accordance with a permit granted under the *Planning and Environment Act* but where only one or two particular persons work as prostitutes. Section 23(2) and (3) contains further provisions in relation to the s 23(1) exemption.

Section 60 of the *Planning and Environment Act* specifies certain things that the responsible authority must consider in deciding whether an application for a permit should be granted. It also specifies other matters that may be considered if the circumstances appear to so require. Without limiting that section, s 73 of the *Sex Work Act* specifies further things that must be considered by the responsible authority before deciding on a permit application for the use or development of land for the purpose of a brothel. These are:

    (a) any other brothel in the neighbourhood;
    (b) the affect of the operation of a brothel on children in the neighbourhood;
    (c) in the case of land within the area of the City of Melbourne bounded by Spring, Flinders, Spencer and Latrobe Streets, whether the land is within 200 m of a place of worship, hospital, school, kindergarten, children's services centre or of any other facility or place regularly frequented by children for recreational or cultural activities and, if so, the effect on the community of a brothel being located within that distance of that facility or place;
    (d) other land used within the neighbourhood involving similar hours of operation and creating similar amounts of noise or traffic (including pedestrian traffic);
    (e) any guidelines about the size or location of brothels issued by the Minister administering the *Planning and Environment Act 1987*;
    (f) the amenity of the neighbourhood;
    (g) the provision of off-street parking;
    (h) landscaping of the site;
    (i) access to the site;
    (j) the proposed size of the brothel and the number of people that it is proposed will be working in it;
    (k) the proposed method and hours of operation of the brothel.

In relation to Ministerial guidelines referred to in para (e) above, none had been issued by the Minister for Planning specifically in relation to the *Sex Work Act* at the time it came into force on 14 June 1995. However, two guideline documents dealing with the same subject matter had been issued before 14 June 1995. The first of these was *Guidelines on the Location of Brothels* (Melbourne, Ministry of Planning and Environment, 1984). That document was replaced by a subsequent guideline found in No 24, September 1987, of the Ministry's *Planning Notes* series. Section 73 of the *Sex Work Act*, discussed below, deals with the matters formerly dealt with by these documents.

As to consideration in para (c) relating to the central City of Melbourne area, there is no guidance in s 73 as to how the specified distance of 200 metres is to be measured. But s 74(2) specifies a method of measuring distances for the purpose of distances specified in s 74(1). In s 74, distances are to be measured according to any route that reasonably may be used in travelling. The Tribunal has held that the distance must be a practical, on-the-ground distance, not "as the crow flies", and requires a "planning unit" to "planning unit" approach (ie from "land" to "land", not from front door to front door): *Yang v Darebin CC* [2006] VCAT 746.

In relation to s 73(b), there is a difference between a brothel being located in an area "regularly frequented by children" and a child or children being in or attending premises in the same area, such as a parent's place of business. In *Cahill v Greater Shepparton CC* [2006] VCAT 925, the Tribunal held that, while an industrial area in which a brothel was proposed to be located could be frequented by children, none of the activities in that area made it a place "regularly frequented" by children. See also *A'I v Whitehorse CC* [2006] VCAT 2549.

Section 74(1) compels refusal by the responsible authority of a brothel permit application where its requirements are not met, whereas the matters specified in s 73, although they must be considered, do not dictate mandatory refusal.

Under s 74(1), an application for a brothel permit must be refused if:
- (a) the land is within an area zoned by a planning scheme as being primarily for residential use;
- (b) if the land is within 100 m of a dwelling other than a caretaker's house with that distance being reduced to 50 m in the case of such a dwelling located between Spring, Flinders, Spencer and Latrobe Streets in the city of Melbourne;
- (c) except within that specified central City of Melbourne area if the land is within 200 m of a place of worship, hospital, school, kindergarten, children's services centre or of any other facility or place regularly frequented by children for recreational or cultural activities.

Section 74(1)(d) prohibits a proposed brothel from having more than six rooms to be used for prostitution unless special circumstances exist as set out in guidelines issued by the Minister administering the *Planning and Environment Act 1987*. No such guidelines created in contemplation of this provision were in existence at the coming into operation of the *Sex Work Act*. The then existing guidelines, referred to above in relation to s 73(e), are not really applicable to s 74(1)(d).

Section 75(1) provides that a person must not, at any one time, have an interest in more than one permit granted by a responsible authority for a use or development of land for the purposes of the operation of a brothel. In fact, this subsection makes such conduct an offence punishable with a penalty of up to six years' imprisonment, 600 penalty units, or both. For the financial year 2009–2010, a penalty unit was $116.82.

The position in relation to brothel permits is not so flexible as in relation to other permits in as much as a permit applicant must hold a licence (see s 72(a)) and a licence must be held by a person carrying on business as a prostitution service provider (see s 22(1)). However, both of these provisions are subject to the exemption provided by s 23(1) in favour of small owner-operated brothels.

Section 75(1) focuses on an interest in a brothel permit. It prohibits a person from having at any one time an interest in more than one current licence authorising the carrying on of a brothel business or an interest in more than one unexpired permit granted for the use of land for the purpose of the operation of a brothel, being a permit under which the use has started.

Section 75(2) provides that a person has an interest in a licence if it was granted to that person or an associate of that person, whether alone or jointly with any other person.

Section 75(3) goes on to specify what association between two persons means for the purposes of this section. One is associated with one's spouse, domestic partner, business partner and a person one has entered a business arrangement or relationship with in respect of the use, occupation, management or otherwise of land. Furthermore, one is associated with a person who conducts a business from which one derives income. Also, a body corporate is associated, for this purpose, with a related body corporate within the meaning of s 9 of the *Corporations Act 2001* (Cth).

See the *Planning Appeal Casenotes* volume in Byard, Code, Porritt and Testro, *Planning and Environment Service Victoria* in Further Reading for some examples of principles that have been applied in deciding permit applications relating to brothels. Case Notes inserted before Service 57 relate to cases decided on the basis of things as they stood before the coming into operation of the *Sex Work Act* on 14 June 1995. Case Notes relating to brothel cases inserted by Service 57 or later services have been decided on the basis of the law after the commencement of that Act.

Review by VCAT of decisions by the Business Licensing Authority on applications for licences must not be confused with review of decisions by responsible authorities on planning permit applications for brothels. Section 36A of the *Sex Work Act* sets out the matters which the Business Licensing Authority must consider when determining licence applications. Section 37 sets out the circumstances in which that authority must refuse a licence application. Section 38 sets out the matters that must be considered by the authority in determining the suitability of an applicant to carry on a business as a prostitution service provider. Section 56 provides that persons whose interests are affected by the decision of the authority may apply to the Tribunal for review of that decision.

Gaming machines

By virtue of Amendment VC39 to cl 52.28 of the VPPs on 18 October 2006, a planning permit is now required for all new gaming machines in Victoria. Previous "as of right" provisions for the installation and use of gaming machines were removed by the amendment. Clause 52.28-2 provides that a permit is required to install or use a gambling machine, with two exceptions. The first is that a gaming machine is prohibited by cl 52.28-3 or cl 52.28-4. The second is that the gaming machine is in an approved venue under the *Gambling Regulation Act 2003* on 18 October 2006 and the maximum number of gaming machines for the approved venue is not exceeded.

Clause 52.28-3 prohibits the installation or use of a gaming machine on land specified in a schedule to the clause. Clause 52.28-4 prohibits the installation or use of a gaming machine in a strip shopping centre if the strip shopping centre is specified in a schedule to the clause or the schedule provides that a gaming machine is prohibited in all strip shopping centres on land covered by the planning scheme. A strip shopping centre is defined as an area that meets all the following requirements:

- it is zoned for business use;

- it consists of at least two separate buildings on at least two separate and adjoining lots;
- it is in an area in which a significant proportion of the buildings are shops;
- it is an area in which a significant proportion of the lots abut a road accessible to the public generally;

but does not include the Capital City Zone in the Melbourne Planning Scheme.

Decision guidelines at cl 52.28-6 require the responsible authority, before deciding on a permit application, to consider, as appropriate, in addition to the SPPF and LPPF, including the MSS and local planning policies:

The compatibility of the proposal with adjoining land uses.

The capability of the site to accommodate the proposal.

Whether the gaming premises provides a full range of hotel facilities or services to patrons or a full range of club facilities or services to members and patrons.

In recent years in some municipalities, planning scheme amendments have been approved which introduce gaming policies into the LPPF and also introduce schedules to cll 52.28-3 and 52.28-4. For example, schedules to these clauses in the Greater Bendigo Planning Scheme, inserted by a planning scheme amendment in March 2009, prohibit gaming machines in specified shopping complexes, and specified strip shopping centres in the municipality. It seems likely that more municipalities will go down this path in an attempt to more closely control the location of gaming venues.

Applications for review of the decisions of responsible authorities on planning permit applications made pursuant to cl 52.28 may be made to VCAT. However, there is little point in seeking a planning permit to install or use a gaming machine unless an approval of premises as suitable for gambling is given by the Victorian Commission for Gambling (the Gambling Commission) pursuant to the *Gambling Regulation Act 2003*. Section 3.3.2(1) provides that an approval of premises as suitable for gambling may be given for premises to which a pub licence, a club licence or a racing club licence applies, but s 3.3.2(3) also provides that, despite sub-s (1), an approval cannot be given for prescribed premises or premises of a prescribed class.

Section 3.3.7 of that Act sets out the matters to be considered by the Gambling Commission in determining an application for approval. Section 3.3.7(1) provides that the Gambling Commission must not grant an application for approval of premises as suitable for gambling unless it is satisfied that:

(a) The applicant has authority to make the application is respect of the premises; and
(b) The premises are, or on the completion of building works, will be suitable for the management and operation of gaming machines; and
(c) The net economic and social impact of approval will not be detrimental to the well being of the community of the municipal district in which the premises are located.

In addition, the Gambling Commission must consider whether the size, layout and facilities of the premises are or will be suitable, and any submission made by a responsible authority pursuant to s 3.3.6, or it must seek the views of the responsible authority if it has not made a submission and must consider those views. Section

3.3.14 provides that an applicant for approval of premises may apply to VCAT for review of the Commission's decision.

In *Romsey Hotel Pty Ltd v Victorian Commission for Gambling Regulation* [2009] VCAT 2275 at [248], Bell J, then VCAT President, observed of s 3.3.7 of the *Gambling Regulation Act*:

> Thus the legislation recognizes the social and economic impact of gaming machines which may be felt in local communities. It makes the impacts in those communities (as defined by reference to the relevant municipal districts) the focus of the no detriment test in s 3.3.7(1)(c). If the net impact will be positive or neutral, the commission has a discretion to grant the approval or amendment. If the net impact will be detrimental, it does not.

The issues of net economic and social impact of approval and how such impact is to be established have been at the heart of some recent Court and Tribunal decisions. In the case from which Bell J's observation above is reproduced, the matter had been remitted back to the Tribunal for determination by the Court of Appeal in *Macedon Ranges SC v Romsey Hotel Pty Ltd* [2008] VSCA 45. The owner of the Romsey Hotel had applied to the Gambling Commission for approval of the hotel premises for gambling. The applicant proposed to install 50 electronic gaming machines (later reduced to 30). The Commission refused the application, stating that it was unable to be satisfied that the social and economic impact of the proposal would not be detrimental to the wellbeing of Romsey and its surrounding area. The Commission's "overwhelming impression" was that "members of the local community find the prospect of gaming at its only hotel so disconcerting that it would have a significant affect on that community". The applicant sought review of that decision by VCAT under s 3.3.14(1) of the *Gambling Regulation Act*. The then Tribunal President, Morris J, set aside the Commission's decision and approved the hotel as premises suitable for gambling: see *Romsey Hotel v Victorian Commission for Gambling Regulation* [2007] VCAT 1. Macedon Shire Council appealed the Tribunal's decision. The Court of Appeal held that the Tribunal erred in its decision because it had failed to take into account the results of a local survey that overwhelmingly opposed the application for 30 gaming machines in the hotel.

The matter was remitted back to the Tribunal and it was heard and determined by Bell J. Further surveys were undertaken by both the applicant and the council and both surveys found that a very sizable proportion of the Romsey community was against the introduction of gaming machines. As there was no fundamental disagreement about results of the surveys, Bell J considered the proposal against the provisions of s 3.3.7(1) of the *Gambling Regulation Act*. He stated that an individual assessment of both social and economic impacts must be made but recognised that the two concepts can run together and in appropriate cases may be considered together. He found that on the basis of the evidence put to him there would be a slightly positive economic impact, but only after taking into account the economic impact of the consumption of gaming machine services. He found that there would be positive social impacts for the great majority of users and there would also be benefits from donations the hotel would make to local sporting and other organisations. However, he found that the significance of the survey data showing opposition to the application was a very important consideration in assessing the social impacts on community wellbeing. In conclusion, on balance he was not satisfied that the net economic and social impact of approval would not be detrimental to the wellbeing of the community. He therefore affirmed the decision of the Gambling Commission to refuse approval.

In *Prizac Investments Pty Ltd v Maribyrnong CC* [2009] VCAT 2616, the Tribunal's decision involved review of a refusal to grant a permit pursuant to cl 52.28 of the Maribyrnong Planning Scheme and a review of an approval by the Gambling Commission under s 3.3.7 of the *Gambling Regulation Act*. In applying the net community benefit test in relation to the planning permit application made pursuant to cl 52.28, the Tribunal stated at para [140]:

> Under Clause 11 it is the State Government's expectation that planning and responsible authorities will endeavour to integrate the range of policies relevant to the issues to be determined and balance conflicting objectives in favour of net community benefit and sustainable development. We accept Mr Townshend's submission that Clause 11 is not a prohibition on the grant of a permit in the absence of net community benefit ... We acknowledge a proposal does not necessarily fail if an applicant cannot demonstrate a net benefit, particularly in a case where there may be neutral benefit.

The Tribunal found at [143] that there would be various benefits that would result from approval of the development, including creating employment, recreation and entertainment facilities.

In relation to approval under s 3.3.7(1) of the *Gambling Regulation Act*, the Tribunal concluded that "the net economic and social impact of the approval will not be detrimental to the wellbeing of the local community". At paras [238]–[239] it said of the surveys undertaken for the applicant and on behalf of the responsible authority (the latter survey showed that 68.7 per cent of respondents were opposed to the proposal):

> We conclude that there will be no net social detriment. The impacts assessed are the marginal impacts of the approved venue that is only those impacts that will occur as a result of the application rather than those that would have occurred in any event.
>
> There will be no increase in gambling venues within the municipality and although a number of people within close proximity to the site are unhappy about the proposal we consider this view would apply equally regarding the location of the nearby existing Powell Hotel and its gaming venue. We do not consider that the surveys indicate there will be an increase in unhappiness or discontent within the community in close proximity to the proposed development as a result of the introduction of gaming, as this community is already in close proximity to a gaming venue.

The Tribunal affirmed the approval of the Gambling Commission and set aside the refusal of the responsible authority.

It should be noted that in the *Romsey Hotel* case there were no other gaming machines in the town and the town was geographically separated from other urban centres.

Works approvals and licences

Where the use or development for which a permit is sought requires a works approval or licence, the Environment Protection Authority (EPA) is specified in schemes as a referral authority in cl 66.02-1 of the VPPs. As a referral authority the EPA may inform the responsible authority that it does not object to the granting of the permit, or does not object to the grant of the permit if certain conditions are included, or that it objects to the granting of a permit on some particular ground: see s 56. Note that, pursuant to s 56, if the EPA, acting as a referral authority, objects to the grant of the permit, the responsible authority must refuse to grant the permit. If the EPA has no objection provided specified conditions are included in any permit issued, such permit must include those conditions and not include other conditions that would conflict with the conditions specified. (See Chapter 2 for the powers of referral authorities.)

Various types of premises are characterised into scheduled activity under the *Environment Protection (Scheduled Premises & Exemptions) Regulations 2007*. Such premises usually require a works approval issued by the EPA before the commencement of building on the premises, or any alterations to pre-existing operations unless the activity is in the course of general maintenance. Works approvals were introduced in 1985 as a necessary precondition to the granting of a licence to discharge waste into the environment so that the authority can have some input at the development stage. A licence will be granted once the requirements of the works approval have been complied with. An application for a licence is basically an administrative procedure.

Under the *Environment Protection Act 1970* responsible authorities are referral authorities for works approval applications. But "referral authority" under the *Environment Protection Act* means something a little different from "referral authority" under the *Planning and Environment Act*. Section 19B of the *Environment Protection Act* requires the EPA to send a copy of the works approval application to the relevant responsible authority under a planning scheme to which the land for which the works application applies: see *Environment Protection Act*, s 19B(3). The responsible authority must inform the EPA as to whether the proposed works are permitted by the planning scheme, or if a permit is required for the works, or if it is considering a planning application for the proposed works, or if the works are prohibited by the scheme: see *Environment Protection Act*, s 19B(4A). The responsible authority has 45 days to respond to the referred application: see s 19B(4A)(b) and (c). The responsible authority must refuse the works approval application if it is prohibited by the scheme unless the EPA has been advised under s 19B(4C)(b) that an amendment to the planning scheme is to be prepared which allows the proposed works to proceed: see s 19B(5)(c). Section 19B(7A) of the *Environment Protection Act* provides that, if a permit is required for the works and the permit has not been issued, any works approval issued by the EPA must include a condition that the works approval does not take effect until a copy of the permit is served on the EPA.

Permits required by responsible authorities and government departments

State legislation does not bind the Commonwealth. Therefore planning schemes, being authorised and made pursuant to a Victorian Act (the *Planning and Environment Act 1987*) do not apply to Commonwealth land. Melbourne, Essendon, Moorabbin and Avalon Airports, for example, are not included in any planning scheme.

Clause 67.01 of VPPs continues the arrangement in place before the introduction of the VPP-based planning schemes whereby virtually all uses and developments are exempt from s 96 of the *Planning and Environment Act*, so that responsible authorities or persons seeking permission on land owned, occupied or managed by responsible authorities must apply to the responsible authority. That is, in the case of responsible authorities, they must apply to themselves.

Section 16 of the Act provides that a planning scheme is binding on every (Victorian) Minister, government department, public authority and municipal council except to the extent that the Governor in Council, on the recommendation of the Minister, directs otherwise by Order published in the *Government Gazette*. This provides a great deal of opportunity for the government of the day to by-pass the provisions of planning schemes. Note that the power conferred by s 16 is in addition to the powers of the Minister to by-pass the normal processes of scheme amendment, call-in permit applications, and call-in applications for review (see Chapter 2). Orders made by the Governor in Council pursuant to s 16 include:

Date of Order	Government Gazette	Area	Minister (Names in Order)
2 February 1988	G5 10 February 1988	All except various areas of and adjacent to the Maribyrnong and Yarra Rivers and Port Phillip Bay	Minister for Conservation, Forests and Lands, Minister for Health, Minister for Education
15 March 1989	G11 15 March 1989	Eastern Arterial Road and Ringwood By-pass	Road Construction Authority
20 March 1990	G12 21 March 1990	Wellington Parade/ Punt Road intersection	Roads Corporation
21 January 1992	G3 22 January 1992	Swanston Walk	Roads Corporation, Public Transport Corporation and Melbourne City Council
13 February 1996	S11 13 February 1996	Albert Park	Melbourne Parks and Waterways, Minister for Conservation and Environment and Secretary of the Department of Conservation and Natural Resources

Date of Order	Government Gazette	Area	Minister (Names in Order)
8 December 2009	G50 10 December 2009	All planning schemes	Minister for Skills and Workforce Department of Conservation and Natural Resources

Source: R Byard, G Code, G Porritt and S Testro, *Planning and Environment Victoria*, Volume 2, para [430,030] (Butterworths).

Under s 95, applications by or on behalf of Ministers or government departments are determined by the responsible authority unless an Order has been made by the Governor in Council that the responsible authority refer in a specified class of application by Ministers or government departments for permits to the Minister: s 95(2). The Governor in Council may determine any application referred to the Minister: s 95(5). If a determination is made to grant the permit, the Minister becomes the responsible authority for the purpose of issuing, administering and enforcing the permit: s 96(7). A determination by the Governor in Council is not subject to review or appeal except to the Supreme Court on a question of law: s 96(6).

It should also be noted that other legislation may modify or set aside the normal processes of planning permit applications, notification, objection and review. An example is the *Major Transport Projects Facilitation Act 2009*, which applies to major projects declared by the Governor in Council on the recommendation of the Premier after being assessed as being of State or regional economic, social or environmental significance. This Act is aimed at expediting major projects in the Victorian Transport Plan, such as Peninsula Link, Melbourne Metro Rail, and the Monash – City Link – West Gate upgrade. It consolidates multiple planning and other approvals often required for transport projects into a single assessment and approval process conducted by the Minister for Planning. There is no review by VCAT of the Minister's decisions.

Chapter 6

VCAT AND PLANNING REVIEWS

A brief overview of VCAT's functions

The Victorian Civil and Administrative Tribunal (VCAT) came into operation on 1 July 1988. It is a multi-jurisdictional body with a President who is a Supreme Court judge. Senior and ordinary members must be either persons who have been admitted to legal practice in Victoria for five years or more or persons who, in the opinion of the Minister, have extensive knowledge or experience in relation to any class of matter in respect of which functions may be exercised by VCAT: *Victorian Civil and Administrative Tribunal Act 1998*, ss 13, 14. Members are appointed by the Governor in Council on the recommendation of the Attorney-General for a period of five years and may be reappointed: s 16.

The Civil Division of VCAT deals with civil disputes involving, *inter alia*, credit, domestic building, real property, retail and residential tenancies. The Administrative Division deals with disputes between people and government, including local government, about land valuation, licences to conduct businesses (such as travel agencies and motor trading), planning, State taxation, Transport Accident Commission decisions and decisions on freedom of information requests. The Human Rights Division deals with matters relating to guardianship and discrimination.

In the Administrative Division of VCAT, the Planning and Environment List deals with disputes arising under the *Planning and Environment Act* and other planning enactments. The members of this list include lawyers with specialist knowledge in town planning, town planners, engineers and architects. Section 25A of the *VCAT Act*, introduced by amendment in 2000, provides that, for a period of two years after a member ceases to be a member, he or she must not represent a party in any proceeding to which the former member was assigned that has been entered in or transferred, unless with the approval of the President.

Jurisdiction of VCAT and its Planning and Environment List

Responsible authorities make decisions on planning permit applications and so exercise a wide range of discretionary powers. To provide a check on the exercise of these powers and at the same time ensure that the effects of contentious development proposals are assessed independently, it is essential that there should be some form of appellate procedure available, not only to the applicant but also to other persons who are affected in some material way by the decisions of responsible authorities. There are two methods of challenging a permit-granting authority. One is by way of judicial review by a court and the other is by way of review by a statutory tribunal. Review by the Supreme Court does not provide a rehearing on the merits of a proposed development. In exercising its powers the Court can only set aside a decision of the responsible authority – it cannot redecide the matter on its merits. Although this power is very important, the Court can have only a minor role in the control of the day-to-day exercise of discretion by responsible authorities in relation to planning permits. A deterrent to bringing an action in the Court is the cost involved.

An alternative avenue of appeal or review to a tribunal, in this case VCAT, has a number of advantages. Firstly, it provides persons affected by the decisions of the responsible authority with a procedure whereby they are able to have their grievance heard on its merits by a tribunal which has wider powers than those of the Supreme Court in hearing matters by way of review. Hearings before VCAT are *de novo*. That is, VCAT reviews the decisions of responsible authorities on the merits and in doing so it has all the functions of the original decision-maker together with any other functions conferred by the relevant enabling enactment (for example, the *Planning and Environment Act*) or its regulations or rules: *VCAT Act*, s 51(1). The Tribunal considers the matter as if for the first time. Secondly, it provides aggrieved persons with the opportunity of having a rehearing of an application before individuals with special knowledge in the field of town planning, and that more often than not leads to better planning decisions because, in more than half the applications for review brought before VCAT, objectors are partly successful in that the form of the development is changed or additional conditions are imposed. Thirdly, the mere presence of a statutory tribunal is a powerful incentive for applicants and responsible authorities to properly consider and make decisions on planning permit applications on their merits in the context of the planning scheme provisions in place rather than on the basis of local political or other considerations. In that sense it is a safeguard against corruption. Fourthly, as each party to a proceeding before VCAT normally bears its own costs (see later in this chapter), there is no significant financial deterrent to bringing a proceeding before it.

VCAT and its Planning and Environment List are given jurisdiction to deal with proceedings arising under "enabling enactments", which is defined in s 3. The *Planning and Environment Act* is a planning enactment pursuant to cl 2 of the Third Schedule to the *VCAT Act* and it bestows jurisdiction via a number of its provisions: see, for example, ss 77–94. Other enabling planning enactments include the *Catchment and Land Protection Act 1994*, the *Environment Protection Act 1970*, the *Extractive Industries Development Act 1995*, the *Subdivision Act 1988*, and the *Heritage Act 1995*: Schedule 1, cl 2.

VCAT has original and review jurisdiction: *VCAT Act*, s 40. Review jurisdiction is that conferred by an enabling enactment to review a decision made by a decision-maker: s 42(1). Review jurisdiction is conferred, for example, by ss 77, 79, and 82 of the *Planning and Environment Act*, dealing with, respectively, review of a refusal to grant a permit, review of a failure to grant a permit within the prescribed time, and review of a decision to grant a permit where there have been objectors. Section 149B of the *Planning and Environment Act* confers a wide original jurisdiction on VCAT to make declarations. A declaration is a decision of a court, judge or tribunal which states authoritatively what the legal position is in relation to a particular issue or question.

The Tribunal has jurisdiction in relation to planning matters under the *Planning and Environment Act* as follows:

- review of a failure by the Minister, a planning authority or panel to comply with procedures in relation to an amendment which has not been approved: s 39;
- review of a refusal to grant a permit: s 77;
- review of a requirement of the responsible authority to give notice of a permit application under s 52(1)(d): s 78(a);
- review of a requirement of the responsible authority to provide more information about a permit application: s 81;
- review of a decision of the responsible authority to give notice of an application to amend a permit application pursuant to s 57A: s 78;
- review of a decision by the responsible authority under s 54A to refuse to extend time within which more information must be given under s 54: s 81(2);
- review of a failure to grant a permit within the prescribed time: s 79;
- review of condition(s) in a permit: s 80;
- review of a refusal to extend time to commence or complete a development: s 81(a);
- review of a failure to extend time within one month of a request to extend time: s 81(b);
- review of a decision to grant a permit: ss 82(1), 82B(1);
- review of a decision by a responsible authority to amend a permit under s 75: s 76C;
- review of a decision of the responsible authority to refuse to amend a permit under s 76: s 76C;
- application to VCAT to amend a permit: ss 87(3), 88, 89(1);
- review of a decision to issue a certificate of compliance that an existing or proposed use or development complies or would comply with the requirements of the planning scheme: s 97P;
- review of a decision to refuse to issue a certificate of compliance, or of failure to issue a certificate of compliance within the prescribed time: s 97P;
- application to VCAT to make an enforcement order: s 114;
- application to VCAT to make an interim enforcement order: s 120;
- application by a specified person for review of a decision by the responsible authority or some other specified body, or a failure to make a decision within reasonable time, in relation to a requirement that something be done or must not be done to the satisfaction of the responsible authority where such requirement is included in a permit condition, s 173 agreement, or an enforcement order: ss 148, 149;

- application by a specified person for a determination if a matter relates to the interpretation of a scheme or permit, whether or not s 6(3) applies to a particular use or development, or the provision of a scheme provision or amendment allowing the continuation of a lawful existing use: s 149A;
- application by a person for a declaration: s 149B;
- application to VCAT to amend a proposed s 173 agreement if the use or development of land is conditional upon the agreement coming into effect and the owner objects to any provision in the agreement: s 184(1);
- application to cancel a s173 agreement if the parties cannot agree that it be cancelled: s 184(3).

Exclusion of courts from hearing or determining planning matters

Section 52(1) of the *VCAT Act* provides that the Supreme Court, County Court and Magistrates Court are excluded from hearing or determining proceedings in which a person "brings in issue the matter of the exercise of, or the failure to exercise, a power under a planning enactment" where the Tribunal has jurisdiction to review the matter or the exercise of or failure to exercise that power and:

- the matter has not been the subject of a proceeding in the Tribunal;
- if it has been the subject of a proceeding in the Tribunal, it has not been determined by the Tribunal;
- it has been determined by the Tribunal and the time for appeal against an order of the Tribunal and the proceeding has not expired; or
- if an appeal has been brought against an order in the proceeding, the appeal has not been determined.

Note that there may be an appeal to the Supreme Court against a decision of the Tribunal on a question of law: *VCAT Act*, s 148 (see later in this chapter). Section 52 applies only to matters involving VCAT's review jurisdiction – it does not apply to an application for a declaration pursuant to s 149B of the *Planning and Environment Act*: *No 2 Pitt Street v Wodonga Rural City Council* [1999] 3 VR 439.

Notwithstanding s 52(1), s 52(2) provides that, if the relevant court is of the opinion that there are "special circumstances" that justify the hearing of a proceeding to which s 52(1) applies, that court may direct that s 52(1) does not apply. "Special circumstances" means something unusual or uncommon, but not as far removed from the ordinary as to be exceptional or extraordinary: *No 2 Pitt Street v Wodonga Rural City Council* [1999] 3 VR 439.

Origins of the Planning and Environment List of VCAT
The Town Planning Appeals Tribunal

Planning legislation from 1949 to 1958 was fairly simple and straightforward and provided minimum appellate rights, particularly to third party objectors such as neighbouring property owners. During this period there was no statutory appeal system provided for in the *Town and Country Planning Act*. However, questions of law could be determined by the Supreme Court of Victoria by way of the common law review procedures. The period from 1958 until 1987 saw a change not only in planning schemes but also in appeal rights. The Victorian legislation in 1958 provided that appeals be heard by the Minister. Section 14(3) of the *Town and Country Planning Act 1958* provided a limited avenue of appeal by an applicant to the Minister for Local Government against the refusal of the responsible authority to grant a planning permit and against any conditions attached to planning consent. Up to 1961, there was no avenue for third parties to appeal against determinations by responsible authorities.

In 1961 third parties were given the right to appeal against the granting of a permit. However, the right of appeal was not to an independent tribunal but to the Minister. The Minister appointed delegates to hear appeals. These delegates presented a report to the Minister, which was considered by him before he gave a decision. The Act was silent in relation to the procedural aspect of appeals, rendering it unsatisfactory, because it did not provide the basic requirements for a fair and impartial hearing. As a consequence, an appeal to the Minister was not necessarily directed to an impartial person or body, because the Minister was almost invariably involved in questions of policy related to the hearings before him, and in some instances was the responsible authority whose decision was being appealed. The delegates did not decide the appeal, but the Minister received their recommendations, which could be accepted or rejected by him. The party to the appeal was not informed of the recommendations or the reasons accepted by the Minister in his decision. The delegates did not necessarily have any qualifications in town planning or local government. The sheer volume of appeals to be decided by a busy Minister and the wish to avoid the political "flak" from unpopular decisions also encouraged the move to an independent tribunal.

An independent appeals body, the Town Planning Appeals Tribunal (TPAT) was established by the *Town and Country Planning (Amendment) Act 1968*. The TPAT was set up to hear appeals from applicants and third party objectors with regard to permit applications under both interim development orders (IDOs) and planning schemes. The TPAT was given the power to hear appeals against the determinations of responsible authorities *de novo* (a complete rehearing on the merits of the decision). The legislation made the TPAT the final body of appeal on all matters except on questions of law. The TPAT had no greater power than the respective responsible authorities, and consequently had no right to make a determination that the responsible authority had no power to make. When hearing an appeal the TPAT was bound to apply the same principles that governed the responsible authority at the time of the determination, subject to the following qualifications.

The Tribunal was, by virtue of s 21(1) of the Act, required on the hearing of an appeal to act "without regard to technicalities or legal forms and shall not be bound by the rules of evidence but, subject to the requirements of natural justice, may inform itself on any matter in such manner as it thinks fit". It had, under s 21(1), a mandatory duty to observe the rules of natural justice. While, as a general rule, the TPAT was required to apply the same principles as the responsible authority when it made its decision, it could consider the changes in circumstances that occurred between the determination of the matter by the responsible authority and the appeal hearing. The TPAT normally considered the application some months after the responsible authority had made its determination. This passage of time could be relevant because the TPAT (like VCAT now) considered the application having regard to all relevant facts (including the scheme controls) at the date of the hearing of the appeal (see *Gala Homes and Sales Pty Ltd v MMBW* [1970] VPA 259). If a scheme amendment changed the controls that applied to land which was the subject of an appeal, the appeal was determined (as are Applications for Review before VCAT now) according to the controls that applied at the time of the hearing: *Ungar v City of Malvern* [1979] VR 259.

Proceedings before the TPAT were designed to be informal, the principal aim being to deal with appeals expeditiously. It was not bound by its own decisions; strictly speaking, it did not have a system of precedent. It was, of course, bound by the enabling legislation which set out its powers and duties and also by the decisions of the Supreme Court. Although not bound to follow its own decisions, in several cases it expressed opinions regarding the procedures it would adopt and the basis upon which it would arrive at determinations. Over the years, it was evident that the TPAT was attempting to provide some continuity in procedures by which it resolved substantive issues of fact.

In 1978 an amendment to the *Town and Country Planning Act* (s 21(4J)–(4K)) allowed the Minister to "call in" appeals. The amendment provided that, where the Tribunal or Minister was of the opinion that an appeal "raises major issues of policy" and the determination of the appeal "may have a substantial effect" on achievement or development of planning objectives in a region, the Tribunal was required to hear the appeal but not determine it. Section 21(4J) stated that after the Tribunal had heard all the evidence it must advise the Minister of its opinion and within 30 days of receiving this opinion the Minister was required to refer the appeal to the Governor in Council for decision. The reason for the amendment to s 21 in 1978 was that there had been Tribunal decisions in that year which ran counter to existing government planning policies (see the discussion in Chapter 2 in relation to Tatra Hut in the Dandenong Ranges and the Boole Poole Peninsula on the Gippsland Lakes). It has since been discovered that the call-in power of the Minister, which is still contained in the current legislation (see *VCAT Act*, Schedule 1, cll 58–59, discussed below), can be used to facilitate development instead of frustrating it.

The introduction in 1968 of the TPAT constituted a major means of reviewing determinations made by responsible authorities. The aim of setting up the Tribunal was to allow parties disputing a permit decision to appear personally for a speedy rehearing of the matter on its merits.

The Planning Appeals Board

The planning appeals system was subject to an extensive review in 1977 (the BADAC report; see Further Reading) and, as a result of the recommendations contained in the BADAC report, a new body, the Planning Appeals Board (PAB), was established by the *Planning Appeals Board Act* in 1980. The jurisdiction of this body was more extensive than that of the old TPAT in that it not only took over the TPAT's function of hearing appeals against the granting and refusal of permits by a responsible authority but it also took over the hearing of appeals previously heard by a number of separate appeal bodies. These bodies included the Environment Protection Appeals Board, the Drainage Tribunal and the Arbitrator under the *Local Government Act 1958*. In accord with the BADAC recommendations, s 37 of the *Planning Appeals Board Act 1980* gave the PAB the right to hear allied matters together. It meant that appeals in relation to a discharge licence, a planning permit and the sealing of a plan of subdivision concerning the same property could be heard and determined by the PAB at the same time.

Previously the *Town and Country Planning Act* provided that in hearing an appeal the TPAT was to have regard to a limited number of matters. Although sections like s 21(1) of the old Act, which required the Tribunal to act "according to equity and good conscience and the substantial merits of the case", were retained in the *Planning Appeals Board Act*, more extensive guidelines were provided for the PAB, particularly in relation to planning matters. Section 27 of the *Planning Appeals Board Act* gave the PAB more specific guidelines on matters which should be taken into account in exercising its discretion. For example, it was required to take into account any relevant planning scheme and have regard to any regional strategy plan, any amendment adopted by the responsible authority and any agreement entered into by the parties.

The concept of compulsory conferences was also introduced under the *Planning Appeals Board Act*. Section 44 provided that the Chief Chairman could order a compulsory conference of parties to an appeal, to be conducted either by the Chief Chairman or by a Board member nominated by him. A compulsory conference could only be held if ordered by the Chief Chairman. The objects of compulsory conferences were set out in s 45 of the Act and were to determine what matters were in dispute between parties, to identify questions of law and fact, and to try to settle the dispute between the parties.

Section 28 of the *Planning Appeals Board Act*, unlike the old provisions, set out clearly who could appear on behalf of the parties to proceedings, including the representation of a body corporate. The PAB was given the power to grant leave to a member of an unincorporated association to make a submission on behalf of that association. Under the old provision, a representative of an unincorporated association was held not to have sufficient standing to bring an appeal before the TPAT (see, for example, *Macedon Ranges Conservation Society v Shire of Gisborne No 3* (1976) 7 VPA 232). Like under the old provisions, all parties to an appeal had the right to be represented (by a lawyer, town planner, or whoever else a party chose to engage for that purpose). However, the right to representation was subject to s 28(3), which gave the Chief Chairman a wide discretion to direct at any time before the commencement of a hearing that each party to the appeal conduct his or her own case. This provision was never used.

Section 41 gave the Minister power to call in a matter if it concerned major issues of policy and this was similar to the old s 21(4J)–(4K) discussed earlier. However, the main addition to the section was that any Minister administering an Act under which an appeal was brought could request the Minister for Planning to call in the matter if it raised major issues of policy. This widening of the call-in power to include other Ministers is a striking example of an increasingly corporate style of government. While the original call-in power was inserted to allow the government to veto development, it can also be used to facilitate development, which was apparent in later decisions made by the Minister.

Section 20 of the *Planning Appeals Board Act* provided that only legally qualified members could determine questions of law in proceedings before a division. Section 60 set out determinations by the Board and required that determinations be in writing and be signed by a member or members of the division – a requirement not specified under the old legislation. Section 61 required that (unless all parties to the appeal agreed otherwise) the reasons for determinations were to be given in writing. Section 62 gave the PAB the power to amend a determination with regard to clerical errors or miscalculations. Section 63 (like the old s 22(3)) stated that determinations were final and made the PAB the final body of appeal on matters before it, other than on questions of law. Section 64 dealt with questions of law, which could be referred to the Supreme Court.

The Planning Division of the Administrative Appeals Tribunal

The *Planning Appeals (Amendment) Act 1987* transferred the jurisdiction of the PAB, which exercised its powers under the *Planning Appeals Board Act 1980*, to a special Planning Division of the Administrative Appeals Tribunal (AAT).

The Victorian AAT was established in 1984 under the *Administrative Appeals Tribunal Act*. It reviewed certain administrative decisions made under Victorian legislation. The Tribunal's role was to review such decisions on their merits. It did not have general jurisdiction to supervise administrative decisions, but s 25 of the *Administrative Appeals Tribunal Act* gave it jurisdiction only where the legislation provided that decisions under that Act were to be reviewed by the AAT. For example, there was nothing in the *Administrative Appeals Tribunal Act* which gave the AAT jurisdiction to review decisions made under the *Freedom of Information Act 1982*. However, s 50 of the *Freedom of Information Act* gave the AAT the power to review decisions under that Act.

The *Planning Appeals (Amendment) Act 1987* did not repeal or replace the previous legislation; rather, it added to and amended the provisions of the *Planning Appeals Board Act 1980* and the *Administrative Appeals Tribunal Act 1984*. Planning appeals and allied matters were heard by the Planning Division of the AAT. The jurisdiction of the AAT in planning matters did not radically alter from the jurisdiction of the PAB. The reason for integrating the PAB with the AAT was a perception by the government that placing all administrative tribunals or bodies under the one umbrella was administratively logical and efficient. Also it brought planning appeals under the Attorney-General's Department, thus distancing the independent Tribunal from the Minister responsible for planning, who could be a party to an appeal.

Review by VCAT of the decisions of responsible authorities on planning permit applications

Review of decisions to refuse or grant a permit, of conditions in permits, and of failure to decide within the prescribed time

As set out earlier in this chapter, VCAT has jurisdiction to hear and determine a wide range of applications for review pursuant to the *Planning and Environment Act*. However, the reviews with which most people in the community have involvement with are reviews of refusals to grant a permit pursuant to s 77, of decisions to grant a permit pursuant to s 82(1), of conditions in a permit pursuant to s 80, and of failures to grant a permit within the prescribed time pursuant to s 79. Note that failure to grant within the prescribed time is deemed to be a refusal to grant a permit: s 4(2)(d).

In a paper delivered to the Victorian Tourism Conference 2004 held at the Telstra Dome on 23 March 2004, Morris J stated:

> [T]he role of VCAT in determining Victoria's growth and evolution is overrated. Decisions of VCAT are often hailed as *profound, crucial* or *critical*. In truth, the key decisions are usually made by others; and the key drivers of economic growth, and how growth manifests itself, are economic, social and environmental influences. ... According to the recent discussion paper Better Decisions Faster there are about 45,000 applications for permits in Victoria each year. Dr Michael Buxton and others put the number of applications at 60,000. The number of permit applications which come before VCAT each year is about 2,500*. So of all the planning applications received in Victoria in any one year, councils make the final decision in 95% of them. VCAT's role is confined to only 5% of the planning applications. Admittedly it is often the most difficult and controversial 5% of cases.
>
> * This represents the sum of all applications for review in respect of decisions to grant, refusals and failure to grant a permit; but excludes reviews concerning permit conditions and secondary consents.

VCAT's 2008–2009 Annual Report provides the following data:

- 3,643 applications were received (27 per cent for review of a refusal to grant a permit; 19 per cent for review of a decision to grant a permit; 15 per cent for review of conditions in a permit; 11 per cent for failure to grant within the prescribed time; 6 per cent for an enforcement order; and 1 per cent for other);

- applications involving $2.73 billion were initiated over the course of the year;
- applications involving two or more dwellings on a lot accounted for nearly a third of all applications (31 per cent).

Lodging an Application for Review

The decision of a responsible authority on a planning permit application is communicated to the applicant and any objectors by a Notice of Decision to Grant a Permit or a Notice of Refusal to Grant a Permit. If there have been no objectors and the responsible authority decides to grant a permit, it will issue a permit. Included on the Notice of Decision to Grant, the Notice of Refusal and the permit itself are instructions and information about how to lodge an Application for Review. In the case of a Notice of Decision to Grant, objectors may lodge an Application for Review within 21 days of receiving Notice of Decision to Grant, and the applicant may lodge an Application for Review of any permit condition proposed in the Notice within 60 days of the date of the Notice. In the case of a Notice of Refusal, the permit applicant may lodge an Application for Review within 60 days of the date of the Notice. In the case of a permit being issued without objections being lodged, the applicant may lodge an Application for Review of conditions in the permit within 60 days of the date of issue of the permit. Where the responsible authority has not made a decision within the prescribed time, the applicant may lodge an Application for Review within the prescribed time (which is 60 days from the lodging of the permit application, but that time may be extended by the "stopping of the clock" provisions dealing with requests for further information as discussed in Chapter 5). There is no prescribed time within which an Application for Review of a failure to decide within the prescribed time must be lodged.

These time limits and other information and instructions in relation to making an Application for Review are prescribed by the *Planning and Environment Regulations 2005*, as is the form of the notices. An Application for Review must be lodged with VCAT on a standard Application for Review form available from VCAT (and also available on its website at <www.vcat.vic.gov.au>). The notice must contain the name and address of the applicant (if a number of people lodge a joint application, the name and address of a person to whom notices should be sent should be clearly indicated), and be signed by the applicant or by a person authorised in writing to sign on the applicant's behalf (such as a lawyer or town planner acting on behalf of the applicant), and include the permit application number, the address of the land concerned, including street number (or, if a street number is not available, the title particulars of the land), the interest of the applicant in the permit application (permit applicant or objector, for example), the use or development for which a permit was sought, the nature of the application (of a decision to grant, or of a refusal, for example), and the grounds of the application (except where the application is for review of a failure to determine within the prescribed time). The Application for Review must be accompanied by the prescribed filing fee set out in reg 4 of the *VCAT (Fees) Regulations 2001*. The filing fees for applications for review of refusals, decisions to grant, conditions and failure to determine are expressed in the regulations in terms of fee units and each year a dollar amount per fee unit is set by a notice in the *Government Gazette*.

The time limits for the lodging of an Application for Review may be extended by the Tribunal on its own initiative or on the application of any person: *VCAT Act*, s 126. The Tribunal may, for example, extend the 21-day time limit for lodging an Application for Review by an objector of a decision to grant a permit in circumstances where the objector was out of the country at the time the responsible authority issued the Notice of Decision to Grant, and for some weeks afterwards, and could not be reasonably expected to have been aware that Notice of Decision to Grant had been issued. The Principal Registrar may also waive the filing fee if he or she considers that the payment of it would cause financial hardship: *VCAT Act*, s 132. Guidelines for fee waiver are available on the VCAT website.

The grounds set out by the applicant in the Application for Review form are usually brief. The form states that any amplification of the grounds considered desirable by the applicant may be attached to the review form. For an Application for Review of a refusal, more often than not the grounds set out will be the opposite of the grounds of refusal included in the Notice of Refusal issued by the responsible authority. For an Application for Review of a decision to grant, the applicant should state briefly why the decision is opposed, such as the proposed development would cause unreasonable overshadowing, be unresponsive to the character of the neighbourhood by virtue of its height and bulk, result in unreasonable overlooking, et cetera. For an Application for Review of a condition in a permit, the applicant should state concisely why the condition is resisted, such as the condition is unnecessary or is invalid. In the case of an Application for Review of failure to decide within the prescribed time, it is not necessary to set out grounds, because no decision has been made by the responsible authority. But, in the other instances where grounds are set out, it should be kept in mind that generally these grounds will need to be expanded upon and defended at the VCAT hearing. In setting out the grounds, a wise applicant would keep in mind the submission that he or she intends to make at the hearing and the deficiencies of the proposal which he or she intends to demonstrate by reference to the plans for the proposed development, the characteristics of the subject land, the provisions of the relevant planning scheme, and the characteristics of abutting and nearby land (see below for a discussion on preparing a submission for the review hearing). There is little point in including grounds which are simply not supported by the facts, such as the development would overlook, if the plans show there are no windows on the relevant elevation, or that the development would result in unreasonable overshadowing, if the shadow diagrams demonstrate that no shadow would be cast on any other property.

Notice of the Application for Review and the lodging of grounds of review

The requirements for an applicant to give notice are set out in s 72 of *VCAT Act* and s 83A of the *Planning and Environment Act*. After the Application for Review has been lodged, the Tribunal instructs the applicant to serve a copy of the application on all the other parties within seven days of the date of lodgement. A person who wishes to contest the Application for Review must, within 14 days of being served, lodge with the Tribunal a Statement of Grounds on which that person intends to rely at the hearing: *VCAT Act*, Schedule 1, cl 56; and *VCAT Rules*, rule 5.07. In the event that the Application for Review is of a failure to determine, the lodging of a Statement of Grounds is not required. While parties are not restricted to the grounds set out in the Statement of Grounds, if new grounds are introduced during the hearing the Tribunal is bound to give the other parties time to consider them, and this could result in an adjournment, with the possibility of costs being awarded (see below).

In the event that notice of the permit application was not given by the responsible authority pursuant to s 52 of the *Planning and Environment Act* (as, for example, if the responsible authority refused to grant a permit pursuant to s 52(1A) without first giving notice) the Tribunal requires the applicant for review to serve on those persons the Tribunal requires to be notified a standard Grounds of Review and Application to be Joined as Parties form.

The advice we have given above in relation to the grounds stated in the Application for Review also applies to the grounds included in a Statement of Grounds. There is little point in including grounds that are simply not supported by the facts.

Who are the parties?

Parties who may appear at a review hearing are the applicant for the permit, the responsible authority, a referral authority which objected to the grant of the permit, and objectors who have lodged a Statement of Grounds within time. If a Statement of Grounds has been lodged out of time the person who lodged the statement is informed by the Senior Registrar that it has been lodged out of time and that application should be made at the beginning of the hearing to be joined as party pursuant to s 60 of the *VCAT Act*.

Persons who were not objectors to the permit application may apply to the Tribunal for leave to apply for a review of a decision of the responsible authority to grant a permit, provided at least one objection to the permit application was lodged with the responsible authority and provided no permit has been issued: *Planning and Environment Act*, s 82B. The Tribunal may grant leave if it believes it would be just and fair to do so, in which case the applicant for leave may lodge an Application for Review: *Planning and Environment Act*, s 82B(4) and (5). Persons who were not objectors to the permit application may lodge a Statement of Grounds and make application to be joined as parties pursuant to s 60 of the *VCAT Act*. The Tribunal may order that a person be joined as a party to a proceeding if it considers that the person ought be bound by or have the benefit of an order of the Tribunal in the proceeding, or the person's interests are affected by the proceeding, or for any other reason it is desirable that the person be joined. The Tribunal may make an order on its own initiative or on the application of any person: s 60(2).

Planning schemes may include exemptions in relation to objection and review rights. The exemption in relation to review rights applies only to decisions to grant a permit. As was discussed in Chapter 4, where an Application for Review is of a refusal or a failure to determine a permit application which is exempt, the Tribunal is not bound to consider any Statement of Grounds lodged by objectors because they are not parties to the proceeding, but objectors may be granted leave pursuant to s 98(1)(c) of the *VCAT Act* to make submissions, or they may make application to be joined as a party to the proceeding pursuant to s 60.

An unincorporated association cannot be a party to a proceeding before the Tribunal: *VCAT Act*, s 61(1). However, the Tribunal may permit a submission to be made on behalf of an unincorporated association by a member of the association or a representative of it: s 61(2).

The Major Cases List, the Short Cases List, and practice day hearings

At the start of October 2010 the time between the date an application for review was lodged and the time when the hearing commences had blown out to more than eight months. In response to this unacceptable delay, the Attorney-General announced special funding for 12 months to establish a Major Cases List within the Planning and Environment List to expedite cases involving development worth $5 million and more. The Major Cases List was established in May 2010. The Planning and Environment List Practice Note PNPE8 – Major Cases List states that the following timelines will apply to Major Cases List proceedings:

- 4 weeks – date of lodgement to practice day hearing;
- 6 weeks – date of lodgement to mediation;
- 12 weeks – date of lodgement to date of hearing;
- 4 weeks – last date of hearing to date of decision or interim decision.

The time from lodgement to decision or interim decision is to be 26 weeks, approximately six weeks sooner than the current delay. Whether or not the timelines will be achieved will depend very much on the level of resources made available. The threshold of $5 million seems to us to be on the low side – after all, a development of a dozen or so dwellings would qualify for the list.

There is also the concern that larger developments appear to be getting preferential treatment. In what appears to be an attempt to ward off that sort of concern, the Short Cases List was established in August 2010. In this list, cases will be listed for a short hearing within eight to 10 weeks of lodgement. Cases typically to be included in this list are those where there are limited parties, where the issues are limited in number and extent, the case is capable of being heard in less than two hours, and a site inspection is unlikely to be required: see Planning and Environment List Practice Note PNPE9 – Short Cases List. Written reasons for decisions will not ordinarily be provided (unless requested, or the Member considers them necessary). The most common form of listing in this list is a fixed two-hour hearing at 9: 30 am, 11:30 am or 2:30 pm, with parties given notice of the hearing approximately four to six weeks in advance, or a listing on a practice day, or some other day, without the allocation of a fixed time.

Matters listed for hearing on a practice day are generally listed for hearing at 10:00 am (normally on Fridays) or as soon thereafter as the business of the Tribunal permits. A party or proposed party wishing to initiate a practice day hearing must lodge a Practice Day Request with the Principal Registrar before noon on the day (usually a Thursday) eight days before the day of the proposed hearing. The Request must outline the nature of the order sought, the proposed date of the hearing (which must be within 30 days of the application), and, where it is practical to do so, advise whether the other parties or prospective parties agree to that hearing date: Planning and Environment List Practice Note PNPE6 – Practice Day. PNPE6 sets out at cl 2.1 the matters dealt with at practice days, including the giving of directions, an application to strike out or dismiss a proceeding, an application for an order in relation to procedural deficiency, an application to extend or abridge any time limit, and an application that notice or further notice be given of a proceeding.

Preparing a submission for the review hearing

The following applies in the main to "normal" review hearings, including Major Cases List hearings, and, with suitable modifications, to Short Cases List hearings, keeping in mind that the latter hearings are to take no longer than two hours.

A submission before VCAT may be made orally or in writing. The most common practice is to present a written submission and either read it or speak to it. Enough copies should be available to distribute to all members of the Tribunal and other parties to the proceeding for review (normally six copies will be sufficient). A written submission will set out the arguments relied on by that party to the proceeding for review.

The following VCAT guidelines deal with submissions in relation to Applications for Review:

- *Planning and Environment List General Guidelines*;
- *Responsible Authority Submissions in Planning Appeals*;
- *Submissions in the Planning List*.

Written submissions by the responsible authority must not only support the decision of the responsible authority but should also set the scene by providing the Tribunal with essential background information and include the following:

- a description of the development or use applied for and a description of the subject land;
- the planning controls as they affect the subject land and adjacent land;

- a brief history of the statutory steps taken up to the lodging of the Application for Review – for example, how notice of the permit application was given;
- brief particulars of objections received and submissions made by the applicant;
- the decision of the responsible authority and the reasons for it;
- answers to the appellant's grounds of appeal.

The objectors will usually set out the reasons for objecting to the grant of the permit. The applicant will either support the responsible authority's notice of a decision to grant the permit or argue against the grounds of refusal or contend that the conditions imposed in the permit are not justified. Written submissions by applicants and objectors are often set out in a similar format to that of the responsible authority, but, unless the submittor intends to make any particular points about the subject land and surrounding land, the planning controls, or the history of the application or to support his or her case, it is not necessary to include these in a submission, or, if they are included, it is not necessary to read them out, because the person representing the responsible authority will have already dealt with these matters.

It is important for all parties to understand that their arguments must be related to the plans, the subject site, the surrounding area, and the provisions of the scheme, as appropriate. Proceedings in relation to permit applications for the development of two or more dwellings are the largest single category of review proceedings in the Planning and Environment List. We offer the following advice to objectors about the preparation of submissions opposing the development of two or more dwellings on a lot, but the advice also has more general application:

- don't claim that a proposed development would overlook or overshadow when the plans clearly demonstrate no overlooking or overshadowing is possible;
- even if the proposed development would overshadow or overlook, the test is whether such overlooking or overshadowing would be unreasonable, not that it would occur, so if you think it is unreasonable, explain why you think that;
- don't claim that the proposed development would result in a significant increase in traffic volumes if the proposed development is only two or three dwellings and the local street network effectively accommodates existing volumes;
- don't claim that the proposed development would cause parking congestion in the street if the on-site parking shown on the plans for the occupiers and visitors meets the *ResCode* standards set out at cl 55 of the planning scheme, particularly if there is capacity to accommodate more kerb-side parking in the street near the development;
- don't claim the proposed development would be out of character in the area because it does not mimic the style and appearance of buildings on abutting or nearby land (the test is whether the proposal respects and responds to neighbourhood character – see Chapter 3);
- in developing an argument about how the proposed development does not respect and respond to neighbourhood character, don't rely on a Neighbourhood Character Study, whether or not it is a reference document or an incorporated document in the scheme, if the character of the area in question bears little or

no resemblance to that identified in the study (all too often the precincts or neighbourhoods in such studies are very large and it is not uncommon for a particular area to be very much at odds with the character identified for the precinct or area as a whole);
- if the planning scheme includes an explicit policy in the Local Planning Policy Framework that the existing character of an area is to be maintained and enhanced, don't rely just on pointing that out. If other policies also explicitly identify the area in which the development is to be located as one in which development at higher densities and at a greater scale are encouraged, concentrate on developing an argument that there are circumstances in this particular instance which justify why the policy encouraging higher densities should not be applied;
- don't rely on an argument that a building or precinct has heritage value if it is not subject to a Heritage Overlay (if the style or form of older buildings in the area are important contributors to neighbourhood character, that is a different matter, but you are usually wasting your time arguing that they have heritage significance if they are not subject to an existing Heritage Overlay or one that is the subject of a planning scheme amendment which has progressed through the amendment process to the point where it could be considered a seriously entertained planning proposal – see Chapter 4).

Our general advice to all parties, but particularly to objectors, is always to examine the plans and the provisions of the planning scheme, and, where it may be useful in informing the Tribunal and supporting your argument, take photographs and measure distances and include these in or as appendices to your written submission. In some circumstances it may be appropriate to use a video camera and play the recording at the hearing as part of your submission. But you must examine the plans for the proposed development and the provisions of the planning scheme. We readily acknowledge that plans are not easy to read and planning scheme provisions are often very difficult to understand. If there are a number of objectors who are parties, they should at least consider banding together and engaging a professional to represent them. The Tribunal is not swayed in any way by the number of persons making a submission opposing a development. What counts is a valid argument that is well supported by reference to the plans for the proposal, the provisions of the planning scheme and the characteristics of the subject site and surrounding area.

If the Tribunal makes a decision "on the spot" (that is, gives its decision orally) it will do so either before or after hearing submissions on proposed permit conditions and give an outline of reasons for its decision (see below for a discussion on decisions). If it reserves its decision, it will hear submissions on proposed conditions before closing the hearing. Draft conditions proposed by the responsible authority are required to be filed with the Tribunal and served on the other parties at least a week before the hearing: *VCAT Practice Note Planning and Environment List (No 1) – General Procedures*, cl 4.5. The other parties are advised to examine them closely and be prepared to make at least verbal submissions on those which they oppose and/or those which they believe should be modified or amended. Where the

Tribunal reserves its decision, the hearing of submissions on these conditions does not mean that the Tribunal will grant a permit – if they are not discussed and the Tribunal decides to grant a permit, the parties would need to attend a further hearing to discuss them.

Order of appearance and representation at the hearing

Where an Application for Review is to proceed to hearing, the Principal Registrar is required to fix a day, time and place for the hearing and to notify the appellant and all other persons to whom a copy of the Application for Review notice was sent: *VCAT Act*, s 99. While the procedure of the Planning and Environment List is not as formal as that of a court, nevertheless it is an independent semi-judicial body, making decisions which vitally affect the proprietary rights of land owners. The practice has been not to swear in witnesses and to allow material to be put to it that a court would not consider as evidence. While there is a power to swear in witnesses, this is rarely used in review hearings, although it is used as a matter of course in enforcement proceedings (see Chapter 7). At the hearing, parties are heard one at a time. The order of appearance is fixed by cl 4 of the VCAT *Practice Note Planning and Environment List (No 1) – General Procedures*:

(a) the responsible authority;
(b) any relevant referral or statutory authority;
(c) any objectors and third parties;
(d) any person (not being a party) having a right to be heard (for example, an unincorporated association given leave to make a submission);
(e) the applicant.

This order of appearance will normally be adhered to, unless the Tribunal considers there are sound reasons for departing from it.

Parties can appear personally or be represented by a professional advocate: s 62(1). Section 62(8) of the Act defines "professional advocate" to mean:

(a) a person who is or has been a legal practitioner; or
(b) a person who is or has been an articled clerk or law clerk in Australia; or
(c) a person who holds a degree, diploma, or other qualification in law granted or conferred in Australia; or
(d) a person who in the opinion of the Tribunal, has had substantial experience as an advocate in proceedings of a similar nature to the proceeding before the Tribunal – other than a person who is in a class of person disqualified by the rules from being a professional advocate.

The VCAT *Practice Note Planning and Environment List (No 5)* provides that, on the application of a party under s 62(1)(c) of the Act, the Tribunal will ordinarily permit the party to be represented by any person (whether or not a professional advocate). In practice, parties may be represented by whomever they choose, but the

Tribunal may require a representative who is not a professional advocate to produce an authorisation from the party concerned: s 62(7)(b).

Substitution of amended plans

It is relatively common for a permit applicant to make application at the beginning of the hearing, as a preliminary matter, to substitute amended plans for the plans accompanying the permit application and upon which, in the case of an Application for Review of a refusal or decision to grant, the responsible authority based its decision. The aim of the applicant is usually to remedy deficiencies of the proposed development identified either by the responsible authority or by objectors. Clause 64 of Schedule 1 to the *VCAT Act* confers wide powers on the Tribunal to amend applications for permits, works approvals or licences which are the subject of a proceeding, including the amendment to a use or development different from the use or development mentioned in the application, or to the land to which the application applies. The Tribunal normally exercises its discretion to grant leave to substitute amended plans if it is satisfied that the amendment(s) do not constitute a transformation of the proposal and/or would not raise new planning issues which were not before the responsible authority when it considered the proposal: see *Wilson v Port Phillip CC* [2002] VCAT 811.

To provide parties with advance notice of an application being made at the hearing to amend plans, and to give opportunity to the other parties to examine those plans, cl 11 of the VCAT *Practice Note Planning and Environment List (No 1) – General Procedures*, which came into effect on 1 October 2001, provides that the permit applicant must, at least 20 business days before any date set for hearing of the proceeding, file with the Tribunal and serve on the other parties a Notice of Application to Amend Plans, a clearly readable and scaled copy of the amended plans, and a statement in writing describing the changes from the previous plans. It also provides that, unless the Tribunal otherwise orders, the permit applicant must serve on any objector to or person notified of the permit application a Notice of Application to Amend Plans, standard Application to be Joined as a Party and Statement of Grounds forms, and a statement in writing describing the changes from the previous plans. Persons may have not lodged objections to the original plans but may be concerned about the amended plans proposed to be substituted and therefore are given the opportunity to lodge a Statement of Grounds and be joined as parties.

Witnesses

Parties to the review proceeding may call expert or lay witnesses to give evidence in support of their case. Witnesses are rarely sworn in, but the Tribunal does have the power to require evidence to be given on oath (see *VCAT Act*, s 102(3)) and this is normal practice in enforcement proceedings. In review proceedings it is common for expert witnesses such as sound and traffic engineers, landscape designers, architects and the like to be called to give evidence on technical issues and to give their opinions as experts. Expert witnesses may read their reports, or speak to them, or utilise a combination of both, as their evidence in chief. Normally the Tribunal will have read their reports before the hearing commences (see below in relation to filing and serving of expert reports) and may instruct a witness to focus on part of a report. Local residents may also be called as lay witnesses to give evidence about such matters as cars parked on the site, or noises or smells emanating from the site. After giving their evidence in chief, witness can be cross-examined (asked questions) by the other parties, usually in the same order as the order in which submissions are made. The party who called the witness is entitled, after the conclusion of the cross-examination, to re-examine the witness. This is usually done to clarify any issues raised during cross-examination. Unrepresented parties usually have difficulty in "leading" their own witnesses and in cross-examining other parties' witnesses and tend to veer into making statements and submissions rather than confining themselves to asking questions. The Tribunal generally allows a fair amount of latitude in such circumstances, in recognition that unrepresented parties normally do not have the skills one would expect of a professional advocate such as a lawyer or town planner.

Clause 4.2 of the VCAT *Practice Note Planning List (No 1) – General Procedures* provides that, no later than 10 working days before the hearing of a proceeding, each party must file with the Tribunal and serve on the other parties a copy of the report or statement containing the evidence in chief of any expert witness whose evidence is to be relied on. If such exchange of witness reports does not occur, when the hearing commences one or more parties may not have had enough time to read them and prepare for cross-examination and may seek an adjournment. If an adjournment is granted, this may result in costs being awarded against the party who failed to comply with the provisions of the Practice Note. But an adjournment is not granted automatically – for example, if the report was filed and served less than 10 days before the hearing, but it was a brief report, did not deal with complex technical matters, and the parties have read it, the Tribunal may decide that none of the parties would be disadvantaged by a request for an adjournment being refused.

Practice Note VCAT 2 – Expert Evidence makes it clear that the first duty of an expert witness is to the Tribunal. Clause 3.2 requires an expert witness to make a declaration at the end of his or her report that the witness has made all the inquiries he or she believes are desirable and appropriate and that no relevant matters of significance have been withheld from the Tribunal. Clause 3.1 sets out a detailed list of matters which must be included in the report, including the expert's name and address, qualifications and experience, expertise to make the report, the instructions that define the scope of the report, and the facts, matters and assumptions upon which the report proceeds, and must refer to the documents or other materials the expert has been instructed to consider or take into account when preparing the report, and the literature or other material used in making the report.

In hearing and determining review proceedings, VCAT is an expert tribunal by virtue of the expertise the members of its Planning and Environment List are required to possess: see *VCAT Act*, Schedule 1, cl 52. It is bound by the rules of natural justice but not by the rules of evidence, and may inform itself on any matter as it sees fit: *VCAT Act*, ss 97, 98. It is common practice for the Tribunal to ask questions of witnesses. It is not bound to accept the uncontradicted evidence of an expert witness but must consider it and, as an expert tribunal, assess its value, relevance and the weight it is to be given.

Section 94 of the *VCAT Act* provides that the Tribunal may call in an expert to advise it in respect of any matter arising in a proceeding. Section 95 provides that the Tribunal may refer a question to a special referee for that referee to decide the question or to give an opinion with respect to the question.

Determination of questions of law

Section 107 of the *VCAT Act*, as modified by cl 66 of Schedule 1, provides that, if a question of law arises during a proceeding where the Tribunal is constituted without a judicial member or a member who is a legal practitioner, the question may be decided by the presiding member if the parties agree, or in accordance with the opinion of a judicial member or a member who is a legal practitioner. Questions of law, such as those relating to the interpretation of planning scheme provisions, are raised from time to time in hearings before members who are not legal practitioners, usually, but not always, as preliminary matters before the start of the hearing of submissions. If the parties do not agree to a "non-legal" member determining the question, this may result in an adjournment and reconstitution of the Tribunal for the purpose of determining it. If the parties agree to a "non-legal" member determining it, all the parties must agree: *Rumpf v Mornington SC* [2000] VSC 311; 2 VR 69; 6 VPR 314. However, not all the parties may be at the hearing.

Section 78(2)(b)(ii) provides the power for the Tribunal to strike out a party causing disadvantage to another party. Non-attendance may unnecessarily disadvantage an applicant. If a party does not attend, he or she could be struck out, allowing the parties who remain and are in attendance to give their agreement that the question be determined by the "non-legal" member. But striking out in these circumstances should be exercised with caution. It may well be that the party is running late for the hearing, having been caught up in a traffic jam, or has been involved in an accident. Any disadvantage may be entirely unintentional and the delay may be caused by circumstances beyond the non-attending party's control.

Compulsory conferences and mediation

The concept of compulsory conferences was introduced in 1981 in the *Planning Appeals Act*. The then Minister, in his second reading speech to the Bill, said "It is expected that a proportion of appeals will be disposed of in this way". The provisions relating to compulsory conferences were retained in the *Planning Appeals Act* (Division 3) and are now contained in the *VCAT Act* in Part 3, Division 5. In addition, the *VCAT Act* has specific provisions for mediation and settlement.

Under s 83 of the *VCAT Act* the Tribunal or Principal Registrar may require parties to a proceeding to attend one or more compulsory conferences before a member of the Tribunal or Principal Registrar before the proceeding is heard. The functions of a compulsory conference are to identify and clarify the nature of the issues in dispute in the proceeding, promote a settlement of the proceeding, identify the questions of fact and law to be decided by the Tribunal, and allow directions to be given concerning the conduct of the proceedings: *VCAT Act*, s 83(2). Unless the person presiding otherwise directs, a compulsory conference must be held in private: *VCAT Act*, s 83(4). The conduct of a compulsory conference is at the discretion of the person presiding: *VCAT Act*, s 83(5). Evidence of anything said or done in the course of a compulsory conference is not admissible in any hearing before VCAT, subject to a limited number of exceptions: s 85.

Compulsory conferences are used only rarely, when it is thought that a compulsory conference is thought to be preferable, for some reason, to a directions hearing or a mediation. The *VCAT Act* includes procedures for mediation, which has become an important means of resolving disputes in relation to planning permits. VCAT's Annual Report 2008–2009 shows that, in that year, 294 cases in the Planning and Environment List were finalised at mediation (a success rate of 67 per cent). It should be noted that in many instances it may not be appropriate to refer matters to mediation, even if the parties agree that mediation is appropriate. That is because proceedings before the Planning and Environment List more often than not involve the public interest and public policy as factors to be considered. Simply endorsing a solution that the parties agree to may not be in the public interest or consistent with public policy: see *Dowling v City of Malvern* (1983) 1 PABR 86 and *Aust Defence Industries Ltd v City of Maribyrnong* (1995) 15 AATR 78. It should also be noted that the Tribunal must satisfy itself that the solution to which the parties have agreed is legally valid. For example, the solution agreed to may be a permit condition that does not meet the tests for validity (see Chapter 5).

Section 88 provides that the Tribunal may refer a proceeding to mediation by a person nominated by the Tribunal. In practice, mediators are normally members of the Planning and Environment List who have been trained in mediation. If the mediation is not successful (that is, not settled), the matter will proceed to a hearing as if it had not been to mediation and the mediator cannot subsequently hear it: s 88(6). Evidence of anything said or done in the course of a mediation is not admissible in any hearing before the Tribunal unless all the parties agree otherwise: s 92. The procedure to be followed during mediation is at the discretion of the mediator, subject to the *VCAT Act* and Rules: s 88(7). The Tribunal has published two information leaflets on mediation which are available on the VCAT website (see Further Reading), as is the *VCAT Mediation Code of Conduct*.

Mediation cannot be successful if the parties refuse to settle, or if the person representing one of the parties is not authorised to negotiate and agree to a settlement. Clause 9 of the VCAT *Practice Note Planning and Environment List (No 1) – General Procedures* provides that the Tribunal may give various directions, including that representatives of parties at mediation must be authorised to settle the proceeding. While it does not happen frequently, it is not unknown for responsible authorities to either neglect to, or refuse to, authorise officers representing them at mediation to settle.

Settlement

Section 93 of the *VCAT Act* provides for the settlement of proceedings. If the parties agree to settle a proceeding at any time, the Tribunal may make the necessary orders to effect settlement. While it may make the necessary orders, it does not have to. The settlement of a proceeding in the form of a consent order may occur as a result of mediation, a compulsory conference or a hearing. But, as was explained above by reference to *Dowling v Malvern* and *Aust Defence Industries Ltd v City of Maribyrnong*, the Tribunal must satisfy itself that the settlement proposed is appropriate. It cannot simply "rubber-stamp" a settlement simply because the parties agree.

The decision of the Tribunal

The Tribunal may give a decision and an outline of reasons orally "on the spot" at the conclusion of the hearing, or it may reserve its decision. Either way, it must subsequently produce a written order, and for final orders (as distinct from interim orders) it must give written reasons within 60 days of making the order or such other period as the President authorises: ss 116(1) and 117(1). The wording of a consent order (such as an order formalising agreement between the parties as a result of mediation) provides the reason for the order (it will contain the words "by consent" or similar words which are self-explanatory). In the case of oral reasons, a party may within 14 days request the Tribunal to give written reasons, and within a further 45 days or such longer period as the President authorises, the Tribunal must comply with the request: s 117(2), (3) and (4). The order of the Tribunal comes into effect immediately after it is made (that is, made in writing) or at such other time as specified in it: ss 116(1) and 118. The reasons for an order, whether oral or written, form part of the order: s 117(6). An order must be signed by a member of the Tribunal or the Principal Registrar and have the Tribunal's seal affixed to it: s 116(1)(b) and *VCAT Rules 1998*, rule 4.16.

In practice, final orders in relation to Applications for Review are signed by the member or members who hear the case and are accompanied by written reasons, even when the decision has been given orally "on the spot". The order will affirm, vary or set aside the decision of the responsible authority: see s 51(2). If the effect of the order is to be that a permit is to be issued, it contains the conditions of the permit. If the effect is that the conditions of a permit are amended, the amendment or amendments are specified. Where there has been no decision of the responsible authority because it failed to make a decision within the prescribed time, the order will state that no permit is granted or that a permit is granted subject to conditions and then set out those conditions. A copy of the order is sent to each of the parties by the Principal Registrar.

Pursuant to s 119 the Tribunal may correct an order if it contains a clerical error, an error arising from an accidental slip or omission, a material miscalculation of figures or a material mistake in the description of a person, thing or matter referred to in the order, or a defect in form. The correction may be made on the Tribunal's own initiative or on the application of a party: s 119. If a correction is made, it is signed by the member(s) and a copy of the correction is sent to the parties by the Principal Registrar.

Costs

The general principle underlying proceedings before VCAT is that each party is to bear its own costs: *VCAT Act*, s 109(1). However, VCAT may order costs, to an amount it thinks just, where the circumstances of a particular case are considered to justify such an order: *VCAT Act*, s 109(2), (3). Section 75(1) also provides power for costs to be awarded where the Tribunal summarily dismisses or strikes out all or any part of a proceeding that is in its opinion frivolous, vexatious, misconceived or lacking in substance, or is otherwise an abuse of process. Section 75(2) provides that the Tribunal may order the applicant to pay any other party an amount to compensate that party for any costs, expenses, loss, inconvenience and embarrassment resulting from the proceeding.

Section 109 of the *VCAT Act* provides as follows:

(1) Subject to this Division, each party is to bear their own costs in the proceeding.
(2) At any time, the Tribunal may order that a party pay all or a specified part of the costs of another party in a proceeding.
(3) The Tribunal may make an order under subsection (2) only if it is satisfied that it is fair to do so, having regard to –
   (a) whether a party has conducted the proceeding in a way that unnecessarily disadvantaged another party to the proceeding by conduct such as –
      (i) failing to comply with an order or direction of the Tribunal without reasonable excuse;
      (ii) failing to comply with this Act, the regulations, the rules or an enabling enactment;
      (iii) asking for an adjournment as a result of (i) or (ii);
      (iv) causing an adjournment;
      (v) attempting to deceive another party or the Tribunal;
      (vi) vexatiously conducting the proceeding;
   (b) whether a party has been responsible for prolonging unreasonably the time taken to complete the proceeding;
   (c) the relative strengths of the claims made by each of the parties, including whether a party has made a claim that has no tenable basis in fact or law;
   (d) the nature and complexity of the proceeding;
   (e) any other matter the Tribunal considers relevant.

The effect of s 109(3) of the *VCAT Act* is modified for the purposes of decisions relating to costs in proceedings under the *Planning and Environment Act* by cl 63 of Schedule 1. Clause 63 provides that, in determining whether or not to make an order for costs, the Tribunal may have regard to "whether the proceeding was brought primarily to secure or maintain a direct or indirect commercial advantage of the person who brought the proceeding". The issue of costs is therefore not dependent on the outcome of the proceedings but relates to the conduct of the parties leading up to the hearing, or during the actual proceedings.

The general discretion as to costs also applies to the cancellation or modification of permits in relation to enforcement procedures. But the approach of VCAT with regard to awarding costs in enforcement proceedings (see Chapter 7) is different from the approach taken in planning reviews. There are situations in which VCAT will be required to make an assessment of indirect costs resulting from a statutory right to seek an amendment or cancellation of a permit. For example, under s 87 or s 89 of the Act, VCAT may seek an undertaking from the party seeking cancellation or amendment to accept liability for the costs, loss or damages that may result from a development being unnecessarily interrupted. Similar arrangements can be involved when an enforcement order is sought to prevent a breach or contravention of a planning control. The Tribunal may make an order for costs and compensation for loss or damage where it is satisfied that proceedings have been brought vexatiously or frivolously: *Planning and Environment Act 1987*, s 150(4).

But it is important for objectors to realise that, as a general rule, parties bear their own costs and there is no penalty for exercising a statutory right of lodging an Application for Review. It is only when this right has been abused or a party's conduct or disregard of procedures has prejudiced another party to the review that an application for costs will be entertained.

> 22. [T]he Tribunal, as the planning tribunal in Victoria, is intended to be accessible to the citizens of the State, and that they should not be frightened off from making use of the Tribunal by fear that orders might be made against them for costs, at any rate where they have behaved in a reasonable and bona fide fashion. (*Sinclair v Greater Geelong CC* [2004] VCAT 588)

> 8. The planning review system operates on the basis of a no-cost jurisdiction or no threat of costs for persons bringing the usual or regular type of planning applications, such as reviews of Council decisions and/or conditions (by both permit applicants and objectors). There is strong policy support for the primary rule that each party bear their own costs because town planning is concerned with balancing private and public expectations, which is and should be open to broad public participation. The respective rights of one party to apply for review and the rights of another party to object and resist an application for review are fundamental aspects of the planning system and the success of the system is to a large degree dependent upon the application of the principle that costs are to be assumed where they fall. (*Arforas v Hobsons Bay CC* [2003] VCAT 1877)

> 17. Section 109 of the *VCAT Act* gives the Tribunal a broad discretion in relation to costs. The existence of such discretion enables the Tribunal to do its best to provide a just outcome, subject to the basic principle that each party will usually bear its

own costs. There is much to be said for the existence of such a broad discretion. But equally, it is important that the obligation to pay costs be predictable, as this promotes certainty. A proper balance is likely to be promoted if decisions as to costs are only made after serious and close consideration of the statutory provisions; and then according to principles and practices that develop in relation to particular provisions, or lists.

18. In my opinion, for an award of costs to be made it is not sufficient to demonstrate that the nature of the proceeding has a strong resemblance to inter-parties litigation in a court. Section 109(1) of the *VCAT Act* is designed to cover proceedings in all lists of the tribunal, including those where proceedings are characteristically similar to those conducted in the County Court or Supreme Court. But paragraph (d) of section 109(3) of the *VCAT Act* anticipates that certain types of proceedings will be brought before the tribunal which will be of a character to enable the tribunal to be satisfied that an order should be made as to costs. How are these cases to be identified? No doubt it would be convenient if a list of such cases was published. But I think it would be unwise to essay such a list; that will have to emerge over time.

19. What can be said is this:
It is more likely that the nature and complexity of a proceeding will make it fair to make an order as to costs if:

- the proceeding was in the tribunal's original jurisdiction, not its review jurisdiction;
- the proceeding involved a large number of issues, or a small number of particularly complex issues;
- the proceeding involved a large sum of money or a major issue affecting the welfare of a party or the community;
- the proceeding succeeded and was a type which was required to be brought, either by reason of a statutory duty or by reason of some unlawful or improper conduct by another party which warranted redress;
- the proceeding failed and was a type where a party has asserted a right which it knew, or ought to have known, was tenuous;
- a practice has developed that costs are routinely awarded in a particular type of proceeding, thus making an award of costs more predictable for the proceeding in question. (*Sweetvale Pty Ltd v Minister for Planning* [2004] VCAT 2000)

Costs awarded pursuant to s 109 are not damages, nor are they fines. They are awarded to compensate a party for loss or expense unreasonably and unjustifiably imposed on that party or penalties. Section 109(3) provides that the Tribunal may award costs only if it is satisfied that it is fair to do so, having regard to a number of factors. The first of these, set out in s 109, is that a party has conducted the proceeding in a way that unnecessarily disadvantaged another party to the proceeding.

The second is whether a party has been responsible for unreasonably prolonging the time taken to complete the proceeding. The third is the relative strengths of the claims made by each of the parties, including whether a party has made a claim that has no tenable basis in fact or law. The fourth is the nature and complexity of the processing. The fifth is any other matter the Tribunal considers relevant.

Examples of where VCAT and/or its predecessors have awarded costs include where:

- a hearing which should have finished in a day was adjourned to a later date to allow traffic evidence to be called and that evidence should have been exchanged before the hearing in accordance with Practice Note Planning 1: *Adams v Bayside CC* [2000] VCAT 933;
- plans were substituted for plans accompanying the permit application resulting in inadequate time for the parties to consider the amended plans before the hearing date: *Cohen Chalmers Pty Ltd v City of Stonnington* (1994) 13 AATR 29;
- failure to provide a short statement of grounds resulted in a proceeding continuing which would have been withdrawn if the party had understood the responsible authority's intention for imposing a condition: *Telford v Shire of Buln Buln* (1990) 5 AATR 193;
- appellant objectors failed to appear at the hearing and the permit applicant had been legally represented and had engaged expert witnesses: *Zalcberg v City of Stonnington* (1996) 18 AATR 122;
- the permit applicant withdrew the appeal on the day of the hearing: *City of Kew v MMBW* (1983) 29 APA 341; 1 PABR 82;
- the permit applicant withdrew its appeal before the hearing and following an adjournment: *McDonalds Properties (Aust) Pty Ltd v City of Stonnington* (unreported, 1996/49075, 49104, 49091; editorial comment 22 AATR 2);
- the decision of the responsible authority was inconsistent with the planning scheme provisions and with the decisions of the Tribunal on three previous occasions: *Marzorini v Mitchell SC* [1999] VCAT 1826;
- the actions of the responsible authority were held to be motivated by reasons other than those to which it was properly required to have regard: *Lowther Hall Anglican Grammar School v Moonee Valley CC* (1999) 1 VPR 90;
- the argument on which the responsible authority relied had been rejected by the Tribunal on six previous occasions: *Terence Casey Architects Pty Ltd v Colac Otway SC* [2003] VCAT 1007; 14 VPR 70;
- the responsible authority imposed a condition in a permit requiring a cash in lieu contribution for car parking to appease a neighbouring municipality, which the Tribunal found had been imposed for an ulterior motive and had no basis in fact or law: *Bengold Pty Ltd v Kingston CC* [2001] VCAT 1925; 9 VPR 9;
- the proceedings where sponsored by a third party and were found to be brought vexatiously: *James W Sadler Pty Ltd v City of Keilor* (1992) 11 AATR 176;
- the purpose of lodging an application for review by an objector was to obtain a commercial advantage for the objector's own subdivision: *Oglesby v East Gippsland SC* [2006] VCAT 2475;
- one objector persisted with an application for review after an amendment to the application had reduced a proposed subdivision from 40 to 27 lots, as a result of which the other objectors withdrew their applications for review. The persisting objector indicated at the hearing that the reason she persisted was that in her view the land was inappropriately zoned. The Tribunal found her behaviour unreason-

able and unjustified and unnecessarily disadvantaged the permit applicant: *Green v Ballarat CC* [2006] VCAT 2535.

Part 8.85 of the *Planning Appeals Casenotes* volume of the *Butterworths Planning and Environment Service (Victoria)* contains other examples where costs have been awarded by VCAT and its predecessors in relation to review proceedings. Part 6.5 contains examples of where costs have been awarded in enforcement proceedings.

Section 109(3)(c) of the *VCAT Act* warrants some specific comment. In *Dennis Family Corporation v Casey CC* [2008] VCAT 691 the Tribunal refused an application for an order of costs against a responsible authority arising out of declaration proceedings. Referring specifically to s 109(3)(c), the Tribunal said:

> 14. The relative strengths of the claims appear to refer to the strength of claims of one party compared to the strength of the claims of another. A difficult, doubtful or test case might be necessary to clarify the legal position of the parties. It is probably seldom that an order for costs would be made having regard to this consideration alone where there was a real issue to be tried and real justification for the claims made by the other side. I take it that generally where there is a very weak case for one side, or none at all, that this consideration is likely to lead to an order for costs. I note that the wording says that the absence of a "tenable basis in law or fact" is a consideration within the consideration of the relative strengths of the claims of the parties.
>
> 15. This certainly cannot mean that an unsuccessful party should be required to pay costs because, at the end of the case, that party's claims have been found to be untenable in fact or law to the extent that they were not upheld and were not successful. That would amount to "costs following the event". It would compromise the general rule created in s 109(1).
>
> 16. As I have said, I do not think that the consideration indicates an order for costs where there are strong cases on either side, or perhaps evenly balanced cases on either side.
>
> 17. I am not minded to go so far as to say that a weak case will necessarily indicate an order for costs. The word "untenable" is stronger than "weak". The Macquarie Dictionary, second revision, defines untenable as incapable of being held against attack, incapable of being maintained against argument, as an opinion, scheme etc.
>
> 18. The ethical rules of the Bar, as I recall them, indicate that a barrister has a duty to do his or her best by the client even if the client has a weak case. On the other hand, a different duty applies if the case is so weak as to be unarguable, or "untenable". It extends to a case so weak that it should not be argued or so weak that it would be an abuse to seek to maintain it.
>
> 19. I think "untenable" in the context of s 109(3)(c) means something like so weak as to be unarguable, rather than merely weak.

The "bar" against awarding costs on the basis of s 109(3)(c) is set quite high. However, sometimes a case is so weak that it is unarguable and costs have been awarded on that basis – see, for example, *Anastassiou v Port Phillip CC* [2007] VCAT 248.

Parties, particularly objectors, commonly represent themselves before the Tribunal. The High Court in *Cachia v Hanes* (1994) 120 ALR 385 held that costs did not include time spent by a self-represented litigant preparing and presenting his or her case (except in the case of a self-represented lawyer), and were confined to those incurred for professional legal services. Costs are intended to be reimbursement for costs actually incurred, not as compensation for inconvenience. In *Zalcberg v City of Stonnington* (1996) 18 AATR 122, *Cachia v Hanes* was applied and the council was not awarded the cost of sending an officer to the hearing. In *Cardinia SC v Stoiljkovic (No 2)* [2002] VCAT 918, it was held that costs in relation to s 150(4) (and presumably in relation to other sections, such as s 109) could be awarded to a professional advocate who was not a lawyer. In *Noonan v Boroondara CC* [2001] VCAT 158, it was held that fees of a town planner advocate amounted to expenses or loss under s 75(2). In *Aussie Invest Corporation Pty Ltd v Hobsons Bay CC* [2004] VCAT 2188, Morris J held that the decision of the High Court in *Cachia* did not prevent VCAT making an order that a party pay the costs of an unrepresented party in respect of lost wages and travelling costs incurred in attending a hearing or proceeding, even if the unrepresented party is not a witness in the proceeding, and that the principal judgement in *Cachia* was made in the context of the rules of the New South Wales Supreme Court, which do not apply to VCAT.

In awarding costs the Tribunal normally confines them to the cost of professional representatives preparing for and attending the hearing and the preparation and appearance costs of witnesses called.

Appeals to the Supreme Court on a question of law

Orders of the Tribunal are binding on all parties to the proceeding appeal and are final, subject to the right of appeal by a party to a proceeding on "a question of law" to the Supreme Court: *VCAT Act*, s 148. There are other avenues by which a decision of the Tribunal may be challenged (by application to the Supreme Court under the Supreme Court Rules, and by application to the Supreme Court under the *Administrative Law Act 1978*), but discussion of these is beyond the scope of this book.

Only a party to a proceeding may apply under s 148. "Proceeding" is defined in s 3 to mean a proceeding of the Tribunal. Section 59 sets out who is a party to a proceeding. The right of appeal is confined to a "question of law" and is only permitted with the leave of the Appellate Court: see s 148(1). Put simply, a "question of law" is whether the Tribunal, in making its order, misinterpreted or misconstrued the provisions of legislation, or of subordinate legislation (such as a planning scheme), or whether in hearing and considering the matter it breached one of the rules of natural justice (such as not affording procedural fairness to one or more parties, or taking into account an irrelevant consideration). The error must be a vitiating error of law, or must at least potentially be a vitiating error of law and not just an abstract error: *Johnson v Russell* [2006] VSC 373.

The Appellate Court will be the Court of Appeal if the Tribunal was constituted by either a President or Vice President and the Trial Division of the Supreme Court in any other case: s 148(1). Application for leave to appeal must be made within 28 days after the date of the Order of the Tribunal, or, if the Tribunal gave oral reasons for making an Order and a party requests it to give written reasons pursuant to s 117, within 28 days of when the written reasons are given: s 148(2) and (4). If leave is granted, the appeal must be instituted within 14 days after the day on which the leave is granted.

The courts do not have jurisdiction to review the planning merits of a decision made by the Tribunal. The Supreme Court of Victoria in *City of Camberwell v Nicholson* (unreported, VSC, 2 December 1988) discussed the restrictions on the right of appeal under s 52(1) of the former *Administrative Tribunals Act 1984*, which provided the right of appeal from the AAT on a question of law to the Supreme Court. Ormiston J said:

> I should emphasise that the right of appeal to this Court is confined to questions of law and permits a review only of relevant legal issues and does not entitle the Court to review the evidence so as to substitute its decision for that of the Tribunal, whether on questions of fact or as to the exercise of the relevant discretions. Parliament has entrusted to the Administrative Appeals Tribunal the final decision on these critical questions of fact and as to the manner in which the powers and discretions granted to responsible authorities under the relevant planning legislation should be implemented. My task is to determine only whether the Tribunal has formed a mistaken view as to the relevant law or whether its conclusion is such that nobody could properly reach if it correctly understood that law.

These observations apply equally to appeals pursuant to s 148 of the *VCAT Act*. The orders on an appeal that the Court of Appeal or the Trial Division (as the case requires) may make include an order remitting the proceeding to be heard again by the Tribunal: s 148(c). If the Court makes such an order it must give directions as to whether or not the Tribunal is to be constituted for the rehearing by the same members who made the original order.

As discussed earlier in this chapter, s 52 of the *VCAT Act* excludes the Supreme Court, County Court and Magistrates' Court from hearing disputes involving planning matters where the Tribunal has jurisdiction to review the matter in dispute but the matter has not been referred to the Tribunal or a determination has not yet been made.

Ministerial call-in of applications for review

Clauses 58 and 59 of Schedule 1 to the *VCAT Act* provide for the Minister or other Ministers to call in an application for review and refer it to the Governor in Council for determination. Clause 60 provides that the Tribunal may refer an application for review to the Governor in Council for determination.

Clause 58 applies to a proceeding for review of a decision under the *Planning and Environment Act* if the Minister administering that Act considers that the proceeding raises a major issue of policy and the determination of the proceeding may have a substantial effect on the achievement or development of planning objectives. The Minister may, by notice in writing to the Principal Registrar, call in the proceeding, or invite the Tribunal to hear or continue to hear the proceeding but refer it with recommendations to the Governor in Council for determination. An invitation to refer, as distinct from a direction to refer, implies the Tribunal has the option of declining the invitation.

Clause 59 applies to a proceeding for review of a decision under a planning enactment other than the *Planning and Environment Act* if the Minister administering the planning enactment considers the proceeding raises a major issue of policy. "Planning enactment" is defined in cl 2 of Schedule 1 to the *VCAT Act*. The Minister administering the relevant planning enactment may request the Minister administering the *Planning and Environment Act*, by notice in writing to the Principal Registrar, to call in the proceeding, or invite the Tribunal to hear or continue to hear the proceeding but refer it with recommendations to the Governor in Council for determination. The Minister administering the *Planning and Environment Act* must comply with such a request.

A notice or invitation given under cl 58 or cl 59 has no effect unless it is given before the final determination of the proceeding and no later than seven days before the date fixed for the hearing of the proceeding. A hearing does not include a directions hearing, preliminary hearing or interlocutory hearing: cll 58(5) and 59(6). These subclauses of cll 58 and 59 were inserted into the *VCAT Act* by the *Victorian Civil and Administrative Tribunal (Amendment) Act 2004*, following the decision of Morris J in *Buttigieg v Melton Shire Council* [2004] VCAT 868 that a directions hearing constituted commencement of a hearing.

Other amendments to cll 58 and 59 made by the *Victorian Civil and Administrative Tribunal (Amendment) Act 2004* appear to contain a contradiction. Clauses 58(3) and (4), 59(4) and (5) provide that a notice given by the Minister, either calling in the proceeding or inviting the Tribunal to continue hearing the proceeding but refer it with recommendations for determination by the Governor in Council, has no effect unless it is given before the final determination of the proceeding *and* no later than seven days before the day fixed for the hearing of the proceeding. On the face of it, it would seem that the notice must be given at least seven days before the hearing commences. Yet the notice may invite the Tribunal to hear, or *continue to hear,* the proceeding, and if the Minister calls in a proceeding by notice the Tribunal must not commence *or continue to hear* the proceeding.

It was noted in Chapter 2 that the power of the Minister to call in review proceedings dates back to 1979, when an amendment was made to the then *Town and Country Planning Act 1961* whereby the Minister was given the power to "call in appeals" from the then Planning Appeals Board. This power was retained after the repeal of the *Town and Country Planning Act 1961* and the enactment of the *Planning and Environment Act 1987*. The call-in power was extended by s 41 of the then *Planning Appeals Act 1980* to enable any Minister administering an Act under which an appeal is brought to request the Minister for Planning to call in a matter if it raises major issues of policy, a similar provision to what is now included at cl 59 of Schedule 1 to the *VCAT Act*.

As to what constitutes a major issue of policy or a substantial effect on the achievement or development of planning objectives is not indicated in the Act.

Section 40(2) of the *Planning Appeals Act* allowed the Minister to intervene in what was then called an appeal before the then Planning Appeals Board by making a submission to the Tribunal if he or she believed the matter raised major issues of policy. In 1985 the Planning Appeals Board in *Altona Petrochemical Co Ltd v City of Altona, Italian Soccer Club Altona Inc and Sixth P & C Nominees Pty Ltd* (1985) 3 PABR 143 at 149 held that:

> The Minister is the sole judge on the questions of whether an appeal raises a major issue of policy and in the case of an appeal under the *Town and Country Planning Act 1961*, whether the determination of the appeal may have a substantial effect on the future planning of the area in which the land the subject of the appeal is situated and that neither this Board nor any other person has any right to question any judgment which the Minister has formed as to the matter. An assertion by the Minister that it appears to him that these matters exist is, in our view, conclusive.

Neither the Minister nor the Governor in Council, in exercising powers to call in and determine proceedings pursuant to cll 58 and 59 of Schedule 1 to the *VCAT Act*, is required to give reasons. In *Orientmix Australasia Pty Ltd v City of Melbourne* (1982) 62 LGRA 152 the Minister had called in the appeal under s 41(2) of the *Planning Appeals Act*. The PAB made its recommendation on the appeal to the Minister, who referred the appeal to the Governor in Council for determination under s 41(5) of the Act. The appeal was dismissed. The applicant brought proceedings in the Supreme Court seeking an order requiring the giving of reasons for the decision by the Governor in Council. Fullagar J held at 158:

> This court cannot go behind the Minister's certificate pursuant to s 41(3) of the *Planning Appeals Board Act* that the appeal raises a major issue of policy, and that the court should in any event refrain from ordering a statement of reasons of the Governor or Minister or Cabinet on a matter of policy ...
>
> The considerations against a court of law ordering the Governor in Council to do a positive act, or to order a Minister of the Crown to disclose the reasons for a cabinet decision are, in my opinion, so strong that I would not (as at present advised) make such an order unless express words of a statute authorised the order by mentioning the Governor in Council or the Minister expressly as the object of the order, or unless I felt compelled to do so by binding authority from which there was no possible escape.

Where the Minister called in a matter under s 41 of the then *Planning Appeals Act*, the rules of natural justice did not apply. In *Minister for Planning and Environment v Braybridge* (1988) 2 AATR 82 at 88, Southwell J said:

> I cannot believe that Parliament intended that the Minister's power to call in an appeal should be restricted by his having to confer with all interested parties before doing so. He is not the person who will hear the appeal and decide the appeal. The Governor in Council is the final arbiter although ... generally speaking, this is done on the advice of the responsible Minister.

His Honour did say that the Minister may have an obligation to give the parties an opportunity to be heard before he makes his final recommendation to the Governor in Council but considered that it would "be remarkable if, for example, the Governor in Council or the Full Cabinet, were to grant some oral hearing". In the case before him, there had been no denial of natural justice because the appellant had not requested copies of the submission or a hearing.

The decision is consistent with the *Orientmix* case, where it was held that the rules of natural justice must be observed by the Governor in Council before he makes his decision. The Court was of the opinion (at 156) that:

> If the court is of the opinion that some requirement of natural justice must be observed at some point *before* the act of the governor which constitutes the ultimate exercise of the power, it sees to it (as far as the powers of the court extend) that the requirement is observed by some 'convenient person' involved in the matter.
>
> After the governor has exercised the power, the court might still declare that act of the Governor in Council to be void and might indicate who is a convenient person to comply with the requirement if a new application is made. The 'convenient person' is usually the minister, but if it is not, the court can chose who is.

In *Moonee Valley CC v Quadry Industries Pty Ltd* [1999] VSC 95; 6 VPR 196, the Supreme Court held that a party to a proceeding before the AAT called in by the Minister pursuant to s 41(1) of the *Planning Appeals Act 1980* had a right of appeal to the Supreme Court on a question of law under s 52 of the *AAT Act*, which is now covered by s 148 of the *VCAT Act*.

Permit applications made to the Minister by other Ministers and government departments may also be removed from the normal processes of hearing and determination of review proceedings by VCAT. Pursuant to s 95 of the *Planning and Environment Act*, such applications may be referred for decision to the Governor in Council if "the Governor in Council considers that the overriding interests of the State require the application be so referred": s 95(3)(c). The decision of the Governor in Council "is final and is not subject to review on appeal except in the Supreme Court on a question of law": s 95(6).

Chapter 7

PLANNING ENFORCEMENT

Section 14 of the *Planning and Environment Act 1987* requires responsible authorities to enforce the provisions of schemes. The duty of enforcement extends to the conditions of permits and the provisions of agreements relating to permits and scheme amendments.

The objectives of enforcement

The objectives of the responsible authority in enforcement are to ensure compliance with the scheme, permit conditions and agreements; to prevent threatened breaches of the scheme, permit conditions and agreements; and to punish those responsible for breaches of the scheme, permit conditions and agreements. The choice of enforcement mechanisms provided for by the Act depends on which objective or objectives the responsible authority chooses to pursue in any given situation. Although the responsible authority has a duty to enforce planning controls under the Act, formal proceedings in the form of enforcement orders or prosecutions are used as a last resort. They will only be used where a person has blatantly defied or ignored proper and reasonable requests from the responsible authority that the contravention should cease. Informal procedures such as a quiet talk by the responsible authority's enforcement officer to the person concerned, or a written warning by the responsible authority, may be enough to achieve compliance – the primary objective of enforcement. It is general practice for responsible authorities to first talk to those who have committed the wrong then, if it is not rectified, to follow up with a warning letter, and, if this fails, to commence formal proceedings.

The formal enforcement procedures are those which are set out in Part 6 and ss 87–94 of the *Planning and Environment Act*. The mechanisms provided for are an enforcement order (ss 114–119), an interim enforcement order (ss 120–121), an injunction, an infringement notice (ss 130–132), cancellation of a permit (ss 87–94), and an order to stop development (s 93). Alternatively, a person guilty of an offence under the Act may be prosecuted in the Magistrates' Court (s 126) and there is provision (s 125) to seek an injunction to prevent a threatened conduct or act from occurring, or to require immediate compliance with a particular provision.

Which method used by the responsible authority will depend upon what is being aimed for. Is it to prevent actions from occurring, to ensure compliance with the scheme, or to punish for persistent non-compliance? The responsible authority may find that, where the informal proceedings are ignored, the formal proceedings may be the only means by which a person who has persistently disobeyed the controls may be made to comply.

The primary objective of the responsible authority is to achieve compliance with the planning controls, permit conditions, or provisions of a s 173 agreement and this aim may be different from what neighbours and third parties want. These persons will also want compliance with the provisions of the scheme, but may also want the offender punished. Although they have the right at common law to seek an injunction, it is rarely exercised because of the potential cost of such an action. Under the *Town and Country Planning Act*, neighbours and third parties had no formal right to institute enforcement proceedings. To all intents and purposes, the power to enforce was in the hands of the responsible authority and, if it chose not to act, there was little that members of the community could do. By contrast, the *Planning and Environment Act* (s 114) allows the responsible authority or "any person" to apply to the Victorian Civil and Administrative Tribunal (VCAT) for an enforcement order against a person who has contravened the Act, scheme, permit or agreement. Third parties are therefore given the power under the Act to institute formal proceedings against offenders. However, they should do so with caution. Costs can be awarded for vexatious and frivolous proceedings.

Difficulties of collecting evidence

One of the problems of bringing enforcement proceedings is to obtain sufficient and accurate evidence that an offence has been committed or is about to be committed. For responsible authorities, the enforcement provisions in the Act include the power for an authorised person (as to who may be authorised, see s 133) to enter land at any reasonable time to carry out the provisions in the Act. However, entry must be at a reasonable time and by consent. If consent is refused, two clear days' notice must be given, which provides sufficient time for evidence to be removed or concealed. No notice need be given or consent obtained in relation to brothels. If consent is not given, an authorised officer may obtain a warrant to enter the land from the Magistrates' Court: s 134(1)(c), (2). The warrant permits the authorised person to enter the land without notice to the occupier: s 134(3). The Court is unlikely to issue a warrant in the absence of some evidence that an offence has been committed or is about to be committed, but the gathering of such evidence is the purpose for entering the land. Section 135 sets out the powers of authorised officers who enter land and permits them to take photographs, make sketches or recordings and remove samples. Under s 136, the police are required to assist entry if a request is made by an authorised officer.

Enforcement mechanisms under the Planning and Environment Act 1987

While the informal procedures of enforcement continue to be used, the formal procedures are aimed at persons who persistently fail to comply with the planning controls and are normally used as a last resort.

Prosecution in the Magistrates' Court for breaches of a planning scheme, permit conditions or a s 173 agreement

Prosecution in the Magistrates' Court of persons for breaches of the planning scheme, permit conditions or s 173 agreements is available either as an alternative to, or in addition to, enforcement proceedings in VCAT (see below). But prosecution can only be for an offence that has been committed. It cannot be for an offence that may be threatened or imminent but has not yet occurred. Nor can prosecution remedy damage done, such as removal of trees, or part demolition of a building, or earthworks. But enforcement orders may deal with these situations.

Prosecution proceedings may be initiated without first seeking an enforcement order or interim enforcement order. The proceedings are aimed at punishing the offender if he or she is found guilty, whereas enforcement orders are aimed, in the first instance, at achieving compliance with the planning scheme, permit conditions or s 173 agreement.

The Act is silent as to who may lay a charge in the Magistrates' Court for a breach of a planning scheme, permit condition or s 173 agreement. In these circumstances, the responsible authority or a member of the public may lay a charge. But private citizens should tread very warily in laying a charge, and seek legal advice. To be successful, it must be proved that an offence has been committed, and proved beyond reasonable doubt.

Although prosecution is still an option, the enforcement provisions in the *Planning and Environment Act* are structured so that prosecution is not the only first formal step available. When the Act was first brought into effect, enforcement orders were intended to be used as a first step in most instances. However, there is nothing in the Act to indicate this is the case. The disadvantage of bringing a prosecution in the Magistrates' Court is that the procedures are more formal and complicated in the Court. For example, the standard of proof is "beyond reasonable doubt". This is the criminal burden of proof. Enforcement order proceedings in VCAT are not as onerous because the evidentiary burden of proving a breach is the civil standard of "on the balance of probabilities". Also, unlike the Magistrates' Court, VCAT is not bound by the rules of evidence. What is admissible evidence before VAT may not be admissible in the Court.

The penalties for a person found guilty of a breach of a planning scheme, permit condition or s 173 agreement are set out in s 127 of the *Planning and Environment Act* and are potentially severe. They are a maximum penalty of 1,200 penalty units (approximately $140,000), and, if the breach continues, a further 60 penalty units (approximately $7,000) per day during which the offence continues after conviction. But note that these are maximum penalties – the Court may see fit to impose a penalty significantly lower than the maximum.

The value of a penalty unit is fixed by notification in the *Government Gazette* pursuant to the *Monetary Units Act 2004*. For the financial year 2009–2010 it was fixed at $116.82.

Enforcement orders

Section 114 of the *Planning and Environment Act* provides that the responsible authority or any person (that is, a member of the public) may apply to VCAT for an enforcement order against any person who contravenes the Act, a planning scheme, a condition of a permit, or an agreement under the Act.

Section 67 of the *VCAT Act* sets out how applications to the Tribunal are made. Applications to the Tribunal include enforcement proceedings under ss 114 and 120 of the Act. Section 67 provides that an application to the Tribunal must be in the form and contain the particulars required by the rules and be accompanied by any documents or further information required by the rules. The rules are the *Victorian Civil and Administrative Tribunal Rules 1998*.

The *VCAT Practice Note 4 (Planning and Environment List 4 – PNPE4 – Enforcement orders and interim enforcement orders)* sets out the procedure to be followed in relation to applications for enforcement orders under ss 114 and 120 of the *Planning and Environment Act 1987* and includes as an attachment the form of application to be used. The details to be provided on the form include details of the applicant; details of the person(s) against whom the order is sought; a description of the land; the relevant provisions of the *Planning and Environment Act*; the relevant provisions of the planning scheme, permit conditions or s 173 agreement being contravened; a short statement of the facts relied on; and a draft of the order sought.

While third parties are not required to employ a lawyer in the drafting and lodging of applications, it would be wise to do so, because care must be taken to make sure that the statutory requirements are followed. Section 114(3) of the Act provides that the order can be made against any one or more of the owner, occupier or any other person who has an interest in the land, or any other person by whom or on whose behalf the use or development was, is being, or is to be carried out. The required information must be provided; if not, the application can be rejected by the Principal Registrar of VCAT under s 171(1) of the *VCAT Act*. This will be done if there is, for example, insufficient information contained in the application. The paperwork must be correct. (See, for example, *Morocco v City of Knox* (unreported decision of the AAT, 88/0901, noted (1989) 2 AATR 25); *Jeffs v City of Keilor* (1991) 7 AATR 134 at 136–137; and *Holt v South Gippsland* SC [2003] VCAT 19). If the application is not rejected under s 72(1) of the *VCAT Act*, the applicant must give notice of the application to relevant interested parties (the responsible authority if it is not the applicant, any person against whom the order is sought, the owner of the land, the occupier of the land, and any other person whom the Tribunal considers may be adversely affected by the enforcement order): *Planning and Environment Act*, s 115.

The initial consideration of an application for an enforcement order is a very important stage in the enforcement proceedings. It enables the Principal Registrar to reject the application if the statutory requirements are not complied with. The reason for strict compliance with these provisions is that the application must not only be correct but it must also give sufficient details and information so that the respondents and other parties involved in the enforcement proceedings can determine the nature of the case being brought and the nature of the alleged contravention.

Section 116 of the Act provides that, if there are no objections to an application for the enforcement order, VCAT may make an enforcement order in accordance with s 119 or reject the application. If objections to the application are received, the relevant interested parties must be given an opportunity to be heard or make written submissions in respect of the application: s 117(1). After hearing the parties, VCAT may make an enforcement order or reject the application: s 117(2).

If an order is made, on whom it must be served is set out in s 116 of the *VCAT Act*. Unlike the repealed s 118 of the *Planning and Environment Act*, s 116 of the *VCAT Act* does not specifically list the parties on whom the order is to be served. The wording used is that the Tribunal must give a copy of the order to each party and each other person entitled to notice of the order. It is assumed that the persons on whom the notice of the order is to be served includes the person or persons on whom it is made, the owner of the land, the occupier of the land, any other person who has an interest in the land, and any other person by whom and on whose behalf the use or development concerned was, is being, or is to be carried out. The order is usually served by the responsible authority. An enforcement order made by VCAT under s 119 must specify that there is or will be a contravention of the Act. It may then direct any person against whom the order is made to do any one or more of the following (s 119(b)):

(i) to stop the use or development within a specified period;
(ii) not to start the use or development; or
(iii) to maintain a building in accordance with the order; or
(iv) to do specified things within a specified period –

   (A) to restore the land as nearly as practicable to its condition immediately before the use or development started or to any or to any condition specified in the order or any other condition to the satisfaction of the responsible authority, a Minister, public authority, municipal council, referral authority or other person or body specified in the Order; or
   (B) to otherwise ensure compliance with this Act, or the planning scheme, permit condition or agreement under section 173.

Section 133 of the *VCAT Act* provides that a person who does not comply with a non-monetary order of the Tribunal is guilty of an offence and is liable to a penalty under s 133(1) of the *VCAT Act*. (See s 3 for a definition of a non-monetary order, which is defined to mean an order other than a monetary order. A non-monetary order is an order other than a fine – for example, an order to do a particular act or thing.) The penalty is imprisonment until the person complies with the order or for three months, whichever is the sooner, or a fine of 20 penalty units (approximately $2,400) if the non-compliance continues after the making of an order, plus a further penalty of five penalty units per day after the making of the order up to a maximum total fine of 50 penalty units, or both imprisonment and a fine. Prosecution for non-compliance of an enforcement order or interim enforcement order is in the Magistrates' Court.

Pursuant to s 133 the penalties for breaching an interim enforcement order are the same as those for breaching an enforcement order. While substantial, the fines are less than the general maximum penalties for offences (see the discussion above on prosecution in the Magistrates' Court for breaches of a planning scheme, permit conditions or s 173 agreements).

Interim enforcement orders

VCAT has power in an urgent case to make an interim enforcement order against certain persons. Section 120 of the *Planning and Environment Act* provides that any person who has applied under s 114 for an enforcement order may apply to the Tribunal in an urgent case for an interim enforcement order against any person or persons in relation to whom the enforcement order application was made. Historically, the Tribunal has taken the view that an urgent case is one where an action which may result in irreparable damage has commenced or is threatened, such as where a person has commenced the clearing of bushland but has not obtained the necessary planning permit for such clearing. But the word "urgent" in s 120 was held by the Tribunal in *Stonnington v Blue Emporium Pty Ltd* [2003] VCAT 1954; 15 VPR 267 as "merely an indication by the Parliament that interim enforcement orders are to be made in cases where a prompt decision is desirable, for some reason or another". An application can be made if an action or threatened action will contravene the Act, a planning scheme, a condition of a permit, or an agreement under s 173 of the Act.

In *Rosanna Parklands Protection Association Inc v Banyule CC* [2004] VCAT 2607 the Tribunal stated that, to obtain an interim enforcement order, an applicant must show that, unless prevented by the order, a person will contravene a planning scheme and "that means break the law. It is not sufficient to show that someone is going to 'jump the gun' in relation to a master plan or improperly impact heritage values or environmental values. It is necessary to go further and demonstrate, in the case of an interim order at least on a prima facie basis, that the person, unless restrained, is likely to break the law".

The Tribunal may make an interim enforcement order *ex parte* (without notice to any other person) but before making such an order must consider what the effect of making the order would be, whether the applicant should give an undertaking as to damages, and whether it should hear any other person before making the order: s 120(2) and (3).

However, an application under s 120 can only be made by a responsible authority or any person who has applied to the Tribunal for an enforcement order under s 114 of the Act. The application of a party under s 114 is a condition precedent to the consideration of an application under s 120.

In urgent cases, applications for interim enforcement orders may be made outside normal office hours, or without notice. Such *ex parte* applications are similar to court applications for interim injunctions. An interim enforcement order given pursuant to such an *ex parte* hearing can last for only seven days, during which time a hearing will be arranged where those affected can be heard as to whether the order should continue. The procedure for making such applications has been laid down by the Tribunal in *Practice Note Planning 4 (PNPE4)*, para 7.

The relevant considerations to be taken into account in considering an interim enforcement order are set out in para 6 of PNPE4, which states, *inter alia*:

> 6.1 Interim enforcement orders are intended for urgent cases. They enable the maintenance of existing circumstances pending the hearing of the ordinary enforcement application. An application for an interim enforcement order can only be made by a person who has applied for an enforcement order under s 114 of the Act.
>
> 6.2 An interim enforcement order can operate only for a limited period of time. It will normally operate until determination of the ordinary enforcement order application can be made under s 114 of the Act, but may cease on the date of the happening or event specified in the interim enforcement order. (See Section 120(6) of the Act). An interim enforcement order may be cancelled or amended by the Tribunal. (See s 121 of the Act).
>
> 6.3 An application for an interim enforcement order should be accompanied by sworn evidence. If circumstances allow, this should be done by means of an affidavit swearing to the truth of the contents of the application under Sections 114 and 120 of the Act as set out and in the recommended form and to the truth of the facts to be relied on as the basis for making such an order.
>
> 6.4 Section 120(3)(b) of the Act requires that before making an interim enforcement order, the Tribunal must consider whether the person seeking that order should give an undertaking as to damages. The usual form of the undertaking required by the tribunal is:
>> If the Tribunal decides that an enforcement order should not be made, and a court decides that any person has suffered loss or damage as a result of making this interim enforcement order and further decides that I should compensate for the loss or damage suffered, I undertake that I will pay the amount assessed by the court to that person.

While *Practice Note PNPE4* provides that an application for an interim enforcement order should be supported by sworn evidence, preferably by means of an affidavit, sworn oral evidence may be relied upon if circumstances are so urgent as to preclude even the preparation of an affidavit.

The purpose served by an interim enforcement order is similar to an interim injunction, even though it is strictly not the same as an application for an interim injunction (see *Stonnington City Council v Blue Emporium Pty Ltd* [2003] VCAT 1954 at [3]; 15 VPR 267, and *Greater Geelong City Council v Geelong Markets Pty Ltd* [2004] VCAT 781).

Injunctions

VCAT may by order grant an injunction, including an interim injunction, against any party to a proceeding if it is just and convenient to do so: *VCAT Act*, s 123. The power is exercisable only by a judicial member of the Tribunal and only if a proceeding is afoot. For example, if an application has been made for an enforcement order and that application had not yet been determined, a proceeding would be afoot. If the application has been determined, the proceeding would be at an end. The Tribunal may make an order pursuant to s 123 on the application of any party to the proceeding or on its own initiative.

An injunction is also available under s 125 to restrain a person from contravening an enforcement order or interim enforcement order. A responsible authority or any other person may apply for such an injunction – application is not restricted to the parties to the enforcement order proceedings and, unlike under s 123, the proceedings must be at an end and the order made. The Supreme Court, County Court and Magistrates' Court (with some limitations) have power to grant injunctions. In addition, the common law right to seek an injunction is still available. A person seeking a common law injunction, whether it be to restrain a breach of a planning scheme, permit condition or s 173 agreement, enforcement order or interim enforcement order, must be a person with "sufficient interest" to be granted standing or proceed with the fiat of the Attorney-General. Given the availability of enforcement order and interim enforcement order proceedings, it is unlikely that an application for a common law injunction restraining a breach of the planning scheme permit condition or s 173 agreement would be granted.

Injunctions are discretionary remedies. That is, the courts have a discretion whether or not to award an injunction, even where there is a valid reason for granting one. The courts are unlikely to exercise this discretion where the other avenues under the Act (such as an enforcement order) have not been exhausted.

Infringement notice

An infringement notice is an "on-the-spot fine" similar to an on-the-spot traffic fine, and is used for minor infringements. If the fine is not paid within the prescribed time, proceedings can be brought in the Magistrates' Court. Additional steps required to expiate the offence (that is, steps additional to paying the fine) can be imposed and are set out in s 130(4) and (5) of the Act. Pursuant to the *Infringements Act 2006*, if an offence has been expiated, then committed again and prosecuted, the defendant will be treated as a first offender.

The on-the-spot fine is five penalty points (approximately $585) for a natural person and 10 penalty points (approximately $1,170) for a corporation: s 130(3).

Infringement notices are appropriate where minor offences are committed, but great care must be taken in considering whether or not additional steps should be included in the notice. This is because, if the additional steps or requirements are not spelt out in the notice, the payment of the fine will expiate the offence. Where the offence is of a continuing nature, obviously an infringement notice is inappropriate.

Cancellation of a permit and order to stop development

Within the context of enforcement powers, the failure to comply with conditions in a permit is a situation where the potential cancellation of the permit becomes a powerful incentive to ensure compliance. The power to cancel a permit is in the hands of VCAT. The grounds for cancellation or amendment are set out in s 87(1) and are:

(a) a material mis-statement or concealment of fact in relation to the application for the permit; or
(b) any substantial failure to comply with the conditions of the permit; or
(c) any material mistake in relation to the grant of the permit; or
(d) any material change of circumstances which has occurred since the grant of the permit; or
(e) any failure to give notice in accordance with section 52; or
(f) any failure to comply with section 55, 61(2) or 62(1).

The last two grounds deserve some comment. A s 52 notice refers to the advertising of planning permit applications. Minimum mandatory advertising or notification is to occur to the owners and occupiers of adjoining land as prescribed by s 52. However, s 52(1)(a) has a "let-out" with regard to adjoining owners and occupiers if the responsible authority is satisfied that the grant of the permit would not cause detriment. In addition, under s 52(1)(d), other persons must be notified if the responsible authority considers that the grant of a permit may cause detriment.

Sections 55, 61(2) and 62(1) deal with the requirement to send copies of applications to referral authorities as required by the scheme and the imposition of conditions on the veto (subject to review by VCAT) of applications by these authorities. Non-compliance with these sections is a ground for seeking cancellation or amendment of a permit.

A responsible authority, referral authority, or the owner or occupier of the land concerned may seek cancellation or amendment of a permit. However, under s 89, other parties may also apply for cancellation or amendment, and these parties are persons (or a person) who objected, or would have been entitled to object, to the issue of a permit had they been given notice under s 52 and so had been aware of the fact that a permit had been applied for. The wording of s 89(1) is not at all clear, but it would appear from it that two types of persons under this section may seek cancellation or amendment. The first type consists of persons who objected to the grant of a permit but believe that other people should have been notified but were not. The other type consists of persons who did not object but would have if they had been notified and had been aware of a permit being applied for. This in effect means that, although a review has been determined by VCAT, the matter is not final for the applicant who has been granted a permit. A subsequent application to cancel or amend may be lodged on the grounds that some people should have been notified under s 52 but were not. Clearly, responsible authorities are put under pressure to advertise very widely indeed.

Another reason why responsible authorities should advertise widely and why third parties should be cautious under these provisions is that not only can VCAT stop a development under s 93 of the Act but there is also a right to compensation if injury is suffered under ss 92 and 93.

Pending the hearing of an application (called a request in the Act) to amend or cancel a permit, VCAT may issue an order to stop development. This is to prevent a person acting on a permit already granted, and orders to stop are used in emergency situations. Non-compliance with an order to stop development is an offence under the Act and subject to penalties imposed by the Magistrates' Court pursuant to s 127 of the *Planning and Environment Act*. This acts as a deterrent for non-compliance. Note that, under s 94, an order to stop which is not followed by a decision of VCAT to cancel or amend a permit results in liability for compensation on the part of the responsible authority or the person who initiated the order to stop development. This disincentive for third parties (objectors and others) is necessary to protect permit holders from having matters protracted unnecessarily. The threat of a compensation claim limits applications for orders to stop development, otherwise commercial competitors and vexatious neighbours would cause havoc.

Under s 89(1)(b), third parties may seek cancellation or amendment where there has been a material misstatement or concealment of fact in relation to the application for the permit or there has been a substantial failure to comply with conditions, or where there was a material mistake with regard to the grant of the permit. Third parties are again restricted to objectors or those who would have been entitled to object.

There is a right to compensation (s 94) if the application for cancellation is made frivolously by a third party. Third parties should have concrete evidence to show that there has been a contravention and should have available sufficient facts to prove the contravention.

The conduct of enforcement proceedings before VCAT

The remedies available for successful enforcement and interim enforcement orders are quasi penal and can have serious effects on existing rights. Because of this, VCAT has issued a practice note (*Practice Note Planning PNPE4*) with regard to interim enforcement orders and enforcement orders. Hearings of applications for enforcement orders are different from the normal planning appeal procedures.

The giving of evidence

Sections 97 and 98 of the *VCAT Act* relate to the procedures of VCAT, and evidentiary provisions contained in s 102 of the *Planning and Environment Act* apply to the hearing of enforcement orders. In addition, s 117(1) provides that people be given "a reasonable opportunity to be heard or to make a written submission in respect of the application".

Paragraph 8.1 of PNPE4 states:

> An enforcement order application is not the same as a normal planning application hearing. Evidence is normally given on oath or affirmation rather than by mere assertion or written submissions. Enforcement orders can have serious effects on existing rights. This can mean that facts that are in issue need to be established on the balance of probabilities bearing in mind the relatively serious nature of the proceedings and consequences.

Although evidence not on oath remains admissible, it will not be given the same weight as evidence on oath, so most parties give their evidence on oath. In *Svanosio v Shire of Strathfieldsaye and Colwell* (1989) 2 AATR 26 at 30, the Tribunal gives an insight into the reason why the giving of evidence before it with regard to enforcement orders differs from the normal planning appeal:

> [T]hey are different in their nature to a planning appeal and the making of an enforcement order carries with it serious consequences for a respondent. In the case of the *Mayor, Councillors and Citizens of the City of Traralgon v Sella Ira Pty Ltd and Paul Apostoleris* Appeal P88/01616 (unreported) the Tribunal said:
>
>> The *Planning and Environment Act* heralded a new era in enforcement by providing an alternative to court proceedings and the delays, technicalities and costs that was said to be involved with them. It gave birth to the Enforcement Order which is by its very nature akin to the Court injunction yet recognised by Section 125 of the Act to be a means of enforcement distinct from the injunction.
>>
>> It must be realised by the parties (especially by Responsible Authorities) that an enforcement order hearing is not the same as a planning appeal hearing. This is reflected by the fact that the practice that has been adopted generally in enforcement order applications is for evidence to be on oath and for the parties to present and prove their respective cases and all relevant facts by evidence in proper form – mere assertions in written submissions or from the person representing a party are not good enough.

Onus and standard of proof

The onus of proof in relation to the facts necessary to establish the basis for making an order is upon the parties seeking the relief. In *Cardinia SC v De Haan* [2004] VCAT 942, the Tribunal stated that to "bring an enforcement order it is incumbent on the party bringing such application to provide substantiated evidence to support their allegation" and observed that in this particular case the application brought by the responsible authority "has been brought on an unsubstantiated basis of mere conjecture, without the provision of any evidence whatsoever and has been persisted with, despite the Respondents providing information to the Council". The Tribunal made a costs order for a substantial amount against the responsible authority.

Sections 139–147 of the *Planning and Environment Act* contain a number of evidentiary provisions to facilitate the proving of formal matters by means of certificates and signed statement. The standard of proof is "on the balance of probabilities", but the degree of proof required must be appropriate to the gravity of the matter.

In *Brandtmann v Shire of Lilydale and Barry* (1989) 2 AATR 130 at 133–134 the Tribunal, in referring to the standard of proof required for enforcement proceedings, stated "that it should be similar to that applied in the Supreme Court in applications for injunctions under s 49(2) of the *Town and Country Planning Act* 1961". The Tribunal adopted a passage from the judgement of McInerney J in *City of Prahran v Cameron* [1972] VR 90 at 99 wherein he stated:

> I would add that I agree with the observations of Crockett, J. in *Shire of South Barwon v Winstanley Bell & Co Pty Ltd* (28 September 1970, unreported), that the Applicant need only, in order to succeed, prove its case on the balance of probabilities, but that the degree of proof required to establish the case must be commensurate with the gravity of the fact to be proved: see *Rejfek v McElroy* (1966), 39 ALJR 177, at p 178; [1966] ALR 270, at pp 272, 273.

The balance of probabilities is the evidentiary burden of proof used in civil litigation. This onus or burden of proof is not as great as that of the criminal burden of proof "beyond all reasonable doubt". The latter burden of proof is more onerous, requiring stronger evidence to support the allegation.

Evidence and notes

To simplify the formal rules dealing with evidence and notes, ss 139–149 of the Act specify what is to be considered as conclusive proof of who is an owner, the contents of a scheme, the provision of permits and permit conditions, et cetera. For example, proof of ownership of a property will be a person who is rated in respect of that land, or a copy of a certified copy of a certificate of title.

Keeping everyone honest: the issue of costs in enforcement order proceedings

Section 109 of the *VCAT Act* provides that costs may be awarded in enforcement order proceedings and sets out the circumstances in which costs may be awarded. Costs in relation to review hearings have been discussed in Chapter 6. Under the provisions of the *Planning Appeals Act* the Tribunal indicated in *Svanosio v Shire of Strathfieldsaye and Colwell* (1989) 2 AATR 26 at 31 that there is a difference in the approach of awarding costs in a normal planning review compared with the award of costs in the case of enforcement order applications, the reason being:

> A planning appeal will always concern a prospective use or development which will be authorized by the issue of a permit, whereas Enforcement Order proceedings will usually concern past actions which the proceedings will decide were either authorized or not authorized.
>
> Each case must be judged upon its own merits. However, in many instances, it will be reasonably apparent whether or not the activities complained of are in breach of a planning scheme, permit or agreement. Where a party has acted in a blatant or cavalier way and has ignored proper requests and warnings, the Tribunal is more likely to make an order for costs than in a situation where there is a reasonable dispute about whether or not a contravention has occurred. In these circumstances,

the Tribunal would not wish the threat of an order for costs to act as a deterrent to parties or responsible authorities making a reasonable and legitimate application for an enforcement order.

On the other hand, where an application is petty or vexatious or where an applicant has failed to ensure that all the necessary elements of their case are proven, it may be reasonable for costs to be awarded against an unsuccessful applicant if the respondent has been put to substantial expense or inconvenience in defending the application. Prospective applicants should recognise this and not lightly make applications for enforcement orders without being able to prove the elements of their case.

This view has been confirmed in *Practice Note Planning PNPE4*, para 10, which states:

> The normal rule in proceedings before the Tribunal is that each party must bear their own costs. However, the Tribunal has power to order the payment of costs where it considers that circumstances justify it in doing so. For example, the bringing of a quite unjustified enforcement order application, or a persistent and unjustified failure to comply with planning laws in the face of requests and warnings, may result in orders for costs being made. Such orders have been more common in enforcement order cases than in normal planning applications.

The difference in approach with regard to costs in enforcement proceedings is justified. In particular, it makes applicants aware of the seriousness of seeking an enforcement order. However, it may also have the effect of dissuading third parties from seeking an enforcement order. This may be a problem if the responsible authority chooses not to initiate enforcement proceedings.

The right to award costs against a party seeking an enforcement order has been provided to ensure that frivolous and vexatious applications are deterred. It is also to protect the innocent person who has in fact not contravened the planning scheme, permit conditions or s 173 agreement. Third parties who bring these proceedings for an ulterior motive (for example, to delay the development, or to increase the costs of the development) should be penalised and the provisions with regard to costs and compensation provide penalties for situations where the proceedings are not genuine.

Enforcing enforcement orders

The mechanisms for ensuring compliance with enforcement and interim enforcement orders are: prosecution in the Magistrates' Court for breach of the order; contempt proceedings in VCAT; filing the order in the Supreme Court; and carrying out work required by the order.

Prosecution in the Magistrates' Court for breach of an enforcement order or interim enforcement order

Prosecution in the Magistrates' Court for non-compliance with an enforcement order or interim enforcement order has been referred to above in the discussion of enforcement orders. The responsible authority or any other person may lay a charge for non-compliance. Note that the Court is only required to establish if the order has not been complied with, not that the breach of the planning scheme, permit conditions or s 173 agreement which resulted in the order being made occurred. Note also that the penalties specified in s 133 are set penalties, not maximum penalties. The Court does not have the discretion to impose lighter penalties than those specified.

Contempt proceedings in VCAT

Section 137(1) of the *VCAT Act* sets out when persons are guilty of contempt of the Tribunal, including if they "do any other act which would, if the Tribunal were the Supreme Court, constitute contempt of that Court". The wilful failure to comply with an order of the Supreme Court is punishable as contempt, therefore wilful failure to comply with an order of VCAT is punishable for contempt: see *Thompson v VCAT* [2001] VCAT 4 and *Varvanides v VCAT* [2005] VSCA 231.

The contempt powers may be exercised only by a judicial member of the Tribunal. Section 137(2) provides that, if it is alleged that or appears to the Tribunal that a person is guilty of contempt, the Tribunal may direct the person to be arrested and brought before it, or the Tribunal may issue a warrant for the person's arrest. If the Tribunal finds that a person is guilty of contempt, it may, in the case of a natural person, commit the person to prison for a maximum of five years or impose a fine to a maximum of 1,000 penalty units (approximately $120,000). For a corporation the penalty is a maximum fine of 5,000 penalty units.

Injunction

An injunction should be seen as a last resort in enforcing enforcement orders. Injunctions in relation to enforcement generally were discussed earlier in this chapter.

Filing of VCAT order in the Supreme Court

If an enforcement order is not complied with, s 122(1) of the *VCAT Act* provides that a non-monetary order (an enforcement order falls within the definition of a non-monetary order: see s 3 of the *VCAT Act*) may be enforced by filing in the Supreme Court the following:

(a) a copy of the order certified by a presidential member or principal registrar to be a true copy; and
(b) that person's affidavit as to the noncompliance with the order; and
(c) a certificate from a judicial member stating that the order is appropriate for filing in the Supreme Court.

Once the order is filed under s 122, the order becomes an order of the Supreme Court and can be enforced as such in the Court. If successfully prosecuted, the offender may be found guilty of contempt of the Supreme Court and penalised accordingly.

Carrying out works required by the order

Section 172 of the *Planning and Environment Act* provides that the responsible authority, or with the consent of the Tribunal any other person, may carry out the work required by an enforcement order if it was not carried out within the time specified in the order. The cost of the works may be recovered from the person in default in any court of competent jurisdiction as a debt: see s 123(1)(b).

Section 123(2) provides that the responsible authority, or any other person authorised by the Tribunal, may sell any building, equipment or materials salvaged in carrying out that work if satisfied that such is the property of the land owner or person against whom the order is made, and apply the proceeds of the sale towards the payment of expenses for carrying out the work.

Special circumstances

Brothels and enforcement proceedings

The *Sex Work Act 1994* sets up a system of licensing of brothels and prostitution service providers by the Business Licensing Authority. The system involves registration and licensing of prostitution service providers (brothels and escort agencies) and approval of managers for such establishments. An officer of the relevant responsible authority, authorised in writing to enforce Parts 4 and 5 of the *Sex Work Act*, may enter and inspect premises which he or she believes on reasonable grounds is being used for the purpose of the operation of a brothel. Offences and provisions relating to the proscription of brothels are dealt with by the *Sex Work Act*. Section 80 of that Act provides that an authorised officer of the responsible authority may apply to the Magistrates' Court to declare premises to be a prescribed brothel. Penalties in relation to persons found in, entering or leaving a prescribed brothel, and penalties in relation to the owners and occupiers of prescribed brothels, are set out in s 82 of the *Sex Work Act*.

Government and enforcement proceedings

The *Planning and Environment Act 1987* and planning schemes do not apply to the Commonwealth Government, including Commonwealth instrumentalities. Section 126(4) of the *Planning and Environment Act* provides that the offences under s 126(1)(2) of the Act do not apply to the owner of Crown land. State Government departments and instrumentalities are immune from committing offences under the Act. This means that one rule applies to the governments and a different rule applies to the rest of the community.

Chapter 8

HERITAGE CONSERVATION AND STATUTORY PLANNING

The meaning of the term "heritage conservation" has evolved from the early 1970s, when it referred mainly to the conservation of buildings and areas of historic or architectural significance. These days it may also refer to the conservation of forests, wilderness areas, wildlife habitats, geological formations and landscape features. It may also refer to sites of archaeological importance, shipwreck sites, and both sites and areas of cultural significance to particular groups in society, such as those containing Aboriginal relics and sacred sites. This wider meaning of heritage conservation is reflected by legislation such as the former *Australian Heritage Commission Act 1975* (Cth) and the *Australian Heritage Council Act 2003* (Cth). The *Australian Heritage Council Act* replaced the 1975 Act. This Act was part of the changes that occurred to the national heritage system which commenced on 1 January 2004. The *Australian Heritage Council Act* created the Australian Heritage Council, which, like the former Heritage Commission under the 1975 Act, advises the Commonwealth government on the listing and protection of heritage places and administers the Register of the National Estate. This chapter deals primarily with the controls on land use and development that are aimed at the conservation of buildings and precincts in urban areas. Therefore the bulk of the chapter is devoted to the *Australian Heritage Council Act 2003* (Cth), the *Heritage Act 1995* (Vic) and the *Planning and Environment Act 1997* (Vic). However, due to increasing awareness of World Heritage listing, a brief discussion of the listing process and Commonwealth powers in relation to places on the World Heritage List has also been included.

World Heritage listing and the Environment Protection and Biodiversity Conservation Act 1999 (Cth)

World Heritage listing

In 1974 Australia became a signatory to the Convention for the Protection of the World Cultural and Natural Heritage (the World Heritage Convention), which was adopted in 1972 by the UNESCO General Conference in Paris. Signatories to the World Heritage Convention bind themselves to assist in the identification, protection, conservation and presentation of world heritage properties. The responsibility for identification, protection, conservation and presentation lies with the country in which the property is located. Most of our planet's widely known outstanding natural and cultural sites are on the World Heritage List, such as the Great Wall of China, the Grand Canyon, the Taj Mahal, the Pyramids of Egypt, the Acropolis and Mount Everest. Australia has 17 properties on the World Heritage List: Riversleigh and Naracoorte Fossil Sites, Fraser Island, Shark Bay, Kakadu National Park, the Great Barrier Reef, the Willandra Lakes Region of New South Wales, the Lord Howe Island Group, the South-Western Tasmanian Wilderness, the Central and East Coast Forest Reserves, Uluru–Kata Tjuta National Park, the Wet Tropics of Queensland, Macquarie Island, Heard and McDonald Islands, The Great Blue Mountains Area, Pumululu National Park, the Royal Exhibition Building and Carlton Gardens, and the Lord Howe Island Group.

As only the national governments of member countries of the Convention can nominate areas for the World Heritage List, it is the Commonwealth Government which submits nominations for Australian properties. While nominations may be initiated by State governments or by conservation organisations, the Commonwealth makes its own evaluation of the merits of a nomination using a set of operational guidelines prepared by the World Heritage Committee. Nominations are forwarded by the Commonwealth Government to the World Heritage Committee Secretariat at UNESCO in Paris and are assessed by the World Heritage Bureau. The World Heritage Committee accepts, defers or rejects nominations.

World heritage properties are declared under s 14 of the *Environment Protection and Biodiversity Conservation Act 1999* (Cth). This Act replaced the *World Heritage Properties Conservation Act 1983* (Cth). Section 14(1) of the *Environment Protection and Biodiversity Conservation Act* provides that:

> The Minister may declare a specified property to be a declared Word Heritage Property by notice in the Gazette if:
> (a) the property is a property submitted by the Commonwealth to the World Heritage Committee under Article 11 of the World Heritage Convention as suitable for inclusion in the World Heritage List; or
> (b) the Minister is satisfied that:
>   (i) the property has, or is likely to have, world heritage values; and
>   (ii) some or all of the world heritage values of the property are under threat.

Constitutional issues in the protection of World Heritage areas

Under the Australian Constitution the Commonwealth has no direct power over land use, development and environment protection of land not vested in or owned by it. For Commonwealth land, however, lease agreements, export licences and the decisions of its own departments and instrumentalities are powerful control mechanisms. Matters over which the Commonwealth has exclusive jurisdiction are contained in s 52 of the Constitution, which deals with Commonwealth places and Territories and the Commonwealth public service. The Commonwealth may also legislate on the matters contained in s 51, which contains heads of powers relating to trade and commerce, taxation, external affairs, corporations, and "people of any race". Under s 109 of the Constitution, Commonwealth legislation made under these heads of powers prevails over State legislation. There is also an unwritten "nationhood" power – an implied power for the Commonwealth to enact legislation in order to carry out its responsibilities as a national government – and s 109 also applies to legislation and executive decisions made under this power. The exercise of power under s 51 may be for environmental or heritage purposes, even though the head of power used may be trade and commerce, taxation, or external affairs. In *Murphyores Inc Ltd v Commonwealth* (1976) 136 CLR 1, the High Court upheld the decision of the Commonwealth Government to refuse an export licence for mineral sands mined on Fraser Island in Queensland. The legislation under which an export licence was required was the *Customs Act 1901*, clearly within the trade and commerce power of s 51. The licence was refused on environmental and social grounds, but the High Court ruled that the grounds of refusal were irrelevant, provided that the legislation under which the refusal was made was within the power of the Commonwealth to enact. The power to refuse export licences, or grant licences subject to conditions, is a powerful tool for the Commonwealth in controlling mining and forestry operations, including woodchipping, on both Commonwealth and non-Commonwealth land, regardless of whether or not the land is within an area on the World Heritage List.

The external affairs power of s 51 is also a powerful source of indirect control for the Commonwealth. In *Commonwealth v Tasmania* (1983) 158 CLR 1, otherwise known as the *Tasmanian Dam* case, the High Court found that the Commonwealth may enact domestic legislation if the subject of the legislation is of international concern or if it implements any international agreement or treaty. In this instance, the domestic legislation was the *World Heritage Properties Conservation Act 1983*, enacted by the Whitlam Labor Government. Regulations made under this Act prohibited, without the consent of the relevant federal Minister, construction work to dam the Gordon River below Franklin in Tasmania. This Act followed the *Gordon River Hydro-Electric Power Development Act 1982* (Tas), passed by the Tasmanian Parliament and authorising work to begin on the project. The site of the dam was in an area that had been included on the World Heritage List, following nomination by the Commonwealth Government as a signatory to the UNESCO Convention, so the central issue of the case was whether or not the Commonwealth legislation was constitutional and therefore whether or not it prevailed over the State legislation under s 109. In brief, the Court found that it was, although it struck out all of s 9 of the Act, except s 9(1)(h), on the grounds that it purported to prohibit rather than regulate activities such as mining and tree felling. Prohibition of these activities in all areas on the World Heritage List would not be necessary to achieve the objectives of the treaty. The *Conservation Legislation Amendment Act 1988* (Cth) repealed those parts of the *World Heritage Properties Conservation Act* held to be invalid by the High Court.

The powers of the Commonwealth in relation to World Heritage areas was extended by the judgment in *Richardson v Forestry Commission (Tas)* (1988) 164 CLR 261; 77 ALR 237. The Federal Minister for the Environment sought an injunction from the High Court to prohibit logging in an area that was the subject of the Lemonthyme and Southern Forests Inquiry established by the *Lemonthyme* and *Southern Forests (Commission of Inquiry) Act 1987* (Cth). The Commission of Inquiry was required under that Act to inquire into whether any of the Lemonthyme and Southern Forests area was, or contributed to, a World Heritage area. Section 16 of the Act prohibited logging in the area for the duration of the inquiry without the consent of the Federal Minister for the Environment. The respondent had continued logging in breach of this prohibition. The injunction was granted by Mason CJ, but his Honour reserved a number of constitutional issues to the Full Court. The major issue was the argument put by the Tasmanian Forestry Commission that the legislation establishing the inquiry was invalid in that the prohibition on logging went beyond any legitimate implementation of the World Heritage Convention. However, this argument was rejected, with all seven judges of the Full Court ruling either directly or indirectly that the Commonwealth had a right under the external affairs power to protect potential World Heritage Areas on an interim basis pending identification. This principle was followed by the High Court in *Queensland v Commonwealth* (1988) 86 ALR 519. See also *Tasmanian Conservation Trust Inc v Minister for Resources* (1995) 85 LGERA 296; *Tasmanian Conservation Trust Inc v Minister for Resources* (1996) 30 LGERA 106.

Protection of World Heritage properties under the Environment Protection and Biodiversity Conservation Act 1999

In 1999 the *Environment Protection and Biodiversity Conservation Act* replaced the *Environment (Impact of Proposals) Act 1974*. The Act introduced a scheme for the protection of matters of National Environmental Significance (NES). Under the *Environment Protection and Biodiversity Conservation Act* no action ("action" includes a project, development, undertaking, an activity or series of activities) can be taken if it will have or is likely to have a significant impact on matters of NES without approval from the Minister for Sustainability, Environment, Water, Population and Communities. Declared World Heritage properties are matters listed as matters of NES: *Environment Protection and Biodiversity Conservation Act*, s 12.

If a person proposes to take an action that will have or is likely to have a significant impact on a declared World Heritage property, that action must be referred to the Minister. The Minister will decide whether the action will or is likely to have an impact on a matter of NES. If the Minister decides that the action will have or is likely to have an impact on a matter of NES then the action will require approval under the *Environment Protection and Biodiversity Conservation Act*. It will then become a "controlled action" and environmental impact assessment procedures must be carried out. The procedures for environmental impact assessment are set out in Chapter 4, Part 8 of the *Environment Protection and Biodiversity Conservation Act 1999*. For actions that are controlled actions, the Minister can choose one of the following methods of assessment:

- an accredited assessment process;
- an assessment on preliminary documentation;
- a public environment report;

- an environmental impact statement;
- a public inquiry.

The Minister will decide whether or not to approve the action and what conditions (if any) are to be imposed after consideration of the environmental impact assessment report. If the Minister decides that it is not a controlled action then approval is not required under the *Environment Protection and Biodiversity Conservation Act.*

Actions undertaken without referral to the Minister and without the Minister's approval are subject to severe penalties under the Act. For example, a person who takes an action that is likely to have a significant impact on a matter of NES, without first obtaining approval, can be liable for a civil penalty of up to 5,000 penalty units ($550,000) for an individual and 50,000 penalty units ($5.5 million) for a body corporate: s 12(1). The Act also provides for Management Plans for declared World Heritage properties in Commonwealth areas: ss 316–320. The Act also sets out principles and provides assistance for the protection of declared World Heritage properties: ss 323–324.

National Heritage protection

There have been major changes made by the Commonwealth to the protection of National Heritage. The new heritage system commenced on 1 January 2004. This system was designed to strengthen the protection of the nation's natural and Indigenous and historic heritage. It was also to overcome the duplication of the different assessment and approval processes by the Commonwealth and States. The changes are incorporated in the following Acts:

> *Environment and Heritage Amendment Act (No 1) 2003 (Cth)*
> This amends the *Environment Protection and Biodiversity Conservation Act 1999* and establishes a National Heritage List and a Commonwealth Heritage List. The inclusion of places on these lists will be added to matters of NES under s 12 of the *Environment Protection and Biodiversity Conservation Act.* Places on these lists will be protected by the Act in that no action can be taken that will have or is likely to have a significant impact on these places without approval from the Minister for Environment and Heritage. The amendments to the *Environment Protection and Biodiversity Conservation Act* also provide for the nomination, listing, management and protection of properties on these two lists.
>
> *Australian Heritage Council Act 2003 (Cth)*
> This Act repeals the *Australian Heritage Commission Act 1975* and establishes the Heritage Council. The Council, like the previous Commission, is the advisory body to the Minister for Environment and Heritage.

The Australian Heritage Council

The Australian Heritage Council, like its predecessor, is an independent body of experts whose role is to advise the Minister on the listing and protection of heritage places and to continue the management of the Register of the National Estate. The Council's functions include:

- assessing nominations in relation to the listing of places in the National and the Commonwealth Heritage Lists;
- advising the Minister for Environment and Heritage on specified matters relating to heritage places;
- promoting the identification, assessment and conservation of heritage;
- compiling and maintaining the Register of the National Estate;
- performing functions conferred on it under the *Environment Protection and Biodiversity Conservation Act*.

The National and Commonwealth Heritage Lists

These are new lists and are in addition to the listing of declared World Heritage places and listing on the Register of the National Estate.

The creation of these two additional lists was a response by the Commonwealth Government to the need to protect places of outstanding national heritage and places managed or owned by the Commonwealth Government. Matters that will be placed on the National Heritage List will be places of outstanding heritage value to the nation and include places overseas. They will be places that do not meet the requirements of World Heritage criteria. The National Heritage List contains four listings (two of them being within the Budj Bim National Heritage Landscape in Victoria) and 56 nominations.

The Commonwealth Heritage List is a list of places managed or owned by the Commonwealth government. It includes places and groups of places that are in Commonwealth lands and waters, or under Commonwealth government control, identified by the Minister as having Commonwealth heritage values. There are 334 places listed on the Commonwealth Heritage List, with 15 nominations for listing. Places listed include the General Post Offices in Sydney, Brisbane, Perth, Hobart and Launceston. Mawson Station in Antarctica is also listed.

Both lists have to meet the criteria set out in the Heritage regulations. For example, some of the criteria listed for National and Commonwealth listing are set out below. National Heritage criteria for a place include either or both of the following:

- The place has outstanding heritage value to the nation because of the place's importance in the course or pattern of Australia's natural or cultural history.
- The place has outstanding heritage value to the nation because of the place's possession of uncommon, rare or endangered aspects of Australia's natural or cultural history.

The Commonwealth heritage criteria for a place are either or both of the following:

- The place has significant heritage value because of the place's importance in the course, or pattern, of Australia's natural or cultural heritage.
- The place has significant heritage value because of the place's possession of uncommon, rare or even endangered aspects of Australia's natural or cultural heritage.

Places that are on these lists have been added to s 12 of the *Environment Protection and Biodiversity Conservation Act* as matters of NES under Part 3 of the Act, the effect being that any action that may have a significant impact on these places will need to be referred to the Minister for Environment and Heritage to determine whether or not it is a controlled action that triggers the impact assessment procedures under the Act.

The *Environment Protection and Biodiversity Conservation Act* also will require management plans for heritage areas under the control of Commonwealth government agencies.

Register of the National Estate

The Register of the National Estate, which was set up under the *Australian Heritage Commission Act 1975*, is retained under the *Australian Heritage Council Act 2003*. The Heritage Council takes over the role of the former Heritage Commission in compiling and maintaining the register.

An initiative of the Whitlam Government was the appointment of a Committee of Inquiry into the National Estate under the chairmanship of Hope J. The *Australian Heritage Commission Act 1975* implemented the recommendations of the Hope report and established the Australian Heritage Commission. The Commission had the following responsibilities under s 7 of the Act: compiling the Register of the National Estate; encouraging public interest in, and understanding of, issues relevant to the National Estate; advising the Commonwealth Minister responsible for the environment and other Commonwealth Ministers and departments on how to conserve, improve and present all matters related to the National Estate; and advising the Minister responsible for the environment on expenditure by the Commonwealth for conservation, improvement and presentation of the National Estate. The definition of the "national estate" under s 4(1) of the Act was very broad. For the purpose of the Act it consisted of "... those places, being components of the natural environment of Australia or the cultural environment of Australia, that have aesthetic, historic, scientific or social significance or other special value for future generations as well as for the present community". Places were not required to be of national significance, but merely of significance or other special value for future generations as well as for the present community. The present community could be a local community, as distinct from the national community.

The Register of the National Estate continues under the Australian *Heritage Council Act 2003*. Those nominations not appropriate for the National and Commonwealth Heritage Lists may be appropriate for listing on the Register of the National Estate. The Register of the National Estate lists places that are of natural, cultural and Indigenous heritage. To be placed on the Register, a place must have significant heritage value in that it must be important for current and future generations of Australians.

Like the National and Commonwealth Lists, criteria to be met are set out in s 22(2) of the *Australian Heritage Council Act 2003*. The criteria for listing of a place on the Register of the National Estate are very broad. Places are not required to be of national significance. Under s 3(2) of the Act, "heritage value" has the same meaning as the *Environment Protection and Biodiversity Conservation Act 1999*. Section 528 of that Act, which defines "heritage value" of a place as "including the place's natural and cultural environment having aesthetic, historic, scientific significance or other significance, for current and future generations of Australians".

There are more than 13,000 places on the Register of the National Estate, the largest proportion of which are historic buildings and historic sites. Also included are places of natural significance, which may cover large areas and contain historic and Aboriginal sites. Places on the Register may be on privately-owned land or on public land, including land owned by or vested in State government departments and instrumentalities and local governments. While the Register contains places of significant heritage value for current and future Australians, it also contains many buildings, areas, and sites of only local or regional significance which have been included after nomination by local governments.

Addition of places to the Register of the National Estate

The criteria for determining whether or not an item or place should be included on the Register do not include its existing or potential use and value – the Australian Heritage Council is bound to consider only significance within the context of s 22(2) of the Act, which has led to criticism of the Act, particularly by logging, mining and farming interests. But, as Bates says about the 1975 Act, which is also valid of the 2003 Act (see Further Reading), the major function of the Australian Heritage Council is to alert Australians to their own heritage and not to make decisions based on the merits of competing economic and heritage claims. This function should be seen in the context of the effect of registration, which by itself imposes no constraint on the use or development of a place. Registration therefore has a moral or exhortatory effect only, although the Commonwealth may exercise its powers indirectly to protect places on the Register.

The processes to be used in adding places to or removing them from the Register are prescribed in ss 22 and 23 of the Act. Nominations may be made by State governments, their departments and instrumentalities, local governments and individuals; nominations may be referred to specially appointed panels or experts for comment. Section 22 of the Act provides that the Council must, before placing a place on the Register, advise persons who are owners or occupiers of these places that it is considering inclusion of the place on the Register. Upon being so advised, the person is given a reasonable opportunity to comment in writing as to whether the place should be included in the Register. Similar processes are involved in removing a place from the Register. There are some criticisms that can be made of the procedures for consideration of places nominated for registration: comments are called for and considered after the decision has been made in principle by the Council to register, which may undermine the confidence of those submitting (which in many instances would be owners) that their submissions will be considered dispassionately. There is nothing in the Act that guarantees a hearing at which owners and occupiers of those places or their representatives may present and expand on their comments, nor does the Act guarantee that owners will be notified as part of the process of advertising. In practice, the Commission notifies owners, but the legislation does not compel it to do so.

The effect of registration

It is not widely understood that no legal constraints are imposed on the owners of private property, or on local or State governments, by entry of places on the Register or Interim Register of the National Estate. Nor does entry mean that the public is granted access to a place. Historic places on the Register that are in Commonwealth areas or subject to actions by the Commonwealth are also protected by the *Environment Protection and Biodiversity Conservation Act*. They are the same provisions that protect places on the National and Commonwealth Heritage Lists.

Places on the Register may also be protected under State legislation. For example, some buildings on the Register are also on the Heritage Register under the Victorian *Heritage Act 1995* and therefore any alteration, removal or demolition of these buildings requires a permit from the Heritage Council. Others are subject to heritage controls in planning schemes under the *Planning and Environment Act 1987* (Vic). Under scheme provisions, a planning permit may be required for alteration or demolition of buildings, and for the construction of nearby buildings. Some are protected by both the *Heritage Act* and planning schemes. However, many buildings on the Register of the National Estate are neither on the Heritage Register nor protected by scheme provisions. In the case of some places on the register of the National Estate and/or on the Heritage Register (such as archaeological sites, Aboriginal sacred sites, natural features and wildlife habitats), planning schemes are limited in what they can achieve. Certainly scheme controls over removal of vegetation and topsoil, alteration to topography, and alteration and defacement of rock formations and the like may well be useful, as may be controls on subdivision. However, the most appropriate approach to protecting many such areas is to ensure, if possible, that they are not placed under pressure in the first place. Creating buffer zones by strict control of land use and subdivision in adjacent areas, zoning land for urban expansion elsewhere, and deciding not to build new roads or tracks, or not to upgrade existing roads and tracks, may all be appropriate.

Aboriginal heritage places are subject to the Victorian *Aboriginal Heritage Act 2006*, which repealed the *Archaeological and Aboriginal Relics Preservation Act 1972*. Under the *Aboriginal Heritage Act 2006* (discussed towards the end of this chapter) it is an offence if a person knowingly does an act that harms Aboriginal cultural heritage and at the time the act was done knew that the thing harmed was Aboriginal cultural heritage: s 27. However, such an offence is not committed if, *inter alia*, the person is acting in accordance with a cultural heritage permit or approved cultural heritage management plan (CHMP): s 29. Applications for cultural heritage permits are made to the Secretary of the Department for Victorian Communities, but such a permit must not be granted for an activity for which a CHMP is required: ss 37, 38. The relationship between planning permits and CHMPs is discussed towards the end of this chapter.

The Heritage Act 1995 (Vic)

Background

The Victorian *Heritage Act 1995* establishes the Victorian Heritage Council to, *inter alia*:

- advise the Minister on Victoria's cultural heritage resources and on any steps necessary to protect and conserve them;
- promote public understanding of Victoria's cultural heritage and develop and conduct community information and education programs;
- adopt, and forward to the Minister, World Heritage Strategy Plans and amendments to World Heritage Strategy Plans; and
- add to or remove places from the Victorian Heritage Register.

The Victorian Heritage Register established under the Act includes all buildings on the Register of Historic Buildings under the *Historic Buildings Act 1981*; all buildings remaining on the Register of Government Buildings under the *Historic Buildings Act* as at 23 May 1998; and all historic shipwrecks, historic shipwreck relics and protected zones: s 19. The Act also establishes the Heritage Inventory, which records all places or objects identified as archaeological sites, areas or relics on the register under the *Archaeological and Aboriginal Relics Preservation Act 1972*; all known areas where archaeological relics are located; all known occurrences of archaeological relics; and all persons known to be holding private collections of artifacts or unique specimens that include archaeological relics: s 120. It is beyond the scope of this book to discuss those aspects of the *Heritage Act* dealing with historic shipwrecks or Aboriginal archaeological sites. The focus of the following is mainly on heritage buildings.

The Hamer Liberal Government enacted the *Historic Buildings Act 1974*, which was replaced by the *Historic Buildings Act 1981*. The 1974 Act established the Historic Buildings Preservation Council, which was responsible for identifying, and placing on a Register of Historic Buildings, buildings (defined to include structures and works) of Statewide historical or architectural value, and administering a permit system for the alteration, removal or demolition of buildings on the Register and buildings subject to Interim Preservation Orders (IPOs) (a form of temporary registration imposed while a building was being considered for inclusion on the Register). The 1981 Act made a number of significant changes to the 1974 Act in that it reduced opportunities for public participation, increased the already considerable powers of the Minister in relation to the Register, and weakened the heritage criteria to be used for registration. The 1974 Act provided for any member of the public to nominate a building to the then Historic Buildings Preservation Council to be considered for addition to the Register, but the 1981 Act restricted nomination essentially to owners and the National Trust. The earlier Act empowered the Historic Buildings Preservation Council to take out IPO control over a building, whereas under the later Act the permission of the Minister was required before such temporary registration could be imposed. The 1981 Act also changed the criteria to be used in determining whether or not a building should be added to or removed from the Register from architectural or historic significance alone to architectural or historic importance and the economic effects of registration. The 1981 Act also restricted the right of persons other than the owners and the National Trust to appear at hearings relating to registration. The Cain Labor Government, via the *Historic Buildings (Amendment) Act 1983* and the *Historic Buildings (Further Amendment) Act 1983*, restored to the 1981 Act most of the provisions of the earlier legislation.

The Heritage Act 1995, which came into operation on 23 May 1996, provided for the *Historic Buildings Act 1981* to continue to apply to government buildings for two years. The 1981 Act provided for a separate Register of Government Buildings, which the Minister could add to, remove from or otherwise amend at his or her discretion. Alteration, removal or demolition of buildings on the Register of Government Buildings at the behest of another Minister required consultation with the Minister, and, if no agreement was reached as a result of consultation, the matter was decided by the Governor in Council. Where the Minister was responsible for a building, he or she could not authorise alteration, demolition or removal without the consent of the Governor in Council. On 23 May 1998, the *Historic Buildings Act* was repealed and the two registers were included in the Victorian Heritage Register.

The Victorian Heritage Register

"Place" is defined to include a building, a garden, a tree, the remains of a ship, an archaeological site, a precinct, and land associated with any of these: s 3. "Object" is defined to include an article associated with a ship and an archaeological relic. "Building" is defined as including a structure, work or fixture and any part of a building, work or fixture. There are now approximately 2,300 places on the Heritage Register (which can be accessed from <www.heritage.vic.gov.au>). But clearly the Act applies to more than buildings as the term is normally understood, as may be seen from the following items on the Register:

Victoria Hill Quartz Gold Mines (1854–1855). Happy Valley Road, Victoria Hill Historic Reserve, Bendigo. To the extent of: All the land known as the Victoria Hill Historic Reserve Marked L-1 on diagram number 608053 held by the Executive Director and including all above-ground structures (granite and brick mining machinery foundations, concrete battery foundations and stamping machinery), mullock heaps, open cut and surface workings, and all archaeological deposits and artifacts. Category: Heritage and Archaeological place.

Former Mount Alexander Silk Worm Farm (1872). Dog Rocks Saddle Road, Harcourt. To the extent of: 1. All of the archaeological features marked as follows on Diagram 501835 held by the Executive Director: F1–ruined rectangular granite building F-2 ruined two roomed granite structure F-3 chimney remains F-4 three briar roses F-5 dam F-6 quarry site F-7 granite paving F-8 remains of drain or well. 2. All the land contained within a 250 metres radius of a point with Australian Grid Reference co-ordinates 260650 5900100. Category: Heritage and Archaeological place.

Pipe Organ (1878). St Augustine's Church, Sullivans Street, Inglewood. To the extent of: All of the structure known as the Fincham Pipe Organ currently located in St Augustine's Church, Sullivan Street, Inglewood. Category: Heritage Place.

The *Historic Buildings Acts* of 1974 and 1981 dealt with buildings (which included part of a building and any structure, work or object or any part thereof or appurtenances thereto) on individual sites. The *Heritage Act 1995* provides for registration of a much wider range of "places" – whole precincts (St Vincent Place in Albert Park, for example), trees, cemeteries, gardens and archaeological sites. Whereas the previous legislation applied only to "buildings" of historic or architectural interest, the *Heritage Act* applies to places of "cultural and heritage significance". Only places and objects of State or national significance are included in the Register, which is consistent with the philosophy of the earlier legislation, which was designed to protect a relatively small number of landmark buildings, with buildings of regional and local significance being protected by planning scheme provisions. Land "associated" with a place may be included in the Register. Under the previous legislation, only land in the same ownership as a building could be registered if it was considered that subdivision or development of that land would lessen the historic or architectural importance of a building (a provision designed primarily to maintain the heritage integrity of buildings set in substantial grounds).

The Victorian Heritage Register includes all places in Victoria on the World Heritage List, all places added to it according to processes prescribed by the *Heritage Act* as discussed below, all places on the Register of Historic Buildings under the *Historic Buildings Act 1981*, and those buildings remaining on the Register of Government Buildings under the *Historic Buildings Act 1981*. The Register of Government Buildings has been referred to above. When the Register of Historic Buildings was first established under then *Historic Buildings Act 1974*, it contained 375 buildings. At that time it had long been the practice of the National Trust to grade buildings according to heritage significance and the initial Register was formed by including all the buildings graded A and B by the Trust and approximately half of those graded C. The Trust has long since abandoned the practice of grading and now identifies heritage significance by simply classifying not only buildings but also areas, landscapes, and, in the case of settlements such as Maldon, whole townships. It is widely believed in the general community that classification by the National Trust provides some form of legal constraint on the demolition or alteration of buildings, a belief that may have its origins in the adoption of National Trust graded buildings as the initial Register of Historic Buildings. However, National Trust classification alone carries no legal status at all – control over alteration and demolition of a building depends on its inclusion on the Victorian Heritage Register (or temporary registration under an Interim Protection Order), or it being subject to the Heritage Overlay controls in a planning scheme.

The Heritage Council and the registration process

The Heritage Council consists of 10 members, six of whom must possess recognised skills in one of each of history, archaeology, architectural conservation or architectural history, engineering or building construction, property management, and planning law. One must be appointed by the Minister from a list of three names submitted by the National Trust of Australia (Victoria); and three must be persons having a demonstrated understanding, expertise or interest in Victoria's heritage or in the management of heritage places: s 7. The functions of the Heritage Council are set out at s 8 and include:

- advising the Minister on the state of Victoria's cultural heritage resources and on any steps necessary to protect and conserve them;
- adopting and forwarding to the Minister World Heritage Strategy Plans and amendments to World Heritage Strategy Plans;
- advising government departments and agencies and municipal councils on matters relating to the protection and conservation of places and objects of cultural heritage significance;
- advising the Minister administering the *Planning and Environment Act 1987* on proposed amendments to planning schemes which may affect the protection or conservation of places and objects of cultural heritage significance; and
- adding or removing places or objects from the Heritage Register or amending the registration of a place or object.

The process of registration is now discussed in summary. Any person or body may nominate a place or object for inclusion on the Heritage Register. A nomination must be made in writing to the Executive Director and include reasons, including reasons based on the assessment criteria published by the Heritage Council, as to why the place or object warrants registration: s 23. The Executive Director must give notice to the owner of the nominated place within 14 days of a nomination being accepted: s 29(1). However, the aim of this notification appears to be to ensure that any prospective purchaser of the property is notified of the nomination by the current owner: ss 30–31. Notification at this stage is not aimed at providing the owner with an opportunity to respond to a nomination made by some person or body other than the owner, despite the fact that the Executive Director at this stage may request further information from such nominators: s 28. It would seem that owners of places nominated for registration are only guaranteed of having some say in the matter after the Executive Director has decided to recommend registration to the Heritage Council.

The Executive Director, having considered the nomination, may do one of three things – inform the nominator (and presumably the owner, if the nominator is not the owner) that the place or object does not warrant inclusion on the Heritage Register; refer the nomination to the relevant planning authority or the Minister administering the *Planning and Environment Act 1987* for inclusion of the place in a planning scheme amendment; or recommend to the Heritage Council that the place or object be included in the Heritage Register: s 32. If the Executive Director recommends inclusion on the Heritage Register, the nominator, the relevant municipal council and the owner must be given a statement setting out the terms of the recommendation, including a brief statement of the cultural heritage significance of the place or object, advising that the Heritage Council will make a decision after a period of 60 days from the date of the notice, and advising that the owner make a submission to the Heritage Council and request a hearing of that submission: s 34. Similarly, if the recommendation is that the place or object should not be included on the Heritage Register, the Executive Director must give a statement to the owner, nominator and relevant municipal council setting out the terms of the recommendation, the reason for the recommendation, and an assessment of the cultural heritage significance of the place or object, advising that the Heritage Council will make a decision after a period of 60 days from the date of the notice, and advising that the owner make a submission to the Heritage Council and request a hearing of that submission: s 34A. Notice of the recommendation of the Executive Director to include or not include the place or object on the Heritage Register must be published in a newspaper circulating in the area in which the nominated building or object is located: s 35.

After considering submissions, the Heritage Council must conduct a hearing if the National Trust or a person with a real and substantial interest in the place or object requests a hearing: ss 31(9) and 41(6). After considering the recommendation of the Executive Director and the submissions lodged, and after conducting the hearing (if a hearing is required), the Heritage Council may determine whether or not the place or object should be included on the Register: s 50. However, the Minister may "call in" a recommendation of the Executive Director and determine the matter instead of the Heritage Council: ss 43–45.

The process of registration raises some concerns. The Heritage Council has the role of an appeals body. There is no opportunity for it to initiate the process of registration – that is in the hands of the Executive Director. The power of the Minister to call in a recommendation of the Executive Director is a device for ensuring that the government of the day can ensure registration or non-registration as it sees fit. And, unlike the planning permit system under the *Planning and Environment Act*, objections are called for after the preliminary decision has been made – that is, after the Executive Director has decided to recommend to the Heritage Council that the place or object be registered. It should also be noted that there are no appeal mechanisms in the Act against the decision of the Heritage Council or against the Minister's decision if the Minister calls in the recommendation.

Effect of registration

Like its predecessors, the *Heritage Act* is aimed basically at preventing summary demolition or alteration. Like most planning and related legislation, it is essentially negative in its effects. It does not compel conservation and good repair. All or part of a place or object on the Heritage Register must not be removed or demolished, damaged or despoiled, developed or altered without a permit: s 64 (but s 65 provides an exemption for the requirement for a permit for alteration if the registered place is a church and the alteration is for liturgical purposes). The penalties for such actions are 2,400 penalty units or imprisonment for five years or both in the case of a natural person, and, in the case of a body corporate, 4,800 penalty units: s 64. Currently a penalty unit is approximately $120. Note that the penalties are not "up to a total of" the specified penalty units. The fines and the jail terms set out are not able to be varied by the court. Note that key terms are defined in s 3: "alter", for example, means "to modify, or changes the appearance or physical nature of a place, whether by way of structural or other works, by painting, plastering or other decoration or any other means". The Heritage Council may determine the works or activities that can be carried out in relation to a registered place or object without a permit (such as routine maintenance): s 66.

A Repair Order may be served on the owner of a registered place or object under s 160, but the purpose of such an order is to prevent the place or object building from falling into disrepair, which is not the same as keeping it in good repair. If the Executive Director of the Heritage Council is of the opinion that a registered place or object has been or is being allowed to fall into disrepair to the extent that its conservation is threatened, he or she may, with the consent of the Heritage Council, require the owner to show cause why the Executive Director should not make an order requiring the owner to carry out specified repairs. Failure to show cause may result in the Executive Director, with the consent of the Minister, serving a Repair Order on the owner, specifying the repairs to be carried out and the period within which they are to be done. The owner has the right of appeal to the Victorian Civil and Administrative Tribunal (VCAT). Failure to comply with a Repair Order is an offence under the Act and carries the same penalties as for breach: a penalty of 2,400 penalty units (4,800 penalty units in the case of a body corporate) or five years' imprisonment, or both: s 164. The current value of a penalty unit for is approximately $120.

Sections 55–62 deal with IPOs, which have the effect of temporarily including the place or object, for the period of the order, on the Heritage Register (such as during the period from when a place or object has been nominated for inclusion on the Heritage Register and a final decision as to its inclusion has been made by the Heritage Council or the Minister). A breach of an IPO carries the same penalties as those set out in s 64.

The penalties for a breach of the requirements of the Act are substantial, but it should be remembered that demolishing a building on the Register in the central business district of Melbourne without a permit would be to clear the site for a development worth many millions of dollars. The fines and threat of imprisonment may act as a deterrent, but a further deterrent is provided in theory by s 182, which allows the Governor in Council to sterilise land where an owner has been found guilty of an offence by declaring that the building or land or both shall not be developed or used for up to 10 years.

It should also be noted that ss 166–168 provide that the Executive Director, the Director of Public Prosecutions or any person may bring proceedings in the Supreme Court for an order to remedy or restrain a contravention of the Act (which includes a threatened or apprehended contravention of permit conditions). If the Supreme Court is satisfied that the Act is or will be contravened, it may make any order it thinks fit, including the removal or demolition of any building or works constructed, the reinstatement of a building, works or object to the condition it was in immediately before the contravention: s 168. The discretion given under s 168 is very wide: see *Rajendran v Tonkin* [2004] VSCA 43. Non-compliance with such an order may result in the offender being found to be in contempt, with resulting severe penalties being applied by the Court, including imprisonment.

The permit system

Applications for permits to carry out works or activities are made to the Executive Director, who must cause notice of the application to be published in a newspaper circulating in the area in which the place or object is located if he or she considers the proposed works may detrimentally affect the place or object, and may require the owner of the registered place to display a copy of the notice in a conspicuous position on the site for a period of 14 days: s 68. If notice of the application is given, any person may lodge a written submission, which must be lodged within 14 days: s 69. Section 70(1) provides that the Executive Director must refer to the Heritage Council a copy of an application if it is in a class of application that must be referred to it. Pursuant to s 70(2), the Heritage Council may, by notice published in the *Government Gazette*, determine the classes of applications that must be referred to it. No determination pursuant to s 70(2) has occurred, so in effect it is the Executive Director who determines all permit applications in the first instance (subject to appeal to the Heritage Council if the permit application is refused). If an application is referred to the Heritage Council it must tell the Executive Director that it either objects or does not object to the permit being issued. If it does object then the effect of the objection is similar to the objection of a referral authority under the *Planning and Environment Act* in that the Executive Director must refuse to grant the permit: s 74(2).

Section 73 sets out the matters which must be considered by the Executive Director in determining permit applications, including the extent to which the application, if approved, would affect the cultural heritage significance of the registered place or registered object; if the application relates to a listed place or registered place or object in a World Heritage Environs Area, the extent to which the application, if approved, would affect the values of the listed place or any relevant Approved Heritage Strategy plan; any submissions made under s 69; and the extent to which the application, if refused, would affect the reasonable or economic use of the registered place or registered object, or cause undue financial hardship to the owner in relation to that place.

Refusal of applications by the Executive Director may be appealed to the Heritage Council by the applicant, by the owner of the registered heritage place or registered object, or by a person with a substantial interest in the registered place or registered object. Appeals against conditions in a permit granted by the Executive Director may be appealed by the applicant or owner of the registered place or registered object: s 75(3). The Heritage Council must conduct an appeal hearing if a hearing is requested by the National Trust or, in any other case, unless the appellant agrees to the determination of the appeal without a hearing: s 76(2).

Section 77 provides for review of decisions by VCAT on permit applications required to be referred to the Heritage Council by virtue of s 70. But, as s 70 is inoperative (see above), there is currently no avenue to VCAT for review of decisions on permit applications. The determination of the Heritage Council in relation to appeals is therefore final (except to the Supreme Court on a point of law – the *Heritage Act* is not included in the "planning enactments" listed in Schedule 1 to *Victorian Civil and Administrative Tribunal Act 1998* which are subject to review by VCAT). However, the Minister may call in appeals to the Heritage Council and either determine them or refer them to VCAT for determination: see s 78. There are no criteria specified in the Act which must be satisfied before the Minister may exercise the call-in power. However, pursuant to s 78(1)(b) the Minister may refer an appeal to VCAT only if in the Minister's opinion the determination of the appeal may have a significant effect on the achievement or development of planning and heritage objectives. Note that appeals may be made only in relation to refusals or in relation to conditions in any permit issued by the Executive Director – there is no avenue of appeal by third parties against a decision to grant a permit. These appeal provisions were criticised by VCAT in *Staged Developments Aust v Minister for Planning, Heritage Victoria* [2001] VCAT 1447; 8 VPR 131. This was an appeal referred to VCAT under s 78(1)(b) after the Minister had called it in. The Tribunal was critical of the appeal provisions of the *Heritage Act* and observed that the Heritage Council had been reviewing the decisions of the Executive Director for years without the discipline of it being required to give reasons for its decisions. The *Heritage Act* does not require the Heritage Council to give reasons. The Tribunal stated that in its opinion this was a serious defect in the *Heritage Act*.

Decisions on applications required to be referred to the Heritage Council by the Executive Director pursuant to s 70, should that section become operative, may be appealed to VCAT by the applicant, the owner of the registered place or object, or a person with a significant interest in the registered place or object: ss 77–79. Appeals may be made against the decision of the Executive Director to refuse, or against conditions in any decision to grant such applications. Appeals cannot be made by third parties against a decision to grant a permit. The Minister may call in and determine such appeals as he or she sees fit: ss 80–81. Again, there are no criteria which must be satisfied before the Minister can exercise the call-in power.

Financial assistance

While the Act is aimed primarily at preventing summary demolition and alteration, it does contain provisions for financial assistance to owners. So there should be, for registration of buildings may impose considerable financial burdens on owners, particularly where permission for repairs and renovations is granted subject to conditions that certain types of materials are to be used, such as turned veranda posts, slate roofing and so on. There are no compensation provisions in the Act relating to the impact of registration, or to the effect of IPOs. However, the Heritage Council may, with the consent of the Minister, compulsorily acquire any land which is a registered place or any land on which a registered place is situated and if it does so is bound by the provisions of the *Land Acquisition and Compensation Act 1986* (see Chapter 9 for a discussion of compulsory acquisition).

Section 135 provides for a Heritage Fund. The Executive Director, with the consent of the Heritage Council, may make loans and grants to owners at rates of interest approved by the Treasurer of Victoria, including no interest: ss 140–141. The Heritage Council may, with the consent of the Treasurer, remit or defer Land Tax payable on land that is a registered place, or on land on which a registered place is situated. Finally, with the consent of the relevant rating authority and relevant Minister, the Heritage Council may remit or defer payment of rates, such as municipal rates, payable in respect of land which is a registered place or on which a registered place is situated: s 144.

There are provisions in ss 85–86 for owners of a registered place or land that is a registered place to enter into a covenant with the Heritage Council or the National Trust to bind themselves and future owners as to the use and development of land registered with the buildings or the conservation of the place and any registered object at that place. At first glance this would seem to be an attractive mechanism for ensuring conservation, but, while some owners may be willing to forgo the potential financial rewards of using or developing land associated with a building or structure, the conservation and good repair of the building or structure itself may involve considerable cost. Owners are unlikely to enter into covenants unless those costs are met.

Effective conservation, as distinct from imposing controls preventing summary demolition, relies on making incentives available for owners. Controls do not prevent demolition, damage or alterations to registered places and objects – they simply have the effect of requiring permission, and the absence of incentives, particularly financial incentives, leads to decisions based at least partly on the financial impact of refusal (after all, the matters to be considered in determining permit applications include "the extent to which the application, if refused, would affect the reasonable or economic use of the registered place or object, or cause undue financial hardship to the owner": s 73(1)(b). The end result may well be demolition or other changes which destroy or detract from the integrity of a registered place or object. A major weakness in the past of the way in which the Act was administered was inadequate funding, although in recent years the amount of money available for grants has increased. For the financial year 2009–2010 grants were made totalling $2,355,000. This is not to say that the Act itself is without its problems – the lack of third-party appeal provisions in relation to decisions to grant permits and the call-in powers of the Minister are matters which have been referred to in the discussion above.

Heritage planning and Victorian planning legislation before the Planning and Environment Act 1987

Heritage planning powers before 1972

Limited statutory power for achieving conservation objectives was included in the *Town and Country Planning Act 1944* – the first planning legislation enacted in Victoria. Under s 13 of that Act, planning schemes were to "make provision for such of the matters referred to in the Schedule to this Act with all such particularity as the Minister requires". Clause 5 of the Schedule authorised "The preservation of objects of historical interest or natural beauty". As explained in Chapter 3, in subsequent planning Acts up until the *Planning and Environment Act 1987*, the approach taken to circumscribing the powers of bodies authorised to prepare planning schemes (such as local councils) was the same as that used in the 1944 Act – matters which could be provided for in schemes were specified in a schedule, so that any provision in a scheme not authorised by inclusion in the schedule was therefore *ultra vires*. The same principle applied to interim development orders when they became available as a development control mechanism under s 17 of the *Town and Country Planning Act 1961* – they could include only those provisions authorised by the Third Schedule.

On first reading, cl 5 of the Schedule to the 1944 Act would seem to have authorised the inclusion in schemes of a wide range of provisions dealing not only with heritage conservation of the built environment but also with what we would now call landscape and natural area conservation. The word "preservation", however, does not do justice to what is now generally understood by the term "conservation" as discussed in the introduction to this chapter. Clause 5 did not extend to objects of architectural, scientific, or cultural interest or significance, all of which would be now considered as valid criteria for assessing conservation and/or heritage value. Nor did cl 5 specify the land use and development controls that could be used to achieve preservation of objects of historic interest or natural beauty – there was certainly no reference made to such matters as regulating the use and development of land on which these objects were located or regulating the alteration or removal or demolition of these objects. The term "objects" also provided some difficulty in that it restricted the application of the clause to specific items and specific sites – it did not authorise the inclusion in schemes of the precinct or area controls that were included in Urban Conservation Zones and are now included in Heritage Overlays. The aims of these controls are to control new development to ensure some degree of harmony between old and new in terms of building style, height, bulk, colour, and materials.

In the *Town and Country Planning Act 1958* the matters that could be provided for in schemes were listed in the Second Schedule and cl 5 of this schedule retained exactly the wording of cl 5 of the Schedule to the 1944 Act. Again, no specific controls were authorised to achieve "preservation". The *Town and Country Planning Act 1961* listed the matters that could be provided for in schemes and interim development orders in its Third Schedule. Clause 8 of that schedule provided for the "preservation of objects and areas of scientific historical or architectural interest or natural beauty". The addition of architectural interest broadened the ambit of the clause, as did the inclusion of areas as well as objects, but there was still no specification of the controls that could be utilised to achieve preservation.

Heritage planning powers after 1972

The limitations of the 1961 Act became apparent in the case of Maldon, an almost intact 19th-century gold mining township in north-central Victoria. In 1968 the Shire of Maldon wrote to the then Minister for Local Government, Mr Hamer, requesting assistance for the preparation of a planning scheme for the township. The Minister instructed the Town and Country Planning Board (TCPB), the predecessor of the current Department of Planning and Community Development, to work with the Shire in the preparation of the scheme. The TCPB took out an IDO over the township, as it was empowered to do under the 1961 Act, and was able to control land use and development via the planning permit process while a planning scheme was prepared (subject to appeal, of course, which always made "blanket" IDOs very coarse instruments of development control). However, it soon became clear that, to achieve conservation objectives, control over demolition of individual buildings would be required, but it was not clear that this was authorised by cl 8 of the Third Schedule. Also, it was quickly recognised that the heritage value and integrity of individual buildings relied heavily on their relationship, in terms of building style and bulk, with surrounding and nearby buildings, some of which were not of themselves of historical or architectural interest. Control over demolition and alteration of these other buildings was also necessary, as were powers over the style, bulk, height, colour and so on of new buildings. Clause 8 did not provide the power for these matters to be included in schemes. The *Town and Country Planning (Amendment) Act 1972* replaced cl 8 of the Third Schedule and also added cll 8A and 8B. These new clauses were as follows:

> 8. The conservation and enhancement of buildings, works, objects and sites specified as being of architectural, historical or scientific interest by prohibiting restricting or regulating the pulling down removal alteration decoration or defacement of any such building work or object.
>
> 8A. The conservation and enhancement of areas and objects specified as being of natural beauty or interest or of importance by prohibiting restricting or regulating the

use or development of land in such areas and by prohibiting restricting or regulating the destruction of bushland trees rock formations and other objects.

8B. The conservation and enhancement of the character of an area specified as being of special significance by prohibiting restricting or regulating the use or development of land in the area by prohibiting restricting or regulating the pulling down removal alteration decoration or defacement of any building work site or object or by requiring buildings and works to harmonize in character and appearance with adjacent buildings or with the character of an area or (in the case of an area of historical interest) to conform to the former appearance of the area at some specified period and for such purposes specifying the materials colours and finishes to be used in the external walls of buildings or in the external covering of such walls.

In all clauses the very powerful controls authorised are preceded by the word "specified". In other words, the controls authorised could only be made applicable to sites, objects, buildings, works, or areas, as the case may be, by specifying them in schemes or IDOs. This was done by actually including in the scheme a statement specifying particular site(s), building(s), work(s), object(s) or area(s) as being of architectural, historical or scientific interest, or as being of natural beauty or interest, or as being of special significance. Therefore, in order for a scheme to require a planning permit for, say, demolition of a building, the building would have to be specified in the scheme or IDO as being of historical or scientific interest under cl 8, or be within an area specified as being of special significance under cl 8B. Demolition control could not be included for zones or sites that were not specified in the scheme or IDO as being of special significance, such as normal residential or commercial zones.

The controls that could now be included went a good deal further than simply control of demolition – under both cll 8A and 8B, alterations to existing buildings could be prohibited, restricted or regulated; painting and façade treatment of existing buildings could be controlled under cl 8; painting and decoration, including façade treatment, of proposed buildings as well as existing buildings could be controlled via cl 8B; and proposed buildings could also be controlled under cl 8B in terms of their shape, size, bulk and style in order to conserve and enhance the character of an area. For non-urban areas, controls were made available for areas specified in schemes or interim development orders as being of natural beauty, interest or importance, such as control over the removal of vegetation. With these amendments the days of being required to get a planning permit to paint a house in a heritage area had arrived.

Heritage controls and the issue of compensation

These changes provided the legislative base for a great deal of heritage planning in Victoria during the 1970s and were made, at least partly, in response to the demands of the National Trust of Australia (Victoria), established in 1956, and the demands of a number of residents groups, such as the Carlton Association. These organisations were important in promoting the cause of urban conservation – the National Trust played a major role in securing the Victorian government's recognition of

Maldon as a township requiring protection. Instrumental in furthering the cause of heritage conservation and in providing funds for studies to establish the heritage worth of buildings and areas was the Whitlam Government's National Estate Programme, set up in 1973, and the Australian Heritage Commission, established in 1975 and discussed earlier in this chapter. The Victorian Government also made a significant contribution by making loans and grants available to municipalities for conservation studies, by undertaking studies itself and by funding and providing heritage and architect advisory services to local government. These initiatives bore concrete results – by April 1980, seven approved planning schemes (Bacchus Marsh, Ballarat and District, Cranbourne, Mornington, Maldon, Newham and Woodend, and Portland) and three interim development orders (Geelong Regional, Seymour, and Western Region) specified a total of 465 buildings under cl 8 (see Blake in Further Reading). Also at that time, three schemes (Bacchus Marsh, Echuca, and Maldon) and four IDOs (Beechworth, Chiltern, Geelong Regional and Healesville) contained zones specified under cl 8B and a further 14 schemes were in the process of preparation or amendment to include buildings specified under cl 8, or areas specified under cl 8B. However, uncertainty about whether or not compensation could be claimed for the effects of site-specific and zone-based conservation controls limited their effectiveness, particularly in the metropolitan area and, more specifically, in the central business district of Melbourne, where development pressures combined with very high land values threw the compensation issue into sharp relief.

In 1973 the City of Melbourne took out an IDO which specified the central business district as an area of special significance under cl 8B and required planning permission for the demolition of any building in that area. However, in 1975 the City Council obtained legal advice that refusal of planning permission for demolition may make it liable for compensation and from then on no planning permit for demolition was refused under the interim development order, resulting in the destruction of many 19th century buildings. This did not mean that all buildings of heritage value in the central business district were placed under threat, for the most important were on the Register of Historic Buildings under the *Historic Buildings Act 1974* and so were afforded protection from summary demolition. The historic buildings legislation is discussed earlier in this chapter, but it should be noted that essentially only individual buildings of State or regional significance were included on the Register. Buildings not of sufficient merit to be placed on the Register, yet nevertheless of significant heritage value or streetscape value either individually or as a group, were those that the scheme and IDO provisions authorised by cll 8 and 8B were designed to protect. Many of these were demolished during the late 1970s to make way for high rise office towers, as a result of Melbourne City Council not refusing to grant permits for demolition because of the fear that refusal would give rise to a claim for compensation.

Under s 42(2) of the *Town and Country Planning Act 1961*, compensation could be claimed for loss or damage resulting from the refusal to grant planning permission on the grounds that land is or will be required for a public purpose. This section applied, for example, to proposed public purposes reservations, where land in private ownership was "earmarked" in the scheme or IDO for public sector acquisition and use at a future date. It is common practice and sound planning to identify and reserve future sites for public sector uses, such as government schools, major roads, parks, public hospitals and so on. In the past that was done by applying, as part of the relevant planning scheme, reservations for proposed public purposes to the land concerned. Now it is done by the mechanism of a Public Acquisition Overlay. However, it may be many years before land so identified and set aside is acquired, and during that time the owner, then as now, may apply for planning permission to use and develop the land. The use and development for which permission is sought may be entirely inappropriate, given the future public use envisioned by the reservation, and therefore the responsible authority may have little option but to refuse consent and therefore be served with a loss or damage claim. Under s 42(6) of the *Town and Country Planning Act 1961*, claims for such loss or damage were limited to the difference between the value of the land as affected by the existence of or any provision in a planning scheme or interim development order, and the value of the land as not so affected.

The City of Melbourne's legal advice received in 1975 was, in summary, as follows: under s 42 of the *Town and Country Planning Act 1961* compensation could be claimed for loss or damage suffered as a consequence of being refused planning permission on the grounds that land is or will be required for a public purpose; land was defined in the Act as including works and buildings; refusal of planning permission for demolition was tantamount to requiring the retention of the building for the benefit of the community and could be construed in law as a refusal on the grounds that the building (that is, land within the meaning of the Act) is or will be required for a public purpose; compensation may therefore be claimed for loss or damage for such refusal. According to this advice, compensation could therefore be claimed for both refusals based on the grounds that the building itself had heritage or conservation or special interest qualities, and refusals based on the grounds that, although the building itself did not have heritage or conservation or special interest qualities, it nevertheless was important in maintaining the integrity of nearby buildings which did. Faced with what it believed was the prospect of paying claims for compensation for sites in the central business district to the tune of the difference between the values of sites where the existing building was required to be retained and the values that would apply if they were considered as potential redevelopment sites, it is understandable that the City of Melbourne did not refuse applications for demolition.

The threat of compensation claims for refusal of planning permission to demolish was finally removed beyond any shadow of doubt by the Cain Labor Government in 1982, which not only demonstrates how simply the matter could have been resolved but also raises questions about why previous Liberal governments did not act to remove this barrier to effectively achieving conservation objectives. The *Town and Country Planning (Amendment) Act 1982*, s 4, amended s 42(1) of the principal Act to specifically exclude loss or damage claims arising from any provision in a planning scheme or interim development order authorised by cll 8, 8A and 8B of the Third

Schedule. However, the issue of compensation had already been resolved in 1980, when the Victorian Supreme Court examined in *Van der Meyden v MMBW* [1980] VR 225 the difference between a zone and a reservation. The Van der Meydens owned 100 acres of land in the Shire of Eltham abutting Kinglake National Park. The land was subject to the Melbourne Metropolitan Planning Scheme (MMPS) and also one of the MMBW's IDOs, and was in a Conservation Zone. It was also subject to the Shire of Eltham's IDO. Under the conservation zoning, the land was subject to tree felling controls as provided for in cl 8A of the Third Schedule, and, subject to permission, the land could be used for afforestation, animal husbandry, caretaker's house, car park, home occupation, minor sports ground, minor utility installation, passive recreation, road, and soil removal, with all other uses being prohibited. A detached house could be built, subject to permission, provided that the site was not less than 100 acres. The Shire's "blanket" IDO required planning permission to "use, subdivide, or otherwise develop any land or erect, construct or carry out any buildings or works on the land". The effect of the MMBW controls was particularly severe, approaching what the Gobbo report called loss of beneficial use (see Chapter 9). In 1977 the Van der Meydens applied to the MMBW for planning permits to (a) subdivide their land into three allotments and on each of two of these allotments develop a detached dwelling and outbuildings; and (b) clear all trees, timber and shrubs from their land. The MMBW failed to determine the applications within the statutory two-month period and the Van der Meydens appealed to the then Town Planning Appeals Tribunal against the failure to determine. Pending the appeal hearing, they also unsuccessfully sought permission for subdivision and clearing from the Shire of Eltham under its interim development order and then appealed against the Shire's refusal to grant permission. The appeals all came on for hearing by the Tribunal in August 1978, and the decision of the Tribunal was that the appeals be disallowed. In its statement of reasons the Tribunal said "the decision of the Tribunal is – that the appeals are disallowed on the grounds that the subject land is or will be required for a public purpose or alternatively that the subject land is, pursuant to the appropriate interim development orders, to be reserved for a public purpose within the meaning of Section 42 of the *Town and Country Planning Act*". Mindful of the opportunity provided by these reasons for the Van der Meydens to claim compensation for loss or damage, both the MMBW and the Shire sought review of the Tribunal's determination by the Supreme Court, challenging the Tribunal's conclusions that the land was or was deemed to be reserved for a public purpose. As might be expected, neither the Shire nor the MMBW challenged the Tribunal's determination that the permits should not be granted – they were concerned at the reasons for that determination.

In finding for the MMBW and the Shire, Anderson J noted that the purpose of the Conservation Zone is to confer a benefit on the community, but he also went on to say that "any restriction or prohibition is evidently imposed for the public benefit and for the enhancement of the amenity of the locality and if the view of the Tribunal were correct, namely that the limitation on the use of land in the Conservation Zone was for the benefit of the public, and that therefore land therein was reserved for a public purpose, then the same argument would apply to all restrictions or prohibitions of use, and all land within all zones would be so reserved or required for a public purpose". His Honour said that there must be characteristics additional to placing restrictions on land that distinguish a reservation from a zone and stated that the first of these was the listing in the scheme of public purposes. The Conservation Zone was not in that list. Moreover, land in the Conservation Zone was not public land nor intended to be public land in the sense that it was intended to remain in private ownership and owners had the right to exclude the general public from it. His Honour rejected the notion that a Conservation Zone is an implied reservation, stating that "if land were reserved for a public purpose it would be expressly so reserved, and that it would not impliedly be so reserved merely because a restriction on the private use of land privately owned and occupied might be considered a benefit to the community".

The example of St James Park

While the *Van der Meyden* case dealt with a Rural Conservation Zone, the judgment that a zone cannot be construed as a reservation obviously applied to Urban Conservation Zones as well, including site-specific zones. Until that principle was established, the threat of compensation produced a marked reluctance on the part of authorities to implement conservation controls, as can be illustrated by the saga of St James Park in the then metropolitan municipality of Hawthorn (see Lawson in Further Reading). Soon after its foundation in 1956, the National Trust recognised the heritage value of the St James Park area by classifying several of its outstanding buildings. In 1971, in response to the intrusion of flats and commercial uses into the area, the residents formed the St James Park Association and in 1973 presented a report to the Hawthorn City Council, the MMBW, the TCPB and various politicians. The report included a recommendation that the area be zoned conservation and called for an appropriate scheme amendment. The City of Hawthorn actively supported the St James Park Association, engaging consultants Loder and Bayly to undertake a full conservation study of historic precincts in the municipality, including St James Park, and used the results of that study in its negotiations and discussions with the MMBW on the proposed scheme amendment. However, progress was extremely slow, with Amendment No 120 to the Melbourne Metropolitan Planning Scheme (MMPS) Urban Conservation Residential Zone No 1 finally being placed on exhibition on 13 February 1980, only after the City of Hawthorn had formally agreed to accept responsibility for the zone and therefore responsibility for any compensation claims that might arise. This amendment was gazetted on 18 March 1981.

With the exceptions of the IDO taken out by the City of Melbourne in 1973 and the St James Park Urban Conservation Zone, heritage controls under planning schemes in the metropolitan area date from after the 1982 amendment to the *Town and Country Planning Act 1961*. Amendment 224 to the MMPS was placed on public exhibition in 1983 and gazetted in April 1984, with the provisions of the amendment being implemented via an IDO during the period between exhibition and gazettal. This amendment introduced heritage controls over North and South Carlton, North and South Parkville, East Melbourne, Flemington Hill, Fawkner Park, Royal Park, Princes Park, Carlton Gardens, Dudley Street, Victoria Parade, Fitzroy Gardens, Treasury Gardens, Yarra Park and Kings Domain.

Heritage Conservation and the Planning and Environment Act 1987

Heritage planning powers under the Act

The matters which may be provided for in schemes under the *Planning and Environment Act 1987* are found in s 6. Unlike the *Town and Country Planning Act 1961* and earlier planning legislation, these matters are included in the body of the Act rather than in a schedule appended to it. Under s 6(1) a planning scheme "must seek to further the objectives of planning in Victoria within the area covered by the scheme" and "may make *any* provision which relates to the use, development, protection or conservation of any land in the area". As detailed in Chapter 3, land is defined under s 3 to include buildings and other structures. However, in the context of conservation and heritage controls, it should be noted that development as defined by s 3 includes exterior alteration or exterior decoration of a building, demolition of a building or works, construction or carrying out of works, subdivision or consolidation of land, the placing or relocation of a building or works on land, and the construction or putting up for display of signs or hoardings. It *includes* these things; it is not confined to them. Given the wording of s 6(1), it is difficult to envisage very many provisions devised to implement conservation and heritage objectives that could not be included in a scheme. Controls on internal alteration of a building are provided for by the Heritage Overlay but apply only if a schedule to the overlay identifies the heritage place as one where internal alteration controls apply. Alteration or removal of the interior or parts of the interior of a building included in the Victorian Heritage Register can also be controlled under the *Heritage Act*.

A list of matters that may be included in schemes is provided in s 6(2), but this is prefaced by the words "without limiting sub-section (1)", so clearly the approach taken here is somewhat different from that employed in the *Town and Country Planning Act 1961*, where any matter not listed in the Third Schedule could not be included. The absence of any reference to heritage or natural area conservation in s 6(2) therefore does not preclude schemes from providing for these matters. Indeed the "must" and "may" provisions of s 6(1) not only confer wide powers but also impose a duty to include conservation controls in schemes where there are sites or buildings or areas of scientific, aesthetic, architectural or historical interest or otherwise of special cultural value.

The requirement for schemes to further the objectives of planning in Victoria makes it essential for us to examine which of these relate to conservation generally and to heritage conservation in particular. These objectives are listed in s 4 and include the following:

Section 4(1)(b) "to provide for the protection of natural and man made resources and the maintenance of ecological processes and genetic diversity"

Section 4(1)(d) "to conserve and enhance those buildings, areas or other places which are of scientific, aesthetic architectural or historical interest, or otherwise of special cultural value"

Power to include in schemes provisions relating to both rural or natural area conservation and to heritage and urban conservation is not only given by s 4(1)(b); it is a power that is required to be exercised – it is a duty that is imposed by s 6(1)(a). Those powers are extended by s 4(1)(b), which requires schemes to not only conserve but also enhance buildings, areas or other places of scientific, aesthetic, architectural or historical interest, or otherwise of special cultural value. "Conservation" is defined in s 3 to include preservation, maintenance, sustainable use and restoration of the natural and cultural environment. The duty therefore extends to something more than simple retention – it also includes restoration where that is appropriate. Enhancement could be achieved by the control and management of land use and development on abutting land or surrounding land, including the prohibition of all forms of development on such land, but it also applies to the building or site or area which is the subject of enhancement. But, as there is now no Heritage Zone in planning schemes, the ability of a responsible authority to manage the use of land or abutting land to achieve heritage objectives may well be less than under the old schemes, if that land is not included in the area to which a Heritage Overlay applies. The State standard Heritage Overlay imposes control over development, not the use of land, although cl 43.01-6 of the Heritage Overlay provisions allows for a permit to be granted to use a heritage place for a use which would otherwise be prohibited. Such a permit may only be granted, however, if the schedule to the overlay identifies the heritage place as one where prohibited uses may be permitted, the use will not adversely affect the significance of the heritage place, and the benefits obtained from the use can be demonstrably applied towards the conservation of the heritage place.

The Heritage Overlay provisions

The Heritage Overlay control in planning schemes is designed to apply to the development of cultural places (historic buildings, structures, gardens, and precincts), places significant for their Aboriginal values, and places significant for their natural heritage values (that is, places of geological, paleontological, botanical, zoological, geomorphological or other scientific importance). Local schedules accompanying the overlay specify the places to which it applies and the nature of the controls imposed.

The purpose of the Heritage Overlay set out at cl 43.01 of all schemes includes to conserve and enhance heritage places of natural or cultural significance, to conserve and enhance those elements which contribute to the significance of the heritage place, and to ensure that development does not adversely affect the significance of the heritage place. Pursuant to cl 43.01-1, a permit is required to subdivide or consolidate land; demolish or remove a building; construct a building; externally alter a building by structural work, rendering, sandblasting or in any other way; construct or display a sign; externally paint a building if a schedule to the overlay identifies the heritage pace as one where paint controls apply; externally paint an unpainted surface; internally alter a building if the schedule to the overlay identifies the heritage place as one where internal alteration controls apply; and remove, destroy or lop a tree if the schedule to the overlay identifies the heritage place as one where tree controls apply.

Provisions dealing with exemptions from the requirements, such as the notification under s 52 of adjoining land owners and occupiers and other persons who may be affected by the grant of a permit, from the requirement under s 64 for the responsible authority to give notice of its decision on the permit application if there have been objectors, and from the right of objectors to apply to VCAT for review of the decision, are set out at cl 43.01-4. These exemption provisions are discussed in Chapter 3.

As was discussed in Chapters 3 and 5, it is a long-established principle, articulated by the Full Bench of the Victorian Supreme Court in *National Trust of Australia (Vic) v Australian Temperance and General Mutual Life Assurance Society Ltd* [1976] VR 592, *Salmal Constructions Pty Ltd v Richards* (1998) 99 LGERA 423; 22 AATR 339, and *Shalit v Jackson Clement Burrows Architects Pty Ltd* [2002] VSC 528, and expounded on in *Victorian National Parks Association Inc v Iluka Resources* [2004] VCAT 20, that, in exercising a discretion conferred by a planning scheme provision, the responsible authority (and VCAT on review of that decision) is confined to considerations which are relevant to the purpose of that provision. If the requirement for a permit is triggered only by a Heritage Overlay then consideration must be given only to heritage considerations pursuant to the Heritage Overlay, not to considerations such as amenity, which would arise if an additional requirement for a permit had been triggered by the zoning which applies to the land (such as a Residential 1 zoning).

The decision guidelines at cl 43.01-5 require the responsible authority, before deciding on an application (and VCAT on review) to consider, as appropriate, matters including the significance of the heritage place and whether the proposal will adversely affect its significance, any applicable heritage study and any applicable conservation policy, whether the location, bulk, form and appearance of the proposed building will affect the significance of the heritage place, whether the location, bulk, form and appearance of the building is in keeping with the character of adjacent buildings and the heritage place, and whether the demolition, removal or external alteration will adversely affect the significance of the heritage place.

The Heritage Overlay may be applied to individual sites or to precincts. In the inner metropolitan area very large proportions of some municipalities are subject to Heritage Overlay controls, which may apply to individual places, or whole precincts. In both instances, the decisions to introduce the controls have been based on heritage studies, which are usually included as reference documents in the relevant planning schemes (for a discussion of reference documents and incorporated documents, see Chapter 3). In the case of precinct-wide controls, and sometimes in the case of site-specific Heritage Overlays, these heritage studies may have been very cursory indeed. It is common for these studies to be examined in detail at VCAT hearings.

Often it is only through the research undertaken by architectural historians and other heritage consultants engaged as expert witnesses, and the testing of their research and opinions through cross-examination, that the heritage value of a building, either in architectural or cultural terms, is established: see, for example, *Harding v Port Phillip CC* [2002] VCAT 416 and *Association of Franciscan Order of Friars v Boroondara CC* [2002] VCAT 1085. The heritage place is the land to which the Heritage Overlay applies. In the case of a precinct-based Heritage Overlay, alteration or demolition of a building will normally have less impact on the heritage place than an alteration or demolition of a building in a site-specific Heritage Overlay.

The heritage study on which the decision was based to introduce the Heritage Overlay may be an incorporated document, as distinct from a reference document, in the relevant planning scheme, as in the City of Port Phillip. As an incorporated document the heritage study is part of the planning scheme and in the case of the City of Port Phillip it identifies individual buildings as being significant heritage places. That does not prevent the responsible authority (or VCAT) from enquiring as to what degree of significance a building may have. It may be established, for example, that it has very low significance, as was the case in *Harding v Port Phillip CC*.

Both the demolition of a building and the construction of a new (and usually larger) replacement building trigger the requirement for a planning permit pursuant to the Heritage Overlay. Permission for the use and development of the replacement building may also be required pursuant to the zoning that applies to the land. The decision guidelines for the Heritage Overlay commence with the requirement for the responsible authority to consider, as appropriate, the State Planning Policy Framework (SPPF) and the Local Planning Policy Framework (LPPF), including the Municipal Strategic Statement and local planning policies. Inevitably conflicts arise between heritage polices and other policies such as economic development, urban consolidation or containment, the encouragement of higher density development near public transport nodes and so on. Clause 11 of the SPPF states that it is the State Government's expectation that planning and responsible authorities will endeavour to integrate policies relevant to the issue to be determined and balance conflicting objectives in favour of net community benefit and sustainable development. The clause states "planning and responsible authorities must take account of and give effect to the general principles and the specific policies applicable to the issues before them to ensure integrated decision making". In other words, the introduction to all planning schemes in Victoria recognises and requires that responsible authorities and VCAT balance policies which may sit awkwardly with and even contradict other policies in the relevant planning scheme and arrive at a decision in the interests of the community as a whole. But it has been relatively consistently held by VCAT that, in determining an application for demolition pursuant to a Heritage Overlay, urban consolidation policy or the social and economic advantages to the community which may result from the development of the replacement building are to all intents and purposes irrelevant: *Halliday v Port Phillip CC* [2000] VCAT 545, *Port Phillip v A and M Resi* [2001] VCAT 489, and *Coptic Orthodox Patriarchate Archangel Mikhall and St Anthony Church Inc v Monash CC* [2004] VCAT 948.

Heritage policies in the LPPF of planning schemes, like all policies in the LPPF, must not be applied as if they were regulations. It is not unusual for planning schemes to contain policies for Heritage Overlay areas to the effect that proposals which would result in the loss of heritage building fabric will not be supported, and that upper floor additions to buildings must be set back specified distances from the front façade, or fit within a specified building envelope defined by the angle of sight lines from the street. A policy that loss of building fabric will not be supported is at odds with the provisions of the Heritage Overlay and its decision guidelines, which clearly contemplate that a permit may be granted for the alteration, removal or demolition of a building which will have a detrimental impact on the significance of the heritage place, whether that place be the land to which a site-specific Heritage Overlay applies or land to which a precinct-based Heritage Overlay applies. Each case must be decided on its merits. Similarly, each permit application for extensions must be decided on its merits. Obviously, the extent to which an upper floor extension should be set back from the lower floor façade or fit within an envelope expressed in terms of sight line angles will depend on a number of factors, including the height and bulk of the extension, whether the host building has a parapet (as with many Victorian era buildings), the width of the street from which the extension will be viewed, and whether or not the extension is to a host building on a corner lot: see, for example, *Craig v Port Phillip CC* [2006] VCAT 2161 and *Dooley v Port Phillip* CC [2006] VCAT 2523.

Pursuant to a Heritage Overlay, decisions on demolition and the replacement of the building by a new building are made in two stages. The first stage is whether or not the proposed demolition should be allowed. The second stage is the whether or not the replacement building should be allowed. If the first-stage decision is that the proposed demolition should not be allowed, the permit application fails. But, if the decision is that demolition is justified and should be allowed, the second-stage decision may give rise to a wide range of issues which need to be considered pursuant to both the Heritage Overlay and the zoning which applies to the land. In relation to the Heritage Overlay, what is acceptable in terms of the decision guidelines at cl 43.01-5, such as whether the location, bulk, form and appearance of the proposed building is in keeping with the character and appearance of adjacent buildings and the heritage place? If the land is subject to a site-specific Heritage Overlay and is in a business zone where there is a great variety in building forms, ages, heights and styles, the answer to that question may well be good deal more straightforward than in a precinct-based Heritage Overlay, such as a residential area where there is a good deal of homogeneity in terms of building form, style and age. Reproduction architecture may be more readily acceptable to the local community than contemporary design, but contemporary design *per se* is not unacceptable: see *Colin v Port Phillip CC* [2000] VCAT 2073. At cl 19.03-2 of the SPPF of schemes it is stated in relation to heritage: "New development should respect, but not simply copy, historic precedents and create a worthy legacy for future generations".

Land to which heritage controls may apply

The *Planning and Environment Act* does not require the specification of areas in schemes as a precondition for including conservation and heritage controls, as was required under the *Town and Country Planning Act*. The implications of this are still unclear, but it would seem that theoretically controls on demolition and the design and decoration of buildings may be included in schemes and made applicable to any area, regardless of whether or not the area has heritage qualities. In practice the controls provided for by the Heritage Overlay apply to precincts or specific sites. Certainly the removal of the requirement to specify an area as being of natural beauty or interest or of importance as a precondition for clearing of trees and vegetation, as was required under cl 8A of the Third Schedule to the earlier Act, has enabled the inclusion in schemes of the Statewide requirement to secure a planning permit to remove, destroy or lop native vegetation.

In *Minnawood Pty Ltd v Bayside CC* [2009] VCAT 440 the Tribunal refused to allow the amendment of a permit under s 87A of the *Planning and Environment Act* to allow demolition of a building, even though the land was not included in a Heritage Overlay. The site was Khyat's Hotel, a landmark and "watering hole" in Brighton, in the Residential 1 Zone, and subject to a Design and Development Overlay, but not a Heritage Overlay. The permit allowed the development of 21 dwellings on the site but required the retention of the front part of the hotel. The amendment sought was to allow demolition of the front part of the building. The Tribunal held that the number of objections lodged to the permit application was evidence of the social and cultural significance of Khyat's Hotel, even though the building lacked sufficient architectural significance or integrity to justify it being included in a Heritage Overlay. It refused to amend the permit, despite the fact that the hotel was not subject to a Heritage Overlay and therefore a permit was not required for demolition. However, it must be emphasised that the matter before the Tribunal was an amendment to a permit. Its decision may well have been different if the matter had been an initial permit application to demolish the hotel *in toto*.

In imposing a duty via s 4 to further conservation objectives, the *Planning and Environment Act 1987* goes further than the *Town and Country Planning Act 1961*, which merely authorised the inclusion in schemes of conservation controls. However, this may afford little comfort to those residents' groups and historical societies who have been disappointed by the failure of their local councils to adopt the recommendations of heritage studies that suitable controls be introduced by scheme amendment to protect buildings, sites and precincts. The result has been that buildings and trees viewed by local communities as having important heritage significance have been removed to make way for new development. Councils and residents have been powerless to stop such actions – no planning permit has been required if those buildings or trees were not subject to planning controls on demolition or removal.

In summary, in terms of conservation and heritage planning the *Planning and Environment Act 1987* goes somewhat further than the *Town and Country Planning Act 1961* in that it imposes a duty on planning authorities in that schemes must seek to further conservation and heritage objectives within the context of the other objectives for planning in Victoria. The Act also authorises at least all those scheme controls that were authorised under the old Act, and provides greater flexibility in allowing for different types of controls in the future. However, it is important that the wider issues of conservation planning and heritage planning are not forgotten. Effective conservation of rural and urban sites and areas cannot be achieved through controls alone, which are essentially negative in nature – they do not provide incentive for owners to retain tree cover, protect the landscape, maintain buildings in good repair, or renovate. Incentives such as rating exemptions, taxation relief, grants and loans are essential companion mechanisms for implementing conservation objectives.

Buildings on the Heritage Register and planning permits

Before the approval and gazettal of the VPP-based planning schemes, a dual system of permits operated for buildings on the Registers pursuant to the *Historic Buildings Act* and (more recently) on the Victorian Heritage Register under the *Heritage Act 1995* which were also the subject of heritage controls under planning schemes. Permits were required from both the Historic Buildings Council / Heritage Council and the relevant responsible authority, normally the local council, for any alteration, removal or demolition. This sometimes resulted in a situation such as that which occurred in the City of Geelong, where the council determined to grant a permit under the Geelong Planning Scheme for the demolition of the Bow Truss building, but permission was not granted by the then Historic Buildings Council (HBC). (Following the intervention of the then Premier, Mr Cain, the Bow Truss building was removed from the Register of Historic Buildings and then demolished.) Administratively it would be much neater if only one permit was required, which could be achieved by dispensing with permits under the heritage legislation and making what is now the Heritage Council or its Executive Director a referral authority under the *Planning and Environment Act* for all places on the Register. Under s 61 of the *Planning and Environment Act* referral authorities effectively have the power of veto in that, if a referral authority objects to the grant of a permit, the planning authority must refuse to grant. If the referral authority does not object and the planning authority decides to grant a permit, it must include in the permit any conditions the referral authority requires.

The Heritage Overlay provisions go some way towards implementing such an arrangement. Under the Heritage Overlay, a planning permit is not required to develop a heritage place identified in the schedule to the overlay if the place is included on the Victoria Heritage Register and a permit for the development has been granted under the *Heritage Act* or the development is exempt under s 66 of that Act. While this may appear at first glance to be a useful administrative advance on the past, it should be remembered that, as noted earlier in this chapter, the permit system under the *Heritage Act* is seriously flawed in that it does not provide for third-party appeals against decisions to grant permits.

Planning permits and Aboriginal heritage

The objectives of the *Aboriginal Heritage Act 2006* include "to recognise protect and conserve Aboriginal cultural heritage in Victoria in ways that are based on respect for aboriginal knowledge and cultural and traditional practices": s 3(a). A responsible authority must not grant a planning permit for any "high impact activity" in any "area of cultural heritage sensitivity" (reg 6 of the *Aboriginal Heritage Regulations 2007*) within the meaning of the Act, unless a Cultural Heritage Management Plan (CHMP) has been prepared and approved.

A CHMP involves an assessment of the area to determine the nature of any Aboriginal cultural heritage present, and a written report setting out the results of that assessment and recommendations or measures to be taken before, during and after an activity to manage and protect the Aboriginal cultural heritage identified in the assessment. The written report is the CHMP: s 42. The CHMP must be prepared in accordance with standards prescribed in the regulations: s 53, and *Aboriginal Heritage Regulations 2007*, Part 4.

The preparation of a CHMP is mandatory if the regulations require its preparation, if the proponent or other person is required to prepare an Environment Effects Statement under the *Environment Effects Act 1978* (see Chapter 2), or if the project proponent is required to prepare an impact management plan or comprehensive impact statement in relation to a declared project under the *Major Transport Projects Facilitation Act 2009*: s 46.

Section 52 provides that a decision-maker must not grant a statutory authorisation for the activity unless a CHMP is approved under this part in respect of the activity. A statutory authorisation includes a permit under the *Planning and Environment Act 1987* to use or develop land for all or part of an activity: s 50. Sections 61–67 deal with the approval of a CHMP. Approval requires the approval of any registered Aboriginal parties who have elected to evaluate the plan: ss 55, 62–64. If there is no registered Aboriginal party in relation to the plan, or the relevant registered Aboriginal parties have given notice that they do not wish to evaluate the plan, the Secretary of the Department of Victorian Communities may approve the plan. If the Secretary is the sponsor of the CHMP, it is the Aboriginal Heritage Council established under s 130 of the Act which approves the plan. The sponsor of a CHMP may apply to VCAT for review of a decision to refuse approval of the plan: s 116:

> Pursuant to reg 6 of the *Aboriginal Heritage Regulations 2007*, a CHMP is required if all or part of the activity area for the proposed use or development of land is an area of cultural heritage sensitivity, and all or part of the activity is high impact. Regulations 7–19 set out the uses, development and works exempt from this requirement.

Regulations 20–38 set out the areas of cultural heritage sensitivity in Victoria. They are further defined by reference to map sheets specified in the regulations and, generally speaking, land within specified distances of those areas (such as waterways and land within 200 metres of a waterway), with the exception of land which has been subject to "significant ground disturbance". Aboriginal Affairs Victoria (<www.aboriginalaffairs.vic.gov.au>) provides a free online service for accessing the maps identifying areas of cultural heritage sensitivity.

The regulations set out a long list of "high impact" activities. If the construction of a building or the carrying out of works would result in "significant ground disturbance" and is for or associated with any of a long list of uses and development specified in regs 43–54, it falls within the meaning of "high impact activity".

"Significant ground disturbance" is defined in reg 40 to mean:

> Disturbance of–
> (a) the topsoil or surface rock layer of the ground; or
> (b) a waterway
> by machinery in the course of grading, excavating, digging, dredging or deep ripping, but does not include ploughing other than deep ripping.

"Deep ripping" is defined to mean:

> The ploughing of soil using a ripper or subsoil cultivation tool to a depth of 60 centimetres or more.

Because extensive areas of land can have cultural heritage sensitivity status, the issue of whether or not "significant ground disturbance" has occurred arises. In *Mainstay Australia Pty Ltd v Mornington Peninsula SC* [2009] VCAT 145, the permit applicant sought review of a refusal by the responsible authority to grant a permit for a 60-dwelling retirement village in Rosebud. The preliminary question to be determined by the Tribunal was whether an approved CHMP was required, because, if a CHMP was required, a planning permit could not be granted pursuant to s 52(1) of the *Aboriginal Heritage Act 2006*. It was agreed by the parties that the proposed use and development was not an exempt activity, it was a high-impact activity, and, subject to the issue of significant ground disturbance, the land was in an area of cultural heritage sensitivity. After hearing submissions from Aboriginal Affairs Victoria, the Tribunal set out four levels of inquiry to establish whether significant ground disturbance had occurred: Level 1 – common knowledge; Level 2 – publicly available records; Level 3 – further information from the applicant; and Level 4 – expert advice or opinion. The Tribunal was not persuaded by the applicant, who had made inquiries at all four levels, that the whole of the relevant land had been subject to significant ground disturbance. It held that part of the land had not been subject to significant ground disturbance and therefore was land which is in an area of cultural heritage significance, so a CHMP was required for the proposed activity.

In *Azzure Investment Group Pty Ltd v Mornington Peninsula SC* [2009] VCAT 1600, the applicant sought review of a failure by the responsible authority to grant a permit within the prescribed time for the use and development of land at Tootgarook as a service station, shop and associated uses. It was agreed by the parties that the development was not an exempt activity under the *Aboriginal Heritage Act*, the proposed development was a "high impact" activity" and the land was within an area of cultural heritage significance, being within 200 metres of the high-water mark of the coastal waters of Victoria. The land comprised three separate lots. The Tribunal accepted that, as two of the lots had been entirely covered with buildings and paved surfaces for many years, they had experienced "significant ground disturbance". The remaining lot had an area of 840 square metres, contained a dilapidated dwelling and outbuilding, was serviced with water and a sewer, and contained a redundant septic tank. The Tribunal found that the lot had experienced significant ground disturbance and therefore a CHMP was not required. In doing so the Tribunal commented that applying the levels of inquiry approach set out in *Mainstay* to smaller lots is anomalous and may lead to absurd situations. For instance, if there was no clear evidence of mechanical disturbance on 1 per cent of this lot, would this mean that a CHMP was required for this small, undisturbed area? The Tribunal observed (at 28):

> [F]or smaller subdivided urban lots (say, up to a standard quarter acre block, or perhaps 0.1 hectare in size) I think it is possible for a decision maker to be satisfied, on the balance of probabilities, based on a comparative and contextual approach, that there has been significant ground disturbance of the entire lot for the purpose of the AH regulations. This does not mean that all small urban lots should automatically be considered to have been the subject of past significant ground disturbance. However, in an established urban area, where a reasonable level of inquiry establishes that a lot has been extensively developed, serviced, and used over an extended period with significant site coverage by buildings and works, like mechanical grading or leveling as part of the subdivision, underground servicing, and with small yards or garden areas showing little or no signs of remnant vegetation or undisturbed ground, a finding of 'significant ground disturbance' of the entire lot is certainly open.

Chapter 9

COMPENSATION

There are very few circumstances in which compensation is payable for the impact of planning controls on private land, or indeed for the impact on nearby private land of public sector facilities such as airports, sewage plants and rubbish tips. Compensation is payable where land is compulsorily acquired by any public sector agency, including responsible authorities. This is usually referred to as acquisition compensation. It is also payable in a limited number of other circumstances prescribed by the *Planning and Environment Act 1987* in which no land is acquired. This is usually referred to as planning compensation.

To provide a context for understanding the circumstances in which acquisition compensation and planning compensation are payable, this chapter commences with a general discussion of the compensation issues that arise from both the impact of planning schemes and the development of facilities by the public sector on land set aside for public purposes. But first we will give a brief explanation of terms.

Planning schemes do not apply to Commonwealth land because, under the Australian Constitution, State legislation and therefore State subordinate legislation cannot bind the Commonwealth. Pursuant to the planning schemes in operation before the bringing into effect of the Victoria Planning Provisions (VPP) based planning schemes commencing in late 1998, land was either in a zone or a public purposes reservation. These schemes did not have zones and overlay controls. A public purpose reservation identified land as either being already in public ownership (such as land used for a government school, public road, public hospital, park et cetera) or proposed for a future public use (that is, intended to be acquired at some point in the future by a government department or public sector agency and used for a public purpose). Reservations could be for existing public purposes (that is, the land had been acquired by the public sector and was being used for a public purpose), or for proposed public purposes (that is, the land was still in private ownership but would be acquired by the public sector at some point in the future and used for a public purpose). In the VPP-based schemes brought into operation from late 1998 onwards, *reservations for existing public purposes* were replaced by various *public land zones*, while *reservations for proposed public purposes* were replaced by *Public Acquisition Overlays*. The purpose of the Public Acquisition Overlay stated in the VPPs and included in the State standard zones of every planning scheme in Victoria (see Chapter 3) includes "to reserve land for a public purpose and to ensure that the use or development of land do not prejudice the purpose for which the land is to be acquired".

Compensation issues and the impact of schemes
Betterment

It may seem a little strange to commence a discussion of compensation issues by focusing on betterment. However, it must be understood that the absence of betterment taxation goes some way towards explaining why compensation is not payable in a number of circumstances where equity considerations suggest that it should be.

Planning schemes inevitably impose some degree of interference with property rights. Depending on the zoning of an area, some uses and development will be prohibited and others will require planning consent, which may or may not be granted, or may be granted subject to conditions. Public Acquisition Overlays cast a shadow over land in that they indicate an intention that the land will be acquired in the future for public sector use and, in the interim, the use and development of such land requires planning consent. The use and development subsequently established by the public sector on the land may also have an impact on adjacent and nearby properties – freeways, sewage plants, and other facilities may have a negative impact on property values and on the general amenity levels of nearby land.

However, the impact of planning schemes on property values is not always negative. For example, a rezoning which permits greater intensity of development will cause the value of the area rezoned to climb. New road, rail and tram routes will have a positive effect on properties which benefit from greater access to shopping, work, recreation and so on, provided they are far enough away from the new routes to avoid the negative effects of factors such as noise. The development of land for parks and open space will have a positive effect on adjacent and nearby properties. The increase in the value of property caused by the decisions or actions of planning and other public authorities is called betterment. Betterment is unearned increment, which means that the owner of the land has done nothing to it to cause its value to rise and it is therefore a windfall gain (at least potentially). If it were to be somehow collected (either by an annual tax or by some form of impost levied when the unearned increment was realised; that is, when the property was sold) then theoretically this money could be used to compensate those whose property values fall as a result of planning activity and those whose properties are acquired in the course of implementing a scheme. In that sense, schemes could be self-financing. This is the argument which lies behind the betterment taxing proposals contained in the final report in 1929 of the Metropolitan Town Planning Commission, the first planning scheme prepared for metropolitan Melbourne, and included in the first planning legislation in Victoria in 1944. Included in the matters that could be provided for in schemes under the *Town and Country Planning Act 1944* was the following:

> Provision for ascertaining whether and by what amount (if any) the value of land is increased by the planning scheme, the levying of a betterment rate for the recovery of one half of such amount and for those purposes applying with any necessary adaptations the provisions of any enactments relating to those matters.

This clause was included in every subsequent *Town and Country Planning Act* and was not removed from the legislation until the introduction of the *Planning and Environment Act 1987.*

Betterment rates provided for by planning legislation in the past have never been imposed in Victoria. Part of the reason for this is that there are real difficulties involved in ascertaining the amount by which the value of land increases as a result of planning decisions. Other reasons include the political backlash which would follow the imposition of a betterment tax, and the problem of when the rate is to be collected (annually, at the time of sale, when the land is developed et cetera). On the whole, though, betterment taxation has not been politically acceptable in a country where one of the national hobbies is land speculation. The strategy of speculators large and small is to buy land and then wait until rezoning and/or the availability of services such as water and sewerage inflate its value.

Betterment rates or taxes should not be confused with development contributions levies imposed to fund infrastructure for new development. For example, such levies may be imposed pursuant to an approved Development Contributions Plan included as a part of the relevant planning scheme: see Chapter 3 and the *Planning and Environment Act 1987*, Part 3B. Such levies normally require the payment of a fixed sum per lot. Nor are betterment rates or taxes to be confused with contributions required pursuant to the Growth Areas Infrastructure Contributions (GAIC) provisions in Part 9B of the *Planning and Environment Act*. If a GAIC contribution is required, it is levied at a fixed sum per hectare ($80,000 or $95,000 per hectare, depending on the type of land involved).

The legislation setting up the development corporations which were responsible for constructing the British New Towns after World War II contained provisions for preventing betterment from occurring rather than for collecting it after it had occurred. The strategy was to enable the development corporations to harvest for themselves the betterment that resulted from the servicing and development of land and then use that revenue to meet the costs of developing the new towns. That was done by legislative provisions which allowed the development corporations to acquire land for a new town at green field prices, as if no decision had been made to include it in a new town. A similar mechanism was used in the legislation establishing the Albury-Wodonga Development Corporation in 1973. The Corporation was authorised to acquire property at prices excluding the impact on value of the designation of the new town area. Such a mechanism was also included in the *Development Areas Act 1973*, which was enacted by the Victorian Government during the Whitlam years when the Commonwealth was making housing grants to the States conditional on the States putting machinery in place to establish land commissions. The *Development Areas Act* was used in a very limited way in the late 1970s to stabilise land prices in some parts of the metropolitan rural-urban fringe. It had the potential to make a significant impact on the price of new housing and on the provision of social and physical infrastructure in new housing areas. For example, it could allow public agencies, such as the then Urban Land Authority, the predecessor of VicUrban, to purchase land without public sector services being capitalised into its price. Profits generated by the sale of developed land and housing could then be used to finance in part or whole the infrastructure of new estates. The potential of such an approach to intervening in the land market could only be fully realised if land were able to be compulsorily acquired, as provided for by the *Development Areas Act*, but this has proved to be politically unsustainable in the past and there is no reason why we should expect this to change in the future.

However, the issue of government intervention in the housing market in order to prevent betterment from occurring is a little different from the issue of collecting betterment after it has occurred, regardless of whether this betterment accrues to land which is used for housing or to land used for any other purpose. Without some form of betterment taxation it is impossible for governments to fund an equitable system which would allow those disadvantaged by planning and related government activities to be compensated, a conclusion reached in both the Gobbo Report of 1978 and the Morris Report of 1983 (see Further Reading).

Injurious affection

There is no compensation for injurious affection alone in Victoria. Injurious affection is the detrimental effect on private land of the public use or development of nearby land. The detrimental effect may be expressed by a decline in property values, or by a loss of amenity, or both. The effect on land values of noise and air pollution emanating from freeways is an example of injurious affection. The fall in amenity levels and land values of properties in Alexandra Parade in Melbourne due to the opening of the Eastern Freeway was a classic case of injurious affection. Widespread comment on the unfairness of owners and occupiers not being able to claim compensation, even for undertaking such remedial measures as the double-glazing of windows, was a major reason why the State government appointed the Gobbo inquiry into compensation and planning in 1976.

Injurious affection is not limited to the effect of freeways. The development of sewage plants, toxic waste dumps, landfill rubbish dumps, airports and jails, to name but a few of the public sector facilities which may have a detrimental effect on amenity and land values, may all cause injurious affection. While compensation cannot be claimed for injurious affection alone, it may be claimed in addition to severance where part of a property is acquired for a public purpose. In other words, if part of the properties in Alexandra Parade had been acquired for road widening, compensation would have been able to be claimed for the part of each property acquired, plus for any deleterious effect of that acquisition on the remainder of the property.

The absence of any opportunity to claim compensation for injurious affection alone means that individuals bear the cost of public sector decisions that are aimed at benefiting the community as a whole, but it is difficult to see how governments could afford to pay compensation to those who bear that cost without having access to funds generated by betterment taxes. There are also difficulties associated with establishing criteria for compensation claims for injurious affection. Noise, odour, air pollution and visual intrusion may all cause detrimental effects, but not all these are capable of quantitative measurement. The Gobbo Report recommended that compensation be able to be claimed when noise emanating from future freeways and future rail routes exceeded a threshold decibel level. While noise levels can be quantified, fixing a threshold level and the period of time for which that threshold must be exceeded before a claim may be made is essentially an arbitrary exercise. If you fall just below the threshold you cannot claim, but the detrimental effect you experience may be only very slightly less than the effect on someone who falls above the threshold and is able to claim. If the cause of the detrimental effect is not noise then you cannot claim at all. If claims may be made for the noise impact of future freeways and future rail routes, is it not inequitable that they cannot be made for the noise impacts of existing freeways and existing rail routes? And if they can be made for freeways and rail routes, why not for all roads, trams, airports and all other public sector facilities that cause noise? What about the situations where the impact from other sources of detrimental effect is much more severe than the impact of noise?

These are just some of the difficulties involved in providing an equitable solution to the problem of injurious affection. The Morris Report recommended that there be no compensation for injurious affection but that it be tackled by a comprehensive strategy including better planning, environmental standards to reduce nuisances at their source, remedial measures (such as double glazing) to reduce noise, special grants to local government to improve the amenity of communities affected and, as a last resort, requiring authorities to purchase properties irreparably harmed. However, there is still no right to claim the costs of remedial measures; grants to local government, even if they were made, may have little or no impact on the source of the injurious affection; and there is no legislative requirement for authorities to purchase properties irreparably harmed.

Severance

When part of a property is acquired for a public purpose, such as in an urban area when part of a front garden is acquired for road widening, or a strip through a farm is acquired for a rural freeway, compensation is available for the property acquired, plus for the effect of acquisition on the remainder of the property. The principles on which compensation is paid for the part of the land acquired are discussed below under the heading of "Acquisition", but here we are concerned with the deleterious effect of acquisition on the remainder of the property.

Severance is loss in value of the remainder caused by the acquisition of part of a property. Acquisition of a strip of land through a farm for a road or freeway may cut the farm in two parts, making it much less efficient to operate. The moving of stock and equipment from one part of the farm to the other may become more difficult, or the road or freeway may isolate water supply points for stock on one part only. The acquisition of part of a building site may make it uneconomic to develop the remainder, or make it impossible to gain planning permission because the relevant scheme specifies a minimum site area as a prerequisite for consent and the site now has an area less than that minimum.

The fact that compensation may be claimed for severance but not for injurious affection without acquisition is an anomaly. You may be far better off if you have part of your land acquired than if no part of it is acquired and you experience injurious affection to the point where the value of your property is decimated. The fact that compensation is not payable for injurious affection alone, but it is for severance, tends to encourage public sector agencies to acquire the whole of properties in urban areas. It is common when roads are widened for all of the abutting properties to be acquired, even when this is not strictly necessary to accommodate the road widening. In rural areas the boundaries of farm properties can be an important influence on the siting of new road and freeway routes. It may be financially more appropriate to run the new route along property boundaries than to have it crossing through properties simply because the chances of having to pay compensation for severance would be less.

Planning blight

When a public sector facility or works is proposed but no reservation in the form of a Public Acquisition Overlay for it appears on the relevant planning scheme map, planning blight may occur. For example, alternative routes for a freeway may be proposed for public discussion and consultation but, until a decision is made on its final route and the planning scheme has been amended to show the reservation in the form of a Public Acquisition Overlay to accommodate that route, the values of properties near *all* the proposed routes will fall. Similarly, if a number of alternative sites are proposed for a tip site or a sewage plant, the values of properties near *all* the proposed sites will fall until the final site is decided and a Public Acquisition Overlay is included in the relevant scheme.

Blight is a temporary condition, but for how long may a temporary condition last? How long is a piece of string? If someone has to sell, the price received will be less than the property is worth, simply because it is under the shadow of uncertainty. In some circumstances it may be impossible to find a buyer. In the absence of a reservation in the form of a Public Acquisition Overlay applying to the land as part of the planning scheme, there is no right to claim compensation for the difference between the price received at sale and the price the property would have sold for had it not been blighted. Morris recommended that in these circumstances the Minister have the power to deem land to be reserved and so qualify the seller to claim compensation for "sale at a loss" (see later in this chapter). This recommendation has been given effect by s 113 of the *Planning and Environment Act*, under which the Minister may declare land to be proposed for public purposes. However, there is no right given by this section – the power to declare land as proposed to be reserved is a discretionary power only, which the Minister may exercise as he or she thinks fit.

The longer the consultation process for deciding on one of a number of alternative sites for public facilities which depress surrounding property values, the more likely it is that individuals will be faced with potential financial loss. If lengthy consultation is to occur, the only way in which to safeguard these individuals is for the Minister to declare land to be proposed to be reserved for public purposes, which in turn leads to a drain on the public purse, including the purse of local government if the facility proposed is a municipal rubbish dump, a local park or a council depot.

Loss of development rights

No compensation may be claimed for the loss or diminution of development rights caused by the introduction or amendment of planning controls. For example, a person may purchase an allotment of, say, one hectare in size and intend to build a holiday house on it as allowed by controls in place at that time. In fact, a house may even be an as of right use. A subsequent amendment may make it impossible to build a house or anything else on an allotment of less than five hectares. Existing houses and houses under construction would be protected by the existing use rights provisions contained in s 6(3) of the *Planning and Environment Act*. If a planning permit was required to build a house under the old scheme provisions, a house could be built according to any permit issued. However, if the owner intended to establish the house in the future and had not applied for and been granted a permit at the time the amendment was approved and gazetted, it would be too late – development rights under the old controls have been lost, and as a consequence the value of the property will fall. In may even be impossible to sell the property. Who would want to buy it if it cannot be developed?

A scheme amendment may remove totally the right to develop a particular property, or it may reduce that right. For example, an amendment may reduce the range of uses and development that can be established by prohibiting some uses and development which were formerly permitted as of right or subject to planning consent. Reduction in the potential range of uses and development that may be established normally results in a diminution of property value.

It is sometimes argued that there should be compensation for loss or diminution of development rights, but those mounting this argument usually reject the notion of betterment taxation. In the absence of a betterment tax, this argument is, more often than not, really a plea for the public purse to provide a guarantee against the failure of speculative investment.

Heritage and environmental controls

The issue of compensation for the impact of heritage and like controls was discussed in Chapter 8. Compensation cannot be claimed for the effects of such controls, even where they may lead to what the Gobbo Report called loss of reasonable beneficial use. Perhaps the notion of loss of reasonable beneficial use is best illustrated by using an example in a rural setting. For example, in a particular rural area the planning scheme may prohibit a range of uses, including pig farming and poultry farming. A dairy farmer in this area may wish to change to more intensive types of farming because dairying is not yielding a reasonable return, but the prohibitions on pig farming, poultry farming and other more intensive farming uses would effectively lock the land into its current uneconomic use. The planning scheme may also prohibit subdivision of the land into allotments of less than a specified minimum size (such as 40 hectares), so the option of selling the property for hobby farm or rural residential development is not available.

This scenario is less likely these days because the Farming Zone now in place for most broadacre farming areas in Victoria contains generally more flexible provisions than the zones which preceded it. However, a loss of beneficial use situation may well result from the imposition of planning scheme controls on areas considered to be old and inappropriate subdivisions because of potential environmental impacts. Such areas may have been subdivided many years ago into lots similar in size to those found in suburban areas but have been identified as areas where development in the absence of a reticulated sewerage system may result in serious environmental degradation, such as contamination of water courses, lagoons and ground water by septic tank effluent. Planning controls in place (such as the Restructure Overlay) may have the effect of prohibiting the construction of any dwelling on a lot smaller than, say, five hectares. Lots smaller than this size are therefore unable to be developed and therefore may be unable to be used for any beneficial purpose. The options for owners are to continue to pay rates and hope that the controls may change (which is unlikely) or buy and sell among themselves and then resubdivide so that a smaller number of lots is created, each with an area the same or greater than the threshold size above which a permit may be granted.

Planning scheme controls aimed at achieving conservation or environmental protection objectives are imposed for the benefit of the community and, while they cannot be construed as reserving land for public purposes (see *Van der Meyden v MMBW* [1980] VR 225; *Equity Trustees Executors and Agency Co Ltd v MMBW* [1994] 1 VR 534), it should nevertheless be recognised that they may impose a significant burden on individuals. Loss of beneficial use probably occurs much more frequently than planning authorities and responsible authorities either realise or are prepared to admit.

Compulsory acquisition and compensation

Voluntary acquisition and compulsory acquisition

The law does not recognise absolute private ownership of land. Instead, what is recognised is interests in land. The highest form of interest in land is a tenancy of an estate in fee simple, which is what is meant by ownership. Other forms of interests in land include leaseholds of various duration, and tenancies of various duration. The tenancy of an estate in fee simple provides the right of occupation, enjoyment and use of land which is not limited by time constraints, as is, for example, a leasehold interest or a weekly tenancy interest. The right to use land is limited by the constraints imposed by legislation, such as the constraints imposed by planning legislation and the planning schemes approved under that legislation. The right to enjoy land is limited by the use and development permitted on abutting and nearby land and by the rights of enjoyment and use enjoyed by those who hold interests in that land.

Historically, absolute ownership of land has notionally resided in the Crown, but that notion has been altered somewhat with the advent of Commonwealth Native Title legislation, pursuant to which rights of occupation and use for a variety of purposes, including hunting, fishing and ceremonial activities, may be established on Crown land which has not been transferred to private, fee simple ownership. When Crown land is transferred to fee simple ownership, it is referred to as being alienated from the Crown. Historically, land was alienated from the Crown and transferred to fee simple ownership by, initially, Crown Grants, and then later, as separate colonies were established, by sale. When Crown land is transferred to private ownership, what is being alienated is the right of occupation, enjoyment and use, which of course may be translated into a commodity that can be bought and sold. Those rights may be reclaimed by the public sector (that is, by the Crown or an agent of the Crown) through negotiation and agreement – a process known as voluntary acquisition. However, they may also be reclaimed in the absence of agreement, in circumstances and according to procedures prescribed by legislation. This latter reclamation is known as compulsory acquisition. When land is acquired by the public sector it is sometimes referred to as resumption. What is being resumed is the rights which were granted when the land was originally alienated from the Crown. If land is acquired by a public sector agency on a voluntary basis, the price negotiated with those who hold interests in the land is the compensation paid for relinquishing their rights. In the case of compulsory acquisition the price to be paid in the form of compensation is governed by the provisions of the relevant legislation, which in Victoria is the *Land Acquisition and Compensation Act 1986*.

The implementation of planning schemes inevitably involves the acquisition of land. The extension of existing public facilities or the provision of new public facilities such as airports, government schools, cemeteries, parks, public hospitals, libraries, roads and so on involves the acquisition of land by the public sector. In some instances land may be able to be acquired on a voluntary basis; that is, on the basis of negotiation and agreement. However, in many, and perhaps even in the majority of instances, acquisition will be resisted and the powers of compulsory acquisition will need to be exercised.

The scope of compulsory acquisition powers

The *Planning and Environment Act 1987* confers very wide powers of compulsory acquisition on the Minister and responsible authorities. Under s 172 the Minister or the responsible authority may compulsorily acquire four categories of land. The first of these is "any land which is required for the purposes of any planning scheme, even if the scheme or an amendment to the scheme including the requirement has not been adopted by the relevant planning authority or approved by the Minister": s 172(1)(a). Note that any land may be acquired, and that land is defined by s 3 to include buildings and other structures, land covered with water, and "any estate, interest, easement, servitude, privilege or right over land".

The second category of land which may be compulsorily acquired is vacant and unoccupied land, which, in the opinion of the Minister or responsible authority, it is desirable should be put to an appropriate use to achieve the proper development of the area in accordance with the planning scheme: s 172(1)(b). The third is "any land which is used for any purpose not in conformity with, whether or not actually prohibited by, the planning scheme" which, in the opinion of the Minister or responsible authority, it is desirable should be put to a more appropriate use to achieve the proper development of the area in accordance with the planning scheme: s 172(1)(b). The fourth is land in an area the Governor in Council has declared under s 172(2). The Governor in Council can make a declaration brought into effect by notice published in the *Government Gazette* that it is satisfied that, to enable the better use, development or planning of an area, it is desirable that the Minister or responsible authority compulsorily acquire land in the area.

The procedures to be used in compulsory acquisition and the principles governing the amount to be paid as compensation for such acquisition are found in the *Land Acquisition and Compensation Act 1986.*

Land to be compulsorily acquired must first be reserved

One of the reforms to the compulsory acquisition process recommended in the Morris Report was that land be reserved in a planning scheme before the commencement of compulsory acquisition procedures. The rationale for this recommendation was that reservation (by the introduction of a Proposed Public Purposes Reservation over the land concerned in the days before the advent of the VPP-based schemes, and by a Public Acquisition Overlay thereafter) should only be achieved by a scheme amendment. The processes of scheme amendment would provide the opportunity for those with an interest in the property to contest the decision to acquire. This contesting of the decision would take the form of lodging objecting submissions to the proposed amendment and then, should the planning authority decide not to accommodate these submissions, the presentation of these submissions to a panel appointed by the Minister under s 153 of the *Planning and Environment Act 1987.* In other words, the decisions of public sector agencies about their own works programmes could be subject to some degree of public scrutiny and public accountability. For proposed new roads, freeways, municipal car parks and so on, not only could those whose land is to be acquired lodge submissions and secure a hearing before a panel but also so could others who would be affected. Submittors could canvass the issue of whether or not there was a need for the proposed facility as well as its proposed location or route.

This recommendation has, in the main, been incorporated into the legislation. Section 5(1) of the *Land Acquisition and Compensation Act* states "The authority must not commence to acquire any interest in land under the provisions of the special Act unless the land has been first reserved by or under a planning instrument for a public purpose". Section 172(3) of the *Planning and Environment Act* declares it to be a special Act and also declares the Minister or responsible authority to be an authority within the meaning of the *Land Acquisition and Compensation Act*. Public Acquisition Overlays in planning schemes reserve land for a public purpose (refer to the beginning of this chapter).

Section 20 of the *Planning and Environment Act* empowers the Minister to exempt a planning authority from the notification requirements of s 19, as was explained in Chapter 4. Under s 20(3) this power does not extend to certain amendments, including those which provide for the reservation of land for public purposes. Where an amendment is to reserve land via a Public Acquisition Overlay, at least the owners and occupiers of the land must be notified. However, governments are reluctant to bind themselves to the same procedures they impose on everyone else. The Minister may prepare an amendment to any planning scheme and then may exempt himself or herself under s 20(4) from *any* of the requirements of ss 17, 18 and 19. Matters dealt with in these sections include notification of owners and occupiers. If they do not know about the proposed amendment, they cannot contest the decision to acquire by making a submission to the Minister, nor have submissions referred to a panel. If the Minister exempts himself or herself, the amendment can be prepared and gazetted without any process of public consultation. Therefore, where the planning authority is a council or a person authorised by the Minister to be a planning authority, at least the owners of land proposed to be reserved by an amendment must be notified, given opportunity to make submissions and, if required, have those submissions referred to a panel, which must give them reasonable opportunity to be heard. This may not lead to the report of the panel before which they contest the decision to acquire being taken into account by the planning authority. As was explained in Chapter 4, s 27(2) and (3) allows the Minister to exempt a planning authority from considering a panel's report. However, they cannot be guaranteed even of notification if the Minister is the planning authority.

Bodies which may compulsorily acquire land are not restricted to the Minister and responsible authorities. Municipal councils have compulsory acquisition powers under the *Local Government Act*. Many public authorities may also compulsorily acquire land. It should come as no surprise that the *Land Acquisition and Compensation Act* provides for these authorities a number of exceptions to the general rule that land must be reserved before acquisition. While s 5(1) lays down the general rule that the procedures for compulsory acquisition must not commence until land is reserved, subsequent subsections provide a series of exemptions from this requirement. Section 5(2) provides that this requirement does not apply in respect of prescribed land or land in a prescribed class of land. Therefore, exceptions to the normal requirement may be provided for simply by regulations approved by the Governor in Council. Under the *Land Acquisition and Compensation Regulations 1998* acquisition without prior reservation is authorised in a number of circumstances. The first is for minor road widening where the land to be acquired is less than 10 per cent of the value and also less than 10 per cent of the area of the total allotment. The second is where an easement is acquired, if the acquisition does not reduce the value of the allotment by 10 per cent.

Section 5(3) provides that the requirement of reservation before acquisition does not apply if the Governor in Council certifies, on the recommendation of the Minister, that reservation is "unnecessary, undesirable or contrary to the public interest". This provides the government of the day with the power to make exceptions to the general rule as it sees fit. Section 5(4A) states that the requirement to reserve before acquisition does not apply to any land in respect of which a declaration has been made under s 172(2) of the *Planning and Environment Act*, which allows the Governor in Council to declare that, to enable the better use, development or planning of an area, the Minister or a responsible authority may compulsorily purchase land in the area. Again, this provides very wide and sweeping powers for the government of the day to make exceptions to the general rule. Section 5(4B) provides that reservation before acquisition does not apply to any land which is special project land under s 201F of the *Planning and Environment Act 1987*. Such land is for a project of State or regional significance and the Secretary of the Department of Sustainability and Environment may acquire such land without it first being reserved for a public purpose, provided the Minister has declared by notice published in the *Government Gazette* that it is required for a declared project.

Where the owner is already attempting to sell land, or where the acquiring authority has commenced negotiations with owners to acquire on a voluntary basis, there is no requirement of reservation before acquisition.

The price paid

Where voluntary acquisition occurs, the price paid by the acquiring authority is a matter of negotiation and agreement with the owner and any others who have an interest in the land, such as lease holders. For compulsory acquisition, the amount paid as compensation is governed by the provisions of the *Land Acquisition and Compensation Act 1986*. The most significant element of that price is the market value of the property at the date of acquisition. Market value is defined by s 40 as the "amount of money that would have been paid ... if it had been sold on that date by a willing but not anxious seller to a willing but not anxious purchaser". In other words, the market value of the property is the price that would be paid if it were sold on the open market, either by private sale or by auction.

Where land is not subject to a Public Acquisition Overlay, the market value of the property is not shadowed. However, where the land has been reserved by the introduction of a Public Acquisition Overlay over it, the shadow of the reservation may have a significant effect on the price paid if it were offered for sale on the open market. After all, who would want to buy, for example, a residential property that was reserved for a road widening? The market value of reserved land is the value according to the zoning that applies to the land, ignoring the effect on the value of the land of the Public Acquisition Overlay.

Section 6(2)(i) of the *Planning and Environment Act* provides that a planning scheme may state the provisions of a planning scheme that would apply to reserved land if such land had not been reserved. If a scheme does not show the underlying zoning of reserved land, s 201 provides that it may be shown on a planning certificate, except where the land is already owned by the Crown or a public authority. Under s 198 any person may apply for a planning certificate to the person nominated in the scheme for that purpose or, if no person is nominated, to the responsible authority. A planning certificate is a statement of the scheme controls that apply to a particular allotment. If a planning certificate states that land is wholly or partly reserved for public purposes but does not state the underlying zoning, the applicant may apply under s 201(1) for a declaration of what the underlying zoning is. The application for such a declaration is made to the Minister if the land is owned or controlled by the responsible authority. "Controlled" in this sense means controlled on behalf of a responsible authority, as by a committee of management, for example. If the property is not owned or controlled by the responsible authority, application is made to the person nominated by the scheme or, if no person is nominated, to the responsible authority. Should that declaration not be made within the prescribed time of 45 days, the Minister may make the declaration.

It is doubtful if there is now any need for ss 6(2)(i) and 201 to remain in the *Planning and Environment Act*. When the Act was brought into effect, the VPP-based schemes were not in place. Under the planning schemes at that time, land was included either in a zone or in a public purposes reservation. The notion of the underlying zoning of land – that is, the zoning which would have applied had the public purposes reservation not been in place – was therefore critical to establishing the market value of land to be acquired. Nowadays, generally speaking, all land is zoned and it is the Public Acquisition Overlay that identifies land proposed to be reserved and acquired. The notion of underlying zoning is therefore no longer applicable.

While market value is the key element in the price paid for property that is compulsorily acquired, there are other elements taken into account. Section 41(1) of the *Land Acquisition and Compensation Act* requires that regard must also be had to the following: special value to the claimant; any loss attributable to severance; any loss attributable to disturbance; the enhancement or depreciation of value of other land severed from the acquired part if only part of the property was acquired; and any legal, valuation and other professional expenses necessarily incurred by the claimant.

While discussion in detail of these elements is beyond the scope of this book, nevertheless a brief explanation of what they mean may be useful to the reader. (For further information, see Chapter 11 of Planning Commentary in Byard, Code, Porritt and Testro, *Planning and Environment Service*, Vol 1 Butterworths.)

Special value is defined by s 40 as "the value of any pecuniary advantage, in addition to market value, to a claimant which is incidental to his ownership or occupation of that land". For example, an owner suffering from some physical disability may have had his or her home fitted with ramps, handrails and other aids to mobility.

The cost of installing these facilities will not be reflected in the market value of the property, but they do constitute a special value to the owner.

Loss attributable to disturbance is defined by s 40 and includes the loss of localised goodwill and the costs of dismantling, removing and reinstalling stock, plant, machinery and fittings. It also includes the costs of removal, expenses incurred in advising clients and customers of a new location, reprinting of stationery and the like. These are pecuniary losses experienced as the natural, direct and reasonable consequence of the acquisition. Section s 41(2) limits claims for special value and loss attributable to disturbance. The limitation is as follows:

> Section 41(2) If the market value of the interest in land is assessed on the basis that the land had potential to be used for a purpose other than the purpose for which it was used on the date of acquisition, compensation must not be allowed for –
>
> (a) any special value in respect of any pecuniary advantage that would necessarily have been forgone in realizing that potential; and
> (b) any loss attributable to disturbance that would necessarily have been incurred in realizing that potential.

This limitation is necessary to prevent double-dipping, as illustrated by the example used in para 628 of the Morris Report (see Further Reading):

> The owner of farm land who is compensated on the basis of the value of the land for residential development would not be permitted to recover the costs of dismantling, removing and re-installing farm machinery, as such costs would necessarily have been incurred were the farmer to realise the highest and best use of the land on which the valuation was made.

Severance in relation to injurious affection on the balance of the property not acquired was discussed earlier in this chapter. It means the loss in value of the remainder caused by the acquisition of part of a property. However, the Act also recognises that the purpose to which the severed part is put may have a positive effect on value. That beneficial effect may extend to adjacent or nearby land owned by the claimant. For example, if part of a property were acquired for a park it may well have the effect of enhancing not only the value of the part of the property not acquired but also nearby properties owned by the person from whom land was acquired.

Solatium may be paid at the discretion of the acquiring authority for intangible and non-pecuniary disadvantages resulting from the acquisition. Solatium is provided for by s 44 of the *Land Acquisition and Compensation Act* and by s 100 of the *Planning and Environment Act*. For acquisition under the *Planning and Environment Act*, solatium is available only for residences and the relevant circumstances to be taken into account when determining the amount to be paid (which must not exceed the total amount paid under other headings of claim and is limited to an amount not greater than 10 per cent of the market value of the land) include the interest of the claimant in the property, the length of time the claimant has occupied the property, the claimant's age, and the number, age, and circumstances of other people living with the claimant.

Under s 45 of the *Land Acquisition and Compensation Act*, loans to dispossessed home owners may be made available by the acquiring authority and must be made available if directed by a tribunal or court, which raises the question of how disputes about compensation are resolved (see below). Such loans may be with or without interest and are aimed at bridging the gap where the amount received as compensation is not enough to pay for a comparable residence elsewhere. Under s 45(1)(b) the circumstances in which loans may be granted are restricted to where the market value of the property acquired does not exceed the amount prescribed from time to time by the Governor in Council. Currently that amount is $250,000: *Land Acquisition and Compensation Regulations 1998*, reg 22. Loans must be secured by a mortgage of the interest in the land purchased by the claimant and are repayable in circumstances such as the sale of the house, or if the claimant and the claimant's spouse die.

Other circumstances where compensation is payable under the Planning and Environment Act – planning compensation

Planning compensation is the term normally used when compensation may be payable but no property is acquired. In addition to the circumstances discussed below, compensation claims may arise in relation to enforcement procedures, as discussed in Chapter 7. The possibility of compensation being claimed in relation to applications for cancellation of permits and orders to stop development is a necessary "brake" on these mechanisms to prevent frivolous or vexatious applications.

Sale at a loss of reserved land

Section 98 of the *Planning and Environment Act* lists the circumstances other than acquisition in which compensation is payable. See *City of Nunawading v Day* [1992] VR 211 at 266; 6 AATR 346 at 360, and *Halwood Corporation Ltd v Roads Corporation* (1995) 89 LGRA 280 at 286, for a discussion on the subject matter of a claim for compensation. The matters include where the owner or occupier suffers financial loss as "the natural, direct and reasonable consequence of" land being reserved for a public purpose under a planning scheme; land being shown as reserved for a public purpose in a proposed scheme amendment of which notice has been given under s 19; and land being declared to be a proposed reservation by the Minister under s 113. The power of the Minister to declare land to be a proposed reservation was discussed above in relation to planning blight.

The function of a reservation via a Public Acquisition Overlay is to indicate quite clearly an intention of the public sector to acquire the land to which the overlay applies. However, what happens when an owner has to sell such land, perhaps due to a change in employment or family circumstances, and the authority at whose behest the Public Acquisition Overlay was included in the scheme refuses to purchase it at that time? As authorities do have limited financial resources, it is quite common for them to plan their acquisitions on the basis of a five- or 10-year rolling programme.

If the owner must sell on the open market, the price paid by another purchaser will be less than if the Public Acquisition Overlay was not in place. Under s 106 the owner may claim the "loss on sale", which is the difference between the purchase price and the price that would have been paid had the land not been reserved via the Public Acquisition Overlay. In other words, it is the difference between the price paid by the purchaser and the market value of the property according to the underlying zoning. There are certain procedural matters that have to be attended to by the seller of property in this situation – under s 106(1)(b), notice must be given in writing of the intention to sell not less than 60 days before the sale takes place. This requirement may be waived in the event that the owner and the planning authority have agreed that notice need not be given or, either before or after the sale, the Minister grants an exemption from giving notice on the grounds of hardship.

Only the original owner who sells at a loss may claim. A subsequent owner who purchased at a price lower than market value cannot claim. The rationale is that the new owner was aware or should have been aware of the restriction before purchasing. In *Halwood Corporation* (see above) the Court of Appeal held that an owner who had purchased land after it had been reserved for a public purpose cannot claim compensation for financial loss resulting from the reservation. In *Analed Pty Ltd v Roads Corporation* [1998] VSC 174 the Supreme Court, having applied the principles set out in *Halwood,* held that a purchaser has no right to compensation if the purchaser, at the time of purchase, knew that the land was proposed or under investigation for reservation, even though the reservation was not in place.

Loss on sale may be claimed where land is reserved via a Public Acquisition Overlay or is proposed to be so reserved in a planning scheme amendment which has been drafted and for which notification and exhibition procedures have commenced, and where the Minister has declared land to be proposed to be reserved. The waiving of the requirement for the owner to notify in writing the planning authority under s 106(2) is to accommodate situations such as where the existence of a proposed Public Acquisition Overlay in a scheme amendment becomes known less than 60 days before the sale occurs.

Where sale at a loss has been paid, the planning authority is placed in an unenviable situation if the Public Acquisition Overlay is removed or lapses. Section 107 provides a right for an owner to claim compensation for any financial loss suffered as the natural, direct and reasonable consequence of an amendment which removes a reservation, the lapsing of an amendment which proposed to reserve land, or the cancellation of a Ministerial declaration made under s 113. However, it is probably easier to imagine situations where any of these circumstances may produce a need for planning authorities and public authorities to recover compensation already paid, such as where compensation has been paid for sale at a loss. The person from whom compensation is to be recovered is not the person who received the difference between the sale price and market value but the new owner who benefited from the lower sale price. Section 111 provides for compensation already paid to be recovered from the new owner on demand or within any further agreed period. There is provision under s 111(3) for the amount to be paid when the property is sold or transferred at some point in the future if the Minister administering the *Land Acquisition and Compensation Act* thinks it would cause hardship to the owner to pay on demand.

Refusal of planning consent for reserved land

The owner or occupier may claim compensation for financial loss suffered as the natural, direct and reasonable consequence of a refusal by the responsible authority to grant a permit to use or develop land on the ground that the land is or will be required for a public purpose: s 98(2). Again, the financial loss must an actual loss, not the loss of hoped-for gain. However, where land is reserved and the owner had knowledge of that reservation when it was purchased, any financial loss suffered by the owner where a permit is refused is a consequence of the owner purchasing it with that knowledge rather than as a "natural, direct and reasonable consequence of the reservation": *Halwood Corporation Ltd v Roads Corporation* [1998] 2 VR 439. The right to claim depends on an application being made and then refused on that ground. However, there are three ways in which that refusal may occur. The first is where the responsible authority refuses to grant: s 99(a)(i). The second is where the decision of the responsible authority has been the subject of review proceedings and VCAT directs that a permit must not be granted on the ground that land is or may be required for a public purpose: s 99(a)(ii). The third is where the responsible authority fails to determine the application or imposes a condition unacceptable to the applicant. In any of these circumstances the applicant may seek review before VCAT, in which case VCAT may refuse to grant a permit on the ground that the land is or may be required for a public purpose. For a discussion on the requirements of s 99, see *Halwood Corporation Ltd v Roads Corporation* [1998] 2 VR 439.

The ability to claim compensation for refusal on the grounds that land is, will or may be required for a public purpose may be more apparent than real. As a claim may be made only for the financial loss suffered as the natural, direct and reasonable consequence of refusal, that loss may be very limited, perhaps only to the professional fees incurred in preparing plans and lodging the application, plus the prescribed fee which must accompany the application under s 47(b). In addition, the application must be for something for which a permit could be issued – the application cannot be for a use that either requires no permit or is prohibited by the scheme provisions. A further limitation is imposed by s 108, which states that a claim may be made only by the owner or occupier of the land at the time when the right to claim arose. Persons who acquire land or become occupiers after a permit has been refused on the ground that the land is or will be required for a public purpose may not claim.

Access restricted by closure of a road

The owner or occupier may claim compensation for the financial loss suffered as the natural, direct and reasonable consequence of access to the land being restricted by the closure of a road by a planning scheme. The right to claim does not depend on application for a permit being made or refused but simply on the approval and gazettal of a scheme or amendment under which the road is closed: s 99(c). Again the opportunity to claim may be more apparent than real, for, in many instances, such as the establishment of a pedestrian mall, it may well be that quite the opposite of financial loss occurs. Even if financial loss does occur, it is not enough to allege it – it must be proved, and also proved to be the natural, direct and reasonable consequence of access being restricted.

Inaccurate planning certificate

Planning certificates state the scheme provisions that apply to any area of land. They are required under s 199(1) to contain prescribed information. The information prescribed by reg 57 of the *Planning and Environment Regulations 2005* includes "a description of the provisions of the planning scheme maps which apply to the land" and "a description of any amendment to the planning scheme maps available under section 18 which apply to the land". In other words, the certificate must state the current planning controls which apply to the land, plus the controls on the land proposed in any amendment which has been prepared and has reached the initial stage in the amendment process where a notice of an amendment has been given to the persons and organisations specified in s 17.

All that certificates do is provide a starting point for establishing the controls that apply or are intended to apply after an amendment currently being processed has been approved. Prospective developers really must go to the scheme and changes contained in proposed amendments to establish the nature of the controls that apply or may apply in the relatively near future. However, a certificate which "appears to be produced by authority of an officer of the responsible authority or by a nominated person is conclusive proof that at the date specified in the certificate the facts set out in it were true and correct": s 200(1). Under s 200(2) a person who suffers financial loss because of an error or misstatement in a certificate may recover damages for that loss from the responsible person or the nominated person. No procedure is specified in the *Planning and Environment Act* for recovering such damages. An action would need to be brought in a court.

Time limit on claims, who pays, and how disputes are resolved

Time limit on claims

Subject to s 106(2), a claim for compensation must be made within two years after the following: refusal to grant a permit by the responsible authority on the ground that the land is or will be required for a public purpose; VCAT directs that a planning permit must not be granted on the grounds that the land is or will be required for a public purpose, or disallows any appeal on the ground that the land is or will be required for a public purpose; sale at a loss of land reserved for a public purpose; the gazettal of a planning scheme or an amendment which restricts access to the land by closure of a road: see *Land Acquisition and Compensation Act*, s 37. Section 106(1) of that Act provides that the normal two-year time limit may be abridged by the Governor in Council, extended by the Minister, or extended by agreement or by a court or tribunal.

Who pays?

Section 98(1) of the *Planning and Environment Act 1987* provides that the responsible authority must inform any person who asks it to do so of the person or body from whom compensation may be claimed. For land which is subject to a Public Acquisition Overlay, the Minister or the public authority at whose behest the land was reserved, or is proposed to be reserved under an amendment, has to meet any compensation claim. Section 109 specifies that the Minister or the public authority is liable if the Minister or public authority has asked the planning authority in writing to reserve land under a scheme or scheme amendment. Where the Minister has declared land to be proposed to be reserved under s 113, it is the Minister, or the public authority that requested in writing such a declaration, who is liable. A referral authority is liable for compensation arising from a refusal to grant a permit because the referral authority objected on the ground that the land is or will be required for a public purpose.

However, it should be remembered that planning authorities and responsible authorities may also be liable for claims in relation to land which is subject to a Public Acquisition Overlay. For example, municipal councils may, via the Public Acquisition Overlay, reserve land for future municipal landfills and other rubbish dumps, council depots, council car parks and so on. In these instances they bear the cost of acquisition and the cost of compensation for sale at a loss, and are also liable for claims arising from refusal of planning permission on the ground that the land is or will be required for a public purpose.

Resolution of disputes

If there is a dispute about the amount of compensation to be paid, it may be referred to the Supreme Court or VCAT, depending on the amount in dispute: *Land Acquisition and Compensation Act*, s 81. If the amount in dispute is less than $50,000, the dispute must be determined by VCAT; if it is more than $50,000, it is determined by the Supreme Court or VCAT at the option of the claimant, or, if the claimant does not exercise that option within one month of being requested to do so by the authority, at the option of the authority; "or by the Supreme Court irrespective of the amount, if the Court is satisfied on the application of any party that the claim raises questions of unusual difficulty or of general importance". The "amount in dispute" is defined in s 81(2) as "the amount of the difference between the amount claimed by the claimant and the amount of the final offer made by the Authority before the application is made to the Tribunal in respect of the claim or the matter is referred to the Court".

Chapter 10

WHERE ARE WE HEADING?

Long-standing tensions in the Victorian planning system

In the past, changes to the planning system have been, at least in part, a reflection of the State government's changing responses to a series of enduring problems. These include:

- the related problems of co-ordination of the agencies of government, as well as the co-ordination of bodies directly involved in the preparation and administration of planning controls;
- the respective powers of municipalities and the State government in preparing, administering and changing those controls;
- the provision of third party rights in relation to planning permits and planning scheme amendments; and
- the tensions associated with providing a measure of certainty as well as flexibility in planning controls.

In terms of the power relationships between the levels of the planning system, the way in which the system has been used (and abused) has been as significant as the way it has been altered by legislative change. Since the early 1980s the story of the system has been very much its subjugation to the corporate strategies of the Victorian Government, particularly in relation to economic growth and the stimulations of employment. All too often, planning has appeared to be viewed by the State Government as an impediment to growth, thereby justifying in its eyes Ministerial intervention in planning scheme amendments, the calling-in of permit applications, and the calling-in of applications for review.

The draft Planning and Environment Amendment (General) Bill, released in late 2009, in some respects reflects the ongoing tensions referred to above, while at the same time foreshadowing an increasing level of complexity of process. While some of the changes proposed in the Bill are positive (such as removing the Minister's involvement in ending and amending s 173 agreements and alteration of the processes for ending and amending agreements), we are of the view that the main changes proposed raise some serious issues.

The draft Planning and Environment Amendment (General) Bill

The Department of Planning and Community Development established a Planning Act Review Team to undertake a review of the *Planning and Environment Act* during the course of 2009. In March 2009 a discussion paper, *Modernising Victoria's Planning Act*, was released for comment. Following the receipt of submissions to this paper, the Review Team published seven response papers, proposing "reforms" as follows:

- update the objectives of planning in Victoria;
- improve the operation of the amendment process;
- improve the operation of the permit process;
- introduce a new procedure for the consideration of projects declared as State significant major development;
- improve the operation of s 173 agreements;
- provide for monitoring and reporting on the performance of the planning system through annual reporting; and
- a range of miscellaneous changes to improve the operation of the Act.

Following a round of submissions in response to these papers, the Draft Planning and Environment (General Amendment) Bill and Commentary was released for comment by the Department of Planning and Community Development in December 2009. A total of 167 submissions to the Draft Bill were received during March to May 2010. Since then there has been an eerie silence. It does seem to us that it is unlikely that the great majority of the proposals in the Draft Bill will be translated into law in the near future. However, these proposals seem to indicate the general thrust and direction of the previous Labor Government's thinking and are likely to be the subject of continuing debate among planning professionals and the community and organisations such as residents' groups. We have devoted this last chapter to the main changes to the Act proposed in the Draft Bill which we consider raise very serious questions.

The Draft Bill and associated documents are available on the Department of Planning and Community Development's website at <www.dpcd.vic.gov.au>.

State significant developments

It is proposed to have a separate process for dealing with State significant projects. Classes of developments which may be State significant developments are to be prescribed by regulation. It is suggested that these be developments such as:

- renewable energy and wind facilities worth in excess of 30 MW;
- those which involve capital expenditure greater than $100 million and are in the metropolitan area;
- infrastructure by or on behalf of the State (such as ports, and transport projects except where the *Major Transport Projects Facilitation Act 2009* applies).

The *Major Transport Projects Facilitation Act 2009* applies to major projects declared by the Governor in Council on the recommendation of the Premier after being assessed as being of State or regional economic, social or environmental significance. It is discussed in Chapter 5.

The process proposed for State significant developments is:

- application is made to the Minister for approval of a project as of State significance;
- notification and consultation of project in accordance with the Minister's directions; submissions and the proponent's report on submissions must be referred to a Panel appointed by the Minister (the Panel is not explicitly bound by the rules of natural justice);
- the reporting of the Panel to the Minister;
- the Minister may decide to approve or not approve a project as being of State significance;
- the Minister may amend the relevant planning scheme or grant a permit without any further process; and
- enforcement of any permit granted by the Minister is the duty of the relevant local responsible authority.

The Minister's amendment of the planning scheme and/or the Minister's decision to grant a permit is not subject to appeal to the Victorian Civil and Administrative Tribunal (VCAT) or (presumably) the courts.

The proposed powers of the Minister in relation to such projects are in addition to the Minister's current powers pursuant to s 20(4) of the Act to amend a scheme without any of the normal processes of notification, consideration of submissions, referral to a Panel, Panel hearing and report et cetera. They are also in addition to the Minister's current powers to "call in" a permit application pursuant to ss 97A–97M, and to call in an application for review pursuant to cll 58 and 59 of Schedule 1 to the *VCAT Act*. They inevitably further erode the powers of municipal councils, public participation in decision-making, and independent scrutiny by VCAT of development proposals. It is likely that projects of State significance are likely to be reasonably large projects, which are therefore likely to have environmental and other impacts of a magnitude which makes independent scrutiny even more important.

However, the ability to prescribe by regulation which projects are of State significance allows the Minister and the government of the day to prescribe even small projects which may be of State significance. The suggestions that they be projects worth more than $100 million in the metropolitan area and more than $50 million in non-metropolitan areas indicate that they do not have to be large projects, but they may turn out to be a great deal smaller than that. The question then arises as to whether the State significance track is really a means of ensuring both local employment and investment while at the same time giving favoured treatment to favoured applicants – a question which is already often asked in the community about the exercise of the Minister's current powers.

It also seems a little odd for the local council to be responsible for enforcing the conditions of any permit the Minister grants pursuant this process. It may well be that the local council is opposed to such a permit being granted, or opposed to the conditions in it. That is hardly an incentive to assiduously police it.

Planning scheme amendments

It is proposed to establish separate "tracks" for the assessment of technical and standard amendments. The technical amendment track is to be very similar to the process of amendment pursuant to s 20(4) – amendment by the Minister and notice of the amendment published in the *Government Gazette*. It is proposed that a class of amendments for technical matters will be prescribed. A technical amendment may include: corrections to anomalous provisions and removal of redundant provisions; changes to ensure provisions reflect the policy intent of the planning scheme; amendments to the VPP; and amendments for the introduction of interim provisions.

Under the technical amendment track:

- any person may apply to the Minister to prepare a technical amendment;
- the Minister prepares the amendment;
- the Minister may consult with the planning authority for the relevant planning scheme (this will not be necessary if the planning authority has requested the amendment);
- the Minister approves the amendment;
- a notice regarding the approval of the amendment is published in the *Government Gazette*.

The amendment is not exhibited and the submission and panel steps do not apply. An explanatory report is required but will be simplified.

The standard amendment track is to be the "normal" process as it now stands – notification, submissions, panel hearing etc as discussed in Chapter 4. However, there is nothing in the Draft Bill to suggest that the Minister will not be able, as he or she sees fit, to exempt him- or herself from any of the normal processes for a standard amendment, and approve the amendment.

But the greatest change proposed in relation to amendments is that it is proposed that the Minister may authorise any person (presumably proponents of amendments) to prepare an amendment. Such persons may prepare the amendment, give notice, consider submissions, refer submissions to a panel, and consider the panel's report. The authorised person then makes a recommendation to the planning authority about whether or not the amendment should be approved and submits the amendment to the planning authority for a decision. An authorised person may recommend to the planning authority that an amendment be supported with or without changes, or refused. Before making a recommendation to the planning authority, the authorised person must consider the panel's report.

This has been referred to in the media as the privatisation of planning scheme amendments, which tends to give the impression that proponents can approve their own amendments. That is, of course, a nonsense. The Minister is to retain power over approval of amendments and bringing them into effect. However, the proposed change raises serious questions. How is this proposed process to avoid being compromised or, at the very least, appear to avoid being compromised, by self-interest and bias? A proponent cannot objectively consider submissions nor make an unbiased recommendation to the planning authority that an amendment be adopted. It seems likely to us that, if this proposed change is carried over into an amending Act, approved amendments for which proponents have been authorised to prepare, consider submissions and recommend approval will inevitably be challenged in the Supreme Court.

A "code assess" procedure for some permit applications

It is proposed that a "code assess" procedure will be used for permit applications which are "straightforward, consistent with the zoning of the land, and have limited or no off-site impacts". But we don't know if the procedure will be restricted to these sorts of applications. We will have to wait and see. The classes of application that are code assessable are to be specified in the VPPs. They are to be assessed against objectives and standards set out in planning schemes. The CEO of the relevant council is to be the responsible authority for applications but presumably may delegate to an officer. Applicants may appeal to VCAT if a decision has not been made on an application within 14 days. An applicant may seek review of a refusal or against a condition in a permit. A simplified procedure is to be established at VCAT for hearings, but no detail is provided. Given the 14-day time limit, it is clear that no notification, lodging of objections or considerations of objections is to occur, and therefore no third-party appeal rights are to be available.

One of the main reasons for moving to the VPP-based schemes was to free up zoning controls. The Use Tables accompanying the VPP zones generally contain significantly fewer prohibited Section 3 uses and significantly more Section 2 discretionary uses than the zone Use Tables in the pre-VPP schemes (see Chapter 3). This is quite consistent with the philosophy of transforming schemes into policy-based documents where the policies would drive decision-making on planning permit applications. We cannot have a policy-based planning system and at the same time return to a relatively rigid "tick in the box" process for assessing permit applications. But that is what a "code assess" approach is. A more prescriptive approach may provide more certainty, but it will not produce better outcomes in terms of the built environment, and it will produce these outcomes at the expense of those very safeguards which are likely to produce better outcomes – that is, at the expense of objections and third party rights.

Conditions that can be included in permits

The Commentary to the Bill proposes authorisation of ongoing permit conditions such that the notion of a "spent permit" and the need for s 173 agreements to impose continuing obligations once the permit is "spent" (as for subdivision permits, see Chapter 2) no longer applies. Permit conditions are to be grouped into "finite" and "ongoing" categories, responsible authorities and referral authorities are to be required to use "standard" conditions, to which they will be able to add others if required, and conditions are to be allowed requiring the land owner to enter into an agreement to provide a bond or guarantee which may be forfeited if there is a failure to comply with a permit condition. In addition, the power of responsible authorities to amend permits, particularly endorsed plans, by secondary consents, is to be removed (see Chapter 5 for a discussion of secondary consents).

The removal of secondary consents will mean that amendments to permits will be via the "normal" amendment processes pursuant to s 72. For amendments which do not trigger any additional consent, would not result in any material detriment to any other person and would not transform the proposal (the tests which have to be satisfied now before a secondary consent can be granted), no notification will be necessary. However, even if no notification occurs, presumably neighbours who nevertheless become aware of the application have the right to lodge an objection and seek review before VCAT of a decision to grant the amendment. That is a gauntlet applicants for secondary consents do not currently have to run.

In the absence of secondary consents, permits issued at the direction of VCAT, which cannot be amended pursuant to s 72, must be amended pursuant to s 87. But pursuant to s 87, VCAT may amend a permit only if any of the circumstances set out in that section apply. They do not allow, for example, an amendment to endorsed plans simply because the applicant desires such an amendment. It is proposed that this restriction will be reviewed to introduce an ability for responsible authorities to amend these permits except where VCAT has specified that the permit or part of the permit must not be amended by the responsible authority. How that works out in detail we will have to wait and see. It may well be that the better course of action is to retain secondary consents.

The need for bipartisan agreement and support

To restate what we said, *inter alia*, in Chapter 1, statutory planning is one among a number of mechanisms for implementing policies dealing with land use and development, but it is not particularly relevant for implementing a wide range of overarching polices such as improving public transport, improving physical and social infrastructure, increasing the accessibility of communities to such infrastructure, providing local employment opportunities, reducing the length of journeys to work, and reducing the cost of housing, to name but a few.

The challenges for planning for the metropolitan area, provincial centres and rural areas are perhaps now more pronounced than they have ever been, given expected population growth levels, the impact of climate change on sea levels, community expectations, creaking infrastructure in established urban areas, the need for providing acceptable levels of physical and social infrastructure in developing areas, and runaway housing costs. The sheer financial cost of meeting these challenges is formidable and it is an ongoing cost that will continue over a long period. It seems to us that these challenges can only be met if there is some significant level of bipartisan agreement and support between the political parties on broad strategic planning policies for the State as a whole and its constituent regions, and on the level and staging of funding devoted to at least the major "big ticket" physical and social infrastructure items required across the State over the next 10 to 15 years. There appears to be little or no agreement about these things at the moment. The major parties (at federal as well as State level) appear to be more concerned with positioning themselves for the next election than they are with addressing in a systematic way the challenges which face us. The result is usually a rash of conflicting promises and announcements in the months leading up to elections, all designed to win votes, especially in marginal seats. This is *ad hoc* decision-making, with more spin on decisions than Shane Warne ever imparted to a cricket ball. But the community at large is getting tired of this. In November 2010 the incumbent Labor Government was defeated by the Liberal National coalition, who now hold power by two seats in the lower house. Maybe that will cause the major parties to rethink their approach and explore the possibilities of consensus rather than adversarial politics. If that happens, perhaps we will get the sort of bipartisan agreement and support we think is desperately required. But we are not holding our breath.

Further Reading

Chapter 1

Chadwick, GF, *A Systems View of Planning* Pergamon Press, Oxford, 1971.
Faludi, A, *Planning Theory* Pergamon Press, Oxford, 1973.
McLoughlin, JB, *Urban and Regional Planning: A Systems Approach* Faber and Faber, London, 1969.

Chapter 2

BADAC (Building and Development Approvals Committee) *Report on the Building and Development Control System in Victoria: Part II Planning Controls* Melbourne, Government Printer, 1979.
Byard, R, Code, G, Testro, G, and Porritt, S, *Planning and Environment Victoria* Butterworths. See Chapter 3 of the Planning Commentary in the Planning Volume.
McLoughlin, JB, *Shaping Melbourne's Future? Town Planning, the State and Civil Society* Cambridge University Press, Melbourne, 1992.
Spencer, R "The Development of Strategic Policy Planning in Victoria, Australia" *Town Planning Review*, Vol 56, No 1, 1985.

Chapter 3

Bryant, T, "Removal or Variation of Restrictive Covenants in Victoria" *Local Government Law Journal* Vol 1, No 3, 1996.
Byard, R, Code, G, Testro, G, and Porritt, S, *Planning and Environment Victoria* Butterworths. See Chapters 1, 2, 4 of the Planning Commentary in the Planning Volume and Parts 3 and 4.65 in the Planning Appeal Casenotes Volume.
Department of Planning and Community Development, *Using Victoria's Planning System* (available on the DPCD website at <www.dpcd.vic.gov.au>), Chapter 1.
Paterson, J, Yencken, D, and Gunn, G, *A Mansion or No House* Urban Development Institute of Australia (Victoria), Melbourne, 1976.
Woodcock, I, et al, "Modelling the compact city: capacities and visions for Melbourne" *Australian Planner* Vol 47, No 2, June 2010.

Chapter 4

Bryant, T, "Ministerial Encroachment on the Decision Making Processes under the Planning and Environment Act, 1987 (Vic)" *Local Government Law Journal* Vol 1, No 4, 1996.
Byard, R, Code, G, Testro, G, and Porritt, S, *Planning and Environment Victoria* Butterworths. Planning Chapter 12 of the Planning Commentary in the Planning Volume.
Department of Planning and Community Development, *Using Victoria's Planning System* (available on the DPCD website at <www.dpcd.vic.gov.au>), Chapter 2.

Chapter 5

Byard, R, Code, G, Testro, G, and Porritt, S, *Planning and Environment Victoria* Butterworths. See Chapter 7 of the Planning Commentary in the Planning Volume and the Table of Contents of the Planning Appeal Casenotes Volume.
Department of Planning and Community Development, *Using Victoria's Planning System* (available on the DPCD website at <www.dpcd.vic.gov.au>), Chapter 3.
Department of Sustainability and Municipal Association of Victoria, *Writing Planning Permits* Melbourne, June 2003.

Chapter 6

BADAC (Building and Development Approvals Committee) *Report on the Building and Development Control System in Victoria: Part II Planning Controls* Melbourne, Government Printer, 1979: Chapter 5, Appeals, pp 102–120, 135, 146–147.

Hon Justice K Bell, *One VCAT: President's Review of VCAT* 30 November 2009 (available on the VCAT website at <www.vcat.vic.gov.au>).

Bryant, T, "The Planning Appeals (Amendment) Act 1987" *Law Institute Journal* Vol 61, October 1987.

Bryant, T, "Planning and Environment Act 1987: Economic and Social Considerations" *Law Institute Journal* Vol 62, September 1988; October 1988.

Byard, R, Code, G, Testro, G, and Porritt, S, *Planning and Environment Victoria* Butterworths. See Chapter 13 of the Planning Commentary in the Planning Volume and the Table of Contents for the Planning Appeal Casenotes Volume.

Department of Planning and Community Development, *Using Victoria's Planning System* (available on the DPCD website at <www.dpcd.vic.gov.au>), Chapter 5.

Forge, W, *The Wade House Case* McCulloch Waterloo Press, Melbourne, 1985.

Komesaroff, T, "Costs in the Planning and Environment List of the Victorian Civil and Administrative Tribunal" *Law Institute Journal* June 2002.

Pizer, J, "VCAT – a new era for tribunals in Victoria" *Law Institute Journal* August 1998.

Pizer, J, *Pizer's Annotated VCAT Act* 2nd edn, JNL Nominees Pty Ltd, Melbourne, 2004.

Raff, M, "A History of Land Use Planning Legislation and Rights of Objection in Victoria" *Monash University Law Review* Vol 22, No 90, p 196.

Chapter 7

Byard, R, Code, G, Testro, G, and Porritt, S, *Planning and Environment Victoria* Butterworths. See Chapter 10 of the Planning Commentary in the Planning Volume and Part 6 of the Planning Appeal Casenotes Volume.

Department of Planning and Community Development, *Using Victoria's Planning System* (available on the DPCD website at <www.dpcd.vic.gov.au>), Chapter 7.

Chapter 8

Bates, GM, *Environmental Law in Australia* 6th edn, Butterworths, Sydney, 2010.

Blake, A, "Urban Conservation in the 1980s" *Urban Conservation at the Local Level – Papers from a seminar designed to explore recent developments in Urban Conservation with special emphasis on the role of Local Government* National Trust of Australia (Victoria) Melbourne, March 1980.

Byard, R, Code, G, Testro, G, and Porritt, S, *Planning and Environment Victoria* Butterworths. See Parts 9.150 and 9.155 of the Planning Appeal Casenotes Volume.

Lawson, J, "Urban Conservation within the Metropolitan Area – St James Park" *Urban Conservation at the Local Level – Papers from a seminar designed to explore recent developments in Urban Conservation with special emphasis on the role of Local Government* National Trust of Australia (Victoria) Melbourne, March 1980.

Chapter 9

Byard, R, Code, G, Testro, G, and Porritt, S, *Planning and Environment Victoria* Butterworths. See Chapter 11 of the Planning Commentary in the Planning Volume and Part 10 of the Planning Appeal Casenotes Volume.

Department of Sustainability and Environment, *Using Victoria's Planning System* (available on the DSE website at <www.dse.vic.gov.au>), Chapter 6.

Morris, S, *Land Acquisition and Compensation* Department of Planning, 1987.

Report of the Committee of Enquiry into Town Planning Compensation (The Gobbo Report) Government Printer, Melbourne, 1978.

Chapter 10

Buxton, M, Goodman, R, and Budge, T, "Planning and Deregulation" *Australian Planner* Vol 42, No 2, 2005.

Dawkins, J, "In praise of regulation" *Australian Planner* Vol 33, No 1, 1996.

Draft Planning and Environment Amendment (General) Bill and associated discussion and response papers (available on the Department of Community Development website at <www.dpcd.vic.gov.au>).

Index

Aboriginal heritage places, 202-203, 226-228
  Cultural Heritage Management Plan (CHMP), 226-227
  cultural heritage sensitivity regulations, 226-227
  planning permits, 226-228
Acquisition *see* Compulsory acquisition; Voluntary acquisition
Activity Centre Zone, 25, 121
Administrative Appeals Tribunal (AAT)
  establishment, 154
  functions, 15
  jurisdiction, 155
  Planning Division of, 154-155
Agreements
  land use and development, 49-50
  planning permits, 133-134
  planning scheme amendments, 101-103
  subdivision of land, 31-32, 49-50
Amendments to planning schemes
  abnormal, 94-96
    notification process, exemption, 94-96
  abandonment of proposal, 90
  adoption of, 89-92
    legal status, 90
  agreements and, 101-103
  appeals of
    merits, on the, 100
  application for, 78
  approval, 24, 27, 89-92
    authorisation for, 27, 90
    Ministerial powers, 90-92
    notice of, 92
  assessment, 75
  certification of, 90
  costs, 78-79
  decisions, 8
  exhibition of, 79-81
  fast-tracking, 96
  fees for, 78-79
  gazettal, 27, 89-92
  Green Wedge land, 98-99
  Growth Areas Authority (GAA), 25
  initiation, 78
  interim development orders and, 19
  lapsing of, 93-94
  notification of, 27, 79-81
    exemption from requirements, 94-96
  opposition to, 76
  panel hearings, 84-89 *see also* Panel hearings regarding amendments to planning schemes
  Parliament and, 98-99
  Precinct Structure Plans (PSPs), 25
  preparation, 24, 27
  procedures, 1, 10-11
    reviews relating to, 100-101
  process, 13, 74-79
    abnormal, 94-96
    combined amendment and permit process, 97-98
    exemption from normal process, 94-96
    reform, 251-252
  public consultation regarding, 27, 74
  public interests of, 74-76
  review of, 79, 99-103
    amendment procedures, relating to, 100-101
  revocation of, 92, 98
  stages, 74-76
  standard amendment track, 251-252
  submissions, 4, 76-77
    consideration of, 81-83
    format of, 83
    joint, 81, 83
    lodgement, 81-83
    presentation, 4
    scope, 82-83
  technical amendment track, 251-252
  Upper Yarra Valley and Dandenong Ranges Strategy Plan, 99
  Urban Growth Zones, 92-93, 98-99
  Victoria Planning Provisions (VPPs), 76-77
Appeals
  Administrative Appeals Tribunal *see* Administrative Appeals Tribunal (AAT)
  "call in" by Minister, 28
  merits, on the, 100
  planning appeals, 4
  Planning Appeals Board *see* Planning Appeals Board (PAB)

Appeals *(cont)*
   planning schemes, amendments to *see* Amendments to planning schemes
   Supreme Court, to *see* Supreme Court of Victoria
   Town Planning Appeals Tribunal *see* Town Planning Appeals Tribunal (TPAT)
   VCAT *see* Victorian Civil and Administrative Tribunal (VCAT)
   Victorian Civil and Administrative Tribunal *see* Victorian Civil and Administrative Tribunal (VCAT)
Australian Heritage Commission, 200, 215
   see also Heritage conservation
Australian Heritage Council
   functions, 198-199
   Register of the National Estate, management of, 198, 199
Betterment, 230-232
   collection, 230
   government intervention, 232
   meaning, 230
   rates, 231
   strategic planning, 230-231
Brothels
   enforcement proceedings, 193
   planning permits, 129-130, 137-140
     considerations, 138
   regulation, 1
   review of decisions regarding, 140
Building
   conservation of *see* Heritage conservation; Heritage conservation in Victoria; Victorian Heritage Register
   definition, 40, 204
   demolition controls, 203-204, 205
   Historic Buildings Preservation Council, 203-204
   Interim Preservation Orders (IPOs), 203-204
   permit, 57
     planning permit, distinction, 57, 104
   planning permission, 68-71
   planning schemes *see* Planning schemes
   Register of Historic Buildings, 205
   residential, 71-73
   single dwellings, 68-71
   Victorian Building Regulations (VBRs), 35
   Victorian Heritage Register *see* Victorian Heritage Register
Business zones, 56

Call-in power
   planning permits, 28-29
Community facilities, 2
Community service policies, 10, 13
Compensation
   acquisition *see* Compulsory acquisition; Voluntary acquisition
   betterment *see* Betterment
   cancellation of permit
     frivolous application by third party, 188
   circumstances for, 229
     acquisition, other than, 243-246 *see also* Planning compensation
   claims, time limits on, 246-247
   compulsory acquisition *see* Compulsory acquisition
   development rights, loss of, 235
   environmental controls, 235-236
   heritage conservation controls, 214-218, 235-236
   injurious affection *see* Injurious affection
   planning *see* Planning compensation
   planning blight, 234-5
     temporary nature of, 234
   public acquisition overlays, 229-235, 240, 243-244
   severance, 233-234, 242
   time limits on claims, 246-247
   voluntary acquisition *see* Voluntary acquisition
Compulsory acquisition, 229, 236-243
   authority to acquire land, 239
   community services, land for, 13
   land which may be acquired, categories of, 237-238
   meaning, 237
   price paid, 240-243
     double dipping, 242
     loans, availability of, 243
     loss attributable to disturbance, 242
     market value, 240-241
     special value, 241-242
   reservation of land, 229, 238-240
     exemptions to requirement, 240
     notification requirements, 239
   severance, 233-234, 242
   solatium, 242
   scope of powers, 237-238
Compulsory conferences, 153 *see also* Mediation
   attendance requirements, 167
   functions, 167

INDEX

introduction, 153, 166
Planning Appeals Board, 153
Conservation *see also* Heritage conservation
  definition, 40-41
  policies, 10
Content, form and structure of planning schemes
  agreements, 49-50
  application for planning permit
    information to be provided, 46-47
    Minister, when to made to, 50
    notice requirements, exemptions, 50-52
    review rights, exemptions, 50-52
  decision guidelines, 65-66
  definitions, 66-67
  development contributions, 43-45
  existing use rights, 62-65
  format, standard, 53
  general powers, 39-41
  General Provisions, 62, 65-66
  incorporation of documents, 47-49
  information to be provided, 46-47
  Local Planning Policy Framework (LPPF), 41
  Ministerial control over, 27
  Municipal Strategic Statement (MSS), requirement for, 23, 41
  non-conforming uses, 62-63
  overlays *see* Overlays
  public utility services, provision of, 43-45
  requirements, 22-24
  ResCode provisions, 68-73
  review rights, exemptions, 51
  rights of way
    creation or extinguishment of, 45-46
    restriction, definition, 46
  specific powers, 41-53
  State Planning Policy Framework (SPPF), 22, 41, 53, 54-55
  State standard provisions, 22, 53-54
  Statewide Particular Provisions, 62
  structure, standard, 53
  underlying zoning, 47
  Urban Growth Boundary, inclusion of, 52-53
  Victoria Planning Provisions (VPPs), 53-54
  zones *see* Zoning
Costs
  award of, 171-174
  enforcement proceedings, 190-191
  Victorian Civil and Administrative Tribunal (VCAT), 148, 169-174, 190-191

County Court
  planning matters, exclusion from determining, 150, 175
Covenants
  restrictive, 46, 108, 110, 131
  removal, 131-132
  variation, 131-132
Cultural Heritage Management Plan (CHMP), 226-227
  approval, 226
  preparation, 226
Demolition controls *see* Heritage conservation in Victoria
Development
  contributions, 43-45
  definition, 40, 57, 104
  detrimental effect of *see* Injurious affection
  environmental effect of, 36-38
    Environmental Effects Statement (EES), requirement for, 36-38, 226
  inquiry, 37
  land, of *see* Land
  medium density, 71-73
  opposition to, 14
  permit for *see* Planning permit
  policies *see* Land use policies
  protection from, 1
  provisions, 23
  redevelopment, 1
  regulation, 1
  restrictions, 41-43
  subdivision *see* Subdivision
  trends, research into, 1, 8
  use, distinction, 57-58
Development Assessment Committees (DACs)
  members, 122
  responsible authorities, 25, 121-122
Development contributions, 43-45
Development control *see* Statutory planning
Development policies
  formulation, 1
  implementation, 1-2, 6-7, 10-13
    allocation of resources, by, 2
    heritage conservation, 3-4
    municipal activities and services, 2
    public transport, improving, 2-3
    residential streets, improving, 3
    statutory planning, through, 5
    Local Planning Policy Framework (LPPF), 7
  monitoring of, 6-7

261

Development policies *(cont)*
  State Planning Policy Framework (SPPF), 7
  statement of intent, 1
Documents
  incorporation of, 47-49
  reference documents, distinction, 48
Economic development policies, 10, 12
Enforcement
  cancellation of permit, 179, 187-188, 243
  evidence, collection of, 180
  infringement notice *see* Infringement notices
  injunction *see* Injunctions
  Magistrates' Court, prosecution in, 179, 181-182
  mechanisms, 179, 181-188
  objectives of, 179-180
  orders *see* Enforcement orders; Interim enforcement orders
  permit, cancellation of, 179, 187-188, 243
  planning scheme, of, 25, 179
  proceedings, 188-193
    brothels and, 193 *see also* Brothels
    government exemptions, 193
    prosecution for offence, 179, 181-182
    responsible authority, by, 25, 179-180
  stop orders, 179, 188, 243
Enforcement orders, 179
  application for, 182-183
    consideration of, 183
    lodging, 182
    procedure, 182
  breach, 184
  compliance, 191
  enforcement of, 191-193
    Carrying our works required by order, 193
    contempt proceedings in Victorian Civil and Administrative Tribunal (VCAT), 192
    injunctions, 192
    prosecution in Magistrates' Court, 191-192
    Victorian Civil and Administrative Tribunal (VCAT) order, filing of, 192
  interim *see* Interim enforcement orders
  non-compliance with, 183-184
    prosecution for, 191-192
  non-monetary, 183, 192
  proceedings
    costs, award of, 190-191
  Victorian Civil and Administrative Tribunal (VCAT), by, 183
  filing of order in Supreme Court, 192

Environmental Effects Statement (EES)
  analysis of environment, 36
  Cultural Heritage Management Plan (CHMP) and, 226
  environment, definition, 37
  exhibition of, 27
  preparation, 36
    responsibility for, 37
  when required, 36-37, 226
    Minister's decisions regarding, 37
Environmental impacts of development, 36-38
  assessments, 21, 197-198
  Environmental Effects Statement *see* Environmental Effects Statement (EES)
  inquiry into, 37-38
Environmental Protection Authority (EPA)
  referrals to, 26, 144
  works approval or licence, permits for, 144
Environmental Significance Overlay, 53, 60
Existing use *see also* Land use
  rights, 62-65
  "use" and "purpose", distinction, 64
Farming Zone, 42-43
  agreements, 49
Gaming machines
  planning permits, 140-143
    restrictions, 140-141
    review of decisions, 141
    social and economic impacts, 142-143
Gobbo Report
  injurious affection, 233
Good Design Guide for Medium Density Housing, 72-73
Government departments
  enforcement proceedings and, 193
  planning permits *see* Planning permits
Green Wedge Zone, 52
  amendments to land in, 98-99
Growth Areas Authority (GAA), 25, 92-93
  functions, 92-93
  members, 92
  precinct structure plans, preparation of, 92-93
Heritage conservation
  Aboriginal heritage places, 202-203, 226-228
  Australian Heritage Council, 198-199
  Commonwealth Heritage List, 199-200
  definition, 40-41, 194
  Heritage Overlays *see* Heritage Overlays
  "heritage value", definition, 201

INDEX

National Estate *see* National Estate
National Heritage List, 199-200
National Heritage protection, 198-203 *see also* National Estate
policies, implementation, 3, 12
Victoria, in *see* Heritage conservation in Victoria
World heritage areas, 195-197
World Heritage Convention, 194
World Heritage List, 194-195 *see also* World Heritage List

Heritage conservation in Victoria
Aboriginal heritage places, 202-203
Cultural Heritage Management Plan (CHMP), 226-227
planning permits, 226-228
compensation, 214-218, 235-236
cultural heritage sensitivity regulations, 226-227
demolition controls, 203-204, 205
financial assistance to owners of heritage buildings, 211-212
Heritage Council *see* Victorian Heritage Council
Heritage Overlays *see* Heritage Overlays
Historic Buildings Preservation Council, 203-204
Interim Preservation Orders (IPOs), 203-204
land, application to, 224-225
legislation, 203-212
permit system, 209-211
planning controls, 214
compensation and, 214-218
planning policies, 3-4
implementation, 3, 12
planning powers, 212-214
Heritage Council and, 206-207
1972, after, 213-214
1972, before, 212-213
Planning and Environment Act 1987, under, 219-225
register *see* Victorian Heritage Register
St James Park, 218-219
Victorian Heritage Council *see* Victorian Heritage Council
Victorian Heritage Register *see* Victorian Heritage Register

Heritage Overlays, 42, 52, 56, 60-62, 70, 105, 212, 220-224
application of, 221-222

controls, 220, 221
decision guidelines, 221, 222
planning permits, 225-226
purpose, 220-221
Victorian Heritage Register *see* Victorian Heritage Register

Historic Buildings Preservation Council, 203-204

Industrial zones, 56

Infringement notices, 179, 186-187
Magistrates' Court, enforcement in, 186

Injunctions, 179, 186
enforcement orders, enforcement of, 192
interim, 185, 186
right to seek, 186
Victorian Civil and Administrative Tribunal (VCAT), by, 186

Injurious affection
alone, 232-233, 234
compensation, 232-233
examples of, 232
freeways, effect of, 232
Gobbo Report recommendations, 233
meaning, 232
Morris Report recommendations, 233
severance, for, 232, 234

Interim development orders (IDOs)
amendments to, 19
heritage conservation control, 215-216
intention of, 19
preparation of, 19

Interim enforcement orders, 179
application, 184-185
breach, 184
compliance, 191
considerations for, 185
enforcement of, 191-193
ex parte, 184, 185
purpose, 185
Victorian Civil and Administrative Tribunal (VCAT), by, 184

Interim Preservation Orders (IPOs), 203-204

Land
acquisition of *see* Compulsory acquisition; Voluntary acquisition
covenants *see* Covenants
definition, 40
development of
controls, 1
planning schemes *see* Planning schemes

Land *(cont)*
   heritage conservation *see* Heritage conservation; Heritage conservation in Victoria
   planning schemes *see* Planning schemes
   reservation of, 229, 238-240
   subdivision of *see* Subdivision
   use of *see* Land use

Land use
   controls over, 1, 23
   covenants *see* Covenants
   development, distinction, 57-58
   existing use rights, 62-65
   Local Planning Policy Framework (LPPF), 7
   mining, 26-27
   non-conforming uses, 62-63
   permit for *see* Planning permit
   planning schemes, implementation of, 1-2
   policies, implementation, 1-2, 6-7, 10-13
     allocation of resources, by, 2
     heritage conservation, 3-4
     monitoring of, 6-7
     municipal activities and services, 2
     public transport, improving, 2-3
     residential streets, improving, 3
     statement of intent, 1
     statutory planning, through, 5
   proposed, characterising, 110-111
   provisions, 23
   regulation, 1
   restrictions, 41-43
   State Planning Policy Framework (SPPF), 7
   subdivision *see* Subdivision
   terms, 66-67
   use
     definition, 40
     development, distinction to, 57-58
     permit for *see* Planning permit
   zones *see* Zoning

Licensed premises
   planning permits, 136-137

Local government, 19

Local Planning Policy Framework (LPPF), 41
   amendments, 78
   content, 55-56
   development policies, 7, 55-56
   heritage policies in, 223
   land use, 7

Local provisions
   amendments to, 24

Magistrates' Court
   infringement notice, enforcement, 186
   planning matters, exclusion from determining, 150, 175
   prosecution in, 179, 181-182
     enforcement order, non-compliance, 191-192

Mediation, 166-168
   evidence, 167
   procedure, 167
   provisions, 166
   referral by Victorian Civil and Administrative Tribunal (VCAT), 167-168
   settlements 167-168

Melbourne @ 5 Million, 14, 52

Melbourne 2030, 2, 14, 52, 54

Melbourne Metropolitan Board of Works (MMBW), 16, 20

Melbourne Metropolitan Planning Scheme (MMPS), 17, 20, 22, 24
   responsible authority, as, 25

Mining
   applications to develop land for, 26-27

Minister's powers
   amendment to VPPs, 23
   Environmental Effects Statement (EES), when required, 37
   Planning and Environment Act, under, 27-29
   planning schemes, 22-24
     amendments *see* Amendments to planning schemes
     approval and gazettal of, 24, 27
     "call in" powers, 28-29, 121, 152
     veto, power of, 27-28
   responsible authority and, 25
   veto, of, 27-28
   Victoria Planning Provisions (VPPS), amendment to, 23, 76-77
   Victorian Civil and Administrative Tribunal (VCAT), applications for review, 175-178

Morris Report
   compulsory acquisition, 238, 242
   injurious affection, 233

Municipal councils
   compulsory acquisition of land, authority, 239
   interim development orders, 19
   municipal restructuring, 22
   planning schemes, 19-22, 27
   powers, 29

INDEX

Planning and Environment Act, under, 27-29
responsible authorities, as, 19, 25, 29
State standard provisions
  amendments to, 24
subdivision, certification of plans of *see* Subdivision
Victoria Planning Provisions *see* Victoria Planning Provisions (VPPS)

Municipal Strategic Statement (MSS)
amendments to, 10-11
content, 55
planning scheme requirement, as, 23, 41
regional planning, 18
review of, 23

National Estate
Aboriginal heritage places, 202-203
definition, 200
"heritage value", definition, 201
register, 198, 199, 200-203
  addition of place to, 201-202
  effect of registration, 202-3
  establishment, 200
  listing on, 200-201

Notification
Application for Review by Victorian Civil and Administrative Tribunal (VCAT), 158
combined amendment and permit application, 97-98
planning permits, 33, 114-118
  amendments after notification, 117-118
  amendments to application before notification, 112-113
  combined amendment and permit application, 97-98
  exemptions, 50-52
  Notice of Decision to Grant, 132, 156
  Notice of Refusal, 132, 156
  procedures, 33
planning scheme amendments, of, 27, 79-81
  approval, of, 92
reservation of land, 239

Overlays, 60-62
controls, 23, 41-43, 51
  built form of proposal, over, 23
Environmental Significance Overlay, 53, 60
Heritage Overlay *see* Heritage Overlays
Incorporated Plan Overlay, 52, 60
introduction of, 23
Land Management, 61
Neighbourhood Character Overlay, 70-71
Public Acquisition Overlay, 42, 53, 61, 216
requirements imposed by, 61
responsible authorities, consideration by, 61-62
Vegetation Protection Overlay, 135
Victoria Planning Provisions (VPPs), inclusion in, 60-62
Wildfire Management Overlay, 26, 60, 61

Panel hearings regarding amendments to planning schemes, 84-89
evidence
  expert witnesses, 85
  oral, 85, 87
  written, 85
field inspections by, 86
functions, 84, 85
hearings, public, 87-88
members, 84, 88
  bias of, 88-89
panel reports, 85
  consideration of, 89-90
  public inspection of, 85, 90
Planning Panels Victoria, 84
powers of, 84-85
procedures, 86-87
submissions to
  consideration of, 84
  presentation of, 87
  referral of, 84
  refusal of, 85-86

Plan of subdivision *see* Subdivision

Planning appeals, 4, 7
review of system, 153

Planning Appeals Board (PAB), 153-154
compulsory conferences, 153
determinations, 154
establishment, 15, 153
jurisdiction, 153
powers, 153

Planning authorities, 15-19
discretionary powers, 104
meaning, 19, 24
Minister as, 24
planning schemes, amendments to *see* Amendments to planning schemes
regional *see* Regional planning authorities

Planning blight, 234-5

Planning compensation
access, restricted, 245-246
circumstances where available, 243-246
dispute resolution, 247
inaccurate planning certificate, 246
meaning, 243

Planning compensation *(cont)*
  payment, 247
  reserved land, regarding
    refusal of planning consent, 245
    sale at a loss, 243-245
  road closures, 245-246
  time limits on claims, 246-247
Planning enforcement *see* Enforcement
Planning Panels Victoria
  functions, 84
Planning permit, 4
  agreements and, 133-134
  amendments, 134-136
    grounds, 187
    notification, after, 117-118
  appeals *see* Appeals
  applicant, 105
    legal personality, 109
    personal, 106
  application form, 107-108
  applications, 20-21, 26, 105
    amendment of licence, requiring, 26
    amendments before notification, 112-113
    "code assess" procedure, 252
    combined process, in, 97-98
    decisions, 8
    dual control of, 20, 26
    fees for, 107
    information to be provided, 46-47, 108
    licence to discharge, requiring, 26
    lodgement, 25
    mining, 26-27
    notice requirements, exemptions, 50-52
    personal, 106
    referral of, 112-114
    reforms to process, 252
    responsible authority, 26
    time limits for decisions, 33
    who may apply, 105
    works approval, requiring, 26
  brothels, 136, 137-140
  building, for, 68-71
  building permit, distinction, 57, 104
  cancellation, 107, 179
    application for, 187-188
    enforcement measure, as, 187-188
    grounds, 187
  combined amendment and permit process, 97-98
  conditions, 41-43, 97, 132-133, 253
    compliance with, 179-180
    time, 106-107

  consents, 97
  covenants, removal of *see* Covenants
  determinations, 120-132
    authority to make, 120-121
    checking details of applications, 109-110
    communication of, 132
    considerations, 109-118, 122-124
    delegation of power, 20, 120
    discretion, ambit of, 122-123
    making of, 120-121
    Ministerial "call in", 28-29, 121, 152
    policy, role of, in, 124-127
    responsible authority and, 20, 21, 109-118
    social and economic effects, consideration, 123-124, 127-130
  discretionary powers of authorities, 104
  duration, 106-107
  expiration of, 106-107
  gaming machines, 140-143
  government departments, required by, 145-146
  grant, 105
    notice of decision to, 132
  Heritage Register, buildings on, 225-226
  information, obtaining, 111-112
  land, over, 105-106
  licensed premises, 136-137
  Minister's powers over, 27-29
    "call in", 28-29, 121, 152
  municipal councils, 20-21
  notification, 33, 114-118
    amendments to application before, 112-113
    amendments to permit after, 117-118
    decision, of, 132
    exemptions, 50-52
  objections to, 4, 118-119
    grounds, 119
    referral authority, by, 26
    who may lodge, 118
  permissions, 105
  personal permits, 106
  proposed use, characterising, 110-111
  purpose, 57
  referral authorities, sending to, 113-114 *see also* Referral authorities
  refusal
    notice of, 132
  register, keeping of, 112
  requirement for, 107, 110-111, 145-146
  responsible authority *see* Responsible authorities

INDEX

restrictive covenants *see* Covenants
review of decisions by Victorian Civil and Administrative Tribunal (VCAT), 155-166
"runs with the land", 105-106
single dwellings, 68-71
social and economic effects of proposal, 123-124, 127-130
stop orders, 179, 188, 243
subdivision, for *see* Subdivision
time
    conditions on permit, 106-107
    limits for decisions, 33, 108-109
    works approvals and licences, 144
    zones, application in, 57

Planning policies
conflicts between policies, 7
consultation, 9
development policies *see* Development policies
evaluation of, 1, 8
formulation, 1, 9-10
implementation, 1-2, 6-7, 10-13
    allocation of resources, by, 2
    heritage conservation, 3-4
    municipal activities and services, 2
    public transport, improving, 2-3
    residential streets, improving, 3
land use policies *see* Land use
Melbourne 2030, 2
monitoring of, 6-7
statement of intent, 1
statements of, 9-10, 16

Planning processes
application, 7
case study, 8-14
components, 6
elements, 5-8
planning schemes, relationship to, 21
policies
    formulation, 1, 9-10
    implementation, 2, 10-13
public meetings, 13
statutory planning, 4-5

Planning schemes
acquisition of land *see* Compulsory acquisition; Voluntary acquisition
administration, 1, 4, 25
amendments *see* Amendments to planning schemes
approval, 4
content *see* Content, form and structure of planning schemes
definitions, 66-67
development control, 1
enforcement *see* Enforcement
exemptions, 51-52
form of *see* Content, form and structure of planning schemes
implementation, 1-2
land use *see* Land use
land values, effect on, 2
local provisions, 22, 24
local sections, 21-22
Melbourne Metropolitan Planning Scheme (MMPS), 17, 20, 22, 25
municipal, 1
Municipal Strategic Statement (MSS), requirement for, 23, 41
objectives, 39
planning processes, relationship to, 21
preparation, 4, 24
provisions, 62
reform of, 24
regional sections of, 21-22
requirements, 22
review of, 23
State Planning Policy Framework *see* State Planning Policy Framework (SPPF)
State sections, 21-22
State standard provisions, 22-24, 53-54
structure of *see* Content, form and structure of planning schemes
subdivision, controls regarding *see* Subdivision
terms used in, 66-67
VicCode 1, 34-36
Victoria Planning Provisions *see* Victoria Planning Provisions (VPPs)
works approval and licences *see* Works approval and licences
zones *see* Zoning

Planning systems in Victoria
co-ordination, 248-253
development of, 15
dual controls, 20, 26
Environmental Effects Statement *see* Environmental Effects Statement (EES)
interim development orders *see* Interim development orders (IDOs)
Melbourne Metropolitan Board of Works (MMBW), 16
Melbourne Metropolitan Planning Scheme (MMPS), 17, 20, 22, 25
objectives, 39

Planning systems in Victoria *(cont)*
  Planning and Environment Act, under, 21-29
  Planning Appeals Board *see* Planning Appeals Board (PAB)
  planning authorities, 15-19
  planning schemes *see* Planning schemes
  problems related to, 248
  promotion of, 15
  referral authority *see* Referral authorities
  reform of, 24, 248-254
  regional authorities *see* Regional planning authorities
  State Co-Ordination Council, 16
  State Planning Council (SPC), 15, 16
  State significant developments, 249-251
  structure, 21
  subdivision *see* Subdivision
  tiered hierarchy of
    change from, 21-22
    conflicts between tiers, 19-21
    development, 15
    local government tier, 19
    regional tier, 17-19
    State tier, 16-17
  Town and Country Planning Act 1961, under, 15-21
  Town and Country Planning Board (TCPB), 15
  Town Planning Appeals Tribunal, 15
  tribunals *see* Administrative Appeals Tribunal (AAT); Victorian Civil and Administrative Tribunal (VCAT)
  zones *see* Zoning
Population
  trends, research into, 1, 8
Precinct Structure Plans (PSPs), 25
Public Acquisition Overlay, 13, 42, 53, 61, 216
  compensation, 229-235, 240, 243-244
    claims, liability for, 247
  purpose of, 229, 243
  reserved land, sale at a loss, 243-245
Public Land zones, 56-57
Public transport
  planning, 2-3
Public utility services
  provision of, 43-45
Public works
  definition, 36-37
Referral authorities, 26-27

Environmental Protection Authority (EPA), 26, 144
  mining, applications for, 26-27
  Minister as, 27-28
  planning permits, 113-114 *see also* Planning permits
    objections, 26
    subdivisions, for, 30-31
  VicRoads, referrals to, 26
  works approvals and licences, for, 144
Regional planning authorities, 15, 21-22
  abolition, 18, 22
  Albury-Wodonga Development Corporation, 18
  creation of, 17
  Geelong Regional Commission (GRC), 17, 19, 22
  Geelong Regional Planning Authority, 17, 19, 22
  Latrobe Regional Commission, 18
  Loddon Campaspe Regional Planning Authority, 17, 20
  municipal councils, 20-21
  Upper Yarra Valley and Dandenong Ranges Authority, 17-18
  Westernport Regional Planning Authority, 17, 19
Register of the National Estate *see* National Estate
Register of Titles
  subdivision, registration of plans, 30
ResCode
  medium density development, 71-73
  planning permission, 68-71
  provisions, 68
  residential buildings, 71-73
  single dwellings, 68-71
  subdivision of land, 34-36
Reserved land, 229, 238-240 *see also* Compulsory acquisition; Planning compensation; Public Acquisition Overlay
  compensation
    refusal of planning consent, 245
    sale at a loss, 243-245
Residential streets
  planning, 3
Residential zones *see also* Zoning
  Residential 1 zone, 32, 36, 41, 56
  Residential 2 zone, 36, 51-2, 56
  township, 36, 56
Responsible authorities *see also* Referral authorities

INDEX

conditions imposed by, 41-43
decision guidelines, 65-66
definition, 25
Development Assessment Committees
  (DACs), 25, 121-122
discretionary powers, 104
enforcement by *see* Enforcement
Minister as, 19, 25
municipal councils, 19, 25, 29
overlays, consideration of *see* Overlays
planning permits *see also* Planning permits
  duties regarding, 20, 21, 109-118
  register, keeping of, 112
  requirements, 50, 145-146
regional authorities as, 19
subdivision, for *see* Subdivision
Restrictive covenants, 46, 108, 110, 131-132
Review
  planning appeals, 4
  proceedings, 4
  Minister, determined by, 7
  rights of, 50-52
Rights of way
  creation, 45-46
  extinguishment, 45-46
  restriction, definition, 46
Rural environments
  development, sensitivity to, 8-9
Rural zones, 56-57
Save Our Suburbs, 14
Severance, 233-234, 242
Social and economic impacts
  gaming machines, of, 142-143
  planning permits, 123-124, 127-130
Special purpose zones, 56-57
State Co-Ordination Council, 16
State Planning Council (SPC)
  composition, 16
  establishment, 15, 16
State Planning Policy Framework (SPPF)
  amendments to, 55
  development policies, 7
  form of, 23
  land use, 7
  objectives, 54-55
  planning schemes, 22, 41
  purpose, 54
  subdivisions *see* Subdivision
State standard provisions
  amendments to, 24-25
  planning schemes, 22
  preparation, 22

State standard zones, 56-60
  planning schemes, 22
  Victoria Planning Provisions (VPPs),
    provided by, 56-7
Statutory planning
  bipartisan agreement, 253-254
  development control, 1
  heritage conservation *see* Heritage
    conservation
  meaning, 1
  planning process, and *see* Planning
    processes
  planning schemes *see* Planning schemes
  strategic planning, distinction, 2
Stop orders, 179, 188
Strategic planning
  functions, 1, 2
  limitations, 2-4
  meaning, 1
  planning policies *see* Planning policies
  planning process, and *see* Planning
    processes
  research and policy development, 1
  statements of intent, 1
  statutory planning, distinction, 2
Subdivision
  agreements, 31-32, 49-50
  certification of plans, 21, 30, 33-34
  cluster, 30
  conditions, 31-32
  controls, 11, 29
    land use, 30
  conventional, 30
  matters to be considered, 33
  minimum allotment size, 29-30, 35
  planning permission, applications for, 26,
    29-32, 33-34
  time limits for decisions, 33
  referral authorities, 30-31
  registration of plans, 30
  ResCode, 34-36
  Residential 1 zone, 32, 41
  responsible authorities, 31-33
    matters to be considered by, 33
  sealing a plan of, 30, 34
  strata, 30
  VicCode 1, 34-36
  Victoria Planning Provisions (VPPs),
    regarding, 30
  Victorian Building Regulations (VBRs),
    35

269

Supreme Court of Victoria
  appeal to, from Victorian Civil and Administrative Tribunal (VCAT), 150, 174-175
  planning compensation claims
    dispute resolution, 247
  planning matters, exclusion from determining, 150, 175
  Victorian Civil and Administrative Tribunal (VCAT) order, filing of, 192
Third parties
  appeal, right of, 151
  cancellation of permit, application by, 188
Time
  planning compensation claims, limits on, 246-247
  planning permits
    conditions on, 106-107
    extensions, 107
    limits on decisions, 33, 108-109
    review by Victorian Civil and Administrative Tribunal (VCAT) application, 156-157
    "stopping the clock" provisions, 33, 109
Town and Country Planning Board (TCPB), 151-153
  establishment, 15, 151
  function, 15
  powers, 151-152
Town planning, 1, 105-106
Town Planning Appeals Tribunal (TPAT), 151-153
  determinations, 151
  establishment, 15, 151
  jurisdiction, 15
  Planning Appeals Board (PAB), replacement of functions by, 153
  powers, 151
  proceedings, 152
Underlying zoning, 47
Upper Yarra Valley and Dandenong Ranges Strategy Plan, 99
Urban Growth Boundary
  amendment of, 98-99
  meaning, 52
  planning schemes, inclusion in, 52-53, 98-99
Urban Growth Zone, 52-53
  Precinct Structure Plans (PSPs), 25, 92-93
Urban planning, 1
Use of land *see* Land use

VCAT *see* Victorian Civil and Administrative Tribunal (VCAT)
VicCode 1
  planning permit applications *see* Planning permit
  planning schemes *see* Planning schemes
  responsible authorities *see* Responsible authorities
  subdivision of land, 34-36
VicRoads
  referrals to, 26
Victoria Planning Provisions (VPPs)
  amendment to, 23, 76-77
  preparation of, 77
  General Provisions, 62
  municipal council discretion over, 23
  overlays *see* Overlays
  planning schemes, 22, 53-54
  referral authority provisions, 26
  regional planning, 18, 22
  standard zones *see* Zoning
  State Planning Policy Framework *see* State Planning Policy Framework (SPPF)
  State standard provisions, 22-24, 53-54
  Statewide Particular Provisions, 62
  subdivision requirements, 30
  VicCode 1, 34-36
Victorian Building Regulations **(VBRs)**, 35
Victorian Civil and Administrative Tribunal (VCAT), 15
  appeal
    restrictions on rights of, 175
    Supreme Court, to, 150, 174-175
  applications for review, 28, 50-52, 155-156
    grounds, 157
    lodging, 156-157, 158
    Ministerial call in of, 175-178
    notice of, 158
    time limitations for, 156-157
  compensation claims
    dispute resolution, 247
  compulsory conferences, 166-168
  contempt proceedings, 192
  costs, 148, 169-174, 190-191
    award of, 171-174
  decisions, 168-169
    "on the spot", 162, 168
    reserved, 168
  declarations, 149-150
  determinations
    questions of law, of, 166, 174-175
  divisions of, 147

INDEX

enforcement orders by *see* Enforcement orders; Interim enforcement orders
enforcement proceedings
  costs, 190-191
  evidence, 164, 180, 188-189, 190
  onus of proof, 189-190
  standard of proof, 189-190
  functions, 147
  hearings, 148, 160
  order of appearance, 163
  parties who may appear, 158-159
  representation at, 163-164
  submissions prepared for, 160-163
  substitution of amended plans, 164
  witnesses, 164-166
  interim enforcement orders *see* Interim enforcement orders
  jurisdiction, 147-150
  lists, 159-160
  Major Cases List, 159
  mediation, referral to, 167-168
  members, 147
  orders, 168-169
  Planning and Environment List, 147-150
    Major Cases List, 159
    origins, 151-155
    Short Cases List, 159-160
  practice day hearings, 160
  review by, 42, 155-157
    applications *see* applications for review *above*
    conditions, of, 41-43
    exemption to review rights, 51
    Minister's power of veto, 28
    parties to, 158-159
    planning permit decisions, 155-166
    planning scheme amendments, 100-101
    submissions, 160-163
    witnesses, 164-166
  review jurisdiction, 148-149
  settlement, 168
  Short Cases List, 159-160
  Supreme Court
    appeals to, 150, 174-175
    order, filing of, 192
Victorian Heritage Council
  establishment, 203
  functions, 206
  Heritage Register and, 206-207
  members, 206
Victorian Heritage Register
  buildings, 204-205
  items included on, 204-205
  planning permits, 225-226
  Register of Historic Buildings, 205
  registration
    effect of, 208-209
    process, 206-207
Voluntary acquisition
  compensation, 236-237
  meaning, 237
  price paid, 240
Works approval and licences
  approval, permits for, 144
  Environmental Effects Statement *see* Environmental Effects Statement (EES)
  licence, permits for, 144
  planning permits, 144
  Environmental Protection Authority as referral authority, 144
  works, definition, 40
World Heritage areas
  Commonwealth constitutional issues over, 195-197
  protection of, 195-197
  Tasmanian Dam case, 196
World Heritage List, 194-195
  Australian properties on, 195
  nominations, 195
  Tasmanian Dam case, 196
World heritage properties, 195
  National Environmental Significance (NES), matters of, 197
  protection of, 197-198
Zoning
  business, 56
  conditions, 41-43
  development control, 1, 11, 41-43
  Farming Zone Clause, 42-43
  industrial, 56
  introduction of new zones, 23
  land use controls, 23, 41-43
  mixed use, 36, 56
  planning permits *see* Planning Permits
  provisions, 56-60
  public land, 56-57
  residential, 32, 36, 56
  rural, 56-57
  special purpose, 56-57
  State standard zones, 56-60
  township, 36, 56
  underlying, 47
  Victoria Planning Provisions *see* Victoria Planning Provisions (VPPs)